GETTING INTO BUSINESS

An Introduction to Business

FOURTH EDITION

Wylie A. Walthall

Michael J. Wirth

College of Alameda

HARPER & ROW, PUBLISHERS, New York

Cambridge, Philadelphia, San Francisco, Washington,
London, Mexico City, São Paulo, Singapore, Sydney

1817

To the "Big Three"
Nancy
Lauren
Jason
W. Walthall

To Barbara and our children,
Christina and Mikey, P. T. L.
M. Wirth

Sponsoring Editor: Jayne Maerker
Text Design: Barbara Bert, North 7 Atelier, Ltd.
Cover Design: Barbara Bert, North 7 Atelier, Ltd.
Text Art: Vantage Art, Inc.
Production Manager: Jeanie Berke
Compositor: ComCom Division of Haddon Craftsmen, Inc.
Printer and Binder: R. R. Donnelley & Sons Company

GETTING INTO BUSINESS: An Introduction to Business, Fourth Edition

Library of Congress Cataloging in Publication Data

Walthall, Wylie A.
  Getting into business.

  Includes index.
  1. Business. 2. Management. I. Wirth, Michael J.,
1945–   . II. Title.
HF5351.W317 1987   658   86–14921
ISBN 0–06–046897–1

86 87 88 89 9 8 7 6 5 4 3 2 1

CONTENTS

part 4 BUSINESS OPERATIONS   239

9 MARKETING MANAGEMENT   241

10 THE MARKETING MIX   265

11 FINANCE   293

PREFACE

Although the fourth edition of *Getting Into Business: An Introduction to Business* represents a major revision, the objectives of this book remain the same. The primary goal is to encourage student interest and involvement in the exciting world of business. To this end, every effort has been made to keep the fourth edition clear, concise, and easy to read. The focus is on practical applications rather than theoretical concepts. Organization is straightforward, proceeding from the general to the specific. The text incorporates learning objectives, contemporary issues, self-examination questions, and extensive end-of-chapter exercises aimed at maintaining student interest and encouraging involvement.

MAJOR CHANGES

The fourth edition includes two chapters on marketing entitled "Marketing Management" and "The Marketing Mix," which expand the single chapter coverage in previous editions. The section on computers in Chapter 8 has been revised, expanded, and updated. The coverage of finance has been consolidated into a single chapter with an optional appendix for those readers desiring more information on money, the banking system, and the Federal Reserve. The final chapter has been revised and rewritten with the major focus on international business. There are 17 new issues, such as "Entrepreneurs versus Intrapreneurs," "China Tries the Capitalist Road," "Do You Really Want Tax Reform?," "Is Bigger Better?," "Market Segmentation: Coke Vs. Coke Vs. Coke Vs. . . . ."

In addition to these major changes, the entire textbook has been updated and revised. There is expanded coverage of marketing, computers in business, world business, the role of the entrepreneur, and the social responsibility of business.

ACKNOWL-EDGMENTS

It is impossible to mention all the individuals who made contributions to this book. We are indebted to our colleagues for reviewing the manuscript and offering numerous constructive comments and suggestions. Special thanks go to Susan Chin, John Dahlquist, Fred Ittner, Ralph Marinaro, Alex Pappas, and Ida Pound. We also appreciate the valuable suggestions offered by our students.

We are grateful to the following reviewers who provided positive criticism and many helpful recommendations:

Murray Alpern, Coppin State College
John Anjewierden, Utah Technical College
Frederick R. Blake, Bee County Community College
Patricia A. Cox, Victoria College
Aaron H. Fairbanks, Western Wisconsin Technical Institute
Grover Gillet, Jr., El Centro College
Ric Gorno, Cypress College
William C. Gray, Jr., DeKalb Community College
Charles Edward Haley, Lord Fairfax Community College
Joseph Tyrol, Columbia-Greene Community College

We appreciate their assistance. Of course, all errors and omissions are our responsibility.

Finally, we would like to thank the entire staff at Harper & Row for their expert guidance, assistance, and support.

Wylie A. Walthall
Michael J. Wirth

MEMORANDUM TO THE INSTRUCTOR

To: The Instructor
From: The Authors
Subject: The Why, What, and How of *Getting Into Business: An Introduction to Business*

This textbook was written because we couldn't find one like it on the market. With a combined experience of over three decades of teaching an introductory course in business, we became convinced that a fresh approach was needed. Many of the traditional textbooks tend to be encyclopedic; in our opinion, they are too long and too detailed for an introductory course. As a result, students often become engulfed in an ocean of minutiae and lose sight of key concepts. In short, too many students become turned off.

Getting Into Business attempts to introduce the American business system to college students taking their first course in business. The title is not intended to imply that the book is a manual for starting a small business. Rather, it suggests the major goal of the book: getting the student interested and involved in the exciting world of business. We have tried to make the book concise, uncluttered, lively, and easy to read by emphasizing major principles and concepts rather than detailed explanations. The extensive end-of-chapter exercises provide a means of stimulating student interest and involvement. In short, the book is intended to be used rather than merely carried around like a piece of superfluous baggage.

Organization is straightforward, employing the traditional or functional approach. Each chapter begins with specific learning objectives and concludes with self-examination questions based on these objectives. All chapters include short issues that focus on contemporary business problems and practices. The issues serve to introduce the student to the role and challenge of modern business in our increasingly complex world.

The questions at the end of each chapter assist the student in reviewing major concepts and building his or her business vocabulary. The problems and short cases serve to sharpen analytical skills and encourage the application of principles and techniques described in the chapter.

Student response to *Getting Into Business* has been overwhelmingly positive. It is a textbook that students can and do use. The compact yet flexible design permits instructors to tailor the course to their instructional goals and to the needs of their students.

MEMORANDUM TO THE STUDENT

To: The Student
From: The Authors
Subject: Why This Book Is Worth What You Paid For It and What
You Should Do With It

This book is about American business. As the title states, it's intended to help you understand how the business system works, to introduce you to the major areas of business, and to assist you in selecting a business career. The perspective of the book is that of the manager, who plays the key role in every business firm from General Motors to the corner ice cream store. *Getting Into Business: An Introduction to Business* aims at giving you a taste of the management decision-making process; that is, how managers make decisions.

That, in a nutshell, is what the book is all about. You should also know what it is *not* about: this is not a "how to" manual for starting a business of your own, nor does it provide a sure-fire formula for getting rich in business. (On the other hand, a knowledge of the business world won't stop you from earning a fortune.)

Each chapter is organized the same way. The learning objectives serve as a concise statement of what you should learn from the chapter. Then comes the main body of the chapter, followed by a summary of key points. At the end of each chapter are a number of self-examination questions you can use to test your mastery of the learning objectives. Next you will find questions, exercises, and a few case studies. Most of these will be assigned and they are important. Why? The entire book is based on the assumption that the best way to learn is to do. The idea is summed up by an old Chinese proverb:

> I hear, and I forget;
> I see, and I remember;
> I do, and I understand!

You can think of this textbook as a useful tool for opening up the exciting and fascinating world of business. A little hard work and practice with this tool should yield a substantial profit on your investment.

Good luck!

part **1**

THE
AMERICAN
BUSINESS
SYSTEM

CHAPTER	TITLE
1	Business and Society: A Quick Overview
2	Business and Government
3	Forms of Business Ownership

The first three chapters provide a broad view of business in America. The focus is on the big picture—how business functions in the economic environment, the impact of government on business, and alternative forms of ownership for business enterprises. Chapter 1 describes the U.S. economy and the key role played by business firms. How government assists, regulates, and taxes business is discussed in Chapter 2. Part 1 concludes with Chapter 3's description of the major types of business ownership—sole proprietorships, partnerships, and corporations.

BUSINESS AND SOCIETY: A QUICK OVERVIEW

You are part of the system—the American business system.

Many students have jobs with business firms. Everyone is a consumer. We all buy a variety of goods and services each week. More than likely you will choose a career in business. Either as a consumer or as a potential business manager, you should know something about how our business system operates.

This chapter and the next are intended to give you a look at "The Big Picture"—some of the key principles that influence the operation of business in our society.[1]

CHAPTER OBJECTIVES

1. Define productivity and state four methods of increasing productivity.

2. Name the factors of production.

3. List the major features of capitalism, democratic socialism, and communism.

4. Describe three roles performed by profits in a capitalist economic system.

5. Compare and contrast fiscal policy and monetary policy.

6. Distinguish supply-side economics from demand-side economics.

---

[1]All references used in the text are included in an appendix entitled "Notes" at the end of the textbook.

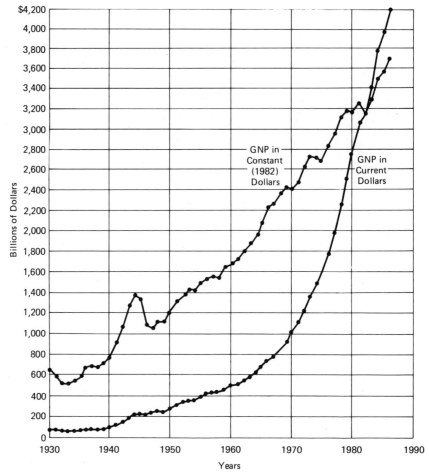

FIGURE 1.1   United States GNP, 1930–1986
Source: Economic Report of the President, 1986. (Note: Data for 1986 are estimates.)

PRODUCTIVITY IS THE NAME OF THE GAME

A few years ago, it was popular to boast that the United States was the richest nation on earth. In one sense this is still true; in another sense, it is not. Our country still produces more goods and services than any other nation. However, although the average income per American is among the highest in the world, the United States is no longer in first place.

Gross National Product (GNP) is the dollar measure of goods and services produced by a country during a year. In other words, if we added up the final selling price of all the automobiles, T-shirts, movie tickets, Frisbees, machine tools, and the millions of other goods and services produced in the United States during the year, the sum would be Gross National Product. Figure 1.1 shows GNP for the years 1930 to 1986. Note that GNP topped $4 trillion ($4,000,000,000,000) in 1986. Also shown is GNP in constant 1982 dollars. This means that the effect of price changes (inflation) has been eliminated so that the figures for each year are in dollars of constant buying power. Note that the difference between the two lines on the graph reflects inflation.

Gross National Product does not tell the whole story. A nation's output must be divided among its citizens. A better measure of a society's standard of living is *output per capita*—the average amount of goods and services produced per individual. The larger a nation's population, the more pieces the economic pie (GNP) must be divided into. We can get an estimate of a country's standard of living by using a simple formula:

$$\frac{\text{GNP}}{\text{Population}} = \text{Output per Capita}$$

Therefore, for example, if a nation has a population of 250 million people and a GNP of $4 trillion, then the average output per capita would be $16,000 worth of goods and services:

$$\frac{\$4,000,000,000,000}{250,000,000} = \$16,000$$

Two factors complicate our calculations: (1) No nation divides its output equally. Some families in the United States have very high incomes while others are relatively poor. (2) Not all of Gross National Product is distributed to individuals. For example, some is used by business firms to invest in new plant and equipment. And, of course, government taxes take a share.

Figure 1.2 shows changes in per capita GNP during this century. Note that GNP is shown in constant 1982 dollars.

Why does the United States have the highest GNP and one of the highest standards of living? The answer can be summed up in one word: *productivity*. Productivity is the measure of output per worker—that is, how much a worker produces during a particular period of time (for example, an hour, a week, or a year). In the United States, average worker productivity is among the highest in the world, and productivity is the basic determinant of standard of living. Increased productivity means more goods and services are available for the citizens of a nation. It can also mean that workers may enjoy more leisure time without having to sacrifice their standard of living.

What accounts for the high level of productivity in the United States? There is no single answer—rather, a combination of factors influence productivity.

Capital Investment   Here the term *capital* refers to the tools, equipment, factories, and machines that are used to produce goods and services. Obviously, capital improves the productivity of workers. A man can dig a ditch

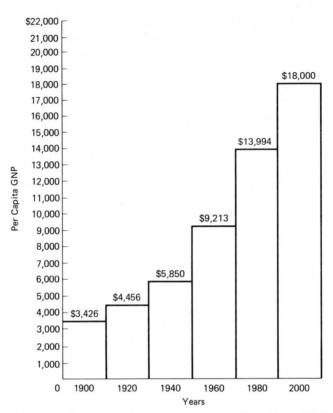

FIGURE 1.2   United States per Capita GNP, 1900–2000 (1982 Dollars)
Source: United States Department of Commerce. (Note: Data for 2000 are estimates.)

faster with a shovel than with his hands, and his output is increased many times if he has a motorized ditch digger. In the United States, the capital investment per worker exceeds $50,000 and in some industries such as oil refining and airlines, the total may top $400,000. Greater capital investment permits each worker to produce more, thereby increasing his or her value to an employer. Increased productivity means higher wages.

Technology

Technology refers to the application of scientific discoveries to develop new and improved products and more efficient methods of production. The growing use of computers by business firms is an example of technology, as is the use of hybrid seeds, which enable farmers to boost crop yields. Technology influences productivity by permitting more output with less effort.

Education, Health, and Training of the Work Force

There are 120 million workers in the United States, roughly 45 percent of the population. On an average these workers enjoy better health and education than do workers in most other parts of the

ISSUE WHAT IS AN ENTREPRENEUR?

The entrepreneur is the essential individual in a capitalistic, free-market system. It is the entrepreneur who launches new enterprises, organizes other factors of production, develops and introduces new products, raises the necessary funds, and risks failure and loss of investment against the chance of earning a profit. The entrepreneur's functions go beyond those performed by employees and managers.

Entrepreneurs possess an outlook and attitudes that make them different from the rest of society. They have a powerful need to be in control, to be decision makers. Whereas the typical professional manager attempts to objectively assess the risks involved in undertaking a new venture, the entrepreneur believes any odds can be overcome through a combination of talent, hard work, and drive. This supreme self-confidence enables entrepreneurs to risk everything on a new business despite past failures. But self-confidence alone is rarely enough for success. Most entrepreneurs fail due to a lack of knowledge about how to run a business combined with inadequate financing. Only about one in five new companies is profitable.

What sparks entrepreneurship? Some experts point to major dislocations or dramatic changes in life-style as key factors in stimulating entrepreneurial efforts. Examples supporting this theory include the large number of entrepreneurs among Vietnam and Cuban refugees and the high proportion of middle-aged women with grown children who start their own companies.

Only a tiny percentage of entrepreneurs "hit it big." Among the success stories are the following:

- In 1977, while still in her twenties, Linda Alvarado quit her job with a Denver, Colorado, consulting firm to launch her own company, Alvarado Construction, Inc. She met with immediate failure. She was unsuccessful in her first four attempts to land management consulting jobs. When

world. Many companies spend millions of dollars a year on training programs to help their employees increase knowledge and skills and thereby boost productivity. Why are you attending college?

Management   Another factor that influences productivity is management. A business firm may adopt the latest technology, own hundreds of

ISSUE   WHAT IS AN ENTREPRENEUR? (Cont.)

she finally got her first job, five banks turned down her request for $20,000 in financing. But she persisted, and by the mid-1980s, she had built a commercial and industrial general contracting firm doing over $10 million in business a year. According to Ms. Alvarado, tenacity is the key to her success: "I may have to go over, under, or around, but there's always a way of doing it." She adds, "You have to believe in your own ability to do it better."

Linda Alvarado has already earned over a million dollars, but most of her profits are ploughed back into the business. Ms. Alvarado's success is partly based on her ability to take advantage of opportunities. "I consider myself an entrepreneur. My skills are marketing, negotiating terms and contracts, administering a business." She is also a strong believer in Hispanic-owned business, and attempts to hire Hispanic subcontractors.

•   Ed Lewis grew up in Harlem. When he was 7 years old, he got his first job; at 10 he began working for a local printer. This led him to enroll in the New York School of Printing. After graduating from Cornell University's School of Industrial Relations, he went to work as an organizer for a printer's union.

In 1968, Mr. Lewis set up his first company. It failed due to lack of experience and inadequate cash. Ten years later, he started GMS Printing, which today is a successful firm in a highly competitive industry.

Mr. Lewis's advice on going into business is short and simple. "Once you make the final decision to start your own business, do as much research as possible . . . find out what the cost factors are, and what you actually need to get started. Find out what resources are available to you, and most important, ask yourself if you are willing to put in the time to make your business a success, remembering to provide excellent service with competitive prices."

He offers some observations on racism, motivation, and

millions of dollars in plant and equipment, employ highly skilled workers, and still fail if it has poor management. American business managers have pioneered in the development of improved organizational and management techniques. Today, some U.S. firms are looking to Japanese and European companies in evolving improved managerial methods.

ISSUE   WHAT IS AN ENTREPRENEUR? (Cont.)

---

success. "I am black. I know that there is racism in our society; I have not let that prevent me from moving ahead. . . . There are some imperfections in our society but you can overcome those imperfections, as long as you persevere and keep going and be the best you can be at whatever you do."

•   A few years ago, Philippe Kahn was broke, an illegal alien, and in danger of being arrested and deported. Today he heads Borland International, one of the most successful software firms in the Silicon Valley.

Bitten by the entrepreneurial bug, Mr. Kahn left his native France for San Jose, California. There he spent his last few dollars to print stationery with the impressive, if somewhat inaccurate, letterhead: Borland International, Worldwide Distributors of Software and Hardware. He mailed letters to dozens of manufacturers suggesting they send him their products for evaluation and possible marketing. Free samples and loaned equipment flooded his office, allowing him to develop software at minimal cost.

Mr. Kahn's attempts to raise money from banks and venture capital firms were largely unsuccessful. "They said I was crazy, that I didn't have any collateral, that I had no real management experience, that no one could make any money selling low-cost software. And besides, I didn't even have a green card."

Ignoring the rejections, Philippe Kahn focused on developing and acquiring software (computer programs) that he sells for prices well below his competitors'. Typically, he markets $200 to $300 programs for less than $100. Says Kahn, "My competitors are just too greedy to make any money."

In only 18 months, Borland's sales topped $2 million a month. Kahn's personal fortune is in the millions. He has received a green card allowing him to work legally in this country and has applied for U.S. citizenship.

To sum up, productivity is the name of the game because it is the key determinant of a nation's standard of living, both present and future. Do you want to be rich? It's easy. Simply develop a high degree of productivity in the production of some good or service that people want. Then you'll have it made.

ISSUE ENTREPRENEURS VERSUS INTRAPRENEURS

Entrepreneurism is the very antithesis of large corporations.

Harold Geneen, former head of ITT, in his book, *Managing*

The more rapidly American business learns to use the entrepreneurial talent inside large organizations, the better. The alternative in a time of rapid change is stagnation and decline.

Gifford Pinchot III, *Intrapreneuring, or Why You Don't Have to Leave the Corporation to Become an Entrepreneur*

Conventional wisdom holds that as corporations grow in size they turn into rigid bureaucracies that stifle innovation and resist change. Threatened by any challenge to the status quo, corporate managers tend to centralize power and create obstacles that discourage entrepreneurial risk-taking among employees. But this dismal picture is changing.

According to Gifford Pinchot III, author of *Intrapreneuring, or Why You Don't Have to Leave the Corporation to Become an Entrepreneur,* in an age of accelerating change, firms that fail to innovate will become noncompetitive dinosaurs. To promote innovation, corporations must create an "intrapreneurial environment" that encourages employees to take risks by eliminating red tape, entrenched procedures, and bureaucratic delays, and, at the same time, develops a spirit of freedom, excitement, and entrepreneurship.

Pinchot maintains that true innovators, both inside and outside the corporation, are driven not by the need for money and power, but by a personal need for achievement. Both entrepreneurs and intrapreneurs are after that thrill of success: "I did it, and it works."

A growing number of U.S. corporations are trying intrapreneurship. General Motors has created the Saturn Corporation, a separate company free from the parent firm's rigid procedures and bureaucracy. Saturn is intended to be GM's entrepreneurial spearhead. International Business Machines has developed the concept of independent business units (IBUs) that operate as separate organizations with control over their own marketing and manufacturing strategies. One IBU was responsible for creating and marketing the IBM personal computer. Other firms adopting intrapreneuring are General Electric, Du Pont, Data General, and AT&T.

In his book, Pinchot lays down "The Intrapreneur's Ten Commandments." The first is, "Come to work each day willing to be fired."

INSTANT ECONOMICS

Economics is the study of how a society or nation produces the goods and services it wants and how they are distributed. The basic problem in economics is that every society has unlimited wants for goods and services, but only limited resources to produce these goods and services. Economic resources are called the *factors of production.* They are: land, labor, capital, and the entrepreneur.

Land means all natural resources including iron ore, timber, petroleum deposits, oceans, lakes, and crop land. *Labor* refers to the physical and mental output necessary to produce goods and services. *Capital* has already been defined as machinery, tools, and equipment—any human-made resource used to produce goods and services. Finally, the *entrepreneur* organizes the other three factors of production in such a way as to produce those goods and services that people will buy. In a broad sense, the entrepreneur is a manager who is responsible for combining land, labor, and capital in the most efficient way. The entrepreneur is also a risk-taker who pits his or her money and talent against the possibility of making a loss rather than a profit.

Given the condition of unlimited human wants and limited resources, every nation must decide what combination of goods and services it will produce. It must ration or economize its scarce resources among alternative uses. In economics, scarcity is the name of the game and economizing is the way it's played. Our business system plays a critically important role in attempting to solve the basic economic problem of scarcity.

CAPITALISM AND OTHER ISMS

Every society must select an economic system—some arrangement of institutions (business firms, government, and farms) and people (workers and managers)—to produce and distribute the products it wants.

Capitalism

Capitalism is an economic system where the means of production (economic resources) are owned and operated by private individuals (or business firms) to make a profit. Pure capitalism is often referred to as *laissez faire capitalism.* This French term means "hands off," or more precisely, noninterference by the government in the affairs of business. In other words, the economic system should not be subjected to government planning, control, or regulation. Capitalism is based on four key principles: (1) right of private property, (2) economic freedom, (3) competition, and (4) the profit motive.

Right of Private Property   The U.S. Constitution guarantees the right of individuals to own, operate, and dispose of property. This guarantee is based partly on the belief that property owned by individuals receives better care. For example, people tend to take better care of a home they own than one they rent. Moreover, the right to own property serves as an incentive for individuals to work hard in order to expand their wealth by acquiring more property. Critics of private property argue that it permits property owners (rich landholders and business firms) to exploit those who have no property and that it leads to a highly unequal distribution of income in our society. Socialism attempts to overcome the unequal distribution of income through government ownership of much property and heavy taxation of high incomes.

Even under pure capitalism, the right of private property is subject to some restrictions. Property owners must pay taxes, and they are subject to *eminent domain* (the right of the government to take private property for public use on paying just compensation). For example, if the state decides to build a highway through your living room, you must sell your home to the government.

Economic Freedom   The principle of economic freedom is often referred to as *freedom of choice* or *freedom of enterprise.* It means that individuals are free to engage in the business of their choice, workers may seek out jobs that suit them, and consumers can select those goods and services on which they wish to spend their incomes.

Economic freedom is rarely complete. Some business activities are illegal—for example, the sale of heroin. Moreover, many types of businesses require very large sums of money to start, which effectively bars most people. It has been estimated that well over a billion dollars would be required to establish a major automobile manufacturing firm. In addition, certain union practices and government licensing laws restrict economic freedom. Some craft unions limit membership to drive up wages. A high school dropout cannot become a doctor. Despite such restrictions, economic freedom is far more extensive under capitalism than under alternative economic systems.

Competition   Under capitalism, business firms compete against each other for the consumer's dollars. Workers compete for desirable jobs and promotions. Competition is the foundation of capitalism and it provides numerous benefits for society. Business managers recognize that they can attract customers and increase sales with low prices. There is also a built-in incentive for business firms to reduce waste and inefficiency—to cut unnecessary costs. Many firms compete by offering customers more and better services. For example, a retail store may offer air conditioning, attractive decor, numerous clerks, free delivery, gift wrapping, and liberal credit.

Competition also encourages firms to improve existing products and develop new ones in an attempt to capture a larger share of the market. Some firms are unable to compete effectively and they tend to fail. From society's standpoint this failure is desirable, because scarce resources are allocated to those firms that are most efficient in fulfilling consumer wants.

Economists distinguish between perfect and imperfect competition. Perfect (or pure) competition refers to an industry with a large number of firms (perhaps tens of thousands) each selling an identical product, with no single firm large enough to influence product price. Very few industries in the United States can be described as perfectly competitive. For example, there are only three companies that produce aluminum in this country, and only four major automobile manufacturers. Most industries are imperfectly competitive. This means that business firms have some control in setting prices for their products. But it would be a mistake to think that competition does not exist in these industries. For example, in what ways does General Motors compete with Ford and Toyota?

The Profit Motive   Profit is the difference between the income from sales and the expenses of doing business:

      Sales
  −Expenses
      Profit

Profit serves as the prime mover in a capitalistic economy. Business managers (or entrepreneurs) will strive to produce the goods and services that consumers want in order to increase sales and earn profits. Therefore, the consumer, by spending his or her dollars, largely determines what goods and services the business system will produce. The pursuit of profit also spurs businesses to develop new products and technology and to invest in capital goods. Profit is a major source of funds for business expansion. The successful (profitable) firm will reinvest part of its earnings by acquiring more plant and equipment, and thus be able to increase productivity and boost wages. In short, profit may be viewed as a report card on the past, as incentive to meet consumer wants, and as a source of funds for capital investment and technological improvement.

Competition is not always present in an industry. Some firms earn profit not through efficiency or by successfully developing improved products but by maintaining a monopoly position. Monopoly is the absence of competition. More on this in the next chapter.

Capitalism is sometimes referred to as the *free-market system* because output and prices are determined by consumers and producers interacting in markets with a minimum of government interference.

Socialism   An alternative to capitalism is socialism. Unfortunately, the term *socialism* is confusing because it has been defined in so many

ISSUE   THE CASE FOR COMPETITION   *Clair Wilcox*

Private enterprise seeks profit. But, to obtain profit, it must serve consumers, for this is the only way to profit that competition will allow.

Human wants are many and growing; the productive resources through which they can be satisfied—land, labor, capital, materials, and power—are scarce. The central problem of economics is to determine how these resources shall be allocated; to decide what goods shall be produced. The goods produced by private enterprise, in a market economy, will be those that the consumer demands. Each time he or she spends a dollar a vote is cast for the production of the thing bought. Dollar votes, recorded in a purchase, express the character of the demands. Where demand for a commodity declines, its price will fall. Where demand increases, price will rise. When producers, in their turn, compete against each other to obtain resources, those with products where demand is weak will find themselves outbid by those with products where demand is strong. Resources will be diverted from the one field to the other, away from producing goods that are wanted less and toward producing goods that are wanted more. Competition is thus the regulator that compels producers to follow the guidance of consumer choice.

Competition operates to enhance quality and reduce price. The producer who wishes to enlarge profits must increase sales. To do so, he or she must offer the consumer more goods for less money. As the producer adds to quality and subtracts from price, rivals are compelled to do the same. Competition also makes for efficiency. It leads some producers to eliminate wastes and cut costs so they may undersell others. It compels others to adopt similar measures in order that they may survive. Competition is congenial to material progress. It keeps the door open to new blood and new ideas. The resulting gains in efficiency open the way to still lower prices. Goods are turned out in increasing volume, and the general plane of living is raised.

The existence of competition is not always assured. Many firms may agree among themselves that they will not compete. Two or more firms may combine to make a single unit. One or a few firms may come to dominate an industry, through the employment of unfair methods or through the enjoyment of special advantages. If the consumer is to reap the benefits of competition, government must make sure that competition is maintained.

ISSUE PROFITS: THE LIFEBLOOD OF THE ECONOMY

Test Question: How much profit does the average business earn on each dollar of sales?

(a) $0.45
(b) $0.33
(c) $0.25
(d) $0.05

In a poll conducted among college students, the majority thought that business firms average $0.45 profit on each dollar of sales. In another poll, which questioned people from all walks of life, the estimate was lower: $0.33. The actual figure is a little less than $0.05. Profits as a percent of Gross National Product have declined by nearly 50 percent in the last 30 years.

Most Americans believe that business profits are much higher than they really are and favor higher taxes on corporate earnings. This attitude reflects a widespread suspicion that somehow profits are a rip-off by greedy corporations that exploit both consumers and employees. Let's review the facts:

- Profits are the driving force in a free-enterprise economy. It is the search for profits that motivates businesses to develop new and better products, reduce costs, and strive to undersell competitors.

- Profits are an economic score card for measuring the efficiency of business. Poorly run firms that make bad decisions and waste resources are likely to have losses rather than profits.

- Profits are a major source of funds for business expansion. Approximately two-thirds of all profits are invested in new plant, equipment, and research. Invested profits create new and better jobs.

- Profits are a reward to investors for risking their money in a business enterprise. Roughly one-third of all corporate profits are paid to stockholders in the form of dividends.

Some economists and business managers are concerned about the relative decline of business profits over the past three decades. They fear that lower profits will lead to economic stagnation with declining growth and fewer jobs in the future.

different ways. To some, any degree of government involvement in the economic system is socialism, while others consider only the Soviet economy as socialist. We shall use the term *democratic socialism* to refer to those economic systems where major industries —such as steel, coal, transportation, and utilities—are owned and operated by the government. However, private ownership of property still exists in democratic socialism and many business firms are privately owned and operated for profit. Examples of democratic-socialist economic systems would include Sweden, Great Britain, and France.

The proponents of democratic socialism claim this system provides more stable employment because during periods of unemployment and recession government-owned industries can hire laid-off workers. In addition, heavy taxation of large incomes coupled with extensive social welfare programs are used to make family incomes more equal.

Critics of socialism maintain that the system severely limits economic freedom and that it reduces the incentive to achieve. They argue that government-owned industries become bogged down in red tape and political interference, which leads to inefficiency, reduced productivity, and higher prices for goods and services.

Communism

Communism is another confusing term. In his famous book *Das Kapital,* Karl Marx, the father of communism, described a future utopian economic system with a classless society and no government at all. However, most people use the term *communism* to refer to the present economies of the Soviet Union and China. In these nations, the state owns and controls virtually all the factories, farms, and other means of production. Moreover, a vast economic plan is developed by the government, which guides all economic activity. Individual economic freedom is subordinated to the government's economic objectives. In addition, political freedom, as we know it in this country, does not exist under communism.

Mixed Economy

Is the U.S. economy capitalistic? Yes and no. There is some government ownership of enterprises such as the Postal Service, Tennessee Valley Authority (TVA), and many local utility companies. Moreover, pure competition is difficult to find in this country. Finally, the government exercises considerable control over individuals and private business firms through taxation, regulation, and a host of social welfare programs (for example, social security and unemployment insurance). For these reasons it would be inaccurate to describe our economic system as laissez faire or pure capitalism. Rather we have a mixed economy—a mixture of pure capitalism and democratic socialism. However, the economy of the United States is closer to capitalism than it is to socialism.

Table 1.1 compares the key features of the three major economic systems.

TABLE 1.1   Comparative Economic Systems

Major Features	Pure Capitalism	Democratic Socialism	Communism
Ownership of property	Private ownership of property (or resources) with a few exceptions	State ownership of major industries, but extensive private ownership of smaller firms	State ownership with some exceptions
Determination of output and prices	Free markets consisting of consumers and producers (seeking profits) determine output and prices	Some government goal setting, planning, price controls, but major reliance on free markets	Central planning by government
Economic freedom	Individuals have broad freedom of choice in seeking jobs and spending incomes	Freedom of choice in seeking jobs, but limited variety of goods available from government monopolies	Some freedom of choice but output determined by a central economic plan
Distribution of income	Incomes based largely on amount and productivity of resources owned by individuals	Extensive government efforts to redistribute income through taxation and compulsory social services	In theory, "from each according to his ability, to each according to his need"; in reality, bonus systems reward productive individuals

The American business system is largely capitalistic, with extensive economic freedom, substantial competition, and emphasis on the profit motive. Most property is owned by private individuals. However, the economic role of government has expanded during the past century.

BUSINESS AND THE ECONOMY

The role of American business is to produce goods and services for society. Figure 1.3 presents a simplified illustration of how a free-enterprise economy operates. The upper loops show the sale of goods and services produced by business firms in response to consumer spending. The lower loops represent the purchase of economic resources (the factors of production) by business firms from private owners. One way to view the economy is in terms of a continuous flow of dollar payments between business firms and the public. This illustration omits government, which plays a significant role in our mixed economy.

Business Cycles

The long-term growth in U.S. GNP has been interrupted by periodic up and down movements in economic activity. These recurring

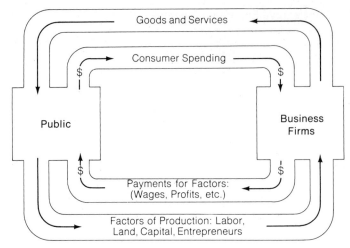

FIGURE 1.3   How the Economy Operates

periods of expansion and contraction are called *business cycles.*
Figure 1.4 shows the stages of the business cycle, which occur over
a number of years.

   During periods of expansion, the nation enjoys economic
prosperity with increased production, employment, and business
profits. However, prosperous times may be accompanied by rising
prices (inflation). Depressions bring sharp drops in output,
large-scale unemployment, and a decline in profits. During the Great
Depression of the 1930s, the output of goods and services fell by
one-third, and one-quarter of the labor force lost their jobs. A
recession is a "mini-depression"—a small and short-lived decline in
economic activity.

**From Keynes to
Supply-side
Economics**

Prior to the depression of the 1930s, most economists, business
managers, and politicians were convinced that government should
maintain a "hands off" attitude toward the economy. However, the
length and severity of the Great Depression caused many people to
call for government action to bring about a recovery. British
economist John Maynard Keynes proposed that the federal
government should intervene directly to fight depressions and halt
inflationary booms. During periods of depression, he advocated
increased government spending to expand the demand for goods and
services and thereby to stimulate production and employment.
Keynes also suggested that tax cuts could be used to stimulate
consumer and business spending during depressions. The opposite
strategy could be used to halt inflationary booms. According to
Keynes, the economy could be "cooled off" through tax increases
and a reduction in government spending.

   Keynes' theories form the basis of modern *fiscal policy*—the
use of government spending and taxing powers to smooth out the

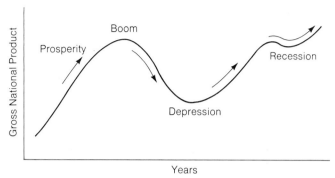

FIGURE 1.4   The Business Cycle

business cycle by taking direct action against depressions and inflationary booms. The management of total spending (or demand) is sometimes called *demand-side economics.*

After World War II, Congress passed the Employment Act of 1946, which made the federal government responsible for using its powers to achieve full employment, stable prices, and a growing economy. The government attempts to achieve these goals through the use of both fiscal policy and monetary policy. *Monetary policy* refers to control of the nation's money supply, which consists of both cash and checking accounts. The supply of money in the economy influences prices, interest rates, output, and employment. Monetary policy is the responsibility of the Federal Reserve Board, a federal agency that exercises control over the nation's banks. Chapter 11 explains the operation of the banking system, the role of the Federal Reserve, and monetary policy in greater detail.

With the election of President Ronald Reagan in 1980, a new group of "supply-side economists" gained influence in economic policymaking. They attacked Keynesian demand-side economics with its emphasis on government deficit spending to stimulate output and employment as inflationary. *Deficit spending* occurs when federal expenditures exceed tax revenues, requiring government borrowing to cover the difference. In contrast, *supply-side economics* calls for reduced government spending on social programs coupled with massive tax cuts aimed at stimulating business investment, boosting work incentives, and increasing personal saving. This strategy is intended to expand the productive capacity of American industry and enhance efficiency, thereby increasing employment and slowing the rate of inflation. The emphasis is on expanding total output (or supply), rather than on increasing total spending (or demand).

World Business and International Trade

One of the most dramatic changes in the last half of this century has been the rapid expansion in world trade and the resulting integration of world economies. Three decades ago, U.S. *exports*— sales of goods and services to foreign countries—accounted for little

---

ISSUE   CHINA TRIES THE CAPITALIST ROAD

It doesn't matter whether a cat is black or white as long as it catches mice.

Chinese Leader Deng Xiaoping

The more you work, the more you get.

Slogan in a Chinese Steel Plant

Since becoming China's supreme leader in 1976, Deng Xiaoping has turned the world's most populous nation upside down. Almost single-handedly, Deng has been trying to transform a huge, bureaucratic, backward communist state into a modern industrial nation. To achieve this goal, he has introduced a number of daring changes.

- Government-controlled agricultural communes have been replaced with family farms, and market incentives were introduced to 800 million rural Chinese.

- The government is abandoning Soviet-style central planning, gradually reducing rigid controls, and forcing state-owned enterprises to compete for business.

- Workers are increasingly paid according to their output, while farmers and small business operators are permitted to keep a portion of profits earned.

- China is actively soliciting investment by Western corporations in an attempt to boost productivity and modernize industry.

- Some Chinese firms have raised funds by selling shares of stock to individuals.

---

more than 5 percent of Gross National Product. Today, close to 8 percent of GNP is devoted to exports, while imports (purchases from abroad) often exceed this figure. Moreover, most other industrialized nations are far more dependent on foreign trade than the United States.

Increasing trade and interdependence has far-reaching implications for American business. It is clear that no major nation can hope to prosper as an economic island. Most economists foresee a further expansion in world trade during the remainder of the century. Trade means increased competition for domestic firms,

ISSUE   CHINA TRIES THE CAPITALIST ROAD (Cont.)

Does all this mean that China has become a capitalist nation? Not by a long shot. In the first place, the government continues to control prices. In a true free-market system, prices move up and down in response to changes in supply and demand. Moreover, most land and capital is still government owned. The government spends 40 percent of its budget subsidizing consumer goods such as grain, rice, and coal to keep prices low. Finally, the Communist party dominates the political system, permitting little dissent and few civil rights.

Some observers refer to China's experiment as "market socialism." It is a long way from Soviet-style communism, but neither is it free-market capitalism.

Why did Deng introduce his revolutionary changes? In the 1960s and 1970s the Chinese economy was stagnating while the population soared past the billion mark. Deng's goal is to quadruple both agricultural and industrial production by the year 2000, while slowing population growth.

Will the plan succeed? On the positive side, agricultural output has grown rapidly in the 1980s, and industrial production is rising at over 10 percent a year. Construction is booming, while foreign trade has reached record levels. However, China is still one of the world's poorest countries and faces many obstacles to growth. Many old-line party bureaucrats feel threatened by reform, and some have attempted to undermine the new system. In addition, there has been an epidemic of corruption as some party officials and enterprise managers have taken advantage of freer conditions to demand kickbacks and bribes and engage in embezzlement and fraud. China also suffers from a shortage of trained managers who can operate effectively in the fast-paced, more open economy. Finally, Deng Xiaoping is in his eighties. Will he live long enough to ensure his reforms survive after he is gone?

forcing American business to develop new and improved products and increase operating efficiency in order to survive. The struggles of the American automobile industry during the 1970s and 1980s are but one example. A growing number of U.S. firms are focusing on international markets rather than relying exclusively on domestic consumers. Success in the international market requires long-range planning, new distribution techniques, and aggressive marketing. Some business, political, and labor leaders are calling for a national policy of closer cooperation among business, labor, and government to successfully meet the challenges of world business.

These and other issues facing American business will be discussed in greater detail in later chapters.

SUMMARY

A nation's total output of goods and services during a year is measured by Gross National Product (GNP). The standard of living of a nation may be estimated by dividing population into GNP to find output per capita.

Productivity can be roughly defined as output per worker during some period of time. Productivity is the basic determinant of a nation's standard of living. There are several ways to raise productivity including increased capital investment, improved technology, more effective management, and expanded education and training for the labor force.

Economics is the study of how goods and services get produced and distributed. Because every nation is faced with unlimited material wants and limited resources, these resources (land, labor, capital, and the entrepreneur) must be rationed. Scarcity means a society must decide what goods and services it wants to produce with its scarce resources.

Every nation must choose some economic system to produce goods and services. Under laissez faire capitalism, property is owned by private individuals or companies. Workers, consumers, and business firms enjoy extensive economic freedom. Competition among business firms results in low prices, improved services, and technological progress. Profit serves as the major incentive for firms to produce those goods and services wanted by consumers.

Democratic socialism provides for government ownership of key industries, heavy taxation of large incomes, and extensive social welfare programs. Under communism, nearly all property is government owned and the economy is operated according to a central plan.

The U.S. economy is a mixture of pure capitalism and democratic socialism.

Business cycles are recurring up and down movements in business activity. Ever since the 1930s, the federal government has attempted to use its taxing and spending powers to prevent depressions and inflationary booms. Fiscal policy is based on theories developed by British economist, John Maynard Keynes. Regulation of the nation's money supply by the Federal Reserve Board is monetary policy. Both fiscal and monetary policies attempt to ensure full employment, steady prices, and a rising standard of living. However, in recent years, many economists have rejected Keynes' demand-side economics and called for tax cuts and reduced federal spending as a means of stimulating production and employment while holding down the rate of inflation. This approach has been termed supply-side economics.

**SELF-
EXAMINATION
QUESTIONS**

The following questions are based on the Chapter Objectives listed at the beginning of this chapter. Test yourself by circling the letter preceding the answer that *best* completes the statement or answers the question. The answers to the Self-Examination Questions are in the appendix at the end of the textbook.

1. Productivity, which measures output per worker, can be increased by: (A) improved management; (B) increased capital investment; (C) expanded technology; (D) improved health, education, and training of the work force; (E) all of these.

2. Supply-side economics: (A) involves reduced government spending and tax cuts; (B) is the same as monetary policy; (C) was developed by John Maynard Keynes; (D) uses government deficit spending to create more jobs; (E) all of these.

3. In the U.S. economy, profits are: (A) about 25 percent of sales; (B) a major incentive for business to develop new and improved products; (C) the cause of monopoly; (D) the difference between government tax revenues and government spending; (E) none of these.

4. Which of the following is *not* a factor of production? (A) entrepreneur; (B) capital; (C) corporation; (D) labor; (E) land.

5. A major feature of pure capitalism is: (A) state ownership of property; (B) an equal distribution of income; (C) the use of markets to determine prices and output; (D) government central planning; (E) fiscal policy.

6. In contrast to fiscal policy, monetary policy refers to: (A) control of the nation's money supply by the Federal Reserve Board; (B) increases in government spending to increase employment; (C) tax cuts to fight inflation; (D) efforts by the U.S. Treasury to repay debts owed to other nations.

APPENDIX A

GRIT AND BEAR
IT: BASIC
BUSINESS
ARITHMETIC

Let's face it, a knowledge of mathematics is essential in business. Modern business managers are relying more and more on the analysis of numerical data to make good decisions. For this reason, most business schools require students to study mathematics through calculus.

This appendix is intended to provide a quick review of basic business arithmetic. It includes examples of addition, subtraction, multiplication, and division of whole numbers, fractions, and decimals. The ability to perform these operations represents the minimum level of arithmetical skill for students considering a career in business.

If you are already proficient in basic arithmetic, then skip this appendix. If not, let's try to refresh your memory.

Example 1   You are employed in the billing department of a fuel company. During March, your firm delivered to Harris & Company the following amounts of coal: 1½ tons, 1¾ tons, 2⅓ tons, and 3⅙ tons. If the price per ton is $121.75, how much does Harris & Company owe?

Solution: Step 1. Express the amounts in fractions with a common denominator (in this case, 12).
Step 2. Find the total tons of coal sold.
Step 3. Multiply the number of tons by the price per ton. (Note: to make the multiplication easier, you can change the fractional ton into a decimal by dividing the denominator into the numerator.)

Illustration:

(1)   1½ = 1⁶⁄₁₂
      1¾ = 1⁹⁄₁₂
      2⅓ = 2⁴⁄₁₂
      3⅙ = 3²⁄₁₂

(2)   7²¹⁄₁₂ = 8⁹⁄₁₂ = 8¾ tons

$$\begin{array}{r} 0.75 \text{ tons} \\ 4\,\overline{\smash{\big)}\,3.00} \\ \underline{2\,8} \\ 20 \\ \underline{20} \end{array}$$

(3)   ¾ tons =

$$\begin{array}{r} \$121.75 \text{ price per ton} \\ \times\ 8.75 \text{ tons} \\ \hline 60875 \\ 85225 \\ 97400 \\ \hline \$1{,}065.3125 = \$1{,}065.31 \end{array}$$

Example 2   You are the new loan officer for the Rockwell Bank. Janice Sung is ready to repay a 9-month loan which is due today. The loan is for $8100 plus interest at 12 percent per year. Ms. Sung wants to know how much to repay. You know the equation for computing simple interest is *PRT,* where *P* is the principal (the amount of the loan), *R* is the interest rate, and *T* is the time expressed as a fraction of a year.

Solution: Step 1. Arrange the numbers according to the equation. Note that 12 percent is $^{12}/_{100}$ and 9 months is $^{9}/_{12}$ of a year.

Step 2. Cancel where possible and multiply.

Step 3. Add the interest to the principal to find the amount owed by Ms. Sung.

Illustration:

$$P \quad \times \quad R \quad \times \quad T \quad = \quad \text{Interest}$$

$$\text{(1) \& (2)} \quad \$8100 \quad \times \quad \frac{12}{100} \quad \times \quad \frac{9}{12} \quad = \quad \frac{729}{1} \quad = \$729$$

(3) $8100 principal
      +729 interest
      $8829 amount owed by Ms. Sung

Example 3   Power's Yamaha, a motorcycle dealership, charges its customers a 15 percent restocking fee on returned parts. Harry Maddox returned an unused camshaft for which he had paid $22.65. What is the amount of Harry's refund?

Solution: Step 1. Multiply $22.65 by 15 percent. (Note: The decimal for 15 percent is 0.15, found by moving the decimal point two places to the left and dropping the percent sign.)

Step 2. Subtract the fee (Step 1) from $22.65 to obtain the net refund.

Illustration:
(1) $ 22.65
      ×0.15
      1.1325
      2.265
      $3.3975 = $3.40 (rounded off)

(2) $22.65 purchase price
       −3.40 fee
       $19.25 refund

Shortcut:
$22.65 × 0.85 = $19.25
(Since 100 − 15 = 85 percent, which is the net percent of the refund on the $22.65.)

Example 4   The Homita Paint Company has received a bulk shipment of red paint in a 500-gallon drum. If the company plans to resell the paint in 2½-gallon cans, how many cans are needed?

Solution: Step 1.   Express 2½ gallons in the equivalent form of $\frac{5}{2}$ gallons.
             Step 2.   Divide $\frac{5}{2}$ into 500 gallons by inverting the fraction and multiplying.

Illustration:
(1) $2\frac{1}{2} = \frac{5}{2}$ ($2\frac{1}{2} = 2 + \frac{1}{2} = \frac{4}{2} + \frac{1}{2} = \frac{5}{2}$)
(2) $500 ÷ \frac{5}{2} = 500 × \frac{2}{5} = \frac{1000}{5} = 200$ cans

Example 5   As a management trainee for an investment advisory company, you have been asked to compute the yield on several stocks and bonds. You know the yield is the percentage return on a security found by dividing the interest or dividend payment by the current price of the security. Compute the yield for:

a.   A bond selling for $400 that pays interest of $48 a year.
b.   Common stock of XYZ Company paying $1.76 per share in dividends and selling for $22 per share.
c.   A preferred stock with a dividend of $15 per share selling for $105.

Solution:
In each case, find the yield by using the following equation:

$$\text{Yield} = \frac{\text{Return (Interest or Dividend)}}{\text{Current Price of Bond or Stock}}$$

Illustration:

(a) $\dfrac{\$48}{\$400} = 12\%$
$$400\ \overline{\smash)48.00}^{\,0.12}$$
          400
          800
          800

(b) $\dfrac{\$1.76}{\$22.00} = 8\%$

$$22\,\overline{\smash{\big)}\,1.76}^{\,0.08}$$
$$\underline{1.76}$$

(c) $\dfrac{\$15}{\$105} = 14.29\%$

$$105\,\overline{\smash{\big)}\,15.00000}^{\,0.14285}$$
$$\underline{105}$$
$$450$$
$$\underline{420}$$
$$300$$
$$\underline{210}$$
$$900$$
$$\underline{840}$$
$$600$$
$$\underline{525}$$
$$75$$

Now test yourself by solving the following problems.

1   What is the yield on a stock selling for $72 and paying a dividend of $9 per share?

2   A $600, 4-month loan with a 9 percent per year interest rate is due. What is the amount of the interest?

3   A customer buys 2¼ yards of red cloth at $4.00 per yard and 3⅜ yards of blue cloth at $4.80 per yard. How much does the customer owe if the sales tax on the purchase is 5%?

APPENDIX B

HOW TO USE THE
*WALL STREET
JOURNAL*

The *Wall Street Journal* is the nation's largest newspaper, with a circulation of over 2 million. Published five days a week, the *Journal* provides up-to-date information on anything that affects business. Coverage ranges from ecology to electronics, from politics to peace talks. Articles are written in a clear, easy-to-read style that helps the nonexpert understand major issues.

The *Journal* has been called "a daily textbook of business." Students may subscribe at special reduced rates through their instructor or use copies available at the college library.

This appendix highlights the key segments of the *Journal,* and provides a simple guide to using "the bible of the business world."

The *Wall Street Journal* is divided into two parts. The first part is headed by the front page, which has five major sections (see p. 29).

The second part of the *Journal* includes medium-length feature stories plus weekly columns on technology, real estate, marketing, small business, and regional trends. Inside the *Journal* is a variety of columns, articles, tables, and advertisements covering business, financial, labor, and government developments plus daily financial statistics.

- *Who's News.* "Who's News" presents management and personnel changes.

- *Stock Quotations.* The *Journal* publishes the prices of stocks and bonds listed on major securities exchanges plus over-the-counter quotations for 1400 securities.

- *Dow Jones Averages.* Dow Jones Averages appear on the next to the last page of each issue. These securities averages— one for 30 industrial stocks, one for 20 transportation stocks, one for 15 utility stocks, and a composite average for all 65 stocks—are popular measures of changes in securities prices widely quoted on television and radio news programs and printed in newspapers throughout the world.

- *Stock Market Columns.* Stock market columns include "Abreast of the Market" and "Heard on the Street," which offer appraisals of market trends plus views and opinions of leading investment authorities.

- *Commodities.* The *Journal* offers daily reports on major commodity markets including price quotations and columns devoted to analyzing current trends in production, consumption, and prices.

- *Financial News.* Financial news covers not only financial markets but also trends in education, ecology, and housing, which influence business and government.

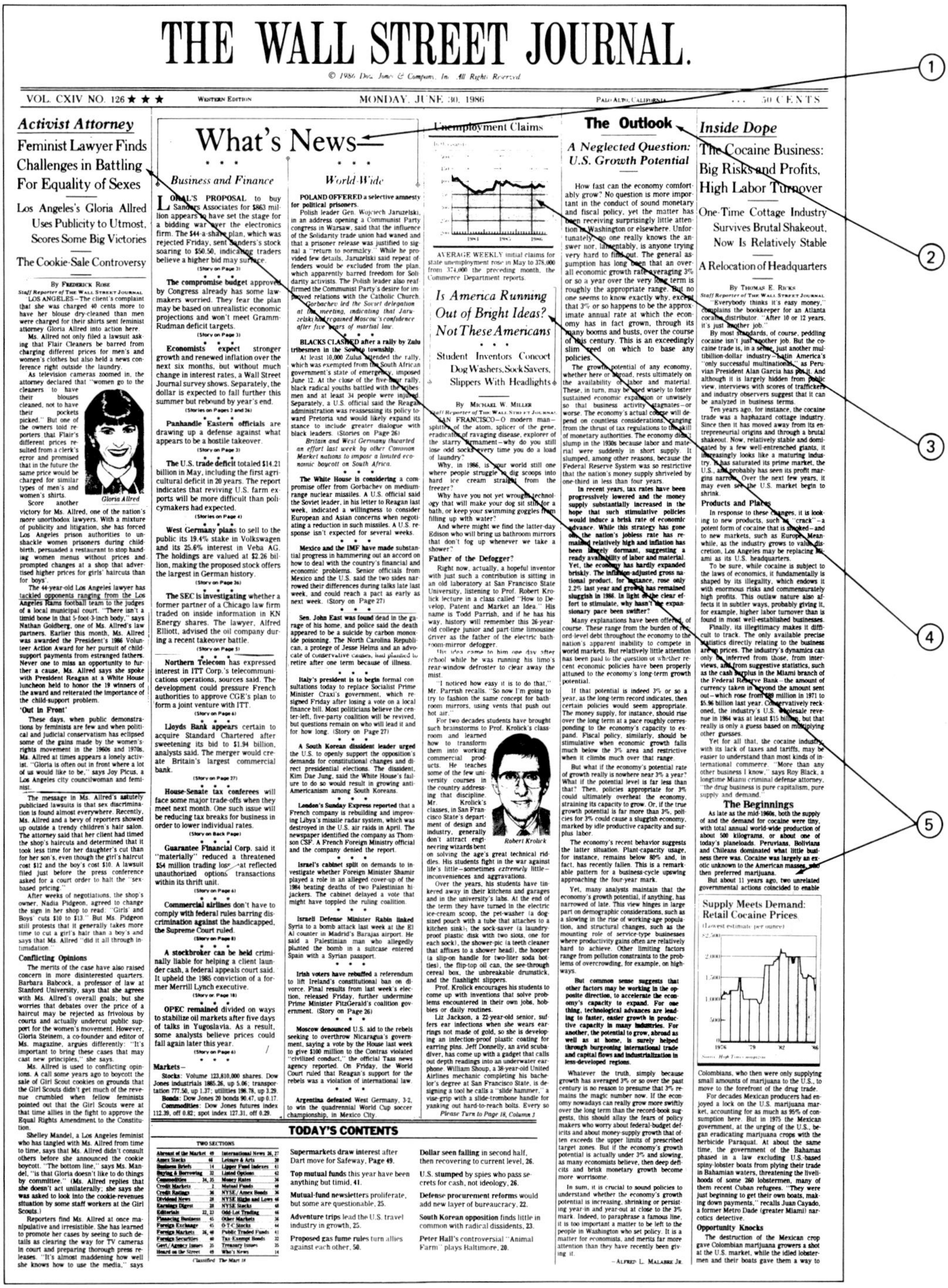

THE WALL STREET JOURNAL.

VOL. CXIV NO. 126 ★ ★ ★   WESTERN EDITION   **MONDAY, JUNE 30, 1986**   PALO ALTO, CALIFORNIA   .... 50 CENTS

Activist Attorney

Feminist Lawyer Finds Challenges in Battling For Equality of Sexes

Los Angeles's Gloria Allred Uses Publicity to Utmost, Scores Some Big Victories

The Cookie-Sale Controversy

By FREDERICK ROSE
Staff Reporter of THE WALL STREET JOURNAL

LOS ANGELES—The client's complaint that she was charged 40 cents more to have her blouse dry-cleaned than men were charged for their shirts sent feminist attorney Gloria Allred into action here.

Ms. Allred not only filed a lawsuit asking that Flair Cleaners be barred from charging different prices for men's and women's clothes but also held a news conference right outside the laundry.

As television cameras zoomed in, the attorney declared that "women go to the cleaners to have their blouses cleaned, not to have their pockets picked." But one of the owners told reporters that Flair's different prices resulted from a clerk's error and promised changes at a shop that advertised higher prices for girls' haircuts than for boys'.

The 44-year-old Los Angeles lawyer has tackled opponents ranging from the Los Angeles Rams football team to the judges of a local municipal court. "There isn't a timid bone in that 5-foot-3-inch body," says Nathan Goldberg, one of Ms. Allred's law partners. Earlier this month, Ms. Allred was awarded the President's 1986 Volunteer Action Award for her pursuit of child-support payments from estranged fathers. Never one to miss an opportunity to further a cause, Ms. Allred says she spoke with President Reagan at a White House luncheon held to honor the 19 winners of the award and reiterated the importance of the child-support problem.

'Out in Front'

These days, when public demonstrations by feminists are few and when political and judicial conservatism has eclipsed some of the gains made by the women's-rights movement in the 1960s and 1970s, Ms. Allred at times appears a lonely activist. "Gloria is often out in front where a lot of us would like to be," says Joy Picus, a Los Angeles city councilwoman and feminist.

The message in Ms. Allred's aptitude and publicized lawsuits is that sex discrimination is found almost everywhere. Recently, Ms. Allred and a few of reporters showed up outside a trendy children's hair salon. The attorney said that her client had timed the shop's haircuts and determined that it took less time for her daughter's cut than for her son's, even though the girl's haircut cost $12 and the boy's cost $10. A lawsuit filed just before the press conference asked for a court order to halt the "sex-based pricing."

After weeks of negotiations, the shop's owner, Nadia Pidgeon, agreed to change the sign in her shop to read: "Girls' and Boys' cuts $10 to $13." But Ms. Pidgeon still protests that it generally takes more time to cut a girl's hair than a boy's and says that Ms. Allred "did it all through intimidation."

Conflicting Charges

The merits of the case have also raised concern in more disinterested quarters. Barbara Babcock, a professor of law at Stanford University, says that she agrees with Ms. Allred's overall goals, but she worries that debates over the price of a haircut may be rejected as frivolous by courts and actually undercut public support for the women's movement. However, Gloria Steinem, a co-founder and editor of Ms. magazine, argues differently: "It's important to bring these cases that may cast new principles," she says.

Ms. Allred is used to conflicting opinions. A call never goes to boycott the sale of Girl Scout cookies on grounds that the Girl Scouts didn't get much of the revenue crumbled when fellow feminists pointed out that the Girl Scouts were at that time allies in the fight to approve the Equal Rights Amendment to the Constitution.

Shelley Mandel, a Los Angeles feminist who has tangled with Ms. Allred from time to time, says that Ms. Allred didn't consult others before she announced the cookie boycott. "The bottom line," says Ms. Mandel, "is that Gloria doesn't like to do things by committee." (Ms. Allred replies that she doesn't act unilaterally; she says she was asked to look into the cookie-revenues question by some staff workers at the Girl Scouts.)

Reporters find Ms. Allred at once manipulative and irresistible. She has learned to promote her cases by seeing to such details as clearing the way for TV cameras in court and preparing thorough press releases. "It's almost maddening how well she knows how to use the media," says

---

What's News—

• • •

Business and Finance

• • •

LORAL'S PROPOSAL to buy Sanders Associates for $863 million appears to have set the stage for a bidding war over the electronics firm. The $44-a-share plan, which was rejected Friday, sent Sanders's stock soaring to $50.50, indicating traders believe a higher bid may survive.

(Story on Page 3)

Economists expect stronger growth and renewed inflation over the next six months, but without much change in interest rates, a Wall Street Journal survey shows. Separately, the dollar is expected to fall further this summer but rebound by year's end.

(Stories on Pages 2 and 34)

Panhandle Eastern officials are drawing up a defense against what appears to be a hostile takeover.

(Story on Page 3)

The U.S. trade deficit totaled $14.21 billion in May, including the first agricultural deficit in 20 years. The report indicates that reviving U.S. farm exports will be more difficult than policymakers had expected.

(Story on Page 3)

West Germany plans to sell to the public its 19.4% stake in Volkswagen and its 25.6% interest in Veba AG. The holdings are valued at $2.26 billion, making the proposed stock offers the largest in German history.

(Story on Page 3)

The SEC is investigating whether a former partner of a Chicago law firm traded on inside information in KN Energy shares. The lawyer, Alfred Elliott, advised the oil company during a recent takeover battle.

(Story on Page 2)

Northern Telecom has expressed interest in ITT Corp.'s telecommunications operations, sources said. The development could pressure French authorities to approve CGE's plan to form a joint venture with ITT.

(Story on Page 3)

Lloyds Bank appears certain to acquire Standard Chartered after sweetening its bid to $1.94 billion, analysts said. The merger would create Britain's largest commercial bank.

(Story on Page 3)

House-Senate tax conferees will face some major trade-offs when they meet next month. One such issue will be reducing tax breaks for business in order to lower individual rates.

(Story on Page 6)

Guarantee Financial Corp. said it "materially" reduced a threatened $54 million trading loss at reflected unauthorized options transactions within its thrift unit.

(Story on Page 4)

Commercial airlines don't have to comply with federal rules barring discrimination against the handicapped, the Supreme Court ruled.

(Story on Page 4)

A stockbroker can be held criminally liable for helping a client launder cash, a federal appeals court said. It upheld the 1985 conviction of a former Merrill Lynch executive.

(Story on Page 4)

OPEC remained divided on ways to stabilize oil markets after five days of talks in Yugoslavia. As a result, some analysts believe prices could fall again later this year.

(Story on Page 3)

Markets—

Stocks: Volume 123,810,000 shares. Dow Jones industrials 1865.26, up 5.06; transportation 777.56, up 1.37; utilities 196.78, up 3.29.

Bonds: Dow Jones 20 bonds 90.47, up 0.17. Commodities: Dow Jones futures index 112.39, off 0.82; spot index 127.31, off 0.29.

World Wide

• • •

POLAND OFFERED a selective amnesty for political prisoners.

Polish leader Gen. Wojciech Jaruzelski, in an address opening a Communist Party congress in Warsaw, said that the influence of the Solidarity trade union had waned and that a prisoner release was justified to signal a "return to normalcy." While he provided few details, Jaruzelski said repeat offenders would be excluded from the plan, which apparently barred freedom for Solidarity activists. The Polish leader also reaffirmed the Communist Party's desire for improved relations with the Catholic Church. Gorbachev led the Soviet delegation at the meeting, indicating that Jaruzelski had regained Moscow's confidence after five years of martial law.

BLACKS CLASHED after a rally by Zulu tribesmen in the Soweto township.

At least 10,000 Zulus attended the rally, which was exempted from the South African government's state of emergency, imposed June 12. At the close of the five-hour rally, black radical youths battled with the tribesmen and at least 34 people were injured. Separately, a U.S. official said the Reagan administration was reassessing its policy toward South Africa and would likely expand its stance to include greater dialogue with black leaders. *(Stories on Page 26)*

Britain and West Germany thwarted an effort last week by other Common Market nations to impose a limited economic boycott on South Africa.

The White House is considering a compromise offer from Gorbachev on medium-range nuclear missiles. A U.S. official said the Soviet leader, in his letter to Reagan last week, indicated a willingness to consider European and Asian concerns when negotiating a reduction in such missiles. A U.S. response isn't expected for several weeks.

Mexico and the IMF have made substantial progress in hammering out an accord on how to deal with the country's financial and economic problems. Senior officials from Mexico and the U.S. said the two sides narrowed their differences during talks late last week, and could reach a pact as early as next week. *(Story on Page 27)*

Sen. John East was found dead in the garage of his home, and police said the death appeared to be a suicide by carbon monoxide poisoning. The North Carolina Republican, a protege of Jesse Helms and an advocate of conservative causes, had pleaded to retire after one term because of illness.

Italy's president is to begin formal consultations today to replace Socialist Prime Minister Craxi's government, which resigned Friday after losing a vote on a local finance bill. Most politicians believe the center-left, five-party coalition will be revived, but questions remain on who will lead it and for how long. *(Story on Page 27)*

A South Korean dissident leader urged the opposition to support the opposition's demands for constitutional changes and direct presidential elections. The dissident, Kim Dae Jung, said the White House's failure to do so would result in growing anti-Americanism among South Koreans.

London's Sunday Express reported that a French company is rebuilding and improving Libya's missile radar system, which was destroyed in the U.S. air raids in April. The newspaper identified the company as Thomson CSF. A French Foreign Ministry official and the company denied the report.

Israel's cabinet split on demands to investigate whether Foreign Minister Shamir played a role in an alleged cover-up of the 1984 beating deaths of two Palestinian hijackers. The cabinet delayed a vote that might have toppled the ruling coalition.

Israeli Defense Minister Rabin linked Syria to a bomb attack last week at the El Al counter in Madrid's Barajas airport. He said a Palestinian man who allegedly planted the bomb in a suitcase entered Spain with a Syrian passport.

Irish voters have rebuffed a referendum to lift Ireland's constitutional ban on divorce. Final results from last week's election, released Friday, further undermine Prime Minister FitzGerald's coalition government. *(Story on Page 26)*

Moscow denounced U.S. aid to the rebels seeking to overthrow Nicaragua's government, saying a vote by the House last week to give $100 million to the Contras violated "civilized conduct," the official Tass news agency reported. On Friday, the World Court ruled that Reagan's support for the rebels was a violation of international law.

Argentina defeated West Germany, 3-2, to win the quadrennial World Cup soccer championship, in Mexico City.

Unemployment Claims

AVERAGE WEEKLY initial claims for state unemployment rose in May to 375,000 from 374,000 the preceding month, the Commerce Department reports.

Is America Running Out of Bright Ideas? Not These Americans

Student Inventors Concoct Dog Washers, Sock Savers, Slippers With Headlights

By MICHAEL W. MILLER
Staff Reporter of THE WALL STREET JOURNAL

SAN FRANCISCO—O modern man—sphinx of the atom, splicer of the gene, eradicator of ravaging disease, explorer of the starry firmament—why do you still nod and shake every time you do a load of laundry?

Why, in 1986, is your world still one where people struggle to dig scoops into hard ice cream straight from the freezer?

Why have you not yet wrought technology that will make your old sink sit, for a bath, or keep your swimming goggles from fitting up with water?

And where might we find the latter-day Edison who will bring us bathroom mirrors that don't fog up whenever we take a shower?

Right now, actually, a hopeful inventor with just such a contribution is sitting in an old laboratory at San Francisco State University, listening to Prof. Robert Krolick lecture in a class called "How to Develop, Patent and Market an Idea." His name is Todd Parrish, and if he has his way, history will remember this 26-year-old college junior and part-time limousine driver as the father of the electric bathroom-mirror defogger.

He also came to him one day after rebait while he was running his limo's rear-window defroster in clear away the mist.

"I noticed how easy it is to do that," Mr. Parrish recalls. "So now I'm going to try to fashion the same concept for bathroom mirrors, using vents that push out hot air."

For two decades students have brought such brainstorms to Prof. Krolick's classroom and learned how to transform them into working commercial products. He teaches some of the few university courses in the country addressing that discipline.

Mr. Krolick's classes, in San Francisco State's department of design and industry, generally don't attract engineering wizards bent on solving the age's great technical riddles. His students fight in the war against life's little—sometimes extremely little—inconveniences and aggravations.

Over the years, his students have toiled away in their kitchens and garages and in the university's labs. At the end of the term they have turned in the electric ice-cream scoop, the pet-washer (a dog sized pouch with a tube that attaches to a kitchen sink), the sock-saver (a laundry-proof plastic disk with two slots, one for each sock), the shower-pic (a teeth cleaner that affixes to a shower head), the hooper (a slip-on handle for two-liter soda bottles), the flip-top oil can, the see-through cereal box, the unbreakable drumstick, and the flashlight slippers.

Prof. Krolick encourages his students to come up with inventions that solve problems encountered in their own jobs, hobbies or daily routines.

Liz Jackson, a 22-year-old senior, suffers ear infections when she wears earrings not made of gold, so she is developing an infection-proof plastic coating for earring pins. Jeff Donnelly, an avid scuba-diver, has come up with a gadget that calls out depth readings into an underwater earphone. William Shoup, a 36-year-old United Airlines mechanic completing his bachelor's degree at San Francisco State, is designing a tool he calls a "slide hammer," a vise-grip with a slide crowbar hooked through its eye that can rip through really tough parts of airplanes.

Whatever the truth, simply because growth has averaged 3% or so over the past century is no reason to presume that 3% remains the magic number now. If the economy nowadays can really grow more swiftly over the long term than the record-book suggests, this should allay the fears of policy makers who worry about federal-budget deficits and about money-supply growth that often exceeds the upper limits of prescribed targets. But if the economy's growth potential is actually under 3% and slowing, as many economists believe, then deep deficits and brisk monetary growth become more worrisome.

In sum, it is crucial to sound policies to understand whether the economy's growth potential is increasing, shrinking or persisting year in and year out at close to the 3% mark. Indeed, to paraphrase a famous line, it is too important a matter to be left to the people in Washington who set policy. It is a matter for economists, and even more attention than they have recently been giving it.

—ALFRED L. MALABRE JR.

The Outlook

A Neglected Question: U.S. Growth Potential

How fast can the economy comfortably grow? No question is more important in the conduct of sound monetary and fiscal policy, yet the matter has been receiving surprisingly little attention in Washington or elsewhere. Unfortunately, no one really knows the answer; for, lamentably, is anyone trying very hard to find out. The general assumption has long been that an overall economic growth rate averaging 3% or so a year over the very long term is roughly the appropriate range. No one seems to know exactly why, except that 3% or so happens to be the approximate annual rate at which the economy has in fact grown, through its many booms and busts, over the course of this century. This is an exceedingly slim reed on which to base any policies.

The growth potential of any economy, whether here or abroad, rests ultimately on the availability of labor and material. These, in turn, may be used widely to foster sustained economic expansion or unwisely so that business activity stagnates—or worse. The economy's actual course will depend on countless considerations, ranging from the thrust of tax regulations to the skill of monetary authorities. The economy didn't slump in the 1930s because labor and material were suddenly in short supply. It slumped, among other reasons, because the Federal Reserve System was so restrictive that the nation's money supply shriveled by one-third in less than four years.

In recent years, tax rates have been progressively lowered and the money supply substantially increased in the hope that such stimulative policies would induce a brisk rate of economic advance. While this strategy has gone far—the nation's jobless rate has remained relatively high and inflation has been largely dormant, suggesting a ready availability of labor and material. Yet, the economy has hardly expanded briskly. The inflation-adjusted gross national product, for instance, rose only 2.2% last year and growth has remained sluggish in 1986. In light of this lack of effort to stimulate, why hasn't the expansionary pace been swifter?

Many explanations have been offered, of course. These range from the burden of record-level debt throughout the economy to the nation's apparent inability to compete in world markets. But relatively little attention has been paid to the question of whether recent economic policies have been properly attuned to the economy's long-term growth potential.

If that potential is indeed 3% or so a year, as the long-term record indicates, then certain policies would seem appropriate. The money supply, for instance, should rise over the long term at a pace roughly corresponding to the economy's capacity to expand. Fiscal policy, similarly, should be stimulative when economic growth falls much below the 3% area and restrictive when it climbs much over that range.

But what if the economy's potential rate of growth really is nowhere near 3% a year? What if the potential level is far less than that? Then, policies appropriate for 3% could ultimately overheat the economy, straining its capacity to grow. Or, if the true growth potential is far more than 3%, policies set for 3% could cause a sluggish economy, marked by idle productive capacity and surplus labor.

The economy's recent behavior regards the latter situation. Plant-capacity usage, for instance, remains below 80% and, in fact, has recently fallen. This is a remarkable pattern for a business-cycle upswing approaching the four-year mark.

But some people suspect that other factors may be working in the opposite direction, to accelerate the economy's capacity to expand. For one thing, technological advances are leading to faster, easier growth in productive capacity in many industries. For another, the potential to grow, abroad as well as at home, is surely helped through burgeoning international trade and capital flows and industrialization in less-developed regions.

Inside Dope

The Cocaine Business: Big Risks and Profits, High Labor Turnover

One-Time Cottage Industry Survives Brutal Shakeout, Now Is Relatively Stable

A Relocation of Headquarters

By THOMAS E. RICKS
Staff Reporter of THE WALL STREET JOURNAL

Everybody thinks it's easy money," complains the bookkeeper for an Atlanta cocaine distributor. "After 10 or 12 years, it's just another job."

By most standards, of course, peddling cocaine isn't just another job. But the cocaine trade is, in a sense, just another multibillion-dollar industry—as its America's "only successful multinational," as Peruvian President Alan Garcia has said. And although it is largely hidden from public view, interviews with scores of traffickers and industry observers suggest that it can be analyzed in business terms.

Ten years ago, for instance, the cocaine trade was a haphazard cottage industry. Since then it has moved away from its entrepreneurial origins and through a brutal shakeout. Now, relatively stable and dominated by a few well-entrenched giants, it increasingly looks like a maturing industry. It has saturated its prime market, the U.S., and probably has seen its margins narrow. Over the next few years, it may even see the U.S. market begin to shrink.

Products and Places

In response to these changes, it is looking to new products, such as "crack"—a potent form of cocaine that is smoked—and to new markets, such as Europe. Meanwhile, as the industry grows to vast dimensions, Los Angeles may be replacing Miami as its U.S. headquarters.

To be sure, while cocaine is subject to the laws of economics, it fundamentally is shaped by its illegality, which endows it with enormous risks and commensurately high profits. This outlaw nature also affects it in subtler ways, probably giving it, for example, higher labor turnover than is found in most well-established businesses.

Finally, its illegitimacy makes it difficult to track. The only available precise statistics directly relating to the business are the prices. The industry's dynamics can only be inferred from those, from interviews, and from suggestive statistics, such as the cash bonus in the Miami branch of the Federal Reserve Bank—the amount of currency taken in beyond the amount sent out—which rose from $89 million in 1971 to $5.96 billion last year. Observers reckon that the industry's U.S. wholesale revenue in 1984 was at least $15 billion, but that really is only a guess based on multiplying other guesses.

Yet for all that, the cocaine industry with its lack of taxes and tariffs, may be easier to understand than most kinds of international commerce. "More than any other business I know," says Roy Black, a longtime Miami criminal defense attorney, "the drug business is pure capitalism, pure supply and demand."

The Beginnings

As late as the mid-1960s, both the supply of and the demand for cocaine were tiny, with total annual world-wide production of about 100 kilograms, or about one of today's planeloads. Peruvians, Bolivians and Chileans dominated what little business there was. Cocaine was largely an exotic unknown to the American masses, and then preferred marijuana.

But about 11 years ago, two unrelated governmental actions coincided to enable

Please Turn to Page 16, Column 3

Colombians, who then were only supplying small amounts of marijuana to the U.S. past century is no reason to presume that part part the cocaine-trafficking business. For decades Mexican producers had enjoyed a lock on the U.S. marijuana market, accounting for as much as 95% of consumption here. But in 1975 the Mexican government began spraying marijuana crops with the herbicide Paraquat. At about the same time, the government of the Bahamas phased in a law excluding U.S.-based spiny-lobster boats from plying their trade in Bahamian waters, threatening the livelihoods of some 360 lobstermen, many of them recent Cuban refugees. "They were just beginning to get their own boats, making poor payments," recalls Juan Clayado, a former Metro Dade (greater Miami) narcotics detective.

Opportunity Knocks

The destruction of the Mexican crop gave Colombian marijuana growers a shot at the U.S. market, while the idled lobstermen and their boats gave them a way to

---

Supply Meets Demand: Retail Cocaine Prices

(Lowest estimate per ounce)

Page annotation legend

1. *What's News* is a daily two-column summary of business, financial, and worldwide news.

2. *Special Weekly Reports* include The Outlook, Labor Letter, Tax Report, Business Bulletin, and Washington Wire.

3. *The Daily Chart* highlights key business and economic statistics such as GNP, business failures, and the index of leading economic indicators.

4. *Feature Articles* are magazine-type articles on a variety of interesting topics.

5. *Survey and Round-Up Reports*, appearing in columns one and six, are lead articles on new trends and surveys on major political, social, and economic developments.

- *Editorial Page.* The *Journal* enjoys an excellent reputation for objectivity, clarity, and fairness in evaluating controversial issues of the day.

- *Journal Advertising. Journal* advertising includes opportunities for businesses, individuals, real estate, and ads covering a variety of products, services, and ideas.

Reading the *Wall Street Journal* can help you to better understand the world of business and should improve your chances for a successful and rewarding career.

Student _____

BUILDING A BUSINESS VOCABULARY

Directions: Match the terms with their definitions by writing the letter in the appropriate blank.

a. Gross National
   Product
b. Output per Capita
c. Productivity
d. Capital Investment
e. Technology
f. Fiscal Policy
g. Business Cycles

h. Factors of
   Production
i. Land
j. Labor
k. Capital
l. Entrepreneur
m. Supply-side
   Economics

n. Monetary Policy
o. Capitalism
p. Laissez Faire
q. Profit
r. Democratic
   Socialism
s. Communism
t. Exports

_K_ 1. Machinery and equipment used to produce other goods and services.

_C_ 2. A measure of output per worker.

_P_ 3. A term that means noninterference by government in the affairs of business.

_A_ 4. Measures a nation's total output of goods and services.

_O_ 5. An economic system with private ownership of the means of production, competition among business firms, broad economic freedom, and emphasis on the profit motive.

_e_ 6. The application of scientific knowledge to production.

_L_ 7. The risk-taker who organizes land, labor, and capital to produce goods or services in the hope of earning a profit.

_S_ 8. An economic system with government ownership of nearly all productive resources that operates according to a central economic plan.

_B_ 9. A measure of a nation's standard of living found by dividing population into GNP.

_J_ 10. Humanpower used to produce goods and services.

_q_ 11. The difference between a firm's sales and its expenses; the incentive for business firms to produce according to consumer wants.

_d_ 12. The purchase of factories, tools, and machinery by business firms to increase the productivity of workers.

_i_ 13. All natural resources created by nature.

_t_ 14. The sale of U.S.-produced goods and services to foreign buyers.

_k_ 15. An economy under which a democratic government owns and operates most major industries and provides its citizens with extensive social services.

_H_ 16. Land, labor, capital, and the entrepreneur.

_F_ 17. The use of federal government taxing and spending powers to achieve full employment, steady prices, and a rising standard of living.

_M_ 18. Government efforts aimed at increasing business investment and boosting work incentives by reducing federal taxes, regulation, and spending on social programs.

_g_ 19. Recurring ups and downs in business activity over a period of years.

_n_ 20. Control of the nation's money supply by the Federal Reserve Board aimed at achieving full employment and growth without inflation.

Student _____

REVIEWING MAJOR CONCEPTS

1. List and briefly explain four methods for increasing productivity. Can you think of a way to boost productivity that is not described in the chapter?

2. Why do many large corporations spend millions of dollars each year on research?

3. Briefly describe two ways the American economic system differs from pure capitalism.

4. Safeway owns and operates thousands of supermarkets. This giant chain cuts costs by purchasing food in large quantities and passes the savings on to consumers in the form of lower prices. How can a small food store compete against Safeway?

5. International Business Machines (IBM), the giant computer maker, spends millions of dollars on training programs for its employees. Why?

6. True or false? Most American business firms operate under perfect (or pure) competition. Explain your answer.

7. Briefly explain how the federal government attempts to move the economy toward full employment, stable prices, and economic growth.

8. How does supply-side economics differ from demand-side economics?

9. Briefly describe how expanded world trade affects American business.

Student _____

b. What steps would you suggest that India take to improve the standard of living of its people?

4. Some socialists believe that profit is a "surplus value" added to the real worth of goods and services. One proposal calls for the government to tax away all business profit. Explain what you think would happen if such a tax became law.

chapter 2

BUSINESS AND GOVERNMENT

Pure (laissez faire) capitalism has never existed in the United States, and it probably never will. From our earliest history government has always exerted some influence on business.

Over the past few decades the economic role of government has accelerated rapidly. One way to gauge this growing influence is to look at spending by local, state, and federal governments. Figure 2.1 illustrates the rise of governmental expenditures over the last 60 years. In 1930, government purchases of goods and services accounted for about 8 percent of GNP; today, the figure is nearly 24 percent.

This chapter is intended to help you explore three areas of government involvement in our economic system: (1) government assistance to business, (2) government regulation of business, and (3) taxation.

CHAPTER OBJECTIVES

1. Describe four ways that government assists business firms.

2. Identify the three purposes of government regulation of business.

3. Describe the three methods used by government to regulate business firms.

4. Compare and contrast the three major antitrust laws.

5. Distinguish between the two major principles of taxation.

6. Explain progressive, proportional, and regressive taxes, giving an example of each.

7. Name the major source of revenue for federal, state, and local government.

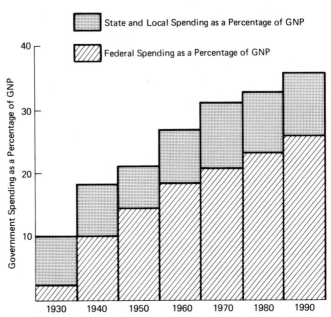

FIGURE 2.1   Federal and State and Local Spending as a Percent of GNP, 1930–1990

Source: Economic Report of the President, 1986. (Note: Data for 1990 are estimated. Total government spending includes both purchases of goods and services and transfer payments (such as Social Security benefits and welfare payments). State and local government spending is slightly understated because federal grants to state and local government are excluded.)

GOVERNMENT ASSISTANCE TO BUSINESS

Government has always acted to promote or assist American business firms. This assistance has often been indirect: by providing a system of laws and courts; by educating the work force; and by coining money to serve as a medium of exchange in business transactions.

For over 200 years the U.S. government has levied *tariffs*—taxes on imported goods—first to raise revenue and then to protect American business firms. Often government makes direct payments to business firms or industries in the form of *subsidies* and outright grants. The farm price support program involves payments to farmers amounting to billions of dollars each year. American shipbuilders also receive government subsidies. During the nineteenth century, millions of acres of public land were given to the railroads to encourage construction of rail lines across the country. More recently, Chrysler Corporation, a major automobile firm and defense contractor, was granted $1.5 billion in government-guaranteed loans to save the firm from bankruptcy.

Government also provides a host of services to American business. Many federal, state, and local agencies collect and publish statistical data that are helpful to business managers in planning future operations. The Department of Commerce provides valuable

ISSUE   DOES FOREIGN TRADE DESTROY U.S. JOBS?

In recent years, a number of major U.S. industries including steel, television sets, and textile goods have cut back on production and laid off tens of thousands of employees. According to the firms and the labor unions involved, the villain is the same in every case: *foreign competition.* They argue that foreign companies are underselling U.S. firms, stealing customers, and destroying the jobs of American workers. A massive campaign has been launched by both business firms and labor unions to secure government "protection" from foreign competition. Such protection takes several forms:

1   *Tariffs* are taxes on imported goods that drive up the prices of foreign products sold in the United States.
2   *Import quotas* place absolute limits on the amount of a foreign product that can be imported each year.
3   *Antidumping Laws* make it illegal for foreign firms to sell products in the United States at less than home prices or below the costs of production.

It is argued that these measures are necessary to protect our high standard of living from the competition of low-wage labor overseas. This argument is disputed by economists who favor free trade. High wages in this country reflect the high productivity of our work force. In other words, the relatively low wages received by workers in India are a result of low productivity. Tariffs and import quotas only result in higher prices to American consumers, a reduction in competition, and special treatment for some business firms. Advocates of free trade emphasize that when foreigners sell in the United States, they use the dollars received to buy and invest in this country, which expands American jobs. Therefore, tariffs and import quotas hurt employers and employees in export industries.

The free-trade arguments are not much comfort to those laid-off workers who cannot find jobs in other industries. So far, the federal government has resisted raising tariffs and imposing stricter quotas. The major thrust of federal action has been toward persuading foreign governments to reduce barriers to U.S. goods and enforcing antidumping laws more strictly.

The issue of free trade raises some difficult questions. Who benefits from and who pays for increased foreign sales in the United States? Are you in favor of higher tariffs and tougher import quotas? Are American managers committed to laissez faire capitalism? Chapter 14 explores international trade in greater depth.

information on a variety of economic activities including Gross National Product, consumer prices, and employment.

The *Small Business Administration,* with offices throughout the country, offers management training, assistance, and loans to small business owners. If you plan to start a business, don't overlook this source of valuable information and possible financing.

Government has actively promoted business in the United States through a variety of services, grants, and assistance programs. Moreover, government purchases of goods and services is the primary source of sales for many firms. Where, for example, would General Motors be today without the billions of dollars of government spending on streets and highways?

GOVERNMENT REGULATION OF BUSINESS

People of the same trade seldom meet together, even for merriment and diversion, but the conversation ends in a conspiracy against the public, or in some contrivance to raise prices.

Adam Smith

During the early nineteenth century, government exercised very little control over American business. Most companies were small, rarely employing more than a few dozen workers, and competition was vigorous. However, after the Civil War a host of new inventions, including the steam engine and advances in metallurgy, brought about the substitution of machinery for human power. The need to purchase expensive machinery led to the widespread adoption of the corporate form of business organization, which permitted business firms to raise money through the sales of stock to the public. Many corporations grew rapidly in size, often employing thousands of workers.

By the 1880s, some industries were dominated by huge monopolies called *trusts.* The Standard Oil Company, under the direction of John D. Rockefeller, controlled 90 percent of the American oil industry, while the United States Steel Corporation accounted for more than two-thirds of all steel production. Competition was eliminated either by deliberately driving smaller firms into bankruptcy or by agreements among competing firms to fix prices at high levels and divide up the market. One of the foundations of capitalism—competition—was being destroyed.

Small business owners, farmers, and the public urged government to take action against the huge monopolies and their unfair business practices. Between 1890 and 1914 a series of federal laws were passed that outlawed monopolies and unfair methods of competition. Theodore Roosevelt, elected president in 1900, proclaimed that "there must be an increase in the supervision exercised by government over business enterprise." The federal government launched an attack on the monopolies by bringing many corporations to trial for violations of the antitrust laws.

Purposes of Government Regulation of Business

There are three major reasons why government intervenes in the affairs of business: (1) to preserve competition, (2) to protect the public welfare, and (3) to regulate "natural monopolies."

Monopoly may be defined as the absence of competition. Without competition there is no incentive for business firms to charge low prices, reduce costs, or develop new and improved products. In other words, you end up paying more for less. The growth of unregulated monopolies is a threat to the capitalist economic system; indeed, capitalism cannot exist without competition. For these reasons, the government, representing the public, steps in to maintain competition and prevent monopoly.

There have always been a few dishonest business managers who have attempted to deceive and cheat the public. For many years, the guiding principle for consumers was *caveat emptor*—"let the buyer beware." If a consumer bought a faulty or overpriced product, it was considered his or her own fault.

At the turn of the century Upton Sinclair wrote a novel called *The Jungle,* describing the filthy conditions in the Chicago meatpacking industry, which often sold diseased meat to the public. The uproar caused by this book resulted in the 1906 passage of the Pure Food and Drug Act, which was aimed at preventing the sale of unsafe food and drugs and forcing manufacturers to accurately label their products. Since then several laws have been passed to protect the public, including the Water Quality Act, the Air Quality Act, the Toy Safety Act, the Consumer Credit Protection Act, and the Fair Packaging and Labeling Act.

Natural Monopolies

Sometimes competition is unworkable. There are some industries in which competition would lead to higher prices and poorer service. Examples include most utilities, such as local telephone, natural gas, and electricity companies. These firms perform essential public services and require a large investment in capital equipment.

Would you be better off if three telephone companies served your local community? This competition would mean three times as many telephone lines as well as the difficulty of trying to call someone served by another company. The increased costs of operating three systems would raise the price of telephone service.

Because of the undesirable effects of competition, most utility companies are considered "natural monopolies." The government grants one firm the exclusive right to provide service to a particular area (a city, county, or state). In return, the government regulates the rates (prices) charged by the utility and sets minimum standards for service.

Methods of Government Regulation

Government attempts to preserve competition, protect the public welfare, and control natural monopolies by: (1) enforcing antitrust laws, (2) establishing regulatory agencies, and (3) occasionally by direct public ownership.

ISSUE TWO CHEERS FOR GOVERNMENT DEREGULATION OF BUSINESS

We rail at government inefficiency and intrusion in our markets, while we call upon the same government to protect our interest, our industry, and our financial institutions.

Paul Volcker, Chairman, Federal Reserve Board

Beginning decades ago the federal government launched a series of programs aimed at solving complex social problems such as cleaning up the environment, increasing employment opportunities for minorities and women, and protecting consumers and workers. These programs gave birth to a host of new government agencies staffed with thousands of federal regulators. In a short time these agencies created an avalanche of rules, regulations, reports, and red tape that buried business firms in paperwork and boosted the cost of doing business.

Overregulation brought a powerful reaction from business and consumers. In 1981 the government embarked on a program of regulatory reform aimed at cutting the number and complexity of federal rules, reducing the staffs and budgets of regulatory agencies, and speeding deregulation of some industries. Although initial reactions to deregulation were generally favorable, within a few months there were a growing

---

At the end of the nineteenth century, the growing power of monopolies, coupled with unfair methods of competition, led to the passage of the *antitrust laws.* Three major acts provide the legal basis for the federal government's continuing efforts to prevent monopoly and unfair business practices.

Antitrust Laws

The *Sherman Act,* passed in 1890, contains two key provisions: (1) monopolies are outlawed, and (2) it is illegal for any person to conspire to monopolize or restrain trade. Individual violators can be fined up to $100,000, sent to prison for 3 years, or both. Corporations may be fined up to $1 million. In addition, convicted individuals or firms can be sued for triple damages by injured parties.

The provisions of the Sherman Act were so broad in scope that the courts had difficulty interpreting their meaning. In 1914, Congress passed the *Clayton Act,* which declares certain business practices to be unfair and illegal when they lead to reduced competition. These unfair practices include:

ISSUE TWO CHEERS FOR GOVERNMENT DEREGULATION
OF BUSINESS (Cont.)

---

number of complaints . . . from business! Soon a number of industries were hard at work blocking deregulation.

Some businesses support government rules because the rules limit competition and keep prices high. Farmers benefit from federal subsidies and market orders (which reduce the supply of fruit and vegetables). Farm organizations have generally opposed efforts to reduce the role of government in agriculture. Companies producing antipollution equipment have lobbied against any attempts to moderate the provisions of the Clean Air Act. They have been joined by firms that have invested in equipment to control emissions who want to make sure their competitors are forced to comply to federal regulations.

When the National Highway Traffic and Safety Administration rescinded a regulation requiring automakers to install air bags or automatic seat belts, the insurance industry launched a counterattack to have the requirement reinstated. Large trucking firms have been joined by the Teamsters Union in fighting deregulation of interstate trucking.

Commenting on the ambivalent attitude of some business firms toward deregulation, Anne Brunsdale of the American Enterprise Institute noted that, "regulatory reform is filled with exceptions and the usual exception is 'me.'"

---

1 *Price discrimination* among competing buyers of the same quantity and quality of a product.

2 *Exclusive contracts* where a firm promises to buy only from one supplier.

3 *Tying contracts* where, for example, a computer manufacturer sells equipment only on the condition that the buyer also purchase all supplies (cards, tape, etc.) from the manufacturer.

4 *Interlocking directorates* that involve one person serving as a director of two or more competing corporations.

5 *Corporate purchases of stock* in competing firms.

The third major antitrust law is the *Federal Trade Commission Act,* also passed in 1914. Under this legislation unfair methods of competition were declared illegal and the Federal Trade Commission (FTC) was created to investigate violations of the antitrust laws. The Wheeler-Lea Act, an amendment to the Federal Trade Commission

---

ISSUE IS FEDERAL SPENDING OUT OF CONTROL?

Budget deficits occur when the federal government spends more than it collects in taxes. Deficits add to the size of the national debt. From 1790 to 1981, a period exceeding 190 years, the national debt grew from $75 million to $1 trillion. But from 1981 to 1986, the debt jumped to $2 trillion! Currently the national debt is about 50 percent of GNP. In 1981, it was less than 35 percent. If deficit spending continues at $200 billion a year, federal IOUs will rise to $3 trillion by the end of 1990.

The problem with deficit spending and a huge national debt is that the Treasury must borrow great sums of money to keep the government operating. The Treasury's heavy demand for money bids up interest rates and, therefore, crowds out business investment. If interest rates are high, business firms are less likely to borrow funds to expand or modernize operations. Without such investment, the economy will not create as many new jobs or grow as rapidly. The current deficit is forcing the Treasury to borrow about 30 percent of all funds available for investment.

The Federal Reserve can reduce interest rates by increasing the supply of money (printing more dollars). Increasing the money supply too rapidly, however, tends to increase the rate of inflation. As President Reagan said, "Only the threat of

---

Act, was passed in 1938 giving the FTC the power to investigate cases of false and misleading advertising.

ANTITRUST IN ACTION

The two largest, most costly, and complicated antitrust suits in the history of the U.S. Department of Justice were settled on January 8, 1982. The suits were against American Telephone & Telegraph Company (AT&T) and International Business Machines (IBM), two giant corporations that dominated their respective industries.

AT&T, commonly referred to as Ma Bell, was accused of numerous violations of the antitrust laws, particularly the Sherman Act. At that time, Ma Bell controlled 80 percent of the U.S. telephone market and was not allowing competing firms to hook up to the Bell long-distance network. The government charged AT&T with conspiring to monopolize telecommunications services. The firm spent an estimated $360 million on legal costs before agreeing to settle out of court.

The giant phone company agreed to divest itself of 22 telephone operating companies. The divested companies would

ISSUE   IS FEDERAL SPENDING OUT OF CONTROL? (Cont.)

indefinitely prolonged budget deficits threatens the continuation of sustained noninflationary growth and prosperity." Unfortunately, growing budget deficits are exactly what the United States has experienced during the 1980s.

The solution seems simple: Cut government spending, raise taxes, or both. The problem is, which programs should be cut—military spending (for example, "Star Wars") or social services (for example, Social Security) or what? Any cuts in government programs are vigorously opposed by those who benefit from the spending, and tax increases are generally unpopular among voters. The result is deficit spending.

In late 1985, Congress passed the Gramm-Rudman Act, which requires the federal deficit be reduced each year until it is eliminated in 1991. If Congress fails to cut spending or raise taxes to meet the target reductions, the law requires automatic cuts in federal spending evenly divided between defense and domestic programs.

The Gramm-Rudman Act has been attacked as politically irresponsible, economically destructive, and socially unfair as well as possibly unconstitutional. However, its defenders contend that Gramm-Rudman offers the only workable means of reducing federal spending and eliminating the deficit. What do you think?

remain natural monopolies in their geographic areas, but only for local calls. AT&T was permitted to keep Western Electric (its manufacturing facility) and Bell Research Laboratories as well as its profitable long-distance network. However, competing firms were allowed to offer long-distance service and sell telephone equipment.

Several hours later, the Justice Department dropped its suit against IBM. In 1969, IBM was charged with monopolizing the computer industry. At that time, IBM accounted for an estimated 70 percent of mainframe (large) computer sales. Originally, the government had sought to break up IBM into several competing companies.

After 13 years, 2500 depositions, 66 million pages of documents, and an army of lawyers, Assistant Attorney General William Baxter concluded, "This case is without merit and should be dismissed. What we learned today is that a company that is large and has a large market share should be allowed to compete aggressively. Period."

By 1982, IBM's share of the mainframe market had declined to 62 percent. Today the firm faces significant competition in the minicomputer and personal computer markets both domestically and from abroad.

Did the Justice Department's decision to drop these suits serve the best interests of the public and the U.S. economy? Should the suits have been brought in the first place?

Government Regulatory Agencies

The Federal Trade Commission and the Justice Department have brought lawsuits against hundreds of business firms for violating the provisions of the Sherman, Clayton, FTC, and Wheeler-Lea Acts. Some of these suits have dragged through the courts for years. In an attempt to avoid the delays of court actions, federal and state governments have established dozens of *regulatory agencies* that exercise control over various industries. The Interstate Commerce Commission (ICC) regulates railroads and trucking firms that operate across state lines. The Federal Reserve Board (FRB) supervises the commercial banking system, while the Securities and Exchange Commission (SEC) oversees the securities industry. At the state level the California Public Utilities Commission, for example, establishes the rates charged by natural monopolies and ensures that consumers receive adequate services. These agencies offer the advantages of rapid action as well as flexibility. If a business firm disagrees with the decision of an agency, it can appeal to the courts.

Government Ownership

In a relatively few cases the U.S. government owns and operates business enterprises. At the federal level examples include the United States Postal Service, retail stores on military posts, the United States Government Printing Office and certain hydroelectric power facilities such as Hoover Dam and Tennessee Valley Authority. Many cities operate water, electric, and natural gas distribution systems, while a few states maintain monopoly ownership of retail liquor stores.

TAXATION

The wisdom of man never yet contrived a system of taxation that would operate with perfect equality.

Andrew Jackson

Local, state, and federal governments levy taxes on both individuals and business firms. Most people believe the purpose of taxation is to raise revenue for financing government-produced goods and services. This is only partly true. Taxation is also used to control the level of economic activity and to regulate the production and sale of certain products.

You will recall that the Employment Act of 1946 made the federal government responsible for ensuring full employment, keeping prices stable, and promoting economic growth (a rising standard of living). Taxes are used to control the income and spending of both individuals and business firms, and the level of government spending influences employment, prices, and growth.

Some products and activities are taxed, not to raise revenue, but to control their use. Taxes on narcotics and gambling require detailed recordkeeping, which provides information to detect illegal activities. Heavy taxes on gasoline have been suggested as one method of conserving energy. Somewhat different reasoning is used to justify high taxes on cigarettes and liquor. Since these products are considered sinful or unhealthy, they are heavily taxed. Following this reasoning, perhaps we should tax war or even deep breathing in smoggy cities.

Principles of Taxation

Two major principles are used to measure the fairness of taxes.

The *benefits principle* maintains that people should pay taxes according to the amount of government goods and services each receives. For example, if you consume $1000 worth of public services a year, you should pay that amount in taxes. Applying the benefits principle raises two problems. How can an individual measure the dollar benefits he or she receives from public education, national defense, or police protection? Moreover, if the benefits principle were applied for everyone, what would happen to welfare programs and free public education? Nevertheless, some taxes do conform to the benefits principle; for example, most gasoline tax revenues are used to build and maintain streets and highways.

The *ability-to-pay principle* holds that each person should pay taxes according to his or her financial ability as measured by wealth or income. In other words, the rich should pay more taxes than the poor. Can you think of a tax based on this principle?

Tax Rates

Taxes are often judged on whether they are progressive, proportional, or regressive. These terms refer to the relationship between the *tax base* and the *tax rate.* The tax base is what is being taxed—for example, income, property, or spending. The tax rate is the percent of the tax base that is paid in taxes.

Progressive Tax   A progressive tax is one whose rate increases as the tax base increases. The illustration in Table 2.1 shows the tax rate rising from 5 to 50 percent as income increases from $100 to $100,000. High incomes are taxed at a larger percent than are low incomes. The federal individual income tax, with rates beginning at 0 percent and rising to 50 percent, is an example of a progressive tax.

Proportional Tax   A proportional tax is one whose rate remains constant as the tax base increases. Table 2.1 shows a fixed tax rate of 20 percent regardless of income. A property tax where all real estate is taxed at 10 percent may be considered proportional when property value is used as the base.

TABLE 2.1 Progressive, Proportional, and Regressive Taxes (Hypothetical Data)

Tax Base (Income)	Progressive Tax		Proportional Tax		Regressive Tax	
	Rate	Amount	Rate	Amount	Rate	Amount
$ 100	5%	$ 5	20%	$ 20	30%	$ 30
1,000	10	100	20	200	20	200
10,000	25	2,500	20	2,000	10	1,000
100,000	50	50,000	20	20,000	5	5,000

Regressive Tax   A regressive tax is the opposite of a progressive one; the tax rate declines as the tax base rises.

Some taxes that appear to be proportional are actually regressive in effect. A general sales tax of 5 percent is proportional when spending is used as the tax base; but if income is the tax base, the tax is regressive. Table 2.2 demonstrates this point.

The poor family must spend all its income, and its sales tax payments are $200 (5 percent of $4000). However, the rich family saves one-half its income, and therefore, the sales tax represents only 2½ percent of family income. To sum up, using income as a tax base, the poor family is taxed at twice the rate of the wealthy family. Some states exempt food, rent, and prescription drugs from the sales tax to reduce its regressive effect.

Major Taxes

What are the major sources of revenue and the main expenditures of federal, state, and local governments? Figure 2.2 provides a summary of how each level of government raises tax revenue as well as how these funds are spent.

Individual Income Tax   Over one-third of all federal tax revenue comes from the individual income tax. The tax rates begin at 0 percent of taxable income and rise to 50 percent. Remember that the tax is not levied on total income, but on taxable income. Here is how the tax is computed:

Taxable Income = Total Income − (Exemptions and Deductions)

Tax Owed = Taxable Income × Tax Rate

TABLE 2.2   The Regressive Effect of a General Sales Tax

	Poor Family	Rich Family
Annual Income	$ 4,000	$ 200,000
Spending	4,000	100,000
5% Sales Tax	200	5,000
Tax Paid as a Percent of Income	5%	2½ %

WHERE IT COMES FROM . . .

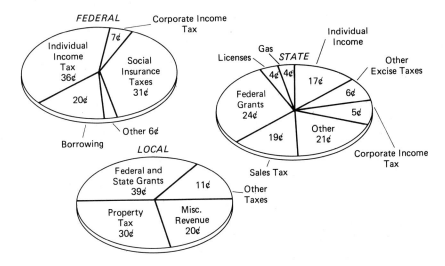

WHERE IT GOES . . .

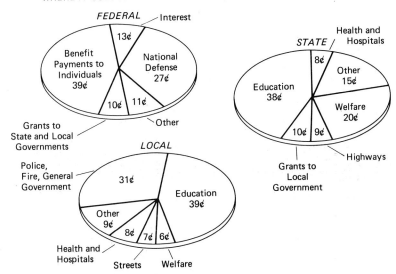

FIGURE 2.2   Sources and Uses of Tax Dollars
Sources: Economic Report of the President, 1986; United States Department of Commerce, *State Government Finances, 1984;* United States Department of Commerce, *Local Government Finances in Selected Metropolitan Areas and Large Counties, 1983–1984.*

The federal government allows taxpayers to reduce total income by $1040 for each dependent.[1] For example, a family consisting of a husband and wife and one child can deduct $3120 (3 × $1040) in *exemptions. Deductions* fall into two main categories:

[1]The $1040 figure is for 1985. This is adjusted annually for inflation.

(1) business deductions, which are the expenses of doing business such as wages, advertising, supplies, and so on; and (2) individual deductions, which include charitable contributions, interest paid, state and local taxes, large medical expenses, and so on.

After subtracting all exemptions and deductions from income, you have taxable income. Now, using a tax table, you find the appropriate rate and compute what you owe. Of course, most workers have a part of their paychecks withheld each pay period to cover their income tax.

In addition to the federal government, many states also levy a tax on income.

Corporation Income Tax   The earnings (or profits) of corporations are taxed by the federal government and some state governments. The federal corporation income tax, which accounts for about 7 percent of federal revenues, has five tax rates: (1) On the first $25,000, 15 percent; (2) $25,001–50,000, 18 percent; (3) $50,001–75,000, 30 percent; (4) $75,001–100,000, 40 percent; and (5) over $100,000, 46 percent. This means that large corporations pay over 40 percent of their taxable earnings in taxes.

Sales Taxes   The vast majority of state governments levy a tax on the sale of goods (and sometimes services) to the consumer. This is a major source of revenue for most states. (Remember that a general sales tax is regressive in effect if income is used as the tax base.)

Property Taxes   A major source of support for local government is the property tax. It is levied on the value of land and buildings owned by individuals and business firms. In some localities personal property (such as furniture) and business inventories are also subject to the property tax.

Social Security Taxes   Payroll taxes, paid by both employers and employees, provide for unemployment insurance: old age, survivors, and disability insurance plus medicare, and workers' compensation. Federal social security taxes account for over 25 percent of all federal tax revenues. In 1986 the rate was 7.15 percent for both the employer and employee on the first $42,000 of taxable wages. This tax is somewhat regressive, taking a larger proportion of the low- and medium-income workers' earnings than it does from high-income individuals.

Other Taxes   Both state and federal governments levy *excise taxes* on selected products and services including gasoline, tires, cigarettes, liquor, and telephone service. Although these taxes are paid by the manufacturer or retailer, they are normally passed on to the consumer in higher prices.

Death taxes are levied by federal and state governments against the wealth left by deceased persons. As Benjamin Franklin said, "Only two things in life are certain—death and taxes—and I resent they don't come in that order." Sometimes they do come in that order, Ben.

Tax Loopholes

A *tax loophole* is a legal way of avoiding or reducing taxes. Most loopholes are based on provisions in the tax laws that give certain types of income special treatment. These provisions are of special benefit to high-income individuals who may "shelter" a substantial portion of their incomes from taxes. Among the most common loopholes are:

- **Municipal Bonds**—Interest paid on bonds sold by state and local governments is not subject to the federal individual income tax.

- **Capital Gains**—A long-term capital gain is the profit realized on securities or property held for a year or more. Such profits are taxed at a maximum of 20 percent of the gain.

- **Expense Accounts**—The cost of travel, meals, and entertainment can often be written off as business expenses by executives.

Taxation and Business Decisions

Many business decisions are influenced by tax considerations. For example, in deciding on the location of a new plant, management should consider local taxes. The accounting system used by a company must conform to standards established by the Internal Revenue Service. The purchase of new equipment is influenced by investment tax credits. If a corporation wants to raise money by selling securities, it must take into account that bond interest may be deducted as an expense, thereby reducing corporate income taxes, while dividends on stock are not deductible. Even a firm's choice of legal ownership form—proprietorship, partnership, or corporation—is influenced by different tax treatment.

SUMMARY

The role of government in the American economy has expanded rapidly over the past century. This expansion is partly a result of the growing demand for government-produced goods and services—highways, education, parks, national defense, space exploration, and police protection, to name a few. A growing population and inflation (rising prices) have also caused government spending to increase.

Government has always assisted American business through

ISSUE DO YOU REALLY WANT TAX REFORM?

Where you stand on a issue depends on where you sit.

Anonymous

Every few years, Congress passes a tax reform law aimed at simplifying taxes. The result is usually the opposite—the federal tax code becomes more complex, confusing, and difficult to apply. The explosion of exemptions, exclusions, credits, deductions, and special allowances have forced many individuals and corporations to hire costly accountants and lawyers to find ways to minimize taxes. Business investment decisions are often made to avoid taxes rather than to increase productivity and efficiency. The "underground economy," where much individual and business income goes unreported, is growing faster than the legal economy. The federal government loses more than $100 billion a year due to tax cheating. Of course, cheating is encouraged by high marginal tax rates (up to 50 percent for individuals and 46 percent for corporations).

Would you favor a federal income tax system that is easy to understand, difficult to evade, and uniformly imposed on all individuals and corporations? One tax proposal would:

- Allow no loopholes, exclusions, or special allowances.

- Levy a flat rate of 20 percent on all income, business and personal.

- Be so simple that tax returns could be completed on a form the size of a postcard.

grants and subsidies, tariffs, loans, and maintaining a system of courts and laws to facilitate trade.

At the end of the nineteenth century, the federal government began to take steps to fight monopoly and halt unfair business practices in order to preserve competition and protect the public welfare. The major antitrust laws—the Sherman Act, the Clayton Act, and the Federal Trade Commission Act—serve as the legal framework for government intervention. In addition, a series of regulatory agencies have been established to oversee certain industries. In a few cases, government has assumed ownership and

ISSUE   DO YOU REALLY WANT TAX REFORM? (Cont.)

A flat tax of only 20 percent would reduce the incentive to evade tax, and it would be harder to "hide" income if there were no exclusions. Investment decisions would be based on profitability rather than tax avoidance. Best of all, this system would be easy to understand.

Does this sound too good to be true? Maybe it is. Everyone wants taxes to be fair and uncomplicated. Yet, what is fair to one person will be seen as unfair by another. Remember, our tax proposal:

• Allows no tax credits for business investment, which promotes productivity and economic growth.

• Prohibits exclusions for dependents, which will raise taxes paid by large families.

• Provides for proportional, rather than progressive, tax rates so that the rich and poor are taxed at the same percent.

• Permits no deductions or allowances for charitable contributions, the blind or elderly, those in debt, or homeowners.

Everyone can think of good reasons for some exceptions, deductions, and exemptions. The problem is that the tax code is so crammed with such "worthwhile cases" that the law has become complicated, confusing, and frustrating. It is human nature to view a special allowance as "fair" when we benefit from it and "unfair" when others qualify and we do not.

Would you vote for the simplified tax system described in this issue? If not, what is your ideal tax system?

operation of some businesses such as the Postal Service, federal power projects, and some local utilities.

Taxation is used to regulate the level of economic activity, to raise funds for public goods and services, and to control the production of certain products. Most taxes are based on either the ability-to-pay or the benefits principle. A tax may be progressive, proportional, or regressive depending on the relationship between the tax base and the tax rates.

The major progressive tax in the United States is the federal individual income tax whose rates range from 0 to 50 percent of taxable income. The corporation income tax is levied on corporate profits. Local governments derive a large proportion of their revenue from the property tax and grants, while state governments rely primarily on grants, sales, and excise taxes. Tax loopholes are provisions in the tax laws that enable individuals and corporations to avoid or reduce taxes paid.

Business managers must give careful consideration to the tax consequences of most business decisions.

SELF-EXAMINATION QUESTIONS

The following questions are based on the Chapter Objectives listed at the beginning of this chapter. Test yourself by circling the letter preceding the answer that *best* completes the statement or answers the question. The answers to the Self-Examination Questions are in the appendix at the end of the textbook.

1. Government assistance to business has taken the form of: (A) subsidies; (B) tariffs; (C) government-guaranteed loans; (D) land grants; (E) all of these.

2. Which of the following is *not* a major goal of government regulation of business? (A) to preserve competition; (B) to increase the size of government; (C) to protect the public welfare; (D) to set prices and services standards for natural monopolies.

3. In the United States the *least common* method of government control over business has been: (A) the use of regulatory agencies; (B) the enforcement of antitrust laws; (C) through public ownership; (D) the use of taxes and tariffs.

4. The antitrust law that outlaws monopolies and makes it illegal to attempt to monopolize is called the: (A) Sherman Act; (B) Clayton Act; (C) Federal Trade Commission Act; (D) Anti-monopoly Law.

5. The amount of taxes people pay should depend on their income or wealth. This principle is called: (A) the fairness doctrine; (B) the benefits principle; (C) regressive taxation; (D) the ability-to-pay principle.

6. If the tax rate remains constant regardless of changes in the tax base, the tax is called: (A) progressive; (B) regressive; (C) proportional; (D) none of these.

7. The single largest source of revenues for the federal government is: (A) social security; (B) corporate income tax; (C) sales tax; (D) individual income tax.

Student _____

BUILDING A BUSINESS VOCABULARY

Directions: Match the terms with their definitions by writing the letter in the appropriate blank.

a. Caveat Emptor
b. Interlocking Directorates
c. Individual Income Tax
d. Tariffs
e. Benefits Principle
f. Regressive Tax
g. Tax Loopholes
h. Regulatory Agencies
i. FTC
j. Monopoly
k. Antitrust Laws

l. Progressive Tax
m. Property Tax
n. Subsidy
o. Municipal Bonds
p. Exclusive Contract
q. Natural Monopolies
r. Small Business Administration
s. Ability-to-Pay Principle
t. Exemptions and Deductions
u. Capital Gains

___d___ 1. Taxes levied on imported goods.

___R___ 2. A federal agency that provides advice, training, and loans to small businesses.

___j___ 3. The absence of competition in an industry dominated by one firm or a few large firms.

___k___ 4. Legislation intended to prevent monopoly and unfair methods of competition.

___A___ 5. Let the buyer beware.

___q___ 6. Government-regulated utilities that are given an exclusive right to provide service in a certain area.

___b___ 7. Competing corporations having the same people serving on their boards of directors.

___i___ 8. A federal agency responsible for investigating unfair business practices and false advertising.

___e___ 9. Individuals paying taxes according to the value of government goods and services that they receive.

___p___ 10. An agreement whereby a business firm is required to purchase only from one supplier.

___f___ 11. The tax rate decreases as the tax base increases.

_C___ 12. The major source of revenue for the federal government.

_L___ 13. A type of tax that takes a larger percent of income from a rich family than from a poor family.

_S___ 14. The amount of taxes paid should reflect the financial ability of the taxpayer.

_I___ 15. The difference between total income and taxable income.

_n___ 16. Assistance by the government in the form of a special payment to a business firm.

_M___ 17. A tax that provides a major source of revenue for local governments.

_h___ 18. Government-established commissions that serve as watchdogs over certain industries.

_u___ 19. Profits on property held a year or more that are taxed at a maximum of 20 percent of the gain.

_g___ 20. Legal means of avoiding or reducing taxes.

_o___ 21. Tax-free bonds sold by state and local governments.

Student _____

REVIEWING MAJOR CONCEPTS

1. Briefly describe the major provisions of the following antitrust laws:

   a. Sherman Act.

   1.) Monopolies are outlawed

   2) Illegal for anyone to conspire to Monopolize OR restrain trade

   b. Clayton Act.

   gives 5 provisions to Sherman
   1. price discrimination
   2. exclusive contracts
   3. tying agreements
   4. Buying of othe busin. Stalks
   5. Interlocking directories

   c. Federal Trade Commission Act.

   gives the government the right to investigate possible violations in the Anti-Trust laws

   d. Wheeler-Lea Act.

   a provision to the FTC allowing gov. to investigate false adv.

2. Why has government spending grown so rapidly over the past 50 years?

3. "If government would only stop interfering with business and return to free enterprise we would all be better off." Do you agree or disagree? Explain your answer.

4. In the space provided, designate whether each of the following taxes is (A) progressive, (B) proportional, or (C) regressive when income is used as the base.

_A_ a. Federal Corporation Income Tax
_C_ b. General Sales Tax
_B_ c. Property Tax
_C_ d. Individual Income Tax
_C_ e. Social Security Taxes

5. List four ways in which the federal government assists business.

1 tarrifs

2 Quotas on foreign trade

3 Subsidies

4 Taxes

6. How can people legally avoid paying taxes? Give two examples.

1. Municiple bonds

2. writing off business expenses

7. Some people feel that huge corporations should be broken up into smaller companies to increase competition. For example, it has been suggested that General Motors might be divided into five or six independent automobile firms. Would you support this plan? Why or why not?

Student _____

SOLVING PROBLEMS AND CASES

1. The table below represents the 1985 federal income tax rate schedule for married couples. In 1985 the personal exemption was $1040 per dependent. Use the table to answer the following questions:

Married Couples Filing Joint Returns

Taxable Income		Amount of Tax	
Not over $3,540		0	
Over—	But not over—		of the amount over—
$ 3,540	$ 5,720	$ 11%	$ 3,540
5,720	7,910	239.80 + 12%	5,720
7,910	12,390	502.60 + 14%	7,910
12,390	16,650	1,129.80 + 16%	12,390
16,650	21,020	1,811.40 + 18%	16,650
21,020	25,600	2,598.00 + 22%	21,020
25,600	31,120	3,605.60 + 25%	25,600
31,120	36,630	4,985.60 + 28%	31,120
36,630	47,670	6,528.40 + 33%	36,630
47,670	62,450	10,171.60 + 38%	47,670
62,450	89,090	15,788.00 + 42%	62,450
89,090	113,860	26,976.80 + 45%	89,090
113,860	169,020	38,123.30 + 49%	113,860
169,020	. . . . . .	65,151.70 + 50%	169,020

a. Mr. and Mrs. Watt have one child. Their total income in 1985 was $20,000 and their deductions amount to $5880. How much tax do they owe? What is their average tax rate? (*Hint:* To find the average tax rate, divide the tax owed by taxable income and express the answer as a percent.)

b. In 1985 Mr. and Mrs. Kent earned a total income of $25,000. They claim 12 dependents including themselves and have deductions of $9020. What is their tax?

c. Mr. and Mrs. Starr are a childless couple who both work in motion pictures. Their 1985 total income (mostly from dividends, interest, and royalties) was $331,100 and their deductions amounted to $60,000. Compute their income tax and average tax rate.

2. Read the first issue in this chapter on foreign trade. Suppose the federal government increases the tariff on foreign steel by $1000 per ton. Briefly explain the effect on each of the following individuals.

a. A steelworker employed by U.S. Steel Corporation.

b. A secretary interested in buying a new Oldsmobile.

c. A soybean farmer in Arkansas.

d. A U.S. Steel stockholder.

e. An aircraft machinist in Seattle.

Student _____

3. *Case:* Poe Products

Frank Truly has been employed for over a year as a salesman for Poe Products, a large manufacturer of farm equipment. Although he likes his job and is well paid, Frank is concerned about several events that have occurred during the past months.

Last October he attended an industry convention where he overheard executives from several companies discussing plans for establishing standard prices for various types of farm equipment.

The following January, Poe Products brought out a revolutionary new grape harvester that made competing products obsolete. Frank's sales manager suggested that customers be informed that the new harvester would be available only if the farmer promised to buy all equipment from Poe. In agreeing to this plan, the customer would be given a special 10 percent price discount on the harvester.

In May, Frank was surprised to read an advertisement for a Poe tractor that made claims that he knew were untrue. Just last week, Frank learned that one of the directors of Poe Products is also a director for a major competitor.

Frank has asked for your assistance. He wants to know if Poe Products is engaged in any illegal activities and, if so, which laws are being violated. In addition, he would like your advice on what, if anything, he should do.

chapter **3**

FORMS OF BUSINESS OWNERSHIP

The first two chapters have provided a broad overview of the economic and political environment of American business. Now we turn our attention to the business firm itself.

Suppose you are planning to start a business. One of the first decisions you must make is the best form of ownership for your firm. Should you select the proprietorship, partnership, or corporation? There is no right answer to this question. Business firms differ in many ways: in the type of products and services they produce and sell; in size; in their need for funds; in the personal characteristics of the owner(s). The most appropriate form of ownership is determined by weighing the advantages and disadvantages of each type of organization against the requirements of the particular firm.

This chapter describes the major features of the proprietorship, partnership, and corporation.

CHAPTER OBJECTIVES

1. Contrast and compare the proprietorship, partnership, and corporation.

2. Give three advantages and three disadvantages of each form of ownership.

3. State three ways that a limited partnership differs from a general partnership.

4. List three factors that may influence the sharing of profits and losses in a partnership.

5. Give the main advantage of S corporations and state three of their requirements.

6. Diagram the structure of a corporation showing the board of directors, employees, officers (or managers), and stockholders.

7. Name and briefly describe the three major types of corporate mergers.

TABLE 3.1 Forms of Business Ownership in the United States

	Proprietorships	Partnerships	Corporations	Total
Number of Firms	10,106,000	1,514,000	2,926,000	14,546,000
Percent of Total Firms	70%	10%	20%	100%
Percent Volume of Sales	6%	4%	90%	100%

Source: *Statistical Abstract of the United States, 1985.*

Table 3.1 compares the three major types of ownership in terms of number of firms and combined sales. What is the most popular form of business ownership? Which form generates the greatest sales?

THE PROPRIETOR- SHIP

The proprietorship, sometimes called the *single* or *sole proprietorship,* is a firm owned and controlled by one individual who receives all of the profit and takes all of the risks. It is by far the most popular type of organization in the United States, accounting for seven out of ten firms. Proprietorships are particularly common in the fields of retailing and personal services. Most neighborhood stores and shops are solely owned. In addition, nearly 3 million farms are operated as proprietorships.

Advantages of the Proprietorship

The popularity of the proprietorship stems from its three key advantages: (1) ease of formation, (2) freedom and speed of action, and (3) maximum incentive.

Ease of Formation   A college student needed additional income but was unable to find a job flexible enough to fit her schedule. After carefully considering the alternatives, she decided to go into business for herself, operating a home janitorial service. She duplicated 100 advertisements, distributed them to likely prospects, and within a week she had signed up six customers with jobs scheduled at her convenience. She was in business! In a short time, she was clearing several hundred dollars a month.

The proprietor needs no state charter. Since there is little or no red tape, organizational expenses are low. A business license may cost a few dollars, but that is about it in terms of legal formalities.

Freedom and Speed of Action   Since the proprietor is the sole owner, there is no need to consult with stockholders or partners. This encourages rapid decision making, and enables the proprietor to make the most of opportunities. For example, the owner of a grocery store can take advantage of a special price on several crates of peaches offered by a farmer who is anxious to make an immediate sale. The single proprietorship enjoys flexibility usually unmatched by the partnership and corporation.

Maximum Incentive   Why do many proprietors work 10 to 14 hours a day, 6 or 7 days a week? For one reason, they directly reap the benefits of their efforts. The store owner who stays open in the evening for the convenience of customers recognizes that the additional income need not be shared with others. There is also the personal satisfaction involved in working for yourself. If the business is a success, the proprietor can take all the credit.

Disadvantages of the Proprietorship

Partly offsetting the advantages of proprietorship are four disadvantages: (1) unlimited liability, (2) limited life, (3) limited funds for expansion, and (4) lack of specialized management.

Unlimited Liability   Perhaps the major disadvantage of the single proprietorship is that the owner is liable to an unlimited extent for the debts of the business. If the firm fails, its creditors can claim not only the business assets of the proprietorship, but the personal assets of the owners as well. Suppose, for example, Todd's Shoes, a retail store, goes bankrupt with $4,000 in assets and $10,000 in liabilities (or debts). If Mr. Todd has a personal savings account, his creditors may lay claim to it to cover the $6,000 in unpaid debts. Thus the unlimited liability feature of the proprietorship makes the owner highly vulnerable in case of poor business decisions or plain bad luck.

Limited Life   In the eyes of the law, the proprietorship and its owner are considered one and the same. Therefore, if the proprietor dies, is imprisoned, or is otherwise incapacitated, this terminates the proprietorship. If the heirs attempt to operate the business after the proprietor's death, legally a new firm has been created.

Limited Funds for Expansion   It is difficult for a proprietor to raise money for business expansion. Normally, funds are limited to personal savings and what can be borrowed. Although a proprietorship may have a good credit rating (due to the unlimited liability of the owner), banks and other financial institutions are hesitant to extend long-term loans for expansion due to the firm's limited life. After all, the proprietorship is truly a one-person business, and if the owner dies, so does the firm. This is one reason few proprietorships ever grow into large companies.

Lack of Specialized Management   As the sole owner and manager, the proprietor is required to be skilled in a variety of management jobs. For example, the owner of Todd's Shoes must be the purchasing agent, advertising manager, financial manager, sales manager, and so on. It is very unlikely that one person will be expert at all these jobs. Nor is it easy for a proprietor to hire good management assistance. Ambitious and talented employees may prefer to seek jobs with a partnership or corporation, where the opportunities for advancement are greater.

THE PARTNERSHIP

In terms of both volume of sales and number of firms, the partnership is the least popular form of business ownership. While it is true that the partnership possesses some significant weaknesses, in some circumstances it is the best choice for a firm.

A *partnership* may be defined as an association of two or more persons as co-owners of a business. There is no limit on the number of partners, although nearly three-quarters of all partnerships have only two owners. Partnerships are common in personal service industries such as law, medicine, real estate, and insurance as well as in retailing.

One of the world's most famous partnerships was formed when Steven Jobs and Steven Wozniak created Apple Computer. Steven Wozniak provided technical expertise while Steven Jobs contributed motivational and marketing skills. As the partnership grew and needed additional capital, Apple Computer eventually became a corporation.

Advantages of the Partnership

In comparison to the proprietorship, the partnership enjoys three significant advantages: (1) more funds for expansion, (2) improved credit rating, and (3) increased specialization of management.

More Funds for Expansion   It is not unusual for a proprietorship to convert to a partnership in order to raise needed funds. A business firm may be highly successful and still run short of finances. One way to overcome this problem is by inviting an investor to become a partner in the firm. Of course, the existing owner must give up a share of the ownership, but this may be offset by greater profits through expansion of the business.

Improved Credit Rating   As a rule, the partnership enjoys the best credit rating of the three forms of business ownership. This is because each general partner has unlimited liability for the debts of the business. Suppliers are much more willing to provide credit when two or more owners are liable to an unlimited extent.

Increased Specialization of Management   A law firm in a large western city has five partners, each of whom is a specialist in a different area of the law—contracts, taxes, personal liability, criminal, and corporate law. Through the advantages of specialization, the firm can offer its clients a wider range of expert assistance than any single attorney. In operating a retail store, two partners may divide responsibilities according to their interests or talents. For example, one owner may handle sales and advertising while the other takes charge of purchasing, accounting, and finance. The partners will consult on general management decisions, in the hope that two heads are better than one.

Disadvantages of the Partnership

Why are partnerships relatively unpopular? There are four main reasons: (1) unlimited liability, (2) divided authority, (3) limited life, and (4) frozen investment.

Unlimited Liability   All general partners are liable to an unlimited extent for the debts of the partnership. Suppose, for example, that a firm with three owners fails after going deeply into debt. If two of the partners have no personal assets, the firm's creditors can collect all debts from the third partner. The partnership is a highly risky form of ownership, particularly for a partner with substantial personal wealth.

Divided Authority   It is often said that choosing a good partner is more difficult than choosing a spouse. Each partner is held responsible for the decisions of all partners. A poor decision by one owner is binding on the firm. With authority spread among two or more owners, it is easy for disputes to arise, and unresolved disputes may lead to termination of the business. Moreover, a dishonest or stupid partner can destroy a business and financially ruin the co-owners as well.

Limited Life   Under the law, the death, imprisonment, or incapacitation of any partner terminates the partnership. If the firm is reorganized to include a new partner, legally a new firm has been created. Can you imagine the problems this causes in a large partnership with dozens of partners?

Frozen Investment   It is often difficult for an owner to withdraw from a partnership. If a partner wishes to sell his or her share of the business, the new partner must be accepted by all of the other partners.

The Partnership Agreement

An agreement to form a partnership may be oral or written. A word to the wise: if you ever decide to enter a partnership, insist on a written agreement. This simple precaution may save you a great deal of disagreement, grief, and financial loss.

A partnership agreement simply states the rules under which the business will operate. It normally includes: (1) the name of the firm; (2) the amount invested by each partner; (3) how profits and losses are to be divided; (4) the duties and responsibilities of each partner; (5) the length of life of the partnership; (6) any provisions for payment of salaries or interest on investment; and (7) the method by which a partner may withdraw from the partnership.

The Limited Partnership

The unlimited liability feature of the general partnership often discourages investors from becoming co-owners. A *limited partnership* may be used to overcome this disadvantage. This type of firm consists of at least one general partner with unlimited liability and any number of limited partners whose liability is restricted to their investment in the business. However, limited partners may not take an active role in the management of the firm. Most states require that a limited partnership have a formal written agreement on file with the county clerk. This requirement provides public notice to creditors that some of the firm's partners have limited liability.

The limited partnership is frequently used to finance ventures such as Broadway shows, equipment leasing, and real estate speculations where the risks are great, but the potential profits are large. (See Figure 3.1.)

Division of Profits and Losses in the Partnership

One of the first decisions that must be made by the partners in a new firm is how profits and losses are to be shared. Any formula should take into consideration the amount invested in the business by each owner, the skill and experience of the partners, and the time devoted to the business. If there is no agreement covering profits and losses, they are shared equally.

A common method of dividing profits and losses is according to the amount invested by each partner. Suppose, for example, that Partner A invests $8,000 and Partner B invests $12,000. If the profit at the end of the first year is $10,000, it will be divided in the following way:

Partner	Investment	% Invested	×	Profit	=	Share of Profit
A	$ 8,000	$\frac{8,000}{20,000} = 40\%$	×	$10,000	=	$ 4,000
B	12,000	$\frac{12,000}{20,000} = 60\%$	×	10,000	=	6,000
Totals	$ 20,000	$\frac{20,000}{20,000} = 100\%$	×	$10,000	=	$10,000

THE CORPORATION

Now we turn to the most complicated, and in many ways the most important, form of ownership. Corporations account for 90 percent of the business transacted in the United States despite the fact that they represent only about one-fifth of the total firms. Many corporations are as small as most proprietorships and partnerships, but the 500 largest corporations produce two-thirds of our nation's goods and services.

What is the *corporation?* The most famous definition was written in 1819 by Chief Justice John Marshall: "A corporation is an artificial being, invisible, intangible, and existing only in contemplation of the law." This definition means that the corporation is a *legal entity* (or legal person) created by the law and granted certain rights by the state. Since the corporation is

---

LIMITED PARTNERSHIP ADVANTAGES

With the public limited partnership concept, investors in NLI 4 can participate in the growing equipment leasing industry in an efficient manner that provides a number of important benefits.

■ **Experienced Management** — A professional management team is responsible for all partnership decisions and day-to-day operations. Integrated's team of acquisition, administration and disposition experts works on your behalf throughout the life of the partnership.

■ **Limited Liability** — Unlike some investments, your financial liability is limited to the amount of your investment in NLI 4.

■ **Increased Buying Power** — A limited partnership allows investors to "pool" their capital thus giving them greater buying power than they would normally have on their own. Larger and more sophisticated types of equipment can be purchased on more attractive terms than could be arranged by a single investor.

■ **Diversification** — By pooling investors' capital and thus increasing buying power, a partnership can purchase many different types of equipment on lease to a wide variety of companies in different industries. (Amount of partnership proceeds will determine how much equipment is actually purchased.) This balance can substantially reduce the risk normally associated with "putting all of your eggs in one basket" with any one direct investment.

■ **Flow Through of Benefits** — Since a limited partnership is not a taxable entity in itself, all of the benefits associated with a partnership's equipment ownership flow through directly to investors.

■ **Direct Share of Profits** — Unlike buying common stock in a corporation, a partnership investment can allow the investor to share directly in cash proceeds from sale or re-lease of the partnership's assets through increased cash distributions, rather than hoping a stock price will go up or a dividend will be paid.

$50,000,000

NATIONAL LEASE INCOME FUND 4,

A CALIFORNIA LIMITED PARTNERSHIP
100,000 LIMITED PARTNERSHIP UNITS ($500 PER UNIT)
MINIMUM INVESTMENT — 5 Units ($2,500)
(2 Units or $1,000 for an Individual Retirement Account)

INTEGRATED RESOURCES MARKETING, INC.

FIGURE 3.1   Promotional Material for a Limited Partnership

considered a legal entity, it exists apart from its owners. In the eyes of the law, the proprietorship and proprietor are one and the same as are the partners and the partnership. But the corporation has an identity all its own; it can own property, make contracts, sue, and be sued. None of these rights directly involves its owners.

A corporation is created by applying to a state government for a *charter*. This can be a fairly lengthy and expensive process that includes filing the *articles of incorporation*. This document provides detailed information about the incorporators, the purpose of the

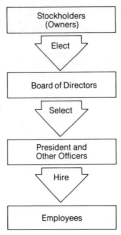

FIGURE 3.2
Corporate Structure

corporation, its bylaws (rules of governance), and the firm's financial structure. The company must conform to state requirements and pay certain fees before a charter is granted.

The Structure of the Corporation

The owners of a corporation are called *stockholders.* They elect a *board of directors* to protect the owner's interests and oversee the operation of the business. In many small corporations, the major stockholders are also directors. The board selects the major corporate officers who are responsible for the day-to-day operation of the firm. Often the president and other key officers are also directors. (See Figure 3.2.)

Advantages of the Corporation

As you might suspect, the corporate form of organization offers owners several significant advantages over both the proprietorship and partnership. These include: (1) limited liability, (2) ease of transferring ownership, (3) continuous life, (4) ease of raising funds for expansion, and (5) specialized management.

Limited Liability   The key advantage of the corporation is that stockholders are limited in liability to the extent of their investment. In other words, their personal wealth is safe from the claims of creditors if the corporation fails. The limited liability feature stems from the fact that a corporation is considered a legal entity, separate from its owners.

Ease of Transferring Ownership   Stockholders of a corporation can transfer their ownership simply by selling their shares of stock. The stock of large corporations is usually traded on organized stock exchanges, where millions of shares are bought and sold daily.

Neither the other stockholders nor the corporation itself can prevent an owner from disposing of his or her shares.

Continuous Life   The corporation, like Superman, is immortal. The death, incapacitation, or imprisonment of a stockholder, director, or officer does not terminate the corporation.

Ease of Raising Funds for Expansion   Almost without exception, the giant business firms in the United States are corporations. This popularity is derived from the ability of corporations to raise money for expansion by selling *corporate securities* (stocks and bonds) to the public. Investors find stock attractive because of the corporation's limited liability and continuous life as well as the ease of transferring ownership.

Specialized Management   Large corporations are divided into departments or divisions, each of which is headed by a manager. These professional managers are often experts in a particular area of business—for example, production, marketing, finance, or purchasing. Management by specialists can lead to improved decision making and greater efficiency.

Disadvantages of the Corporation

The drawbacks of the corporate form of organization are fourfold: (1) double taxation, (2) expense and difficulty of organization, (3) employee apathy, and (4) government regulation.

Double Taxation   In Chapter 2 we pointed out that the profits earned by corporations are subject to taxation by the federal government. Moreover, any dividends (distribution of profits) are taxed as personal income to stockholders under the individual income tax.[1] It should be noted that neither the profits of the proprietorship nor the partnership are subject to special taxes. Instead, profits are considered income earned by the proprietor or partner and are subject only to the individual income tax.

The special tax on corporate profits is a result of its legal status. Since the corporation is considered a legal entity, its earnings are taxable, and dividends paid from aftertax profits are also subject to taxation as income to stockholders.

S Corporations

Small firms can enjoy the benefits of the corporate form of ownership while avoiding double taxation. *S corporations* (formerly called Subchapter S corporations) pay no corporate income taxes. Earnings, whether or not distributed, are "passed through" directly to stockholders according to their percentage ownership of stock. For example, if you owned 30 percent of an S corporation, you must declare 30 percent of its earnings as taxable personal income.

[1]At the time of this printing, up to $100 ($200 for joint returns) of qualifying dividends may be excluded from taxable income.

To qualify for S corporation status, a firm must:

- Be chartered in the United States.

- Have the agreement of all stockholders to be taxed as an S corporation.

- Have only one class of stock (although not all shares need to have the same voting rights).

- Permit only individuals, estates, or certain trusts as stockholders.

While S corporations avoid the double tax on a federal level, some states do not recognize S corporations and impose state income taxes on both corporate earnings and profits distributed as cash dividends.

Expense and Difficulty of Organization   The process of applying for and receiving a corporate charter from the state may require several months and cost hundreds or even thousands of dollars. Normally the assistance of a corporate attorney is required to complete the articles of incorporation. In addition, there are incorporation fees to be paid to the state.

Employee Apathy   Several years ago, a large corporation experienced a major increase in employee theft. Several employees were caught pilfering and were questioned about their motives. In nearly every case, the same response was given: "I wasn't hurting anyone."

This incident illustrates a key problem faced by many giant corporations. Employees may come to feel they are working for a huge impersonal machine with no concern for their welfare. In the corporation, there is no owner-manager to personify the firm. Employees rarely see top management, and they wouldn't know a stockholder if they bumped into one.

Government Regulation   To a far greater extent than the proprietorship or partnership, the corporation is the target of regulation by state and federal government. Corporations must register in all states where they conduct business. The Securities and Exchange Commission requires detailed financial reports from large corporations. Indeed, the variety and number of reports required by various governmental agencies can represent a major expense of doing business. Table 3.2 summarizes some of the main features of sole proprietorships, partnerships, and corporations.

Before choosing a form of business, it is wise to consult both a lawyer and an accountant to be certain that your firm will meet all governmental and legal requirements.

TABLE 3.2   Characteristics of Forms of Ownership

Characteristics	Sole Proprietorship	Partnership		Corporation	
		General	Limited	Regular	S
Number of owners	One	Two or more	At least one general partner and one or more limited partners	One or more stockholders	No more than 35 stock-holders
Liability	Unlimited	Unlimited	Unlimited for general partners, limited for all others	Limited	Limited
Taxation of profits	Profits taxed as personal income	Profits taxed as personal income		Double tax: 1. Corporate income tax on profits 2. Individual income tax on dividends	No federal corporate income tax; profits taxed as personal income
Distribution of profits	All profits and losses go to the sole owner	Profits and losses are divided equally by partners unless otherwise stated in the partnership agreement		Profits and losses allocated to stockholders based on the number of shares owned	

ISSUE WOMEN IN BUSINESS

One of the most significant changes in the U.S. business system is the dramatic increase in female employment. Let's review the facts:

- Well over half the population is female.

- In the past 20 years the number of women in the work force has doubled.

- Women filled two-thirds of the 10 million new jobs created in the last decade.

- The average pay for working women is about 64 percent that of the average for men.

The surge of women into business began in the early 1970s when 4 out of 10 adult females worked. It is expected that 6 out of 10 adult females will be employed in the next decade. In terms of relative pay, however, progress has been less impressive. Until this decade, women's pay was stuck at about 60 cents for every dollar earned by males.

What accounts for this pay gap? While much of it is due to discrimination, other factors are also involved. Most women have traditionally crowded into low-paying "pink-collar" occupations such as clerical, sales, nursing, and teaching. As more people compete for jobs in these fields, employers have found it less necessary to increase wages to attract or keep qualified personnel. Economists point out that since the flood of women into business is comparatively recent, females have less work experience than males. In addition, part of the difference in earnings reflects the fact that women tend to enter and leave the labor market more frequently than males. Most studies reveal that when women and men do the same work and have the same experience, pay tends to be similar.

As more women move into traditional male occupations, the pay gap should close. Since 1980, women's wages have moved from 60 to 64 percent of men's wages, and most experts expect this trend to continue and even accelerate for the rest of the century.

Who Controls the Corporation?

In theory at least, the corporation is the most democratic of institutions. It would appear that stockholders can exercise substantial control over the firm's activities by electing directors. This is true in many small- and medium-size corporations. However, in the case of most giant corporations, with hundreds of thousands of stockholders, the owners have little influence over how the firm is run. A stockholder who is disappointed with the performance of the company or its management is much more likely to sell his or her shares than to engage in an expensive fight to replace the directors.

Does this mean that control of the corporation is in the hands of the board of directors? After all, the directors have the right to declare dividends, select the corporate officers, and approve or reject major management decisions. In fact, the boards of directors of many large corporations serve as little more than rubber stamps for recommendations presented by the president and other top executives. Increasingly, the control of giant corporations is passing into the hands of professional managers who may not be major stockholders.

The separation of ownership and control in today's huge corporations raises a puzzling question: For whose benefit should the corporations be run? The stockholders? The management? The employees? The consumer? Society as a whole? Or all of these?

Corporate Mergers How have some corporations grown so huge? Many have expanded through internal growth using reinvested profits to enlarge operations. IBM is a case in point. The giant computer maker ploughs back a large part of its earnings in research and capital investment. An even faster means of corporate expansion is through mergers.

A merger occurs when two or more firms combine into a single company. Recent examples include the Philip Morris acquisition of General Foods and the Capital Cities Communications purchase of American Broadcasting Company. Even IBM followed the merger approach in 1984 when it acquired ROLM corporation.

There are three major types of mergers: (1) horizontal; (2) vertical; and (3) conglomerate. A *horizontal merger* occurs when two or more firms producing the same product or in a related field of business combine. An example is the merger of two banks. In contrast, a *vertical merger* involves firms in different stages of production from raw materials to final sales. Large supermarket chains have moved into manufacturing and food processing by acquiring their own bakeries, meat-packing plants, and canning operations. Large oil companies such as Exxon control production from drilling to the sale of gasoline through their own chains of service stations. A *conglomerate merger* occurs when a firm takes over other companies in totally unrelated fields. Over the past 20 years, there was a wave of conglomerate mergers as firms such as ITT, Gulf & Western, and Beatrice purchased dozens of companies operating in different industries. Conglomerates are based on the notion that good management can manage any type of business. This often proved untrue. In the 1980s, many large conglomerates have been selling off billions of dollars of subsidiaries.

ISSUE IS BIGGER BETTER?

The decade of the 1980s has witnessed a wave of mergers that is producing giant corporations with vast economic power. In 1984 alone, there were 2543 corporate mergers with a combined value of $122 billion. Since 1980, 62 of the 500 largest U.S. corporations have been swallowed up by other firms. A few examples will serve to illustrate this trend.

- In 1984, Chevron, Inc., purchased Gulf Oil Company for $13.3 billion in the largest corporate merger in history.

- A year later, General Motors paid $5 billion for Hughes Aircraft to gain access to Hughes' technical know-how.

- In 1986, General Electric Company purchased RCA Corporation for $6.28 billion in cash, creating a huge communications, defense, and consumer products conglomerate.

What factors are behind this accelerating trend toward corporate acquisition? In some cases, mergers permit companies to acquire assets at bargain prices. According to Edward Hennessy, chairman of Allied Corporation, which acquired Bendix Corporation in 1982 and Signal Corporation in 1985, "It is cheaper to buy than to start from scratch." In addition, many observers feel that mergers make sense if U.S. companies are to compete successfully in global markets. Simply put, bigness may increase efficiency and provide greater clout in the world marketplace. This has been the view of the Reagan administration, which has shown little inclination for government antitrust action aimed at blocking large-scale mergers.

Many economists and business managers argue that mergers have a healthy effect on the economy by promoting more efficient production, encouraging effective management, and rewarding stockholders. According to James Goldsmith, chairman of General Oriental Investments, Ltd., everyone benefits from corporate takeovers: "Stockholders . . . get a

Mergers may involve several different financial arrangements. Sometimes a large firm makes an outright cash purchase of a second firm's assets. More commonly, a corporation will make an offer to purchase for cash the common stock held by the owners of the

---

ISSUE   IS BIGGER BETTER? (Cont.)

---

high price for their shares . . . the community in general gets a more competitive industry, [and] assets, once in the hands of tired management, are transferred to more vigorous and entrepreneurial hands."

Not everyone shares this enthusiasm for the merger wave. Opponents argue that mergers cause unemployment, disrupt communities, and create mountains of unmanageable debt. Since many acquisitions are aimed at cutting costs, the result may be massive layoffs. When Chevron took over Gulf Oil, 16,000 Gulf employees lost their jobs. Moreover, Pittsburgh suffered from the closure of Gulf's headquarters and the loss of the firm's support for cultural and educational institutions. Since most acquisitions are financed by borrowing large sums of money to buy out the company's stockholders, the acquiring firm is often saddled with huge interest payments that may reduce profits.

The most telling argument against mergers is that so many of them do not work. According to a study by McKinsey & Company of corporate mergers from 1972 to 1983, nearly half the acquisitions did not earn enough to justify their purchase price. Mobil's acquisition of Montgomery Ward and Exxon's purchase of Reliance Electric have been troubled by large losses. The fact is, some giant corporations become bureaucratic dinosaurs, plagued by slow decision making, poor morale, and excessive complexity. In addition, concentrated economic power resulting from mergers may enable a few managers of megacorporations to exert undue influence on government officials.

The opponents of the merger movement are uncertain what should be done. A few propose government ownership of major industries. Some call for more vigorous enforcement of existing antitrust laws with the federal government intervening more frequently to block mergers. Others favor restrictions on corporate borrowing to finance acquisitions. Still others believe that the merger wave will die out of its own accord as acquisitions become more expensive and less profitable.

What is your solution?

---

second firm. Another widely used method is for the acquiring company to offer to exchange its stocks or bonds for the common stock of another firm.

Both horizontal and vertical mergers often have been blocked by the Justice Department under the antitrust laws. Conglomerate mergers have not been subject to strong antitrust action.

SUMMARY

There are three major forms of business ownership: the proprietorship, the partnership, and the corporation. Each has both advantages and disadvantages that must be carefully weighed in deciding which type to choose for a particular business firm.

The proprietorship is a one-owner business. It is easy to start, permits rapid decision making, and provides maximum incentive for the proprietor. The disadvantages include unlimited liability of the proprietor, limited life, the difficulty of raising funds, and the lack of specialized management. Despite these limitations, the proprietorship is by far the most popular form of ownership with over 10 million currently operating in the United States.

A partnership is a business jointly owned by two or more partners. It normally enjoys greater access to financing and more specialization of management than the proprietorship. The partnership's disadvantages are the unlimited liability of all general partners, limited life, frozen investment, and divided authority.

Although the partnership agreement may be written or oral, it is strongly recommended that a written document be executed to avoid misunderstandings.

The limited partnership may be used to overcome the unlimited liability feature of the general partnership. In this form of ownership there must be at least one general partner with unlimited liability, and any number of limited partners whose liability is limited to their investment.

The sharing of profits and losses among partners is often based on the amount invested in the business, the skill and experience of the partners, and the amount of time each owner devotes to the business.

The corporation is a legal entity created by the law and existing apart from its owners. Corporations account for over four-fifths of all business transacted in the United States. The stockholders (owners) of the corporation elect a board of directors, which in turn selects corporate officers to run the firm. Stockholders enjoy limited liability as well as relative ease in transferring ownership. The corporation has an unlimited life and funds may be raised by selling corporate securities to the public. Moreover, there are ample opportunities for specialization of management in large corporations. Disadvantages of the corporation include double taxation, the expense and time required to obtain a charter, employee apathy, and extensive government regulation. S corporations can be formed to avoid the disadvantage of double taxation.

The control of many corporations is largely in the hands of professional managers with relatively little influence exerted by either stockholders or directors. This situation is often referred to as separation of ownership and control.

Corporate mergers occur when two or more firms combine to form a single company. The major types of mergers are horizontal, vertical, and conglomerate.

SELF-EXAMINATION QUESTIONS

The following questions are based on the Chapter Objectives listed at the beginning of the chapter. Test yourself by circling the letter preceding the answer that *best* answers the question or completes the statement. The answers to the Self-Examination Questions are in the appendix at the end of the textbook.

1. Which form of business offers its owner(s) limited liability? (A) proprietorship; (B) general partnership; (C) corporation; (D) all of these.

2. Frozen investment and divided authority are problems most often found in: (A) proprietorships; (B) partnerships; (C) corporations; (D) none of these.

3. In a limited partnership: (A) there generally must be a written partnership agreement; (B) the liability of limited partners is restricted to their investment; (C) there must be at least one partner with unlimited liability; (D) all of these.

4. The most common method for dividing profits and losses in a partnership is according to: (A) the time devoted to the business by each partner; (B) the amounts invested by the partners; (C) the skill and experience of the partners; (D) none of these.

5. The corporation: (A) is a legal entity; (B) requires a charter; (C) exists apart from its owners; (D) all of these.

6. Which type of corporate merger is *least* likely to attract government antitrust action? (A) horizontal; (B) conglomerate; (C) vertical; (D) mergers between competitors.

APPENDIX

IS SMALL
BUSINESS FOR
YOU?

Success in business is largely a matter of luck.
Funny thing—the harder I work, the luckier I am.

Frank K. Shallenberger
Professor of Industrial Management,
Stanford Graduate School of Business
and Founder of Shalco Corporation

The advantages of becoming a small business owner-operator are
many and appealing. Being your own boss, the satisfaction of
building a successful company, the chance to earn big money, and
the independence that comes with making your own decisions are
some of the obvious benefits of starting your own firm. But, consider
this ugly fact: *Over half of all new firms fail within 5 years!* Among
the most common reasons for failure are: (1) lack of experience in
the field, (2) poor planning, (3) inadequate financing, (4) poor
recordkeeping, (5) weak marketing skills, and (6) poor human
relations. If you avoid these mistakes, you reduce your chances of
failing. Let's take a closer look.

Experience

Before taking the plunge, you should build up your knowledge and
skills by working in the field you plan to enter, taking business and
occupational courses, and doing some careful research. Some experts
suggest that you have at least 3 years of experience, part of it in
management, before opening your own firm.

Planning

Not planning ahead guarantees failure. There are hundreds of things
to consider before getting started.[1] Your business plan, commonly
called a *prospectus,* should cover, among other things: (1) a clear
description of the proposed business, (2) identification of the market,
(3) the form of business ownership, (4) a statement of objectives, and
(5) a summary of legal and accounting requirements.

 1 The description of proposed business includes the specific
good(s) or service(s) you plan to sell; the "image" you want
your business to have; and the reasons why customers will buy
from your firm instead of some other (product features,
customer service, location).
 2 Identification of the market spells out in detail the
characteristics and location of people most likely to buy your
product; the price, promotion, and distribution that will best
reach your prospective customers and maximize profits; and the
location of firms that will compete with or complement your
product.
 3 Determining the form of ownership for your business
entails weighing the strengths and weaknesses of each type

[1]The Small Business Administration publishes an excellent planning guide for starting
a business entitled, "Checklist for Going Into Business," #2016, Forth Worth, TX, 1981.

against the requirements of the enterprise. If you select the sole proprietorship, determine the necessary qualifications for the owner-managers and the required investment of time and money. For the partnership, spell out the type of partnership, limited or general; the qualifications, authority, and responsibility of each partner; the division of profits and losses; and the required investment of time and money of each partner. If you decide to incorporate, select the type of corporation, regular or S, and specify the qualifications and personnel needed for key positions.

4   The statement of objectives should include the reasons for starting the business, and the expected monthly sales, profits, and capital investment for the first 3 years.

5   Specify the accounting and legal requirements of your firm including the type of accounting system, manual or electronic; the license, fee, tax, and zoning requirements; and the insurance needs of the firm.

One approach to planning is to make up a prospectus in loose-leaf binder form. Divide the binder into sections covering the major areas of operation—for example, financing, marketing, merchandise, personnel, and operations. Continue to add to and revise the prospectus until you are satisfied with your plan. However, don't overlook the fact that planning is a continuous process. You must devote time to updating and revising your plans in the light of changing conditions.

Financing

Famous last words: "If I'd only had a little more cash, my business would have made it." Probably the most important part of your plan focuses on estimating your financial needs and identifying sources of funds such as bank loans, the Small Business Administration, friends, relatives, and partners. Two things to remember: (1) you'll need a reserve for unforeseen emergencies; and (2) successful businesses often run short of cash due to the need to build inventories, extend credit, and acquire more facilities and equipment.

Recordkeeping

A good accounting and record system is essential to a successful business. If you haven't taken a course in accounting, do so. A firm's books should reveal what's selling best, which products or services should be dropped, where costs can be cut, how to use employee time more effectively, and other valuable information. Finally, good records can help you stay clear of trouble with various government agencies.

Marketing

The beginning and end of a successful business is satisfying customers. It is your market that determines location, merchandise, prices, advertising, and promotion. Goods and services do not sell themselves. To succeed in business, you must develop a comprehensive marketing strategy based on identifying who your customers are and what they want and need.

Human Relations

Finding, hiring, and motivating good employees is another key to success in business. Deciding what must be done and what it takes to do it is the first step in selecting employees. A good manager cares about the welfare of employees, but no small business can afford to carry deadwood. As the firm expands, be prepared to delegate increased authority to employees so you won't become too busy to plan.

Where to Find Help

If all this sounds like too much of a hassle, perhaps you should forget about starting your own business. Remember the odds of success are pretty long. However, there are several sources of assistance.

The *Small Business Administration* (SBA) is a federal agency that offers small-business persons management training and financial assistance. It also helps small firms in getting federal contracts. SBA training programs include short courses, workshops, and conferences. There are hundreds of SBA publications covering nearly every aspect of business operations. SBA financial assistance may be through direct loans or loans guaranteed to local banks. Small Business Administration offices are located in major cities throughout the United States. *Service Corps of Retired Executives* (SCORE) offers advice by experienced managers to small-business operators.

Management

Most business failures are due to poor management. Carefully study the material in Chapter 4 before launching your new business.

Books for Further Assistance

The following list of books can give you more information and aid in starting your own business.

> **1** Bafaro, Hohanna and Freedman, Melvin H. *Entrepreneur's Information Source Book* (New York: Entrepreneurs Productions, 1985).
> **2** Coffee, Robert and Scase, Richard. *Women In Charge: The Experience of Female Entrepreneurs* (Massachusetts: Allen & Unwin, 1985).
> **3** Cook, James. *The Start Up Entrepreneur: How You Can Succeed at Building Your Own Company or Enterprise Starting from Scratch* (New York: Dutton, 1986).
> **4** Drucker, Peter F. *Innovation & Entrepreneurship: Practices & Principles* (New York: Harper & Row, 1985).
> **5** Easton, Thomas A. and Conant, Ralph W. *Cutting Loose: From Employee To Entrepreneur* (Illinois: Probus Publishing, 1985).

Student _____

BUILDING A BUSINESS VOCABULARY

Directions: Match the terms with their definitions by writing the letter in the appropriate blank.

a. Legal Entity
b. Limited Liability
c. Frozen Investment
d. Partnership
e. Conglomerate
f. Unlimited Liability
g. Limited Partners
h. S Corporation

i. Horizontal Merger
j. Charter
k. Vertical Merger
l. Corporate Securities
m. Proprietorship
n. Stockholders
o. Board of Directors
p. Corporation

_M_ 1. The most popular form of business ownership in the United States.

_F_ 2. The creditors of a firm may claim the owner's personal assets to cover unpaid business debts.

_N_ 3. The owners of the corporation.

_A_ 4. Refers to the corporation's special legal status as having an existence separate from its owners.

_O_ 5. The elected representatives of the stockholders who are responsible for selecting the officers of the corporation and declaring dividends.

_B_ 6. The liability of owners is restricted to the amount of their investment.

_K_ 7. A merger that combines firms in different stages of production.

_J_ 8. A document granting a corporation the right to exist.

_g_ 9. Owners who are legally forbidden from taking an active part in the management of a firm.

_C_ 10. A term that refers to the difficulty of transferring ownership in a partnership.

_d_ 11. A type of firm with two or more owners each of whom has unlimited liability.

_____ 12. The combination of two or more firms producing similar products into a single company.

_____ 13. The form of ownership that accounts for the largest volume of business in the United States.

_____ 14. Stocks and bonds.

_____ 15. A firm that uses mergers to gain control of other companies operating in nonrelated fields.

_____ 16. A form of business that pays no corporate income tax because earnings are "passed through" directly to stockholders.

Student _____

REVIEWING MAJOR CONCEPTS

1. Explain what is meant by "double taxation" of corporate profits.

2. Suppose there are three firms of about equal size and financial condition—a proprietorship, a partnership, and a corporation. Which one would probably have the best credit rating? Why?

3. Why is the partnership a relatively unpopular form of business ownership?

4. How does a limited partnership differ from a general partnership?

5. What is the main advantage of S corporations? List three requirements for S corporations.

6. Why are most business firms proprietorships?

7. Who controls General Motors? For whose benefit is the firm being operated?

8. Identify each of the following as a vertical (v), horizontal (h), or conglomerate (c) merger by writing in the correct letter in the space provided.

    _____ a. A textile company buys a helicopter manufacturer.
    _____ b. A steel firm buys a coal company.
    _____ c. Two hotel chains merge.
    _____ d. A department store chain takes over a furniture manufacturer.
    _____ e. An oil company acquires a department store chain.

9. Do mergers of large corporations benefit society or should the government prohibit such combinations? Explain.

Student _____

SOLVING PROBLEMS AND CASES

1. Ms. Dahl, Mr. Yee, and Mr. Marcos formed a partnership and invested $21,000, $9,000, and $6,000, respectively. Profits for the year were $48,000.

   a. If the partnership agreement did not mention how profits were to be divided, how much would each partner receive?

   b. Suppose the partners had agreed to divide profits according to the amount invested by each. How much would each partner receive?

2. Assume you are planning to open a sporting-goods store located in the city where you live. You have estimated that a minimum investment of $15,000 will be required. Based on your own financial resources and business experience, what form of ownership would you choose? Outline the reasons for your choice and explain why you rejected the other alternatives.

3. Place a check (✓) in the appropriate column(s) to indicate whether each of the 12 statements most likely refers to the proprietorship, partnership, or corporation.

	Type of Ownership		
	Proprietorship	Partnership	Corporation
1. The single owner has unlimited liability.			
2. The firm has unlimited life.			
3. Each owner is responsible for the acts of other owners.			
4. Profits of the firm may be taxed twice.			
5. Firm has no existence apart from its single owner.			
6. Every owner has limited liability.			
7. The firm is a legal entity.			
8. The death of any owner brings an end to the firm.			
9. Firm may sell stock to the public.			
10. All decisions can be made without consulting others.			
11. Firm requires written permission of the state to exist.			
12. Divided authority is a common problem.			

part 2

ORGANIZATION AND MANAGEMENT OF THE FIRM

CHAPTER	TITLE
4	Management and Organization
5	Management and People
6	Personnel and Labor Relations

Part 2 focuses on the key role of management. Chapter 4 defines management, presents key management principles, and explores different organizational structures. The challenge of motivating and leading employees is covered in Chapter 5. The final chapter of Part 2 describes the responsibilities of the personnel department in hiring, orienting, training, evaluating, and paying employees, and concludes by examining the relationship between labor unions and employers.

chapter 4

MANAGEMENT AND ORGANIZATION

The preceding chapter was devoted to external forms of organization —the proprietorship, partnership, and corporation. Now we turn our attention to the internal management and organization of the business firm. This chapter introduces the scope and nature of management and explores different organizational structures. The following two chapters focus on the human aspects of management.

Any institution—a church, a college, an army, or a business— must be organized and managed if it is to survive. Here we are primarily concerned with business firms, but the principles of management and organization described in this chapter are applicable to most other institutions as well.

CHAPTER OBJECTIVES

1. Define management and briefly explain why it is important.
2. Name and define four functions of management.
3. Contrast and compare authority and responsibility.
4. Diagram examples of the three major types of internal organization.
5. Distinguish between line and staff managers.
6. List two advantages and two disadvantages of committees.
7. State two problems associated with matrix management.

WHAT IS MANAGEMENT?

A cynic once defined management as the art of getting other people to do your work. There may be an element of truth in this statement, but it would be more accurate to describe *management* as the process of accomplishing tasks by working through and with others.

Suppose 10 students work for a college bookstore. One Friday afternoon they are told to restock the bookshelves, unload a shipment of supplies, and clean the floor. If all the students decide to do their own thing, the result will be mass confusion. On the other hand, suppose one student is selected to supervise the others. This manager can organize the students into groups, divide up the work, and develop teamwork. Through management and organization, the jobs are done faster and better, and no one will miss the Friday evening action.

We noted in Chapter 1 that the factors of production—land, labor, capital, and the entrepreneur—are the economic resources used to produce goods and services. One job of the business manager is similar to that of the entrepreneur: to combine land, labor, and capital in the most efficient manner in order to produce maximum output at the lowest cost. In this sense, we may define management as the skillful combining of people, materials, and machines to accomplish organizational objectives.

Still another dimension of management is decision making. The manager's job involves deciding what to do, how and when it should be done, and by whom. One chief executive put it this way: "My job is to make decisions. If I make more good ones than bad ones, the company is likely to earn money. But if I make too many poor decisions, the company suffers and I'll be looking for another job."

The Importance of Management

Without doubt the single most important determinant of the success of a firm is the quality of its management. You want proof? Take a look at Figure 4.1. This chart indicates that 9 out of every 10 business failures are the result of inexperienced or ineffective management.

As a firm expands in size, the problems of management become increasingly complex. For example, when a firm grows from 10 to 50 employees, the difficulty of maintaining effective management and control may increase *more* than fivefold. The problems of preserving good communications—getting the right word to the right people at the right time—are complicated by increasing size. One executive summed up the problem of size in these words: "Large-scale management is in a battle to the death with complexity. The contestants are joined, and the outcome is still uncertain."

Some companies have grown beyond the ability of their managers to control them. The result has often been bankruptcy. In giant corporations with tens of thousands of employees, good management is essential to avoid chaos.

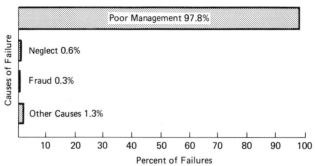

FIGURE 4.1 Why Business Firms Fail
Source: Dun & Bradstreet, Inc.

Levels of Management

A large firm may employ hundreds or even thousands of managers operating at different levels within the organization. It is convenient to classify management into three categories: top, middle, and operating management. Figure 4.2 shows a simplified organization chart for a corporation illustrating the three levels of management.

There is some dispute as to whether a corporation's board of directors should be considered a part of management. We shall exclude the board of directors since they are often relatively inactive. (For the exception, see the Issue entitled, "Who's Number One?") *Top management* includes the president and vice-presidents. *Middle management* refers to the plant managers and the major department heads. *Operating managers* are concerned with direct supervision of the nonmanagerial employees of the firm.

There are endless examples of managers who have moved to new jobs in totally different institutions and enjoyed a high degree of success. Indeed, it has been estimated that one-half of all managers will switch jobs in the next decade. What accounts for the mobility of management? The explanation is that managers, particularly at the upper levels, perform essentially the same functions no matter the type of organization for which they work. Therefore, a person who is a good manager in one firm will usually do an equally good job after moving to another firm.

The term *universality of management* means that management skills have transferability. The jobs performed by all managers are much the same. What are these functions of management?

What Do Managers Do?

The functions of management refer to the essential jobs performed by every manager. We may identify eight key functions: (1) setting objectives; (2) making policies; (3) planning; (4) organizing; (5) staffing; (6) directing; (7) controlling; and (8) coordinating.

Setting Objectives   The most important management function is establishing organizational goals. *Objectives* provide direction for

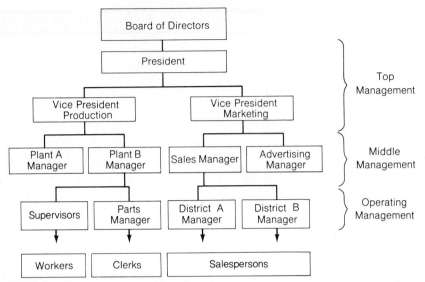

FIGURE 4.2   Top, Middle, and Operating Management

the organization; they serve as targets to guide all activities within the firm. Without clearly stated objectives, the people in an organization tend to work at cross-purposes; the result is confusion, conflict, and inefficiency. For individuals as well as organizations the first rule for success is to clearly define your goals and then to concentrate every effort toward achieving these goals.

At the top management level objectives tend to be broad in scope. Robert Townsend, in his book *Up the Organization,* describes how it took Avis Rent-A-Car 6 months to define its single objective: "We want to become the fastest-growing company with the highest profit margins in the business of renting and leasing vehicles without drivers."

At the lower levels of management, objectives may be more specific. For example, the sales department of a television manufacturer might establish a goal of increasing sales by 10 percent within 12 months. At the supervisor's level, a typical objective might be to reduce worker accidents by one-half in the next month.

The importance of organization objectives is underlined by Marshall E. Dimock, a long-time student of management:

> The first step . . . is the clear determination of objectives, for you cannot make valid detailed plans for either your program or your strategy until you know where you are going. The determination of objectives influences policy, organization, personnel, leadership, and control. Fixing your objectives is like identifying the North Star—you sight your compass on it and then use it as the means of getting back on track when you tend to stray.

ISSUE WHO'S NUMBER ONE?

The goal of many aspiring managers is to climb the corporate ladder to the top—the president of the company. However, in many large corporations, the president or chief operating officer is second in command. The chairman of the board is the chief executive officer (CEO).

The board of directors often selects the president to be the successor to the CEO. This makes the relationship between the president and the chairman a very sensitive one. The CEO typically wants to maintain personal direction and control over the firm. If the president is too forceful and independent, making unilateral decisions without keeping the chairman informed, the CEO may become irritated and hostile. Conversely, bowing to the wishes of the CEO in all matters may convince the board of directors that the president does not possess the strength and independence necessary to head the company.

According to Frank R. Beaudine, the chairman of an international executive search firm, the corporate president should insist on a clear definition of his or her authority and responsibilities and strive to establish effective relationships with both the board and the CEO. Mr. Beaudine advises the new president to listen and learn, get to know the company, and keep the CEO informed. He warns that presidents of large corporations are in a risky position, but for most, the risks are worth it.

Making Policies   A *policy* is a general rule that guides an organization in achieving its objectives. It goes without saying that policies must be consistent with objectives. Suppose a store has a goal of treating all customers fairly and equally. It might then develop a policy stating that no special price discounts will be offered to any single customer that is not available to all customers.

There can always be too much of a good thing. Some organizations attempt to develop policies to cover nearly every conceivable situation. In other words, they attempt to prepackage all decisions. This practice can kill initiative and stifle incentive. To sum up, policies should be simple, easy to understand, and limited in number.

Planning   The purpose of *planning* is to define courses of action to achieve objectives. It involves determining *what* should be done, *how* it should be done, *when,* and *by whom.* Objectives provide the framework for all planning.

A simplified example can be used to illustrate the planning process. The XYZ Company has set a goal of doubling production in the next 3 years. Deciding what should be done to achieve this goal involves examining alternative courses of action—adding to the existing plant, building a second plant, or perhaps subcontracting work to other firms. After carefully comparing the advantages and disadvantages of each alternative, management may choose the alternative of building another plant.

The "how" part of the plan involves a host of interrelated decisions. How shall the new plant be financed? Where will it be located? What is the best plant layout and design? What steps should be taken to hire and train additional production workers? Planning also requires the development of a detailed timetable to avoid confusion and delay. Each segment of the plan must be carefully scheduled to ensure the smooth execution of the plan. For example, it would be foolish to postpone financing until the last minute, since the lack of funds could delay construction.

Usually one manager is put in charge of executing the plan. This executive is provided with the necessary authority and resources to carry out the plan and is held accountable for its success or failure.

Effective planning is a challenging and often frustrating task. Managers engaged in planning should remind themselves of Murphy's Laws:

1   Nothing is as simple as it looks.
2   Everything takes longer than it should.
3   If anything can go wrong it will.

Despite these words of caution, effective planning is essential for business success.

Organizing   *Organizing* involves arranging people, machines, materials, and work to best carry out plans and achieve objectives. Organization provides the means for translating plans into action.

As a business firm grows, the need for organization increases. The process of organizing involves identifying those activities to be undertaken, dividing the firm into segments (departments or divisions), and assigning specific activities.

Figure 4.2 showed a firm with two major departments: one responsible for producing goods and the other for selling them. Each department is further divided into segments, each of which is responsible for specific activities.

Staffing   This management function involves recruiting, hiring, and training the right people to carry out plans. An IBM executive put it this way: "The point is that it's not enough to recruit good people; you must know what needs to be accomplished—your

FIGURE 4.3   The Functions of Management

objectives and plans—and make your recruitment decisions in these terms." We shall explore the *staffing* function in more detail in Chapter 6.

Directing   Managers must supervise the actions of others to accomplish objectives. All institutions consist of human beings, and *directing* is the management of people. It is the manager's responsibility to ensure that employees are carrying out their assignments in accordance with plans and objectives. The effectiveness of a manager is often measured in terms of how well he or she works with people.

Controlling   The *controlling* function includes all steps required to ensure that the activities of a firm are conforming to plans. The control process answers the question: How well are we doing? It also involves correcting or modifying activities that do not conform to plans.

Most business firms establish control systems that measure actual performance against established standards and provide information feedback to management. An example is a cost-accounting system. Suppose that plans call for a product to be manufactured at a cost of $1.10, but actual cost per unit is $1.25. Using this information, management can attempt to correct the production process, or failing this, adjust the standard cost upward.

Coordinating   *Coordination* means teamwork. No organization can operate efficiently without teamwork. It is the manager's job to ensure that individuals and departments work together toward common goals.

Figure 4.3 summarizes the functions of management. Objectives

ISSUE PERSPECTIVES ON MANAGEMENT

The following selections are intended to help you capture the flavor of management—to better understand what management is and what managers do.

Management is the marshalling of manpower, resources, and strategy to get a job done.
   Marshall E. Dimock, *The Executive in Action* (Harper, 1945)

A three-sentence course on business management: You read a book from the beginning to the end. You run a business the opposite way. You start with the end (goal), and then you do everything you can to reach it.
      Harold Geneen, *Managing* (New York: Doubleday, 1984)

And Moses chose able men out of all Israel and made them heads over the people, rulers of thousands, rulers of hundreds, rulers of fifties, and rulers of tens. And they judged the people of all seasons: the hard cases they brought unto Moses, but every small matter they judged themselves.
                                        Exodus 18:25–26

The No. 1 managerial productivity problem in America is, quite simply, managers who are out of touch with their people and out of touch with their customers.
      Thomas Peters and Nancy Austin, *A Passion for Excellence*
                              (New York: Random House, 1985)

The best managers think of themselves as playing coaches. They should be the first on the field in the morning and the last to leave at night. . . . A good manager is a blocking back whenever and wherever needed. No job is too menial for him if it helps one of his players advance toward his objective. . . . In business, he identifies company objectives and gets his players to see them as their objectives.
      Robert Townsend, *Up the Organization* (Greenwich: Fawcett
                                                 Crest, 1970)

The only things that evolve by themselves in an organization are disorder, friction, and malperformance.
      Peter Drucker, *Management* (New York: Harper & Row,
                                                      1974)

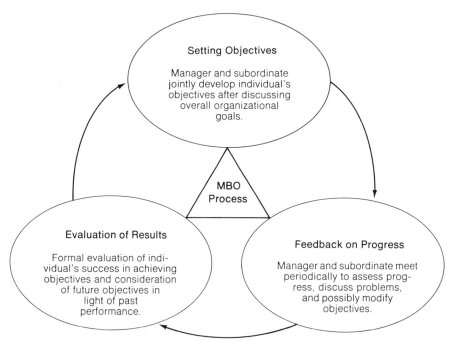

FIGURE 4.4   The Management-by-Objectives Process

serve as the starting point for all activities within the firm. Policies are rules that guide behavior. Plans define courses of action to achieve objectives, while organization involves arranging resources and work to carry out plans. Management must hire the right personnel, provide direction and control, and develop teamwork within the organization.

Management by Objectives (MBO)

We have already described the key role of objectives in guiding the activities of managers and employees in an organization. A growing number of business firms have adopted a formal process for establishing organizational objectives and evaluating performance in terms of these objectives. This process, known as *management by objectives* or *MBO,* is based on the belief that clearly defined objectives are essential for effective group effort.

MBO has been described as a process whereby the members of an organization jointly set objectives that serve as targets for managing the organization. The distinguishing feature of MBO is the emphasis on results. Success is measured in terms of achieving objectives.

How does management by objectives work? Figure 4.4 illustrates the major steps in the process. The first step is establishing specific objectives at every level in the organization. This step requires extensive discussions between managers and their subordinates to develop agreed-upon goals. The emphasis is on participation in goal setting, since the MBO process aims at merging individual goals with those of the organization.

Objectives should be quantified for better measurement. For example, a production manager may set a goal of reducing unit production costs by 5 percent in the next 12 months. Specific objectives serve as the basis for developing plans and strategies aimed at achieving broader objectives.

An effective MBO program should provide a feedback system to keep individuals posted on their progress in meeting their goals. Many firms schedule regular meetings between managers and subordinates to review progress, solve problems, and assist in planning. At the end of the performance period, a final evaluation is made to measure the extent to which objectives were met. This evaluation serves as a means of recognizing achievement and considering future objectives for the next performance period.

MBO is not a guarantee of success. However, many firms have found that management by objectives is an effective tool for improving planning and control, for increasing effective communications, and for generating enthusiasm and creativity.

PRINCIPLES OF MANAGEMENT

Over the years, certain rules of good organization and management have been developed. These principles have evolved through the experiences of thousands of managers in many diverse types of institutions. They provide a set of guidelines for effective management.

Unity of Command

No employee in an organization should report to more than one boss. The *unity of command* principle is intended to avoid confusion as to which manager is in charge. Without unity of command, there may be conflicting orders, low employee morale, and chaos.

Authority and Responsibility

Authority is the right to make decisions and the power to direct others. The extent of each manager's authority must be clearly defined in order to avoid conflict within the organization.

Responsibility involves being held accountable for accomplishing certain tasks. Everyone in an organization, from the president to the janitor, has certain responsibilities. Each person is answerable to someone in authority for carrying out his or her responsibilities. It is important that each individual fully understand these responsibilities. For this reason, many firms follow the practice of listing responsibilities and duties in writing.

It is obvious that authority and responsibility are closely related. It would be foolish to make a manager responsible for a certain activity and give the manager no authority. The guiding principle is: *Enough authority must be delegated to carry out responsibilities assigned.* In other words, you can't hold a person

ISSUE A MENU FOR SUCCESSFUL MANAGEMENT?

In Search of Excellence, coauthored by Thomas L. Peters and Robert H. Waterman, Jr., has sold over 5 million copies, making it the best selling book on corporate management in history. Published in 1982 at a time when many U.S. firms were being battered by foreign competition, the book's central theme was immensely appealing to Americans: U.S. corporations could compete successfully by focusing on the needs of their customers and employees, by fighting bureaucracy, and by sticking to the business they know best.

The authors offered 43 "excellent companies" as examples of well-managed U.S. corporations. They also identified "The Eight Attributes of Excellence":

1 *Bias for Action* Doing something—anything—rather than sending an idea through endless cycles of analyses and committee reports.
2 *Staying Close to the Customer* Learning customer preferences and catering to them.
3 *Autonomy and Entrepreneurship* Breaking the corporation into small companies and encouraging them to think independently and competitively.
4 *Productivity Through People* Creating in all employees the awareness that their best efforts are essential and that they will share in the rewards of the company's success.
5 *Hands-on, Value Driven* Insisting that executives keep in touch with the firm's essential business and promote a strong corporate culture.
6 *Stick to the Knitting* Concentrating on those areas that are best understood and most profitable.
7 *Simple Form, Lean Staff* Keeping to a minimum the number of upper-level managers and layers of administration.
8 *Simultaneous Loose-Tight Properties* Fostering a climate where there is dedication to the central values of the company combined with tolerance for all employees who accept those values.

Not everyone greeted *In Search of Excellence* with uncritical acclaim. Peter Drucker, well-known author of numerous books on management, attacked it as a "book for juveniles" that oversimplifies the complexities of managing large corporations.

Peters and Waterman responded that their purpose was to identify those qualities of good management that are too often ignored, not to write a comprehensive text on management.

accountable for activities unless you give that person adequate power to control them.

Delegation of Authority

All authority is originally vested in the owner(s) of the firm. Authority is delegated to the president and other managers. *Delegation of authority* relieves managers of unnecessary work. For example, the president of a large corporation should not spend his or her time supervising machine operators. Many firms follow the policy of having decisions made at the lowest possible level of management. In other words, the manager closest to the problem deals with it. This policy reduces the work load of top managers and encourages initiative at the middle- and operating-management levels.

Span of Control

The number of persons reporting to one manager is called the *span of control.* A broad span of control can raise employee morale and improve communications by reducing the number of levels of management. But a broad span of control may also overburden managers and limit the time they have to spend with each subordinate. Figure 4.5 compares two alternative organizations. Company A has a broad span of control while Company B has a limited one. Each firm employs 288 workers. Company A has only two levels of management while Company B uses four levels. Which organizational pattern is better? There is no right answer to this question. It depends on the type of work being done, the skill of the managers, and the need for supervision.

There is a general agreement that the span of control should be narrower at the top-management level than for operating managers. This is because activities become diverse and problems more complex at the upper levels of an organization. The "rule of seven" states that no more than seven subordinates should report to one executive at the top-management level. Of course, this is only a rule of thumb. Some firms use a rule of three; others, a rule of eight.

Organizational Stability

Business firms should have the ability to adjust quickly to the loss of key managers. In these days of executive "job-hopping" any organization can expect to lose personnel. A danger to guard against is the "one-person department" headed by an executive who refuses to delegate authority. If the executive resigns or is incapacitated, there will be no one with the experience or knowledge to take over the position.

Some corporations establish programs designed to groom junior managers to take over key jobs. Such programs are intended to prevent disruption of operations through the loss of managers.

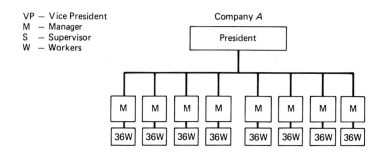

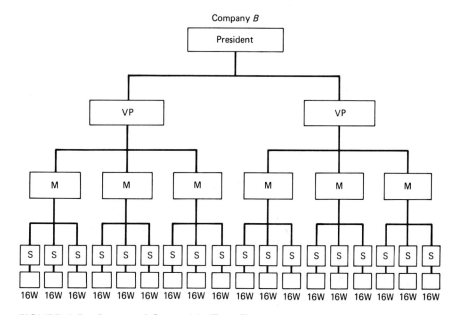

FIGURE 4.5   Spans of Control in Two Firms

Organizational Change

No organizational structure should be "carved in stone." In our society, change is the name of the game, and institutions that fail to adapt to change die. For this reason, management must continually review and revise objectives and plans in terms of changing conditions. The organization of the firm should also be subjected to periodic review to determine if modification or revision is required. For example, it might be better for the company as a whole if one department is dissolved, and its functions taken over by another department.

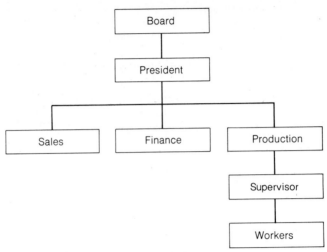

FIGURE 4.6 Line Organization

TYPES OF INTERNAL ORGANIZA-TION

Every firm with more than one person requires some form of organization. In small firms, the organization may be informal. For example, when Sharon Valdez opened her travel agency last March, she had the following conversation with her two employees, John Chin and Lois Medsker. "Lois, you're in charge of air, ship, and bus reservations. John, you take care of all accommodations bookings. Lois, when I'm here, see me if you have any questions; when I'm busy, check with John." In a few short sentences an organization has been created, complete with lines of authority and areas of responsibility.

In larger firms, more complex and formal organization is required. There are three major types of internal organization structures: (1) line; (2) functional; and (3) line-and-staff.

Line Organization

By far the simplest organization is the *line* type. There is a straight line flow of authority from the board of directors to the workers, as shown in Figure 4.6.

The line organization has several advantages. It is easy to understand, and everyone reports to a single supervisor, thereby preserving unity of command. It encourages speedy decisions because only one manager is in charge of each area. Also, "buck passing" tends to be reduced since responsibility is clearly defined.

The line organization is not without weaknesses. The major disadvantage is that each manager is assumed to be skilled in the many different aspects of the job. For example, the sales manager in Figure 4.6 must make decisions in the areas of advertising, market

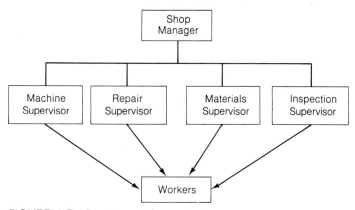

FIGURE 4.7   Functional Organization

research, supervision of the sales force, pricing, and so forth. It is unlikely that one person will have the time and knowledge to handle all of these activities effectively. The line organization may also make it difficult to coordinate different functional areas, such as sales, production, and finance.

Although the line organization is widely used by small firms, it is rarely found in large corporations.

Functional or Staff Organization

In the late nineteenth century, Frederick Taylor, an early student of management and organization, developed the *functional* or *staff* organization to overcome the problem of having too many duties for line managers. Each employee reports to several specialists, each of whom is an expert in one part of the worker's job. Taylor's plan is illustrated in Figure 4.7.

The overwhelming disadvantage of the functional organization is obvious: each worker has more than one boss. Unity of command is violated, thereby leading to divided authority, buck passing, and confusion. For this reason, the functional organization in its pure form is rarely used today.

Line-and-Staff Organization

Nearly all large corporations use some form of *line-and-staff* organization, which combines the best features of the line and functional types. Line officers still retain the right to make decisions and issue orders. Staff specialists are available to provide assistance to line officers. Their jobs include solving special problems, interpreting technical information, assisting in planning, and generally supporting line executives. Staff specialists do *not* have line authority. Their function is to provide advice and make recommendations, *not* to give orders. Figure 4.8 shows a typical line-and-staff organization with five staff positions.

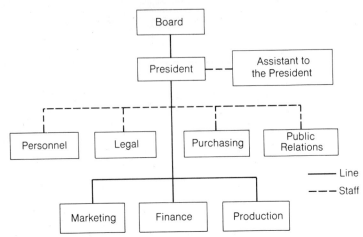

FIGURE 4.8   Line-and-Staff Organization

The obvious strength of the line-and-staff organization is that unity of command and clearly established responsibility and authority are preserved, while at the same time, expert assistance is available from the staff. This frees line executives from being bogged down in details. If the marketing manager in Figure 4.8 needs to hire five additional salespersons, assistance is available from the personnel department. If the executive is negotiating a contract with a customer, the legal department provides legal advice.

The line-and-staff organization does tend to be expensive because of the added cost of staff specialists. Decision making may be somewhat slowed through the involvement of staff. Another serious problem is that staff officers are often tempted to assume line authority. This can undermine the effectiveness of the line executives and result in confusion and conflict. Figure 4.9 depicts the staff specialist's functions.

COMMITTEES

Institutions are rarely managed solely through committees, yet most large organizations make widespread use of a variety of committees. There are, of course, many different types of committees—temporary or permanent, advisory, decision making, or information gathering.

Most managers are either highly enthusiastic about committees or unalterably opposed to them. Opponents claim committees waste time and slow down the decision-making process. Managers who must devote hours to endless meetings do not have the time to carry out their assigned responsibilities. Moreover, committee decisions are, by necessity, compromises. As the saying goes, "A camel is a horse designed by a committee." Finally, it is impossible to pinpoint

THIS IS A LINE ORGANIZATION.

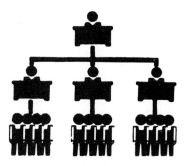

It means that each person has ONE BOSS—Unity of Command.

THIS IS A LINE AND STAFF OR-GANIZATION.

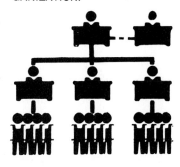

This still means that each person has one boss. The STAFF SPECIALIST helps the boss do a more effective job.

THE STAFF SPECIALIST investi-gates, plans, advises, SERVES.

A supervisor directs the work of others and delegates some authority to others. The supervisor needs help on problems involving policy interpretation, company plans, engineering changes, technical information, etc. Staff Services—THE STAFF SPECIAL-IST PROVIDES THIS HELP.

THE STAFF SPECIALIST doesn't give orders to line—doesn't per-form line duties. STAFF SPECIAL-ISTS SOLVE SPECIAL PRO-BLEMS.

FIGURE 4.9   What Does the Staff Specialist Do?
Courtesy Exxon Corporation.

responsibility for committee decisions. How can you hold an entire group accountable?

On the other hand, proponents argue that committees provide an opportunity to solve complex problems by pooling information. If no one person possesses all the necessary knowledge to make an educated decision, it makes sense to call together a group of individuals and share information. In some cases many heads are better than one.

It is also argued that committees lead to improved communications. Each member of a committee gains a better understanding of other people's problems and viewpoints. Widespread use of committees also results in broad participation in the decision-making process, which encourages understanding of, and enthusiastic support for, decisions. People are more likely to support a decision when they have participated in making it.

Is the committee a useful management tool or just a time waster? Perhaps we should form a committee to come up with an answer.

MATRIX MANAGEMENT

As firms grow in size, they become more complex. Many large firms respond to complexity by adopting increasingly complicated organizational structures. *Matrix management* is a variation of the line-and-staff structure which adds horizontal lines of authority to traditional vertical ones. The result is a sophisticated and flexible structure that puts an emphasis on management by compromise. It was developed in the 1960s by the National Aeronautics and Space Administration (NASA) and several aerospace companies to manage the extremely complicated Apollo and Mercury space programs. The idea was to bring together individuals from diverse backgrounds (scientists, accountants, technicians, production managers, etc.) and create project teams to undertake the complex mission of developing and launching space vehicles.

Figure 4.10 presents a simplified example of matrix management. Notice that equal authority is given to product managers and functional managers such as engineering, production, marketing, and finance. Product managers are in charge of product teams consisting of members from the four functional areas. This leads to divided authority—each team member is jointly responsible to a product-manager and a functional manager. The result is inevitable conflict. However, according to the proponents of matrix management, this conflict is healthy. It forces team members to weigh conflicting viewpoints and come up with plans of action that satisfy both managers. Decisions are made at the lowest possible level in the organization by managers who are most familiar with the problems. Moreover, matrix management encourages rapid decision making, greater organizational flexibility, and improved productivity. The structure puts an emphasis on teamwork and good human relations skills.

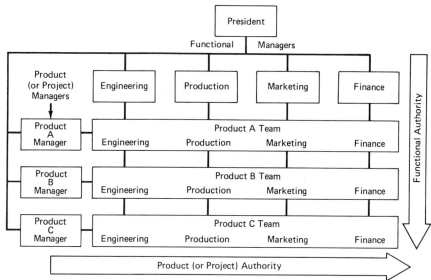

FIGURE 4.10   Matrix Management

Today, matrix management is viewed with less enthusiasm than it was a decade ago. A number of firms that have experimented with this complicated structure have run into major problems. The matrix structure is difficult to implement, often requiring 4 to 5 years of effort before it becomes operationally efficient. During this period management turnover is high among those executives that have difficulty adopting to the unique demands of the matrix approach. Managers are unsure to whom they report. Organizational goals and innovation may be sacrificed to the need to compromise and satisfy different supervisors. According to Thomas Peters and Robert Waterman, Jr., authors of *In Search of Excellence,* "It [matrix management] . . . regularly degenerates into anarchy and rapidly becomes bureaucratic and non-creative."

SUMMARY

Management may be described as the art of working through others to accomplish tasks. Poor management is the major reason for business failure. As firms grow in size, they become increasingly complex. This makes effective management essential to avoid chaos.

All managers, regardless of the type of organization, perform eight major functions (or jobs): (1) setting objectives; (2) making policies; (3) planning; (4) organizing; (5) staffing; (6) directing; (7) controlling; and (8) coordinating.

Management by objectives (MBO) is a process used by many business firms to establish organizational objectives and evaluate results in terms of achieving these objectives.

ISSUE   WOMEN IN MANAGEMENT

It has been little more than a decade since business firms launched a concerted effort to hire more women in management positions. In some ways progress has been impressive. According to census figures, the number of female managers has doubled since 1972 to 3.5 million. However, these gross figures hide a disturbing fact: Very few women hold top management positions in large corporations. Only one of *Fortune* magazine's top 500 U.S. firms is headed by a woman, and there are only a handful of senior female executives in major corporations.

What accounts for the lack of progress by female managers? Partly it is due to insufficient experience. Since most women managers have been hired in the last 10 years, they have not had enough time to gain entry into the higher levels of management. But discrimination also plays a role. Women managers report that it is harder for them to advance to top-level positions due to sexist stereotyping and male-dominated corporate politics.

A common complaint is that senior male managers often do not feel comfortable with women, and therefore pass them over for top-level promotions. Another problem that handicaps women managers is that they do not receive the same constructive criticism as males. They claim that there is a widespread reluctance among men to criticize women, which deprives women managers of opportunities to learn from their mistakes. In addition, some observers believe that the lack of progress of female managers may be partly attributed to the reduced commitment of the federal government to affirmative action.

There are other problems as well. Both female and male experts believe that some women managers sabotage their careers by choosing relatively safe staff positions rather than the higher risk line jobs. In most corporations the fast track to top management is through the line organization.

Another obstacle to advancement is motherhood. Some

Several principles of management have evolved over the years: (1) no employee should report to more than one manager; (2) enough authority must be delegated to carry out responsibilities assigned; (3) decisions should be made at the lowest possible level of management; (4) too many people reporting to one manager can result in loss of control and overworked executives; (5) business firms should establish procedures to minimize disruption from the

ISSUE WOMEN IN MANAGEMENT (Cont.)

firms fear a loss of investment in women managers who take lengthy maternity leaves or fail to return to their jobs after having a child. A related concern is that women may be more reluctant to move to take a new position. One study found that twice as many men as women had relocated for their firms.

Whether because of discrimination or lack of job satisfaction, women are leaving large corporations in record numbers to go into business for themselves. The number of new businesses owned by women is increasing at three times the male rate. According to Kay Koplovitz, who heads her own cable TV company, "The best way to get to the top for a woman is to start there."

Several forces are at work that will increase the number of women executives taking over top jobs in corporations.

- Thousands of ambitious and talented women are in the ranks of middle management, and inevitably, after 20 years of experience, many will be promoted to top jobs.

- Male views are changing. According to a survey published by the *Harvard Business Review*, there has been a dramatic increase in the number of males holding favorable views toward women executives.

- A growing number of firms are setting up programs aimed at encouraging female managers. Some companies are restructuring jobs so there is productive part-time work for managers, and less damage is done to careers for managers who are absent for months or who are unwilling to relocate.

- Powerful economic forces are on the side of women managers. Increased worldwide competition is forcing corporations to seek out the most talented managers regardless of sex.

loss of key personnel; and (6) any organizational structure should be subject to review and revision.

There are three major types of internal organization. The line organization is simple, easy to understand, and preserves unity of command. However, it requires managers to be skilled in many different areas. The functional or staff organization provides for management by specialists, but it violates unity of command. The line-and-staff organization combines line officers with decision-making authority and staff specialists who give advice and assistance. Line-and-staff organization is common in large corporations.

Committees are useful for pooling information, improving communications, and encouraging widespread participation in decision making. However, committees have been criticized for wasting the time of managers and making "watered-down" decisions.

Matrix management, a variation of the line-and-staff organization, uses a system of teams or committees to provide flexible management of complex organizations.

SELF-EXAMINATION QUESTIONS

The following questions are based on the Chapter Objectives listed at the beginning of the chapter. Test yourself by circling the letter preceding the answer that *best* completes the statement or answers the question. The answers to the Self-Examination Questions are in the appendix at the end of the textbook.

1. Management: (A) may be defined as the skillful combining of people, materials, and machines to achieve organizational objectives; (B) involves goal setting, policymaking, and planning; (C) is the single most important determinant of a firm's success; (D) all of these.

2. The management function that involves defining courses of action to achieve objectives is called: (A) policymaking; (B) planning; (C) organizing; (D) controlling; (E) none of these.

3. An important management function is: (A) setting objectives; (B) demanding authority; (C) serving on committees; (D) universality of management.

4. Authority: (A) is the same as responsibility; (B) means being held accountable for accomplishing certain tasks; (C) involves the right to make decisions and direct others; (D) all of these.

5. The type of internal organization most commonly found in small firms is the: (A) line organization; (B) functional organization; (C) line-and-staff organization; (D) none of these.

6. Managers who have no order-giving authority but specialize in problem solving, planning, and providing assistance are known as: (A) line managers; (B) staff managers; (C) command advisers; (D) drones; (E) none of these.

7. Committees may: (A) slow the decision-making process; (B) encourage broad participation in decision making; (C) improve communications within a firm; (D) waste time; (E) all of these.

APPENDIX

TIME
MANAGEMENT

Never before have we had so little time in which to do so much.

Franklin D. Roosevelt

Have you ever wondered why a few individuals accomplish so much every day while most others never seem to find enough time to achieve their goals? The difference between the two groups is effective time management. If you want to make better use of your time, here are five steps that will help you accomplish more in less time:

1 *Find out how you spend your time.* Most people have no clear idea of how they use their time. For at least one week, keep an hour-by-hour log of the time you spend sleeping, eating, resting, working, attending school, socializing, and so forth.

2 *Set goals and establish priorities.* Once you discover how you spend your time, you can decide if you want to devote more or less to various activities. Instead of being a slave to time, put yourself in control by setting specific, measurable goals and by establishing clear priorities.

It is important to set objectives that can be reached in the near future. Long-term goals can be divided into a series of shorter, specific objectives. For example, if your goal is an *A* grade in a course, a short-term objective of completing the first assignment accurately and on time will help you in achieving your goal.

It is equally important to prioritize your goals. This means ranking your goals according to importance and urgency. Alan Lakein, an expert on time management, suggests dividing goals into three categories: A, B, and C. Your highest priority goals belong in the A category; B goals are of medium importance; those activities with little urgency or significance fit in the C category. Goals should be reviewed periodically. Some C goals can be moved into A or B categories, while others may be eliminated entirely.

3 *Determine and meet deadlines.* Specific actions leading to achievement of goals should be written down. When setting deadlines, be realistic—build in enough flexibility to allow for unexpected interruptions. Pocket calendars, appointment books, and daily planners are useful tools for reminding you what to do and when to do it.

4 *Work smarter, not harder or longer.* Here are eight time-savers that will help you get more done in a given period of time.

    a. Avoid interruptions.

    b. Delegate work to others when possible.

    c. Say no to people who want you to spend time on

activities of minor importance (for example, C priority items).

d. Develop an organized routine. In other words, "plan your work and work your plan."

e. Keep your work area neat and orderly.

f. Use waiting time effectively. For example, bring a textbook when going to a doctor appointment.

g. Do not work too long on any one project. Breaks and variety tend to increase productivity.

h. Handle paper work only once if possible.

i. Keep files current and organized. Remember: "When in doubt, throw it out."

5 *Review the preceding steps and modify as necessary.*

Time is a precious commodity; once spent it can never be reclaimed. If you are not fully satisfied with the way you are using your time, *now* is the time to start on step one.

Student _____

BUILDING A BUSINESS VOCABULARY

Directions: Match the terms with their definitions by writing the letter in the appropriate box.

a. Span of Control
b. Line Organization
c. Objectives
d. Planning
e. Authority
f. Management
g. Policy
h. Organizing
i. Line-and-Staff Organization
j. Unity of Command
k. Responsibility
l. Management by Objectives
m. Matrix Management
n. Functional or Staff Organization
o. Directing
p. Coordination
q. Universality of Management

___g___ 1. A general rule that guides an organization in achieving its objectives.

___q___ 2. Management skills have transferability.

___e___ 3. The right to act, decide, and command.

___b___ 4. A type of organization commonly used by small business firms.

___d___ 5. Deciding what should be done, how and when it should be done, and who should be responsible for it.

___a___ 6. The number of subordinates reporting to one supervisor or manager.

___i___ 7. An organization consisting of managers assisted by specialists who provide advice and support.

___K___ 8. Being held answerable for the accomplishment of assigned tasks.

___H___ 9. Arranging employees, machines, material, and work to carry out plans and accomplish objectives.

___n___ 10. A type of internal organization in which each worker is supervised by several specialists.

___P___ 11. Developing teamwork among individuals and departments in an organization.

___J___ 12. An employee should have only one boss.

_C_ 13. Goals that provide direction for an organization.

_O_ 14. The face-to-face supervision of employees.

_F_ 15. The process of accomplishing objectives by working through others.

_L_ 16. A formal process for establishing organizational objectives and evaluating performance in terms of these objectives.

_M_ 17. A variation of the line-and-staff organization that adds horizontal lines of authority from product or project managers to traditional vertical lines of authority from functional managers.

Student _____

REVIEWING MAJOR CONCEPTS

1. How do you explain the fact that former corporation executives are often very successful in managing government agencies?

2. "Many heads are better than one. Therefore, all organizations should be managed through a system of committees." Do you agree or disagree? Explain your answer.

3. Describe two policies in effect at your college.

4. Complete the following table by listing two major advantages and two disadvantages for each form of organization.

Organization	Major Advantage	Major Disadvantage
Line	easy to understand Unity of command Speedy decissions	difficult for one Boss to cordinate and advise the many departments of the bus.
Functional	Many advisors to specialize in specific jobs	More than 1 boss
Line-and-Staff	line mgrs still maintain Unity of Command expert assistance	more expensive decisions slowed down could be authoraty conflict
Matrix Management		difficult to implement 4-5 year to develope Compromising non creative high mgmt turnover for those who don't confrum

5. On which *two* of the eight functions of management would the president of General Electric devote the most time? On which *two* would a production supervisor spend the majority of time?

Student _____

SOLVING PROBLEMS AND CASES

1. You have been hired as general manager and coach of the California Comets, a new professional basketball team. There are eight management functions listed below. Using your basketball team, give an example of each function. (*Hint:* What are the objectives of a professional basketball team? What policies might the team have? What types of plans would the Comets need?)

   a. Setting Objectives.

   b. Making Policies.

   c. Planning.

   d. Organizing.

e. Staffing.

f. Directing.

g. Controlling.

h. Coordinating.

Student _____

2. *Case:* Winton Shoe Company

The production manager of the Winton Shoe Company has ordered several major design changes in the company's line of women's shoes. She claims that the changes (lower heels and simpler buckles) will reduce production costs and at the same time result in a better quality shoe. However, the sales manager is held accountable for any loss in sales. He alone is responsible for achieving sales objectives, although he has no control over changes in the product. What principle of management is involved here? If you were the president of Winton Shoe Company, what would you do?

3. Draw a line-and-staff organization chart showing the following positions: Production Supervisors, Vice-President for Marketing, Board of Directors, Personnel Department (staff), Chief Accountant, Director of Advertising, Vice-President for Finance, District Sales Managers, President, Legal Department (staff), and Vice-President for Production.

Student _____

4. *Case:* Mercury Machine Tools, Inc.

Two months ago Mr. Vance Edwards became president of Mercury Machine Tools, Inc., known in the industry as MMT. Mr. Edwards had been an executive for one of MMT's major rivals. He decided to spend a week "nosing around" in order to get acquainted with how MMT operates. In talking with his management team and visiting various departments he discovered the following:

a. The marketing vice-president has 11 district sales managers, the advertising manager, and the head of market research reporting directly to him.
b. The production supervisors in the plant are not permitted to change worker assignments without first checking with the plant manager.
c. The head of the purchasing department (a staff specialist) has been issuing directives to the parts manager who reports to the plant manager.
d. The financial manager is jointly responsible to the marketing vice-president and production vice-president.
e. One of the district sales managers resigned 6 months ago and no replacement has been found. Meanwhile, district sales have dropped 25 percent.
f. The advertising manager and director of market research are feuding and have not spoken to each other for nearly a year.

Mr. Edwards has asked you, his assistant, to prepare a brief report outlining any problems you can find and suggesting possible solutions.

MANAGEMENT AND PEOPLE

Business is people. Every organization consists of groups of people—employees and managers—working together. Psychologists have long recognized that each human being is a unique combination of abilities, aptitudes, and personality traits. In short, no two individuals are exactly alike. This fact makes personnel management —the management of people—a challenging and vital part of every manager's job.

This chapter deals with the *people* part of management. It focuses on management's efforts to increase employee morale and motivation through effective human relations and work-improvement programs.

CHAPTER OBJECTIVES

1. Contrast and compare the motivational theories of Mayo, Maslow, and Herzberg.

2. Name three factors that build morale.

3. Briefly describe McGregor's Theory X and Theory Y and Ouchi's Theory Z.

4. Give an example of decision making under the autocratic leadership style and under the participative leadership style.

5. List and describe three types of quality of work-life (QWL) programs.

HUMAN RELATIONS IN BUSINESS

Morale is to all other factors as four is to one.

Napoleon

The success of a business is largely dependent on the degree to which its employees are motivated to carry out assigned duties and work toward achieving the firm's objectives. Until a few decades ago, managers often viewed workers as little more than commodities to be purchased at a low price and worked hard for long hours. However, a few managers, concerned for the workers' welfare, made efforts to increase wages, improve working conditions, and boost morale. The result was often astonishing gains in productivity. It began to dawn on employers that treating workers like human beings could pay off in dollars and cents! Today, managers are increasingly concerned with the relationship between employee morale and productivity.

The Hawthorne Experiments

The human relations movement gained impetus from the Hawthorne Experiments conducted by Elton Mayo of Harvard University at the Hawthorne Works of the Western Electric Company during the 1920s and 1930s. The research began as an attempt to measure the effect of illumination on worker output, but the experiments were broadened to include changes in rest periods, working hours, and other conditions. The researchers were astonished to find that however they changed working conditions production increased, even when the working conditions were deliberately changed for the worse. Mayo and his associates concluded that the workers involved in the experiments enjoyed the attention they received, and their feeling of increased recognition and participation motivated them to boost output. It appeared that social and psychological factors might be more important than physical working conditions in determining productivity! The widespread publicity given the Hawthorne Experiments caused many managers to rethink their approaches to personnel management.

Motivation and Needs

One of the most widely accepted theories of human motivation was developed by Abraham Maslow. According to Maslow, human beings are motivated by needs arranged in the form of a hierarchy illustrated in Figure 5.1. Basic needs are physical or material in nature—the need for food, clothing, and shelter are examples. A hungry person is motivated to seek food. A secure job and insurance are ways of satisfying safety needs. When these material needs are satisfied, human behavior is influenced by social and psychological needs, which include recognition, social acceptance, self-respect, as well as self-realization through a sense of accomplishment.

Frederick Herzberg's experiments in human motivation complement and confirm Maslow's theories. Herzberg tried to determine what job traits or characteristics were sources of

FIGURE 5.1   Maslow's Hierarchy of Needs

satisfaction or dissatisfaction for employees. He divided job traits into two categories—maintenance factors and motivational factors.

Maintenance factors, such as pay, working conditions, fringe benefits, and security, maintain or preserve employee satisfaction. Herzberg contends that these factors are not strong motivators but must be present if worker dissatisfaction is to be avoided. In short, the presence of these factors will not motivate workers, but their absence will cause poor morale and dissatisfaction.

According to Herzberg, recognition, fulfillment of potential, appreciation, and the challenge of work itself are the key factors that motivate employees. Herzberg calls these *motivational factors.* He believes that jobs should be structured to maximize employee satisfaction in these areas.

Until the middle of the twentieth century, most workers were motivated by monetary incentives; that is, by money to meet basic needs. However, the substantial increase in per capita income during this century has meant that the vast majority of workers can now satisfy their material needs.

Many business firms and labor unions still attempt to satisfy and motivate employees solely through increased wages and fringe benefits. Elton Mayo referred to this approach as the "rabble hypothesis" because it assumes that workers are a mob of money-grubbing rabble with no social goals or self-esteem. Money is important to workers and will motivate those who have not satisfied their basic needs. However, both Maslow and Herzberg agree that higher-level needs such as recognition and self-esteem are the primary motivators for most American workers. Greater emphasis on satisfying social, psychological, and self-fulfillment needs is likely to improve employee motivation.

Morale

Morale influences people's "willingness to work." It is a reflection of workers' attitudes toward their jobs and the firm. Morale is determined by the extent that employees' work satisfies their needs.

Obviously, there is a close relationship between employee morale and productivity. Effective managers attempt to improve morale by identifying worker needs and undertaking activities to fulfill these needs.

Although morale is intangible and difficult to measure, there are some indicators that can be used to gauge the level of employee morale. Labor turnover measures the number and frequency of employee resignations. A high rate of labor turnover is often a signal of low morale. Increased absenteeism suggests declining morale, as does low productivity. A drop in productivity should alert management to possible morale problems. Frequent strikes are another indicator of worker dissatisfaction.

It is management's responsibility to build good morale by providing a work climate that motivates workers by meeting their needs. This, of course, is not always an easy task. However, a good human relations program begins by recognizing the social and psychological needs of human beings.

What factors tend to build morale? This is a complex question, and space does not permit a comprehensive answer. However, it is possible to identify a few factors that contribute to good morale.

Recognition   It goes without saying that human beings want their efforts to be recognized and acknowledged. A few words of encouragement and praise can be very effective in boosting an employee's morale. Many large firms publish house organs—company newspapers or magazines—that contain articles and announcements about employees and their jobs. Is there anyone who does not like to see his or her name in print?

Some time ago, a textile firm sponsored a daily music program on a local radio station that was piped into the company's offices. Instead of commercials, spot announcements praised the work of outstanding employees. Management claimed that productivity increased by 125 percent as a result of the program.

Preserving Self-Respect   An individual's dignity and self-esteem influence his or her attitude toward work. A supervisor must be careful not to needlessly damage an employee's self-respect. One rule of thumb is to praise publicly, but criticize privately. A public reprimand causes an employee to lose face before fellow workers, and it may result in permanent hostility and poor morale.

Stressing Job Importance   Workers engaged in assembly-line operations perform the same simple task thousands of times a day. These employees may come to feel like cogs in a giant machine, and as a result, morale may decline. Management can undertake a program to emphasize to the worker the importance of a job by relating the task to the operation of the completed product. For example, workers who install automobile brakes might be shown a motion picture stressing the prevention of automobile accidents through properly functioning brakes.

Good Communications   Some managers think of communications as getting "the word" to the workers. But effective communication is more than a one-way street. Employees must be able to transmit their problems and suggestions to management without being confronted with excessive delays and red tape.

Good communications involve transmitting understanding. Whenever possible, employees should be given the reasons for an order. Suppose, for example, the manager of a department store issues the following directive to all store personnel: "Effective next Monday, this store shall open one hour later and close one hour later." This announcement is likely to generate hostility since no explanation is offered for the change and because the employees were not consulted about the later hours.

The lack of effective communications can lead to rumors that are likely to cause anxiety and undermine morale. When an organization is undergoing change, management should endeavor to keep all employees informed of the latest developments in order to reduce rumors.

Prompt Handling of Complaints and Grievances   Closely related to good communications is effectively dealing with employee complaints and grievances. Management should welcome workers' requests to discuss grievances because getting the problem out into the open is the first step toward solving it. The very act of voicing a complaint serves as a safety valve. Unexpressed grievances tend to become internalized and can cause frustration out of proportion to the problem.

Some firms have adopted an open-door policy for handling grievances whereby the worker may take a complaint up the chain of command until satisfied. For example, if a production worker is not satisfied with the supervisor's solution to the grievance, it is next taken to the plant manager, and so on until it is resolved. Other firms submit unresolved grievances to arbitration, a procedure described in Chapter 6.

The Key Role of Leadership

Leadership may be defined as the act of persuading and directing others in order to gain their enthusiastic participation and support. In one sense, all managers are leaders. No single factor has more influence on employee morale than the leadership of the supervisor. The manager's actions create the atmosphere in which subordinates operate. Methods of issuing orders, fairness and consideration, and even a sense of humor will influence worker behavior.

Styles of leadership are based on certain assumptions as to how people are motivated and how they react to work. Douglas McGregor has categorized such assumptions into two theories, which

ISSUE MANAGEMENT AND THE ART OF LISTENING

Poor listening is one of the most significant problems facing business today.

J. Paul Lyet, Chairman and Chief Executive Officer, Sperry Corporation

A stereotypical view of management is the self-assured executive issuing a stream of decisive orders to attentive subordinates, who then carry out those orders with dispatch and enthusiasm. In sharp contrast to this distorted image, studies show that managers typically spend 40 percent of their time listening. It follows that an important management skill is the ability to listen effectively.

Most people do not listen well. According to one test, the average person retains and understands only half of what is said. There is a natural tendency to "tune out" people and to listen selectively. This means we hear only what we want to hear. To fully understand what is being communicated, the listener should attempt to stand in the speaker's shoes. This means adopting the speaker's frame of reference to fully grasp his or her meaning. Other suggestions for improving listening skills include:

- Give the speaker your full attention. Resist distractions and try to avoid interruptions.

- Keep your emotions in check. Do not dismiss what the speaker is saying merely because of poor delivery. Concentrate on content, not personality or style.

- Focus on the central theme and the key ideas that are being communicated rather than becoming bogged down in details.

- Take advantage of the fact that your mind works four times as fast as speech to analyze and summarize what is being said.

- Learn to read nonverbal messages. *How* a person says something is often more important than the actual words. Remember that body language is a powerful method of communication.

Listening is a skill that can be developed through practice. Improving your listening skills can help you reduce mistakes in your business and personal life, and enhance your effectiveness as an employee and manager.

TABLE 5.1 McGregor's Theory X and Theory Y

Theory X	Theory Y
1. People dislike work and will avoid it if possible. 2. Most people must be directed, coerced, and threatened with punishment to make them work toward company objectives. 3. People dislike responsibility, have little ambition, and want security above all.	1. People do not hate work; it's as normal as rest or play. 2. People don't have to be coerced or threatened. They will commit themselves to mutual objectives and work hard to achieve them if their needs are satisfied in the process. 3. Under the right conditions people will seek responsibility and bring to bear all their energy, imagination, and creativity in solving business problems.

he calls Theory X and Theory Y. These theories are summarized in Table 5.1.

Theory X, which McGregor calls the traditional view, assumes that organizational objectives are not compatible with human goals. In contrast, *Theory Y* suggests a participative approach to management, which emphasizes the involvement of employees in the decision-making process so that they will be more highly motivated.

McGregor suggests that the Theory Y approach is the more desirable one for managers to adopt. However, research suggests that the Theory X approach works well under some circumstances and ineffectively in others. The same is true for Theory Y. For example, a participative approach may be inappropriate for emergencies. If there was a fire in your classroom, would you want to establish a committee and involve all students in the decision on how to evacuate the building? The best approach seems to depend on the nature of the work being done and the needs of the people involved. In organizations where work and procedures are formalized and the tasks to be accomplished are predictable, Theory X may prove the more appropriate approach. Theory Y appears to work better where there is an emphasis on innovation and problem solving.

Styles of leadership range from totally autocratic to participative. (See Figure 5.2.) Some managers believe that the autocratic manager who makes all the decisions and gives orders that are carried out without question is outdated. They may prefer participative leadership, where subordinates are encouraged to involve themselves in the decision-making process, while the leader attempts to develop group consensus. Obviously there is an infinite variety of leadership styles, each of which will work in different circumstances. The most appropriate leadership style depends on the

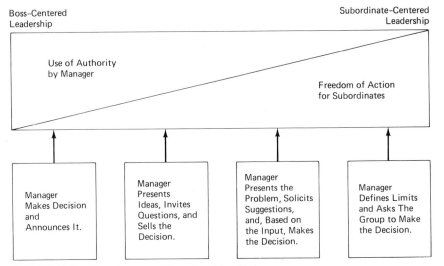

FIGURE 5.2   The Range of Leadership Styles
Source: Adapted from Robert Tannenbaum and Warren H. Schmidt, "How to Choose a Leadership Pattern," *Harvard Business Review,* May–June, 1973, p. 164.

personality of the leader, the nature of the subordinates, and the type of work being performed. For example, the leadership style that is effective for an assembly-line supervisor might be totally ineffective in managing a group of scientists in a research laboratory.

The truth is that very little is known about leadership. Good leaders come in all shapes, sizes, colors, and sexes. We do know two things about leadership: (1) leaders lead, and (2) leadership is critically important to the success of any enterprise.

Perhaps the ultimate in leadership was described 25 centuries ago by the Chinese poet Lao-tzu:

A leader is best when people barely know he exists,
Not so good when people obey and acclaim him,
Worse when people despise him.
Fail to honor people, and they fail to honor you.
But a good leader, who talks little,
When his work is done, his aim is fulfilled,
The people will say, "We did it ourselves."

BEYOND HUMAN RELATIONS: THE QUALITY OF WORK-LIFE MOVEMENT

We have run out of dumb people to handle those dumb jobs.

Robert Ford, Personnel Director,
American Telephone and Telegraph Co.

In the 1970s and 1980s, many managers began to realize that the changing goals and values of American workers required a new approach to human relations. Triggered by tougher foreign

---

ISSUE THEORY Z: A STEP BEYOND THEORY Y?

For more than a decade, American executives have been studying Japanese management hoping to discover the secret of Japan's remarkable economic success. One of the most popular books on this subject is William G. Ouchi's *Theory Z: How American Business Can Meet the Japanese Challenge.*

Theory Z is a basic approach to management that suggests that involved workers are the key to increased productivity. Among Ouchi's major recommendations:

- Management must develop a clear statement of the company's purpose and philosophy and articulate it throughout the organization. This encourages employee identification with the enterprise.

- Collective decision making promotes involvement and facilitates implementation of decisions.

- Management and employee training should aim at developing a broad knowledge of overall operations rather than encouraging specialization.

- Career progression should be slow with greater commitment to lifelong employment.

Theory Z emphasizes the close relationship between employee self-esteem and productivity. However, Ouchi cautions that his theory is not a quick fix for productivity problems. Only by taking the long view and instituting basic changes over an extended period can firms benefit from Theory Z.

---

competition and sagging productivity, a number of firms attempted to restructure workplace relationships in such a way as to appeal to employee values. This modern approach to human relations is often called the *quality of work-life* (QWL) movement. However, it is also referred to as human resources development, work improvement, humanization of work, and work reform.

What Is QWL?

One of the most dehumanizing assumptions ever made is that workers work and managers think. When we give shop floor workers control over their work, they are enormously thoughtful.

Michael Sonduck,
Corporate Manager for Work Improvement,
Digital Equipment Corp.

The quality of work-life movement is rooted in the belief that human beings are the most important factor in any situation. For years the key to increasing productivity was thought to be more capital investment and increasing specialization—the breaking down of all work into small component parts, assigning each worker a tiny task, and relying on assembly-line processes. Specialization has been carried to great extremes in factories and offices. Recently, however, there has been a growing recognition that the advantages of specialization may be more than offset by worker boredom and alienation. Moreover, traditional human relations efforts are not always successful in combating declining productivity, rising absenteeism, and increasing labor turnover.

One of the major features of QWL is the concern with the nature of work itself—the focus on restructuring and reorganizing the relationships among people, machines, and jobs. The underlying assumption is that the nature and structure of work shapes human attitudes and behavior. Accordingly, employee motivation is influenced more by the structure of work and degree of employee involvement than by reward systems (better pay) or good human relation practices (recognition and improved communications). As Peter Drucker observed in his classic book on management, "It is not human nature but the structure of job and work that, in effect, determines how people will act and what management they will require."

A second dimension of QWL is developing a climate of trust between labor and management with emphasis on greater cooperation in achieving common goals. The traditional adversarial relationship is being replaced by efforts to gain worker involvement in problem solving and decision making. This requires a major change in managerial style.

QWL Programs

It is difficult to offer a concise description of quality of work-life programs because they encompass a host of interrelated activities, all of which reflect the growing concern for better management of human resources. Among the most widely adopted QWL programs are (1) job redesign, (2) job rotation, and (3) participative management.

Job Redesign is a counterattack on labor specialization. The first step is *job enlargement,* which involves expanding typical assembly-line and office jobs by the addition of more complex tasks. Lengthening the work cycle—the amount of time a worker has to complete a job—is accomplished by expanding the number of tasks and duties assigned to an employee. The purpose is not to make the work harder, but to overcome worker boredom and dissatisfaction by making jobs more varied and interesting.

An extension of job redesign is *job enrichment.* The purpose is to reshape jobs to provide workers with more responsibility, challenge, and independence with the goal of enhancing employee self-esteem and sense of accomplishment. Broader in scope than job enlargement, job enrichment is not limited to office and factory workers but extends to sales, professional, and managerial personnel.

Job Rotation means training all members of a work group to be capable of doing each other's jobs. Such groups are often paid for what they know rather than what they do.

Participative Management refers to systematic efforts to get more people involved in planning and making decisions about activities that affect them and their jobs. *Quality circles,* or worker committees that analyze and solve quality problems, are the most widely used technique for encouraging worker participation. Such groups have been used for years in Japan and are credited for that country's reputation for high-quality goods.

The Shift in Management Philosophy

Successful quality of work-life programs require a fundamental change in attitude throughout the organization, and the change must be supported from the top. Most important is a shift in management style from the traditional boss-employee type of decision making to a participative process. This requires greater delegation of authority, increased sharing of information with employees, greater job security, and the sharing of gains from increased productivity. With participative management, the role of the supervisor shifts from that of an overseer primarily concerned with directing and controlling to that of a coordinator and teacher.

It is difficult for managers to give up authority and control. Some managers feel that the participative process robs them of hard earned status and prestige. Others are threatened by the success of subordinates. Moreover, QWL programs make the first-line supervisor's job difficult and demanding. Firms have found that the prerequisite to successfully introducing work-improvement programs is educating management to understand and support the participative process.

The rapid increase in the number of firms introducing QWL activities reflects a growing awareness of the competitive advantages of such programs. In other words, QWL efforts can pay off in dollars and cents by reducing absenteeism, labor turnover, and worker errors while boosting morale, product quality, and productivity.

The leaders in the quality of work-life movement have been such innovative firms as General Foods, Procter & Gamble, Xerox, People Express, General Motors, and Ford.

People Express, the fastest growing discount airline, operates without traditional supervisors, secretaries, or organizational charts. Every employee is a stockholder. Profits, decision making, and a sense of belonging are shared by all employees. Work is completed

---

ISSUE MANAGEMENT JAPANESE STYLE

Over the past 2 decades the Japanese business system has outperformed every major industrial nation on earth. During the 1960s and early 1970s, Japan's GNP increased at a rate of more than 10 percent a year. By the 1980s, Japan had become the world's leader in the production of such goods as automobiles, television sets, and home audio equipment.

One of the secrets of the Japanese performance lies in their unique management system, which is built on what has been called the *wa* spirit. *Wa* means harmony, a sense of affection, commitment, and responsibility by members of an organization or firm toward each other. Contrary to Western thought, which tends to focus on differences, the Japanese emphasize the unity and harmony of things. While Americans tend to think of themselves as individuals, the Japanese view themselves as members of a group. Thus the Japanese corporation is seen as a community sharing common interests.

The Japanese style of management is based on four major features: (1) managers are highly success oriented; (2) employees are loyal to their jobs and to the company; (3) decision making is a "bottom-to-top" process; and (4) consensus is based on achieving mutual agreement through discussion. The loyalty of Japanese employees stems from a sense of belonging enhanced by a system of lifetime employment. Moreover, management encourages employees to initiate proposals for solving problems; decisions are not imposed from above. Everyone who is involved in the implementation of a decision participates in making it. This bottom-to-top process creates two problems: first, decision making is slow; and second, it is difficult to pinpoint responsibility. However, once the decision is made,

---

by teams of three or four people that move from job to job. Team managers are viewed as coaches that guide and encourage team members.

General Motors and Toyota formed a joint venture known as NUMMI, New United Motor Manufacturing, Inc., that manufactures subcompact cars using the Japanese style of management. Even the lowest level workers are involved in decision making, including whether to stop the assembly line for quality defects. There are only four supervisory levels, instead of six or seven common to most traditional U.S. automobile plants. Decisions are made by teams of workers. Employees are even allowed to design their own production areas.

ISSUE MANAGEMENT JAPANESE STYLE (Cont.)

---

implementation is speedy because everyone understands what is required.

Most American managers have studied the Japanese system with a mixture of envy and enthusiasm. However, the Japanese management style does not offer a quick solution to the problems of American business. Much of Japan's economic success stems from cultural traits that are centuries old. Nevertheless, the Japanese have been successful in transferring many of their managerial techniques to companies they operate in the United States staffed mainly with American workers and managers.

Many U.S. firms, however, have encountered difficulty in sustaining programs that encourage worker participation and quality circles. Union officials often fear their role as workers' representatives will be undermined if employees and management use quality circles to solve production problems, increase output, and improve quality. According to Norman Meyer, president of United Automobile Workers Local 699, "the cardinal rule here is that you don't discuss contractual matters in the quality of work-life groups."

Participative management assumes that employees possess the necessary education, attitude, and skill to effectively participate. Hewlett-Packard found that some of its employees lack the arithmetic skills to make simple calculations measuring variations in output.

Finally, management may view quality of work-life programs as a threat to their jobs or may simply perfer a more autocratic style of leadership. In short, to be effective, quality of work-life programs must have the support of management, the union, and employees.

Donald Peterson, Chairman of Ford Motor Company, states the renewed confidence of management in today's worker:

> We're discovering that, more than anything else, people are the source of a corporation's strength. From my point of view, this is a very positive development, because people and their job satisfaction, their morale, and their management support structure make a great deal of difference in whether or not we succeed in today's competitive business environment.

The underlying assumption of QWL is that efforts to restructure work and humanize the workplace can contribute as much to increased productivity as capital investment and technological improvement. However, firms seeking a quick fix for their productivity problems by adopting QWL programs are likely to be disappointed. Successful programs require time and commitment. As Gene Kofke, director of work relations at American Telephone and Telegraph Company, puts it, "The worst enemy that quality of work life has is the impatience for quick and finite results." Moreover, QWL programs that aim only at boosting productivity soon lose worker support. Successful programs combine productivity goals with improved worker satisfaction.

Figure 5.3 illustrates one company's QWL program.

SUMMARY

The Hawthorne Experiments led many managers to recognize that worker motivation and morale influence productivity. According to Maslow's hierarchy-of-needs theory, human beings are motivated by both material and nonmaterial needs. Of particular importance are psychological and social needs, which include recognition, social acceptance, and self-respect. Herzberg divided job traits into maintenance factors, which preserve employee satisfaction, and motivational factors such as recognition and fulfillment of potential.

Some of the major indicators of worker morale are labor turnover, absenteeism, productivity, and the number of grievances. Management can help to build high morale by praising good performance, preserving employees' self-esteem, stressing job importance, establishing good communication, and providing for the effective handling of grievances.

Leadership is the art of gaining the enthusiastic participation and support of others in achieving the leader's goals. Styles of leadership differ according to the leader's personality, the type of work being performed, and the education and skills of the employees. McGregor's Theory X and Theory Y represent two contrasting views of how people are motivated and how they react to work.

The quality of work-life (QWL) movement represents a recent trend in personnel management that aims at improving the quality of work by restructuring jobs and expanding employee involvement in productive activities. Common QWL activities include job redesign, job rotation, and participative management.

SELF-EXAMINATION QUESTIONS

The following questions are based on the Chapter Objectives listed at the beginning of the chapter. Test yourself by circling the letter preceding the answer that *best* completes the statement or answers the question. The answers to the Self-Examination Questions are in the appendix at the end of the textbook.

Much has been written about Japanese management style.

Quality circles, lifetime employment, corporate anthems, exercise programs, etc.

The implication is that the style of Japanese management is superior to that of American management. And that for Japanese companies, this particular style works both at home and abroad.

But did you know that this style is not universally practiced in Japan? In many Japanese companies, employment tenure varies, quality circles don't exist, the boss is the boss.

And did you know that many American companies have an even better record of management than some Japanese companies? We believe that one of these companies is Motorola. Why? It all starts with our respect for the dignity of the individual employee. We apply this philosophy in many employee-related programs.

Our Participative Management Program brings our people together in work teams that regularly, openly and effectively communicate ideas and solutions that help improve quality and productivity. In the process, many employees tell us that the program also enhances their job satisfaction.

Motorola's Technology Ladder provides opportunities for technical people, such as design engineers, to progress in professional esteem, rank and compensation in a way comparable to administrators and officers.

Our ten-year service club rewards employee dedication and loyalty with special protection for continued employment and benefits. And in an industry noted for both explosive growth and high mobility, almost one-quarter of our U.S. employees have been with us for more than a decade.

Are employee exercise programs, company songs and lifetime employment the best ways to increase productivity?

Our open door policy enables employees to voice a grievance all the way up to the Chairman. It's rarely needed, but it's there. And it works. These and other programs reflect our respect for, and commitment to, the individual and the team. Their continuing effectiveness is reflected in the direct and open, non-union relationship among all our people, whether production workers, engineers or office workers. All of this works for us as we work for you.

Meeting Japan's Challenge requires an enlightened management style—demonstrated by our participative management style that respects the dignity of the individual.

 **MOTOROLA** A World Leader in Electronics

Quality and productivity through employee participation in management.

FIGURE 5.3   An Advertisement Promoting Motorola's QWL Program

1.   The American psychologist whose experiments at Western Electric Company led to the conclusion that social and psychological factors are more important than working conditions in affecting productivity is: (A) Elton Mayo; (B) Douglas McGregor; (C) Frederick Herzberg; (D) Abraham Maslow; (E) none of these.

2.   Who developed a hierarchy of human needs to explain motivation? (A) Elton Mayo; (B) Douglas McGregor; (C) Frederick Herzberg; (D) Abraham Maslow; (E) none of these.

3.   The theory that divides job traits into maintenance factors that preserve satisfaction and motivational factors that motivate employees was developed by: (A) Elton Mayo; (B) Douglas McGregor; (C) Frederick Herzberg; (D) Abraham Maslow; (E) none of these.

4.   Which of the following is *not* a factor that builds employee morale? (A) praising good performance; (B) increasing labor turnover; (C) stressing job importance; (D) improving communications; (E) handling grievances promptly.

5.   A manager who uses threats and coercion to motivate employees is committed to: (A) Theory X; (B) Theory Y; (C) Theory Z; (D) all of these; (E) none of these.

6.   What style of leadership is involved when a manager defines a problem, describes budget limitations, and then encourages his or her subordinates to find a solution? (A) autocratic; (B) Theory A; (C) laissez faire; (D) participative; (E) disastrous.

7.   Which of the following programs are part of the quality of work-life movement? (A) job redesign; (B) job rotation; (C) participative management; (D) all of these; (E) none of these.

Student _____

BUILDING A BUSINESS VOCABULARY

Directions: Match the terms with their definitions by writing the letter in the appropriate blank.

a. Morale
b. Theory Z
c. Leadership
d. Elton Mayo Hathorne eX
e. Participative Management
f. Theory X
g. Quality of Work-Life (QWL) Movement

h. Quality Circle
i. Frederick Herzberg
j. Job Enlargement
k. Job Enrichment
l. Job Rotation
m. Theory Y
n. Abraham Maslow
o. Douglas McGregor

 1. A theory based on Japanese management techniques that emphasizes employee identification with the firm through collective decision making, nonspecialized training, and lifelong employment.

 2. An American psychologist whose experiments suggested that working conditions are less important than social and psychological factors in motivating employees.

 3. A redesign of jobs with the goal of adding greater challenge, responsibility, variety, and independence.

 4. The attitude of workers toward their jobs and the firm.

 5. Organized efforts to gain increased involvement by employees in planning and decision-making activities that concern them and their work.

 6. Expanding the number of tasks and duties assigned a worker so that jobs become more interesting.

 7. Persuading and directing others in order to gain their enthusiastic participation and support.

 8. Training all members of a work team to be capable of doing each other's jobs.

 9. The assumption that people dislike work and responsibility and must be coerced to work toward company objectives.

_____ 10. A student of human motivation who divided job characteristics into two categories: maintenance factors and motivational factors.

_____ 11. The theory that under the right conditions people will seek responsibility and enthusiastically work toward mutually determined goals.

_____ 12. An approach to increasing job satisfaction and worker productivity by restructuring and reorganizing jobs and developing a climate of trust and cooperation between labor and management.

_____ 13. A psychologist who theorized that human beings are motivated by unfulfilled needs arranged in a hierarchy from basic needs to social and psychological needs.

_____ 14. A group of workers and managers who meet together to analyze and solve problems.

_____ 15. The person who labeled the traditional view of management Theory X and the participative approach to management Theory Y.

Student _____

REVIEWING MAJOR CONCEPTS

1. What was the major conclusion drawn from the Hawthorne Experiments? Why were the Hawthorne Experiments important?

2. Why are social and psychological needs probably more important than material and safety needs in motivating most American workers?

3. Why should management be interested in employee morale?

4. Which of McGregor's two theories do you think accurately reflects most people's attitudes toward work? Explain your choice.

5. What is the quality of work-life (QWL) movement? How does it differ from traditional human relations programs?

6. Describe four methods for improving listening skills.

Student _____

SOLVING PROBLEMS AND CASES

1. *Case:* Arnoba Janitorial Services

   Dolores Arnoba is the hard-driving owner and manager of a successful janitorial services firm with more than 150 employees. Ms. Arnoba started in business 25 years ago working out of her home with her son as her only assistant. Working 12 to 16 hours a day, she built a profitable firm with contracts to perform janitorial services for 45 companies located in a middle-sized western city.

   Ms. Arnoba pays her workers top wages, but she has always opposed such fringe benefits as paid vacations, health insurance, and coffee breaks. Recently she noticed that customer complaints had been rising, and she bawled out two supervisors in front of their work crews for sloppy work. In recent weeks several employees have quit and absenteeism has been rising.

   Yesterday, Ms. Arnoba learned that four workers have been trying to persuade the other employees to form a union. Her first reaction was to "fire the troublemakers." She told her son, "Workers today are soft and lazy. I pay top wages and I expect hard work. What's wrong with those people anyway?" If you were Ms. Arnoba's son, what would you say to her?

2. *Case:* Dixie State Bank

The Dixie State Bank, established in 1870, operates six branch banks in a southern state. High operating costs have cut profits in recent years, and last month a new president was selected by the board of directors and given the task of increasing earnings.

The staff at each branch typically consists of a branch manager, a loan officer, an operations officer, five tellers, three machine operators, and two or three clerks. Although management personnel have been employed by the bank for an average of 15 years, the turnover among nonmanagement employees is high. One of the major problems common to all branches is that the work load varies greatly according to the time of week and month. The tellers are swamped on Fridays and on traditional paydays, while the machine operators and clerks are busiest during the first part of the week.

Yesterday, the president submitted to the board a revolutionary reorganization plan calling for the following changes:

• Employees at each branch would be organized into a work team, and all employees would be trained to perform each team member's job.

• Management personnel would be expected to help out at a teller's window during periods of peak traffic.

• Team members would be encouraged to make job assignments, schedule coffee breaks, and interview prospective employees.

• Each branch team would be responsible for generating new business, and a system of bonuses would be used as rewards for attracting new customers. Moreover, team members would vote on pay raises for fellow employees.

As a member of the Dixie Board of Directors, would you vote for this plan? Explain why or why not. What problems do you foresee if the plan is adopted?

Student _____

3. *Case:* Continental Airlines

The following comments were made by Robert F. Six, former president and chief executive officer of Continental Airlines, when accepting the "Man of the Year" award from UCLA's Executive Program Association:

> It has been my observation that a desperate management in a frantic effort to implement employee communication frequently treats its people like spoiled brats. The use of brainstorming sessions, of management chats, of this endless search for a two-way street whereby employer and employee may vent their souls and fall in love with each other misuses work time and shows depressingly small success.
>
> So, too, does the ancient plea that "My door is always open—bring me your problems." This is guaranteed to turn on every whiner, lackey, and neurotic on the property. If you enjoy playing priest or psychiatrist, this is great fun, but it has nothing to do with the motivation of the employees.
>
> May I suggest that there are many millions of workers who actually, honest-to-God, like their jobs and are proud of their skills? Accepted doctrine seems to insist that employees hate work, hate the boss, and have to be cuddled and cajoled into punching a clock because they would much rather be down at the library improving their minds or out on the beach playing in the sand.
>
> Ladies and gentlemen, despite what you hear, most people enjoy going to work in the morning. Honest! They find their tasks interesting—even challenging—their fellow workers like-minded people with whom they can share occupational concerns. Many grow to be their friends. The cadence of the job has a healthy rhythm. Their rewards are tangible and satisfying.

Are Mr. Six's comments inconsistent with the theories presented in this chapter? Explain why or why not using specific examples.

4. The Homework Committee

Meet with two other students in this class and form a committee to complete the homework for Chapter 6, Personnel and Labor Relations. This case is to be turned in with the homework for Chapter 6.

a. List the names of the committee members.

b. State the responsibilities of each member.

c. Specify the meeting time(s) and place(s).

d. State the advantages and limitations of completing homework assignments by committee.

chapter 6

PERSONNEL AND LABOR RELATIONS

This chapter again focuses on the people part of business. In every organization, someone is in charge of recruiting, selecting, and training employees and keeping them motivated and productive. Large firms have created personnel departments to provide specialized services related to employees. One important responsibility of many personnel departments is labor relations, which refers to the relations between employers and labor unions.

CHAPTER OBJECTIVES

1. Briefly describe four major responsibilities of the personnel department.

2. List three key steps in the hiring process.

3. Compare and contrast the time rate, piece rate, and straight salary methods of compensation.

4. Identify the two major types of labor unions and give an example of each.

5. Cite three reasons for the slowdown in growth of labor union membership.

6. Describe the key provisions of the Wagner Act, the Taft-Hartley Act, and the Landrum-Griffin Act.

7. Contrast and compare collective bargaining, mediation, and arbitration.

8. Identify the following activities as tools of labor or management: strike, secondary boycott, lockout, injunction, primary boycott.

ER/LABOR REPRESENTATIVE
Career oppty in employee relations & labor for listed mfg co. in rural No. Ca. location. To $38,000. Resumes to **Dunn Agency, 830 Market St., Ste. 502, San Francisco, CA 94102.**

SALES REPRESENTATIVE
For leading NY distributor of cosmetics & fragrances. Openings available in all areas of USA. Please call **Rita Master at (516) 273-4000 collect.**

ADMINISTRATIVE ASSISTANT
Top Secretarial skills required for company President with multiple interests. College required. Stable. Mature. Intelligent. Palo Alto area. Send resume & salary history to **Box WB 5, Wall Street Journal.**

FIGURE 6.1 Management Recruiting
Reprinted by permission of the *Wall Street Journal.*

PERSONNEL MANAGEMENT

In a broad sense, the management of personnel is the responsibility of every manager in an organization. However, personnel departments headed by a personnel manager are common in large corporations and in other public and private institutions. It should be noted that the *personnel manager* is usually a staff position whose primary responsibility is to provide assistance in personnel matters to other departments. Typically, the personnel department is concerned with (1) hiring; (2) orientating; (3) training; (4) evaluating; and (5) compensating employees. More recently, health and safety programs and equal employment opportunity procedures are usually administered by personnel departments.

Hiring

The hiring process begins with a careful analysis of the position to be filled. This study is used to develop *job specifications,* which describe the qualifications needed to perform the job.

Recruiting is the process of actively seeking out prospective employees and encouraging them to apply for open positions. Recruiting may involve classified advertising (see Figure 6.1), the use of private employment agencies, public employment services, and visits by company recruiters to schools and colleges.

Selection of new employees is a very important process. Many firms find their freedom to fire unsatisfactory employees severely limited by union contracts, company policies, and civil rights legislation. Therefore, every effort must be made to hire the right individual for the position or the company may be stuck with an unsatisfactory employee for many years.

The selection process normally begins with the *application form,* which provides information on the applicant's personal characteristics, work experience, education, and so forth. The application form serves as a screening device for eliminating those applicants who obviously do not have the necessary qualifications for the position. A typical application form is shown in Figure 6.2.

The most important part of the hiring process is the *interview.*

Victor Corporation

Employment Application

PRINT IN INK OR TYPE. IF ADDITIONAL SPACE IS NEEDED, USE SEPARATE SHEET.

FOR OFFICE USE ONLY
DATE EMPLOYED
TITLE
SALARY
ENGAGED BY
TITLE

NAME LAST FIRST INITIAL			SOCIAL SECURITY NUMBER (VOLUNTARY)
ADDRESS STREET CITY STATE ZIP CODE			
TELEPHONE NUMBER	MINIMUM SALARY REQUIREMENT	DATE AVAILABLE	DATE OF APPLICATION
POSITION DESIRED			

MILITARY SERVICE DATA	BRANCH OF SERVICE		DUTIES
DATE OF INDUCTION	DATE OF DISCHARGE	RANK AT DISCHARGE	TYPE OF DISCHARGE

LAW VIOLATIONS List any felony convictions.

EDUCATIONAL RECORD (NAME AND ADDRESS)			
LAST ELEMENTARY SCHOOL	1 2 3 4 5 6 7 8		
LAST HIGH SCHOOL	9 10 11 12		
JUNIOR COLLEGE	MAJOR FIELD	DEGREE	
COLLEGE OR UNIVERSITY	MAJOR FIELD	DEGREE	
COLLEGE OR UNIVERSITY	MAJOR FIELD	DEGREE	

EMPLOYMENT DATA

COMPANY NAME	FROM: MO. YR.	BEGINNING SALARY	JOB TITLE
ADDRESS	TO: MO. YR.	ENDING SALARY	JOB DUTIES
CITY STATE		REASON FOR LEAVING	
SUPERVISOR			
COMPANY NAME	FROM: MO. YR.	BEGINNING SALARY	JOB TITLE
ADDRESS	TO: MO. YR.	ENDING SALARY	JOB DUTIES
CITY STATE		REASON FOR LEAVING	
SUPERVISOR			
COMPANY NAME	FROM: MO. YR.	BEGINNING SALARY	JOB TITLE
ADDRESS	TO: MO. YR.	ENDING SALARY	JOB DUTIES
CITY STATE		REASON FOR LEAVING	
SUPERVISOR			

TWO PERSONAL REFERENCES (NOT RELATIVES OR PERSONS YOU HAVE WORKED FOR)

NAME	MAILING ADDRESS	STATE	TEL. NO. IF KNOWN	BUSINESS OR PROFESSION

Signature ________________ Date ________________

FIGURE 6.2 Employment Application Form

Face-to-face contact with the applicant permits the interviewer to gain additional information not available from the application form, and to generally evaluate the applicant's qualifications for the position. The interviewer attempts to assess the applicant's attitudes, interests, and personal characteristics that affect job performance. An interview also provides the applicant with an opportunity to ask questions about the firm, the job, and the conditions of employment. Some firms use a series of interviews beginning with a preliminary or screening interview and ending with a final selection interview.

ISSUE   WHAT'S YOUR JOB PSYCHOLOGY?

A job is more than a way of earning a living; it is a means of achieving self-esteem, status, and personal satisfaction. Of course everyone wants a job that is rewarding and satisfying. Your job success depends to a large extent on your attitudes and personal characteristics—that is, on your job psychology.

A job represents a contract between an employer and an employee that entails responsibilities for both parties. The employer has an obligation to pay the employee what he or she is worth, to provide opportunities for advancement, and to reward superior performance. The employee's responsibility begins with a commitment of time, energy, and effort to the firm's success. In other words, an employee should identify with the firm's goals.

When you take a job, the first thing to find out is what is expected of you in terms of performance and behavior. Your first question should be "What can I contribute?" not "What's in it for me?" Be realistic enough to recognize that no job is exciting and satisfying all the time. Your employer expects you to get the job done on time even if it is difficult and unpleasant. In short, you are expected to produce! After all, you are accepting the firm's money. Taking a job without a commitment to deliver to the best of your ability is dishonest.

Probably the single most important reason for job failure is the inability to get along with others. Your interpersonal relations with your coworkers can make or break you. A little courtesy and kindness can go a long way. Do not act superior,

Many employers make use of *testing* in the selection process. There are various types of tests designed to measure different characteristics.

1   *Performance Tests* are used to measure skills such as typing and shorthand accuracy and speed.
2   *Aptitude Tests* attempt to determine an individual's potential proficiency for certain types of work such as clerical or assembly jobs.
3   *Psychological Tests* try to measure motivation and personality traits of the applicant.

Psychological tests have been criticized for being invalid and an inaccurate predictor of motivation and performance. In addition,

ISSUE WHAT'S YOUR JOB PSYCHOLOGY? (Cont.)

even if you think you are. Remember that acts of hostility toward others are usually a reflection of your own feelings of dissatisfaction or inadequacy.

Another determinant of job success is your personal image —how others view and react to you. Your image depends on a number of factors, including your appearance, tact, poise, and honesty. The way you dress as well as your personal grooming influence the reactions of coworkers, customers, and your employer. Most firms have an easily recognized appearance model. If you feel your dress and grooming are no one's business but your own, then you had better find a job where these factors are unimportant.

Tact is skill in not offending others. Try to develop an awareness of people's feelings and sensitivities. A good rule to keep in mind is that no one likes to be criticized. Poise is a combination of confidence (but not overconfidence) and dignity that engender respect from others. It is a reflection of personal competence and self-assurance mixed with humility. In short, poise is the ability to laugh at oneself and yet not be a fool.

If you were an employer, would you hire or promote a dishonest person? Of course not! Be worthy of other people's trust. Remember, your reputation for personal honesty will follow you throughout your career.

Technical skill and intellectual brilliance are rarely key factors in job success. Far more important are the employee's attitudes and personal characteristics. Do you have a positive job psychology?

there are charges that the tests are culturally and racially biased. Finally, some people believe that psychological testing is an invasion of privacy.

Despite these criticisms, most major employers use psychological tests in the initial selection process as well as in evaluating employees for promotion. In recent years, the tests have been revised and upgraded to overcome the criticisms of being biased and unrealistic. The growing use of psychological tests is based on the surging costs of hiring the wrong people for jobs and management's demand for more objective predictors of performance.

The selection procedure may include physical examinations to determine if the applicant has any health problems or disabilities that would interfere with performance on the job.

Orientation

The purposes of *orientation* are to introduce new employees to the work environment and to ensure they are familiar with company policies and procedures. Employees are usually apprehensive when starting a new job. An orientation program can ease this apprehension by explaining to workers what is expected of them and by introducing them to fellow employees. An effective orientation program can reduce labor turnover by helping new employees adjust quickly to the work environment.

Training

The purpose of training is to provide employees with the knowledge and skills to perform their duties effectively. Training methods vary from firm to firm. Probably the most common method is *on-the-job training* where an employee attempts to develop skills while actually performing a job. Often an experienced worker will be assigned to provide guidance and assistance.

Vestibule training takes place in a special area away from the job site. Necessary materials and equipment are available for practice. Computers can be used to stimulate the job environment. An example is training airline pilots with flight simulators. The advantage of vestibule training is that it provides an environment similar to the actual workplace where workers can make mistakes without grave consequences.

Some firms use *formal classroom training,* particularly in management development programs. A variety of instructional techniques including lectures, discussions, role-playing, and audiovisual presentations may be used.

Evaluating

Most large organizations have developed formal procedures for rating the performance of employees. The purpose of evaluation is to provide information for determining wages and salaries and for promotions. In addition, an effective evaluation process can serve to assist employees in recognizing and overcoming their shortcomings. One type of evaluation form is presented in Figure 6.3.

Compensating

Wage and salary administration is one of the most complex responsibilities of the personnel department. A fair and equitable system of compensation is a major determinant of employee morale. Interestingly enough, studies have shown that the relative differences in compensation paid to various workers is often more important than the absolute size of the paycheck. This is because employees tend to measure their status by comparing their income to that of other workers.

There are several methods of compensation:

Time Rate   Time rate systems pay workers according to the amount of time spent on the job. For example, the employee may be

PERFORMANCE APPRAISAL SUMMARY   **Confidential**

I.   GENERAL INFORMATION

EMPLOYEE NAME		POSITION TITLE		EMPLOYEE NO.
COMPANY		LOCATION		DIVISION

DEPARTMENT	NO.	OCCUP. CD. 1	OCCUP. CD. 2	OCCUP. CD. 3	OCCUP. CD. 4	OCCUP. CD. 5
SALARY GRADE	PRESENT SALARY	EFFECTIVE DATE		TYPE INCREASE		
DATE LAST PERFORMANCE REVIEW		DATE OF HIRE		DATE ENTERED PRESENT POSITION		

II. POSITION FUNCTION

Have individual objectives been established?   (if no explain in remarks section)   ☐ Yes   ☐ No

If employee has both functional and organizational reporting responsibilities or dual reporting requirements, has this appraisal been discussed with the other manager?   ☐ Yes   ☐ No

Have the objectives of the affirmative action program been reviewed this period?   ☐ Yes   ☐ No

Have accident prevention results been reviewed and individual objective established?   ☐ Yes   ☐ No

Has the Corporation's policy statement relative to Anti-Trust law compliance been reviewed this period?   ☐ Yes   ☐ No

Has the Corporation's policy statement relative to employee Conflict of Interest been reviewed this period?   ☐ Yes   ☐ No

III.   PERFORMANCE EVALUATION (See Salary Administration Policy for Performance Definitions.)

☐ 1.   OUTSTANDING

☐ 2.   EXCEEDS POSITION REQUIREMENTS

☐ 3.   MEETS POSITION REQUIREMENTS

☐ 4.   MEETS MINIMUM REQUIREMENTS

☐ 5.   UNSATISFACTORY (not eligible for merit salary consideration)

Date Prepared _____

Covering period from _____

To _____

V. REMARKS   *(Use Remarks Section as needed to elaborate on any section of Summary)*

PREPARED BY	POSITION	TELEPHONE NUMBER

PERSONNEL COPY

FIGURE 6.3   Employee Evaluation Form
Courtesy Moore Business Forms, Inc.

paid at a rate of $8 per hour for a 40-hour week and $12 per hour for overtime above 40 hours.[1]

---

[1]Most employees are covered by the Fair Labor Standards Act, which requires hours worked in excess of 40 a week be compensated at one-and-one-half times the regular hourly rate.

ISSUE   TWO-TIER PAY: LONG-TERM TREND OR QUICK FIX?

Two-tier salary contracts have become a major point of contention in the area of employee compensation. Under such contracts, newly hired workers are paid less than current employees for the same job.

The major purpose of two-tier arrangements is to reduce labor costs without hurting existing employees. The contracts have become increasingly common in such industries as airlines, retailing, steel, and trucking where unionized firms are fighting for survival against foreign competition or nonunion companies.

According to the Bureau of Labor Statistics, one-third of all new contracts contain some form of two-tier pay. Even the huge U.S. Postal Service recently negotiated a two-tier contract that provides starting pay for new letter carriers and postal clerks that is $3000 below current employees.

Some experts predict the use of two-tier systems will become increasingly widespread. Unions initially accepted such contracts as preferable to layoffs and general pay cuts. However, there is growing union opposition to two-tier contracts because they alienate new employees and lead to dissension among union members.

Even managers are having second thoughts. Two-tier systems rarely solve a firm's long-term financial problems, but they can cause discontent, lower morale, and reduce productivity. Gordon Kirby, director of industrial relations for the California Trucking Association, concludes, "Two-tier systems aren't panaceas; they're a quick fix."

Piece Rate   Piece rate systems base the employee's pay on output. There is a built-in incentive for the worker to increase production. An example is a system that pays a worker at the rate of $0.10 per unit. If the worker produces 500 units per day, he or she earns $50; if output increases to 570 units, earnings would be $57 per day. This piece rate system is commonly used to compensate sales personnel who work on a commission basis.

Straight Salary   Usually managers and most white-collar employees such as clerks, secretaries, and other office workers are paid a fixed amount each month or year. Today, more firms are augmenting salaries with bonuses based on productivity. Sometimes salaried workers are not eligible for overtime pay.

ISSUE DO-IT-YOURSELF FRINGE BENEFITS

An important trend in personnel management is allowing employees to select their fringe benefits cafeteria-style. Such programs typically group benefits under two categories, basic and optional. Basics might include vacation time dependent on length of service, minimum health insurance coverages, and a limited pension program. The employee then can use credits to choose among such optional benefits as additional vacation time, full health coverage, dental and eye care, company-paid life insurance, and increased employer payments to retirement programs.

Flexible fringe benefits programs are particularly appealing to the growing number of two-income families. These programs permit employees to avoid duplication of benefits and tailor a benefits package to their individual needs.

Employers claim the plans reduce employee turnover and serve as a valuable aid to recruitment. In addition, flexible plans give the impression of providing employees with increased benefits without adding significantly to costs.

Do-it-yourself packages have several drawbacks. The cost of setting up such programs can exceed $1 million for larger firms. Since most cafeteria-type plans permit employees to adjust benefits once a year, paperwork costs can be high. Finally, the tax treatment of flexible fringe benefits is still unsettled.

Managers with experience administering flexible programs suggest that companies start plans gradually, with a few options, and add additional benefits as knowledge is gained. They point out that time is needed to shape programs for individual firms and to communicate the nature of the programs to employees.

Profit Sharing   Profit sharing is used by some firms to encourage increased production, reduce labor turnover, and promote employee loyalty. A portion of aftertax profits are set aside for distribution to workers in the form of a bonus. Profit sharing plans have met with mixed results. If profits decline, worker bonuses are reduced and morale may drop. Moreover, such plans may result in lower earnings for stockholders.

Fringe Benefits   Fringe benefits refer to noncash payments that often take the form of company-paid health, accident, and life insurance; pension plans; rest periods; paid holidays and vacations; company-subsidized cafeterias; and a variety of other benefits. In recent years fringe benefits have grown increasingly important. Today, fringe benefits account for 30 to 40 percent of labor costs, and this share is growing.

Health and Safety Programs

There are several reasons why management must devote time, money, and effort to developing an effective program aimed at protecting the health and safety of employees. In the first place, a humane manager is concerned with minimizing suffering, illness, and fatalities among employees. Second, the Occupational Safety and Health Administration (OSHA) is seeking to reduce health and safety hazards in the workplace. Finally, employee accidents and illness reduce productivity and raise labor costs.

Equal Employment Opportunities

There are numerous federal and state laws that attempt to promote equal employment opportunities. Title VII of the Civil Rights Act of 1964 prohibits discrimination based on race, religion, sex, and national origin in employment practices. It established the Equal Employment Opportunity Commission (EEOC) as the federal regulatory agency charged with preventing job bias and discrimination. The EEOC investigates charges of discrimination, seeks court orders to halt discriminatory practices, and implements affirmative action programs. The major thrust of affirmative action is developing programs for recruiting, selection, and promotion aimed at overcoming the effects of past discrimination by increasing employment opportunities for minorities, women, older workers, and the handicapped.

LABOR RELATIONS

A specialized area of personnel management is *labor relations,* which refers to management's relations with labor unions. In many American industries, all or nearly all of the workers are union members. Wages and conditions of employment are negotiated through a process called *collective bargaining.* What unions are and how they operate is best understood by briefly reviewing the historical development of labor unions in the United States.

The American Labor Movement

Even before the Revolutionary War, groups of craft workers banded together in an attempt to improve their bargaining position with employers. However, most early unions failed, largely because of internal conflicts and the strong opposition of employers.

In 1886, a cigar maker named Samuel Gompers helped to found the American Federation of Labor (AFL), which was a voluntary association of craft unions. Except for one year, Gompers was president of the AFL until 1924. He was a staunch believer in *business unionism,* a philosophy based on three guidelines: (1) unions should be organized by crafts such as carpenters and machinists; (2) labor should focus on "bread-and-butter" issues such as higher wages, better working conditions, and shorter hours; and

---

ISSUE THE AFFIRMATIVE ACTION CONTROVERSY

Affirmative action is a hotly debated issue. Advocates argue that affirmative action programs are necessary to provide opportunities for people that have been traditionally discriminated against in employment, including women, minorities, the aged, and the handicapped. Without affirmative action, the antidiscrimination laws would be meaningless since there would be no enforceable method of assuring equality of opportunity. Supporters claim affirmative action offers the only way to break the vicious circle of past discrimination, which is a prerequisite for a just and equitable society.

Opponents of affirmative action maintain that such programs in effect establish numeric hiring quotas for selected groups that must be met by certain deadlines. The fear of being labeled "racist" or "sexist" plus the cost of potential litigation forces employers to fulfill quotas rather than hire on the basis of merit or qualifications. According to William Bradford Reynolds, chief of the Justice Department's Civil Rights Division, "We really made a mistake to try to cure discrimination with discrimination."

Critics of affirmative action further argue that women and minorities, as well as the aged and handicapped, now receive preferential treatment. They complain that affirmative action programs increase government bureaucracy and regulation, leading to time-consuming court cases and wasted tax dollars.

Under current laws, it is the government's responsibility to protect workers from discriminatory employment practices. The challenge is how to make up for past discriminatory practices without engaging in "reverse discrimination."

---

(3) unions should operate within the framework of the capitalist system and not become deeply involved in politics.

Union membership grew steadily and by 1920 there were 5 million members. However, in the 1920s employers launched a concerted counterattack against the unions, and by the end of the decade membership had dropped to barely 3 million workers.

In the 1930s the turning point came for the American labor movement. The Great Depression led to the election of Franklin Roosevelt and a Democratic congress with strong labor support. The federal government encouraged union growth and passed a series of laws that were favorable to organized labor. In 1935 a group of labor leaders broke with the AFL and formed the Congress of Industrial Organizations (CIO) to organize workers in mass-production industries such as steel, automobiles, and rubber. In the next 10

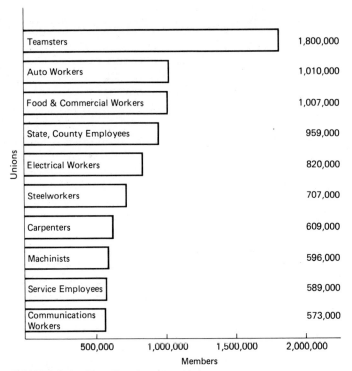

FIGURE 6.4   The Ten Largest Unions
Source: United States Department of Labor, Bureau of Labor Statistics, 1985.

years the number of unionized workers increased fivefold, and by 1978 union membership stood at over 20 million.

In 1955, after 20 years of competition, the American Federation of Labor and the Congress of Industrial Organizations merged to form the AFL-CIO. Not all unions are affiliated with the AFL-CIO. Major independent unions include the Teamsters, United Automobile Workers, and United Mine Workers. Figure 6.4 shows the largest unions in the United States.

Types of Unions   There are two major categories of unions—craft and industrial.

1   *Craft Unions* consist of skilled workers organized by crafts or trades such as electricians, plumbers, and musicians. Most craft unions are associated with the AFL.
2   *Industrial Unions* are organized on an industrywide basis and their members are normally semiskilled or unskilled production-line workers. Examples of industrial unions include the United Rubber Workers and United Steel Workers. The majority of industrial unions are associated with the CIO.

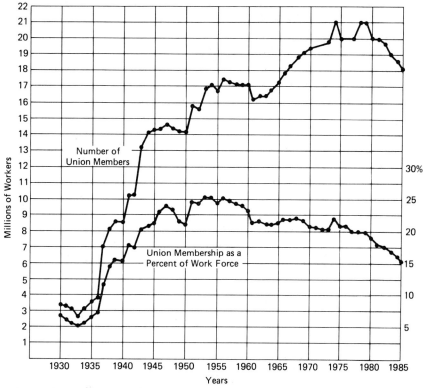

FIGURE 6.5   Union Membership, 1930–1985
Source: United States Department of Labor, Bureau of Labor
Statistics, *Handbook of Labor Statistics, 1985.*

Unions: Problems and Prospects   The tremendous growth of the
labor movement during the 1930s and 1940s has slowed in recent
years. Figure 6.5 shows union membership and the percent of the
total labor force that is unionized. It is interesting to note that the
percent of the labor force belonging to unions reached a peak of
about 25 percent in the early 1950s, and in the last 35 years union
membership has failed to keep pace with the growth in the labor
force.

There are several factors that explain why unions have not
matched the rapid growth in membership achieved during the 1930s
and 1940s. The major strength of the unions has always been among
blue-collar workers—that is, skilled craft workers and
production-line employees. However, the structure of the American
work force has changed drastically in the past few decades. While
the blue-collar work force has declined in size, the number of
white-collar workers (office and service workers, sales personnel,
and most government employees) is growing at a rapid pace. The
unions have spent millions of dollars in attempts to organize
white-collar workers. These efforts have been successful in some
cases—for example, many government employees have joined

unions. But the fact remains, the vast majority of white-collar workers remain unorganized.

The public's attitude toward unions has changed. In the 1930s many people viewed the unions as underdogs fighting for worker rights against selfish "fat-cat corporations." But the growing wealth and power of many unions caused the public to become less sympathetic. This change in attitude was reflected in labor laws passed in the 1940s and 1950s that sought to limit union power and check the corrupt practices of a few union leaders.

Today many industrial unions are feeling the impact of increasing foreign competition, which has made workers less willing to strike when the result may be lost jobs. In the automobile, steel, and rubber industries there is a trend toward "givebacks" where unions forego previously won benefits in order to increase job security. Another trend is the growing popularity of "preventive labor relations consultants," or "union-busting consulting firms" as they are called by union officials. These law firms counsel management on how to prevent employees from joining unions and strategies for getting existing unions voted out by employees. The consultants claim their goal is to create a union-free environment by teaching management to be more responsive to employee needs. However, union representatives claim the consulting firms advocate psychological warfare based on fear, intimidation, and isolation.

What does the future hold for unions? There is evidence that organized labor is undergoing fundamental changes. (See the issue entitled "Has Organized Labor Turned the Corner?") In the older, "smokestack" industries, American firms have taken a competitive beating in the global marketplace. Hundreds of thousands of workers have been laid off, many of them permanently. Both labor and management are beginning to realize that the old adversarial model of labor relations no longer works. The time has come for cooperation in achieving common goals: higher productivity, lower costs, and improved quality.

An example of cooperative labor relations is the contract between the United Automobile Workers (UAW) and General Motors covering GM's new Saturn plant. GM invited the UAW to participate in the planning of the Saturn project, setting the stage for conciliatory bargaining. During contract negotiations, the union agreed to give up restrictive work rules that hamper productivity and to accept salaries (not hourly wages) that are only 80 percent of the amount paid in the rest of the industry. The remaining 20 percent may be made up through profit sharing and an incentive plan based on worker productivity. In return, GM guaranteed lifetime job security for 80 percent of the workers and offered them a greater voice in decision making.

Labor Laws

Federal, state, and local governments have passed hundreds of laws that have influenced labor-management relations. For example, the

Clayton Act contains a provision that exempts labor unions from prosecution under the antitrust laws. Three important pieces of labor legislation are the Wagner Act, the Taft-Hartley Act, and the Landrum-Griffin Act.

Wagner Act   In 1935, Congress passed the National Labor Relations Act, commonly known as the Wagner Act. This law was intended to encourage the growth of unions by guaranteeing workers the right to organize and bargain collectively. Prior to the passage of the Wagner Act, employers were free to fight unions with almost any method including firing union members, using strikebreakers and armed guards, and by refusing to meet with union representatives.

The Wagner Act also established the National Labor Relations Board (NLRB) to investigate charges of unfair labor practices, and to hold elections to determine if the majority of workers in a particular plant want to be represented by a union.

Taft-Hartley Act   After World War II, organized labor called a series of major strikes aimed at securing large wage increases. Public opinion turned antiunion, and in 1947, Congress passed the Labor Management Relations Act, commonly called the Taft-Hartley Act. The law was an attempt to correct some of the abuses of organized labor and to restore the balance of power between unions and business firms.

The Taft-Hartley Act outlawed certain unfair labor practices by unions. The closed shop, which prevents employers from hiring nonunion members, was made illegal, as was the practice of featherbedding, which requires employers to limit production or employ more workers than actually needed. Secondary boycotts, described later in this chapter, were also outlawed.

The Taft-Hartley Act also contains a provision that permits the president of the United States to secure a court order postponing a strike for 80 days whenever the strike threatens the national health and safety. This is known as the 80-day "cooling-off" injunction, and it requires striking workers to return to work.

The most controversial part of the Taft-Hartley Act is Section 14b, which permits individual states to pass laws prohibiting the union shop. These so-called *right-to-work laws* make it illegal for a worker to be forced to join a union to keep his job. At this time, 20 states have "right-to-work" laws, but none of these states is highly industrialized.

Landrum-Griffin Act   During the 1950s a congressional committee investigated charges of racketeering and corruption on the part of some labor leaders. As a result, the Labor Management Reporting and Disclosure Act, also known as the Landrum-Griffin Act, was passed in 1959. This law requires unions to report the handling of union funds, particularly financial arrangements with union officers.

ISSUE   HAS ORGANIZED LABOR TURNED THE CORNER?

The labor movement is at a point of historical crisis.

Harley Shaiken, Labor Analysis,
Massachusetts Institute of Technology

There have been setbacks and there are enormous problems, [but] a new spirit of solidarity and confidence has been growing within our ranks.

Lane Kirkland, President, AFL-CIO

The facts are not encouraging. Between 1980 and 1984 the U.S. labor force grew 5 percent while union membership dropped 13 percent. According to a 1983 Gallup Poll, the public ranked labor leaders near the bottom in honesty and integrity, ahead only of car salespersons. Even with the concerted support of organized labor, Walter Mondale suffered a landslide loss in the 1984 presidential election. In short, the labor movement is fighting a 30-year decline in membership, public confidence, and political influence.

Despite these setbacks, there is a new mood of cautious optimism in the ranks of organized labor. At its 1985 convention, the AFL-CIO executive council acknowledged that "unions find themselves behind the pace of change" and called for fundamental shifts in direction. Actually, major changes are already underway.

• Unions are making an effort to discover what younger workers want. As a result, there is greater emphasis on pay equity, day care, advancement for women, office automation, and job safety and security.

It attempts to ensure the democratic participation of union members in the election of officers and in the conduct of union affairs. For example, the secret ballot is required in union elections.

Collective Bargaining

The process by which representatives of labor and management attempt to settle their differences through negotiations is called *collective bargaining.* This process requires that the union be recognized by management as the bargaining agent for the employees. Under the Wagner Act, such recognition may be granted voluntarily by management, or when the majority of workers vote to be represented by a union. The degree of union recognition, which

---

ISSUE   HAS ORGANIZED LABOR TURNED THE CORNER?
(Cont.)

- With strikes becoming less effective, unions are turning to research as the basis for bringing economic pressure against adversary firms. Analysis of company finances, creditors, and investments is used to shift pension funds, challenge the election of hostile directors, and pressure creditors to transfer funds out of target banks. This strategy proved decisive in organizing J. P. Stevens, the giant textile firm.

- A number of unions are successfully using radio and television advertising campaigns to publicly protest company demands and present labor's bargaining position. In addition, several unions have launched public relations campaigns to counter the image that organized labor is greedy and inflexible.

- In an effort to better relate to more educated employees, some unions are hiring younger, college-educated organizers, often recruited from university campuses and enrolled in special training programs.

Union shifts in attitudes and strategy are not universal. A number of labor leaders, especially in the construction trades, remain inflexible on pay and work rules despite the fact that nonunion contractors have captured 70 percent of the business in some areas. Another area of concern is the underrepresentation of women in union leadership positions. The AFL-CIO's 35-member executive council has only 2 women members even though women make up 34 percent of union membership and 44 percent of the work force.

---

may vary considerably from firm to firm, is defined by what are called *shop agreements*.

Shop Agreements   There are four major types of shop agreements.

1   The *closed shop* requires that management hire only workers who are already union members. From the union's viewpoint this is highly desirable because the union essentially controls all hiring. The Taft-Hartley Act declared the closed shop illegal, but it still persists in some industries.[2]

---

[2]Federal laws may not apply to firms that operate within a single state.

ISSUE: THE DEBATE ON COMPARABLE WORTH

Comparable worth can be an important tool in the arsenal for attacking employment discrimination.

> Blandina Cardenas Ramirez, U.S. Civil Rights Commissioner

What the comparable worth advocates always ignore is who will bear the cost of the pay increases their system would mandate. The costs will not be borne by . . . employers. They will be borne mainly by women.

> Linda Chavez, Staff Director of the U.S. Commission on Civil Rights

The law seems clear enough: equal pay for equal work. Few people would argue with the principle. But in 1983, the name of the game changed when a federal judge ruled that the state of Washington must pay back wages and raises to women paid less than male workers in "comparable jobs." According to the judge, the Civil Rights Act of 1964 "was designed to bar not only overt employment discrimination, but also practices that are fair in form but discriminatory in operation." Although the decision was reversed by an appellate court, six states have begun to adjust salary schedules for traditional female-dominated occupations to make them more equal to those jobs that traditionally employ men. An additional 25 states and a growing number of private firms are reviewing their pay scales based on comparable worth standards.

The key issue in comparable worth is how can you compare two completely different jobs—for example, clerk-typist and truck driver—and determine their relative values? A number of consulting firms specialize in job rating studies. They begin by identifying job requirements, such as skills, knowledge, problem-solving demands, job hazards and working conditions and then assign points to these qualifications and other specifications. The point totals measure each job's worth.

The advocates of comparable worth point out that women's wages have been stuck at about 60 percent of male wages since the 1920s. Although progress has been made in reducing overt sex discrimination over the last few years, past discrimination forced many females into certain occupational

---

2   The *union shop* permits employers to hire nonunion workers, but all workers must join the union within a specified period of time, usually 30 days after being hired.

ISSUE: THE DEBATE ON COMPARABLE WORTH (Cont.)

and career areas leading to segregation and low wages. Examples include nursing and teaching as well as sales and clerical occupations. Proponents argue that social justice demands pay equity, and only comparable worth offers a means of overcoming the consequences of past segregation and discrimination.

In 1985, the U.S. Civil Rights Commission voted 5 to 2 to oppose the comparable worth doctrine as a remedy to sex bias in the workplace. The majority of the commission maintained that pay differences between men and women are caused not by discrimination but by other factors such as job experience, unequal education, and different turnover rates.

Opponents of comparable worth focus on three main points. First, they argue that the studies used to implement comparable worth programs are inherently subjective. There is no realistic way to compare traditional female and male jobs other than through the marketplace. Second, they claim that implementing comparable worth would be prohibitively expensive. One consultant estimates that eliminating pay differences between traditional male and female occupations would cost over $300 billion and boost inflation by 10 percent. Linda Chavez, staff director for the U.S. Commission on Civil Rights, argues that if comparable worth becomes the law of the land, higher salaries will lead to fewer jobs in traditional female occupations. Finally, argue the critics, comparable worth undermines our economic system by replacing free-market prices reflecting supply and demand with government-imposed price fixing.

The supporters of comparable worth are unconvinced by these arguments. They maintain that job evaluation studies are already widely used by large employers, that the critics exaggerate the cost of implementing pay equity, and that justice demands the widespread adoption of the comparable worth concept. The decision of the appellate court in the state of Washington suit is expected to be appealed to the U.S. Supreme Court.

The conflict continues to rage: Is comparable worth social justice or economic nonsense?

3   Under an *agency shop* agreement, workers need not join the union but nonunion members are required to pay a fee equal to union dues.

4   An *open shop* reflects no formal recognition of the union by management. Workers may join the union or not, at their option.

The Labor Contract   The purpose of collective bargaining is to sign a labor contract. The labor contract is simply a list of rules and procedures that govern the relationship between management and employees. The major provisions covered in most labor contracts include: (1) the life of the contract; (2) union recognition and the shop agreement; (3) wages and hours; (4) fringe benefits; (5) provisions for holidays, vacations, and overtime; (6) layoffs and seniority; and (7) grievance procedures.

Mediation and Arbitration   Should labor and management be unable to reach agreement on the labor contract or some other item of dispute, a third party may be asked to intervene. In *mediation,* a neutral third party listens to the arguments from both sides and attempts to get labor and management to settle their differences. Although the mediator may recommend solutions, neither party is bound to accept those recommendations.

Arbitration is similar to mediation except that both labor and management agree to be bound by the decision of the arbitrator. In other words, arbitrators act as judge and jury, and their decisions are binding on both parties.

Arbitration is commonly used as the last resort in settling grievances. A typical procedure calls for management to select one arbitrator, labor another, and a third arbitrator is selected by the other two. After hearing both sides of the dispute, the board of arbitrators votes to determine a solution.

Labor-Management Conflict

It is inevitable that some disputes between labor and management result in open conflict. Workers feel that they have a right to higher wages, improved working conditions, and job security. On the other hand, management also feels that it has certain prerogatives such as the right to introduce new equipment, to change production procedures, and to hire and fire workers. These different viewpoints often lead to conflicts that involve direct pressure being exerted by both sides.

Union Pressure   The most important union weapon is the *strike.* The walkout strike where workers leave their place of employment is the most widely used. The sitdown strike, where workers remain on the job but refuse to perform work, and the slowdown strike, which involves reducing production, have both been declared illegal by the courts.

Picketing occurs when workers parade in front of their place of employment carrying signs stating that a labor dispute is in progress. Members of other unions will often refuse to cross a picket line, thereby bringing additional pressure on management. There are two major types of boycotts. In a *primary boycott,* union members refuse to purchase an employer's products until their demands are granted. A *secondary boycott* involves taking action against a second firm not involved in the labor dispute in order to bring indirect pressure on an employer. Suppose, for example, that the shoemaker's union is striking the ABC Company, a shoe manufacturer. The union then pickets retail shoe stores that carry ABC shoes to force the stores to stop buying from the ABC Company. Because the secondary boycott involves an "innocent" third party, it was declared unlawful under the Taft-Hartley Act.

Management Pressure   The employer's equivalent of the strike is the *lockout.* Management refuses to allow workers to enter the plant until they drop some demand or halt some activity.

The *injunction* is a court order, obtained by an employer, which prohibits a union from engaging in some activity. Prior to the 1930s the injunction was management's main weapon against unions, but legislation has severely limited its use.

The *blacklist* is a secret list of union members and organizers used by firms in an industry to prevent these people from being hired. Although the blacklist is considered an unfair labor practice under the Wagner Act, it is still used in a few nonunionized industries.

Another illegal antiunion weapon is the *yellow-dog contract* under which as a condition of employment, a worker is required to sign a contract promising not to join a union.

The publicity given to strikes by the news media may lead people to conclude that most collective-bargaining sessions break down and lead to open conflict. This is far from true. The vast majority of labor contracts are negotiated and signed with little fanfare and publicity. Our system of collective bargaining is far from perfect, but it is workable.

SUMMARY

Most large organizations have a personnel department that is responsible for assisting other departments in the areas of hiring, orienting, training, evaluating, and compensating employees. The selection process is critically important because a firm may be saddled with an unsatisfactory employee for many years. This process normally includes screening, interviewing, and testing. The personnel department is often charged with the responsibility of developing and maintaining an effective health and safety program, and administering the firm's equal employment opportunities program.

The term *labor relations* refers to the relations between employers and unions. The American labor movement experienced its most rapid growth in the 1930s and early 1940s, largely as a result of favorable government legislation and the successful organizing of workers in mass-production industries. In 1955 the American Federation of Labor and the Congress of Industrial Organizations merged to form the AFL-CIO. About two-thirds of all union members belong to unions that are associated with the AFL-CIO. Craft unions consist of skilled workers organized by trade, while industrial unions are organized on an industry basis and include semiskilled production workers. The future growth of American unions depends on their ability to organize the white-collar work force.

The Wagner Act (1935) guaranteed workers the right to organize and bargain collectively and established the National Labor Relations Board. The Taft-Hartley Law (1947) sought to limit unfair labor practices by unions, provided for a presidential 80-day "cooling-off" injunction, and permitted states to pass "right-to-work" laws. The Landrum-Griffin Act (1959) required unions to report their financial activities and attempted to guarantee union members' rights.

Collective bargaining refers to negotiations between labor and management for the purpose of signing a labor contract. The bargaining process may include mediation or arbitration, both of which involve the assistance of neutral third parties.

The shop agreement defines the degree of union recognition by management. Four major types of shop agreements are the closed shop, the union shop, the agency shop, and the open shop.

Both unions and management attempt to exert pressure during labor conflicts. Unions may call a strike, picket, and use boycotts. Employers may lock out workers or seek a court injunction against the union. In the past some firms have used blacklisting and the yellow-dog contract to oppose union organizing efforts.

SELF-EXAMINATION QUESTIONS

The following questions are based on the Chapter Objectives listed at the beginning of the chapter. Test yourself by circling the letter preceding the answer that *best* completes the statement or answers the question. The answers to the Self-Examination Questions are in the appendix at the end of the textbook.

1. Which of the following is usually *not* part of the hiring process? (A) orientation; (B) developing job specifications; (C) interviewing; (D) testing; (E) using application forms to screen applicants.

2. Responsibilities of the personnel department typically include: (A) administering health and safety programs; (B) developing procedures for rating employee performance; (C) wage and salary administration; (D) operating training programs; (E) all of these.

3.   A union consisting of skilled workers in a particular trade is a: (A) craft union; (B) industrial union; (C) professional association; (D) board of trade; (E) none of these.

4.   A compensation system where pay is based on employee's output is called: (A) straight salary; (B) time rate; (C) piece rate; (D) profit sharing; (E) none of these.

5.   A major cause of the slowdown in union growth is: (A) the failure to organize blue-collar workers; (B) a decrease in the number of white-collar workers; (C) antiunion activities by the federal government; (D) the relative decline of the blue-collar work force as service and office jobs have expanded; (E) all of these.

6.   A labor law that provides for an 80-day "cooling-off" injunction for certain strikes and permits states to pass "right-to-work" laws is the: (A) Wagner Act; (B) Taft-Hartley Act; (C) Landrum-Griffin Act; (D) Civil Rights Act; (E) none of these.

7.   A technique for settling labor-management disputes where a neutral third party listens to both sides and suggests solutions is called: (A) collective bargaining; (B) mediation; (C) arbitration; (D) blacklisting; (E) none of these.

8.   Which of the following is a legal method of labor union pressure in a dispute? (A) primary boycott; (B) sitdown strike; (C) lockout; (D) secondary boycott; (E) all of these.

Student _____

BUILDING A BUSINESS VOCABULARY

Directions: Match the terms with their definitions by writing the letter in the appropriate blank.

a. Orientation
b. Arbitration
c. Right-to-Work Laws
d. Samuel Gompers
e. Recruiting
f. Agency Shop
g. Injunction
h. Business Unionism
i. Piece Rate System

j. Closed Shop
k. Mediation
l. Personnel Manager
m. Blacklist
n. Union Shop
o. Fringe Benefits
p. Yellow-Dog Contract
q. Secondary Boycott
r. Job Specifications

_____ 1. A staff position responsible for providing assistance in hiring, orientation, training, and compensating employees.

_____ 2. The founder of the American Federation of Labor.

_____ 3. A union activity that brings pressure on one firm by taking action against a second firm.

_____ 4. An agreement that requires all workers to join the union within a stated period of time after being hired.

_____ 5. Labor and management agree to be bound by the decision of a neutral third party.

_____ 6. A list of names used by employers to deny employment to union members and organizers.

_____ 7. An agreement whereby every worker employed by a company must first be a union member.

_____ 8. A court order prohibiting a group or individual from undertaking some activity.

_____ 9. A document signed by employees promising not to join a union.

_____ 10. A union philosophy calling for organization by crafts, concentration on economic issues, and political neutrality.

_____ 11. A list of qualifications required to perform a certain task.

_____ 12. Actively seeking out prospective employees.

_____ 13. An agreement that requires nonunion members to pay fees equal to union dues.

_____ 14. State legislation that outlaws the union shop.

_____ 15. A process intended to help a new employee adjust to the work environment.

_____ 16. A method of compensation based on production.

_____ 17. A method of settling labor disputes whereby a neutral party attempts to reconcile differences by suggesting solutions.

_____ 18. Noncash payments to workers in the form of insurance, holidays, pension plans, and so forth.

Student _____

REVIEWING MAJOR CONCEPTS

1. What major steps are involved in the hiring process? Which one do you consider the most valuable in selecting the best employees?

2. What are the criticisms of psychological testing for selection and evaluation? Have these criticisms reduced the use of such tests? Why or why not?

3. What is the purpose of orientation?

4. Would you prefer to be paid on a piece rate or on a time rate basis? Explain why.

5. Give three reasons why labor union growth has slowed in recent years.

6. Do you expect American unions to grow or decline in membership in the next 10 years? Why?

7. What is the difference between a craft union and an industrial union? Give an example of each.

8. What does the National Labor Relations Board do?

9. "Right-to-work" laws essentially outlaw the union shop. Would you vote for or against such a law for your state? Explain why.

Student _____

SOLVING PROBLEMS AND CASES

1. *Case:* Morton Muffler Company

   The Morton Muffler Company of Cleveland, Ohio, manufactures mufflers for trucks and automobiles. Although the company has expanded in recent years, its sales are closely tied to the ups and downs of the automobile industry.

   In 1977 the management of Morton Muffler adopted an affirmative action program setting targets for hiring and promoting minorities and women. In the past 10 years the proportion of minority employees has increased from 10 to 25 percent while women now make up nearly 30 percent of the firm's work force.

   When collective bargaining negotiations opened last week, the union representatives proposed a seniority clause, providing that the last employee hired shall be the first laid off. The union pointed out that most labor contracts contain such a provision. However, a number of minority and women employees have voiced opposition to the seniority clause.

   An assistant manager for industrial relations, you have been asked to write a brief report analyzing the advantages and disadvantages of the seniority clause and recommending what position the company should take on this issue.

2. *Case:* The Green Food Company

Ms. Hardy has just been promoted to plant manager of a food-processing factory owned by the Green Food Company. Reviewing the past performance of the plant, Ms. Hardy found that worker productivity has been low, and the plant has been struck by the union several times, despite the fact that wages and fringe benefits are generally higher than those paid by other companies in the area.

Mr. Massey, the former plant manager, maintains that the union leaders "are nothing but a bunch of troublemakers." He openly boasts that at the last contract negotiation he "tricked" the union representatives into taking less than the company was prepared to offer. Mr. Massey had also issued instructions to his supervisors to "ignore or take a hard stand on worker grievances to prevent the employees from becoming a bunch of chronic complainers."

The labor contract for the plant expires in 2 weeks. The union is already talking about another strike.

What action should Ms. Hardy take?

Student _____

3. Place a check (✓) in the appropriate column to indicate whether each of the following provisions is a part of the Wagner Act, Taft-Hartley Act, or Landrum-Griffin Act.

	Wagner	Taft-Hartley	Landrum-Griffin
1. Outlaws the closed shop.			
2. Guarantees workers the right to organize.			
3. Established the NLRB.			
4. Provides for an 80-day "cooling-off" injunction.			
5. Permits states to pass "right-to-work" laws.			
6. Aimed at curbing labor racketeering and union corruption.			
7. Prohibits secondary boycotts.			
8. Requires secret ballot election of union officials.			
9. Provides for detailed reporting on the handling of union funds.			
10. Requires that management bargain collectively with authorized union representatives.			

4. Interview a personnel manager and find out:

    a. What are his or her major responsibilities (job description)?

    b. What questions are most likely to be asked during a job interview?

    c. What are the most common reasons that job applicants are not hired?

    d. What tips can the personnel manager offer on applying and interviewing for a job?

THE
TOOLS OF
MANAGEMENT

CHAPTER	TITLE
7	Accounting and Budgeting
8	Statistics and Data Processing

The central theme of Part 3 is that management needs accurate and timely information to make good decisions. Chapter 7 presents the key elements of financial accounting that enables management to measure a firm's performance (profitability) and financial condition. This chapter also introduces the related topics of financial analysis (how to interpret accounting statements) and budgeting (financial forecasting and planning). The first section of Chapter 8 introduces some simple tools for gathering, analyzing, and interpreting statistical information. The major focus in this chapter, however, is on computers and how computers are used in business.

chapter 7

ACCOUNTING AND BUDGETING

On your next vacation you visit the faraway land of Zamm. You soon discover the people speak only Zammian, a language you do not understand. Your vacation is spoiled because you cannot talk with anyone.

Sad story? No sadder than the business manager who does not understand accounting—for accounting is the language of business.

This chapter is intended to introduce you to accounting and the related subjects of financial analysis, budgeting, and forecasting. It won't make you an instant accountant, but it can help you understand some important accounting tools.

CHAPTER OBJECTIVES

1. Name four groups that are interested in a firm's accounting reports.

2. Carefully describe the balance sheet and income statement and distinguish between the two.

3. Name three common ratios used in financial analysis and briefly describe what each measures.

4. Contrast and compare the three major techniques for business forecasting.

5. Explain the structure and purpose of a cash budget.

6. Given information on a firm's sales, fixed costs, and variable costs, calculate the break-even point.

ACCOUNTING: WHO NEEDS IT?

You can't tell whether you have won or lost the game unless you know the score. In business, the scoring system is called *accounting*. It involves recording, classifying, and summarizing business transactions and interpreting their impact on the firm. These transactions are expressed in dollars and cents.

Management needs information to make decisions, and the most important source of information is accounting reports. Accounting reports show where a firm has been, where it is now, and where it may be going in the future. These reports reveal how a firm stands financially. They show what a firm owns and what it owes as well as its sales, expenses, profits, or losses.

Management is not the only group interested in a firm's accounting reports. Government requires accounting data on profits, expenses, and property for tax purposes. Commercial banks will rarely make a business loan without first analyzing a firm's financial reports. Suppliers must estimate the financial strength of a business before extending credit. Owners and potential investors study accounting information to evaluate a firm's future prospects. There is no escape: A successful business requires accurate and up-to-date accounting records.

ACCOUNTING STATEMENTS

The two main financial reports are the balance sheet and the income statement. Together they form a picture of a firm's operations and financial condition.

The Balance Sheet

This statement shows the financial condition of a business firm as of a certain date. It is based on the *accounting equation:*

Assets = Liabilities + Owners' Equity

Assets are anything of value *owned* by a firm such as buildings, equipment, supplies, and merchandise. *Liabilities* are debts—what is *owed* by the firm. In other words, liabilities are the creditors' claims on the assets of the business. *Owners' equity,* sometimes called net worth or capital, reflects the owner's share of the business.

Liabilities appear ahead of owners' equity in the accounting equation and on the balance sheet. This is because liabilities are a preferential right (creditors have first claim on the assets), whereas owners' equity is a residual right (owners get whatever is left). If a firm goes out of business and has to sell its assets, the owner(s) can get only what is left after all the debts are paid. The residual nature of owners' equity is emphasized when liabilities are transferred to the other side of the equation:

Assets − Liabilities = Owners' Equity

TABLE 7.1   Balance Sheet for Hailwood Department Store

Hailwood Department Store Balance Sheet December 31, 1987			
Assets			
Current Assets			
Cash		$ 2,800,000	
Accounts Receivable		10,000,000	
Inventory		43,200,000	
Total Current Assets			$ 56,000,000
Fixed Assets			
Land		26,000,000	
Building	$ 90,000,000		
Less Accumulated Depreciation	36,000,000	54,000,000	
Equipment	20,000,000		
Less Accumulated Depreciation	12,000,000	8,000,000	
Total Fixed Assets			88,000,000
Total Assets			$ 144,000,000
Liabilities and Owners' Equity			
Current Liabilities			
Accounts Payable	$ 17,600,000		
Wages Payable	680,000		
Taxes Payable	520,000		
Total Current Liabilities		$ 18,800,000	
Long-term Liabilities			
Bank Loan (due 1993)	24,000,000		
Mortgage on Building	28,000,000		
Total Long-term Liabilities		52,000,000	
Total Liabilities			$ 70,800,000
Owners' Equity			
Common Stock (1,000,000 shares)	40,000,000		
Retained Earnings	33,200,000		
Total Owners' Equity			73,200,000
Total Liabilities and Owners' Equity			$ 144,000,000

Table 7.1 shows the balance sheet for the Hailwood Department Store on December 31, 1987. Two questions: (1) Can you find the accounting equation in the balance sheet? (2) How did the balance sheet get its name?

Notice the balance sheet is divided into five major sections:

Current Assets   Current assets are cash and other assets that will be converted into cash within 1 year. Cash reflects the total of deposits in the bank plus currency on hand. Accounts receivable are debts owed to the store by its customers—in Hailwood's case, mostly customer charge account purchases. Inventory is the amount of unsold merchandise on hand.

Fixed Assets   Fixed assets are the permanent or long-term assets of the firm that are not directly converted into cash. Notice in Table 7.1 that both buildings and equipment are carried at their original cost less accumulated depreciation. *Depreciation* is the reduction in value of a fixed asset because of wear and tear and obsolescence. Since a fixed asset such as a building has a useful life of several years, the accountant must "write off" or depreciate a portion of its value each year. The $36 million accumulated depreciation shown under the building represents the portion of the $90 million cost that has been written off. The $54 million difference is called the *book value* of the asset. A word of caution: Book value has little relationship to actual market value.

The simplest way of depreciating the value of a fixed asset is called the *straight-line method.* To illustrate, suppose the building that houses the Hailwood Department Store cost $90 million when new and had an estimated life of 15 years. The annual depreciation can be found by dividing the cost of the asset by its estimated life:

Cost   ÷ Estimated Life = Annual Depreciation

$90,000,000 ÷   15 years   = $6,000,000

How old is the Hailwood building as of December 31, 1987?

Current Liabilities   Current liabilities are short-term debts that must be paid within a year or less. Accounts payable consist of debts owed to trade creditors by the firm for the purchase of merchandise, supplies, or other assets on account. Wages payable reflect money owed to employees, while taxes payable are liabilities to federal, state, and local governments.

Long-term Liabilities   Long-term liabilities are long-term debts that are not due within a year. Hailwood has borrowed $24 million from a bank, and it owes another $28 million debt secured by a mortgage on the store.

Owners' Equity   Owners' equity, the owners' share of the corporation, consists of the proceeds from the sale of stock plus profits reinvested in the firm. *Common stock* represents the investment made by the stockholder. *Retained earnings* reflect that portion of profits over the years that has been plowed back into the company.

The balance sheet provides a useful picture of the financial strength of a business firm on a specific date. It presents two views of property (or assets). At the top, property owned by the firm is listed. On the lower half are the liabilities and owners' equity, which comprise the claims on the property. In accounting, when both parts of a statement are equal, it is said to be "in balance," which explains how the balance sheet got its name. The balance sheet for the Hailwood Department Store may be summarized using the accounting equation:

Assets $\quad=\quad$ Liabilities $+$ Owners' Equity

$144,000,000 = $70,800,000 + \quad $73,200,000

The Income Statement

The second major financial report is the income statement, sometimes called the operating statement or profit-and-loss statement. It summarizes a firm's operations over a period of time. The income statement lists income and expenses for a particular period, often a year. Table 7.2 represents a simplified income statement for the Hailwood Department Store covering a period of 12 months.

The single source of revenue for the Hailwood Department Store is the sale of merchandise to customers. The cost of goods sold represents what the store paid for the merchandise sold during the year. The difference between sales and cost of goods sold is called *gross profit.* Operating expenses are listed in some detail so that management can keep track of individual items. Note the depreciation expense, which represents the write-off of the building and equipment for the year 1987. Subtracting total operating expenses from gross profit produces net profit before income taxes.

TABLE 7.2   Income Statement for Hailwood Department Store

Hailwood Department Store Income Statement For the Year Ended December 31, 1987		
Sales		$ 332,000,000
Cost of Goods Sold		246,000,000
Gross Profit		86,000,000
Operating Expenses		
Wage and Salary Expense	$ 41,560,000	
Selling Expenses	7,800,000	
Depreciation Expense—Building	6,000,000	
Depreciation Expense—Equip.	4,000,000	
Administrative Expenses	4,000,000	
Interest Expense	3,900,000	
Property Tax Expense	3,700,000	
Miscellaneous Expense	5,400,000	
Total Operating Expenses		76,360,000
Net Profit Before Taxes		9,640,000
Federal Income Taxes		3,000,000
Net Profit		$ 6,640,000

After deducting federal income taxes, the firm earned a net profit of $6.64 million for the year 1987.

Net profit (sometimes called net income or net earnings) may be distributed to the owners (common stockholders) in dividends, reinvested in the business, or both. If the Hailwood Department Store paid dividends of $2 million, this would leave $4.64 million in retained earnings for reinvestment.

The income statement reveals the amount of sales income, the expenses incurred to generate the sales, and the resulting profit or loss for the period. The main components can be summarized as follows:

> Sales
> — Cost of Goods Sold
> Gross Profit
> — Operating Expenses
> Net Profit (or Net Loss)

FINANCIAL ANALYSIS

Accounting statements provide valuable information on a firm's profitability and financial strength. However, this information must be analyzed and interpreted before it can serve as the basis for management decisions. There are many analytical tools used to explore and interpret accounting statements. Two common techniques are ratio analysis and comparative analysis of income statements. The ratios described below use the data from the financial statements for the Hailwood Department Store (Tables 7.1 and 7.2).

Ratio Analysis

A ratio is a convenient means of comparing two quantities. Ratios are used to explore the relationship between various items appearing on the accounting statements. These ratios can be compared to established standards to discover possible weaknesses or potential problems. Among the most commonly used ratios are: (1) the current ratio; (2) equity-to-debt ratio; (3) net profit as a percent of sales; (4) inventory turnover; (5) rate of return on investment; and (6) profit per share.

Current Ratio   The current ratio measures the ability of a firm to pay its short-term debts.

$$\text{Current Ratio} = \frac{\text{Current Assets}}{\text{Current Liabilities}} = \frac{\$56,000.00}{\$18,800,000} = 2.98 \text{ to } 1$$

For every dollar of current liabilities, the Hailwood Department Store has approximately $3 in current assets. A safe ratio is generally considered to be 2 to 1; a ratio below 1 to 1 is a signal that the firm may experience difficulties paying its short-term debts.

Equity-to-Debt Ratio   The equity-to-debt ratio illustrates the relationship between funds from creditors and owner(s).

$$\text{Equity-to-Debt Ratio} = \frac{\text{Owners' Equity}}{\text{Total Liabilities}} = \frac{\$73,200,000}{\$70,800,000} = 1.03 \text{ to } 1$$

A more conservative ratio would be 2 to 1, and some firms feel it is poor practice to permit the ratio to fall below 1 to 1, where the amount of money invested in the business by the owner(s) is equal to the amount contributed by creditors.

Net Profit as a Percent of Sales   Net profit as a percent of sales shows what percent of sales revenue is converted into profit.

$$\text{Profit as a Percent of Sales} = \frac{\text{Net Profit}}{\text{Sales}} = \frac{\$6,640,000}{\$332,000,000} = 0.02 \text{ or } 2\%$$

Out of each dollar of sales, only 2 cents is profit; the remaining 98 cents is used to pay for the cost of goods sold, operating expenses, and income taxes.

Inventory Turnover   Inventory turnover measures how many times a year the average inventory is "turned over" or sold.

$$\text{Inventory Turnover} = \frac{\text{Cost of Goods Sold}}{\text{Inventory}} = \frac{\$246,000,000}{\$43,200,000} = 5.7$$

This formula shows that Hailwood turns its inventory almost once every 2 months. This turnover would be considered above average performance for a department store. Normally the higher the inventory turnover, the greater the net profit.

Rate of Return on Investment   Rate of return on investment is the key measure of the efficiency of a business firm. This ratio compares net profit to the stockholders' investment.

$$\text{Rate of Return on Investment} = \frac{\text{Net Profit}}{\text{Owners' Equity}} = \frac{\$6,640,000}{\$73,200,000} = 0.0907$$
$$\text{or } 9.1\%$$

The owners of the Hailwood Department Store earned a 9.1 percent return on their investment in 1987. Is this return low in view of the risks of business ownership and when compared to alternative investments?

TABLE 7.3   Selected Business Ratios and Percentages

Line of Business	Current Ratio	Equity to Debt	Net Profit as a Percent of Sales	Inventory Turnover	Rate of Return
Department Stores	3.3	1.8	2.3%	4.7	8.8%
Variety Stores	3.6	2.3	4.5	3.5	15.9
Grocery Stores	2.2	1.4	1.7	17.2	15.2
Auto Equipment	2.5	1.4	3.1	5.1	11.5

Source: Dun & Bradstreet, Inc., 1984.

Profit per Share   Profit or earnings per share is computed by dividing the number of shares of common stock outstanding into net profit:

$$\text{Profit per Share} = \frac{\text{Net Profit}}{\text{Shares of Common Stock}} = \frac{\$6,640,000}{1,000,000} = \$6.64$$

Profit per share is a major determinant of a stock's market price.

Table 7.3 shows the average (median) ratios for several types of business firms. Can you explain why the ratios vary so widely for firms in different lines of business?

Comparative Analysis of the Income Statement

It is often informative to compare the results of operations over a period of years. Such comparisons may reveal trends that would not be apparent from 1 year's results. This type of analysis is more meaningful if accompanied by a percentage breakdown of the income statement. Sales are designated as 100 percent, and all other items are shown as a percent of sales. Table 7.4 shows abbreviated income statements for Zoe's Candy Company covering a period of 3 years.

A glance at the income statements suggests that the firm is doing very well; both sales and profits have risen over the 3-year period. However, closer examination indicates some reasons for concern. Notice that costs of goods sold as a percent of sales has declined each year, leading to a larger gross profit margin. This

TABLE 7.4   Income Statements for Zoe's Candy Company, for the Years 1986–1988

	1986	%	1987	%	1988	%
Sales	$ 200,000	100	$ 250,000	100	$ 320,000	100
Cost of Goods Sold	140,000	70	170,000	68	210,000	66
Gross Profit	60,000	30	80,000	32	110,000	34
Operating Expenses	40,000	20	57,500	23	84,400	26
Net Profit	$ 20,000	10	$ 22,500	9	$ 25,600	8

decline could suggest efficient purchasing. On the other hand, operating expenses have been increasing at an alarming rate, more than offsetting the rise in gross profit. As a result, net profit as a percent of sales has been declining. These trends should alert management to examine operating expenses to determine the causes for the rapid increase and to seek ways to control these costs.

BUSINESS FORECASTING

There is a tide in the affairs of men,
Which, taken at the flood, leads on to fortune.

William Shakespeare

Shakespeare, as usual, was right. If you can accurately predict the future, your fortune is made. Of course, no one has a magic crystal ball, but the successful business manager is vitally concerned with what will happen tomorrow, next month, and 5 years from now. Therefore, managers must attempt to predict the future through business forecasting. Forecasts play a key role in developing sales projections, budgeting, inventory control, and marketing strategy.

Business forecasting techniques fall into three broad categories: subjective forecasting, simple projections, and causal models.

Subjective Forecasting depends heavily on intuition and experience. Since managers must make forecasts nearly every day, they often rely on educated guesswork that combines a knowledge of important facts plus personal judgment. Subjective methods are quick and inexpensive, and they can be surprisingly accurate for near-term forecasts.

Simple Projections are essentially extensions of past and current trends. For example, a sales manager may analyze the sales of a product over the last 4 or 5 years and use this data to project future sales. This method assumes that conditions will not change much in the future and that past performance is a good indicator of what will occur in coming months or years.

Causal Models employ sophisticated mathematical techniques, such as regression analysis, that measure the relationship between variables over time. This sounds complicated, but the basic idea is simple. For example, a liquor store owner orders extra beer when a heat wave is forecast because past experience has shown that beer sales increase when the temperature rises. In the same way, a lumber company might develop a model for forecasting the demand for lumber products by correlating sales to consumer incomes, housing starts, and interest rates.

Regardless of the method used, it is easier to predict the immediate future than it is to make accurate long-term projections. Forecasts, no matter how scientific, cannot eliminate uncertainty; but effective forecasting can reduce the range of uncertainty, thereby minimizing the chance of making major mistakes.

The difficulty of accurate forecasting is underlined by three

---

ISSUE WHAT IS AN ANNUAL REPORT?

Suppose you have a job interview with Universal Widgets, Inc. Where can you find information on what the company does and its future prospects?

Or suppose you have a "hot tip" to buy Universal Widgets stock. How can you check up on the company's profits and sales performance?

Or suppose you are a supplier of widget material who just received your first order from Universal Widgets, known as UW. Should you grant UW credit or insist on cash up front?

The answer to these questions can be found in UW's annual report.

The Securities and Exchange Commission requires all corporations whose stock is publicly owned and traded to publish annual reports and distribute them to stockholders. You can get a copy by writing to the firm's corporate headquarters. Most companies consider their annual report an effective public relations tool.

What will you find in the annual report? Most begin with a letter from the chief executive officer reviewing the past year and describing the company's prospects, usually in glowing terms. Next there is a description of the firm's products and operating divisions complete with color photographs.

Then you come to the "hard data" section of the report,

---

tongue-in-cheek "principles of forecasting" developed by Edgar Fiedler, vice-president of the Conference Board:[1]

- Forecasting is very difficult—especially if it is about the future.

- Those who live by the crystal ball soon learn to eat ground glass.

- Give them a number or give them a date, but never both.

BUDGETING

Why Budget?

A budget is a financial tool for planning future operations. Indeed, the very process of creating a budget forces management to make detailed projections about the future. The budget is also a device for management control. It is used to compare actual performance against budgeted standards. This device enables management to

---

[1]The Conference Board is a private, nonprofit organization that gathers and analyzes economic statistics and makes economic forecasts.

ISSUE WHAT IS AN ANNUAL REPORT? (Cont.)

---

which includes the balance sheet and income statement as well as other financial reports. Be sure to read the notes that accompany the reports. They often contain important information that will help you interpret the numbers in the statements.

Next you will find a 5- or 10-year statistical summary of accounting information. This section is particularly helpful in spotting trends in sales, profits, dividends, and so forth.

Near the back of the annual report there will be an auditor's statement, which tells you if the accounting statements conform to "generally accepted accounting principles." Note that the auditor is an independent accounting firm that reviews the financial reports to ensure they are based on accepted accounting guidelines. Watch out for the term "subject to." This means that the auditor has some doubts about the accounting information presented in the report.

Finally, at the back of the report you will find a list of top management and directors.

Keep in mind that the annual report is written by corporate management. Therefore, it may present a less than candid picture of the company. If you want to know all you can about the firm, you will have to review the business press and statistical services for articles and reports on the corporation. Any good librarian can help you find this information.

---

identify problem areas and take remedial action. For example, if selling expenses are exceeding budgeted estimates, management can investigate the causes and attempt to correct the situation. To sum up, the *budget* is both a means of planning for the future and a control device to ensure conformity to plans.

The budgeting process usually begins with a sales forecast. In large corporations each department develops a budget, which is reviewed, revised, and finally approved by top management. Then a master budget, based on the combined departmental budgets, is developed for the firm as a whole. Frequently, a budget committee reviews all estimates and approves the final projections.

One executive is normally assigned responsibility for administering the budget. This manager collects data on actual performance, compares performance to budgeted standards, and prepares periodic budget status reports.

Two common types of budgets are the cash budget and the projected income statement. In addition, break-even analysis is a valuable planning tool for budget development.

ISSUE RISK, INSURANCE, AND THE BUSINESS MANAGER*

Both individuals and business firms face risks arising from uncertainty about the future. *Risk* refers to the possibility of loss, injury, or damage resulting from unforeseen events. Some, but not all, risks may be reduced or transferred through insurance.

Business firms suffer losses from fire, theft, personal injury, and a variety of other events. Insurance companies sell policies to cover risks in return for an annual payment called a *premium*. The amount of the premium is based on statistical studies that determine the probability of an event occurring. The greater the chance of loss, the higher the premium.

In deciding whether or not to buy insurance, management must consider the financial loss to the business firm should an event occur. If the potential loss is severe, then insurance should be purchased to offset the loss. Some firms elect to reduce the amount of the premium by purchasing deductible insurance. For example, with a $10,000 deductible fire insurance policy, the firm must pay the first $10,000 of damage and the insurance company is liable for the remainder.

The increasingly important field of *risk management* attempts to reduce or transfer the chances of loss through alternatives to insurance. For example, a firm may decide to install a fire sprinkler system in its plant rather than purchase an insurance policy. Sometimes risks can be transferred

---

The Cash Budget

The cash budget reflects the flow of funds through a business firm over a period of time. It is a statement showing projected cash receipts and expenditures, usually for a week, month, or year. Table 7.5 presents a cash budget for the Rossi Wine Company. The first step is to enter the cash balance at the beginning of the year. Next, the expected cash receipts and payments are estimated for the next 12 months. To find the ending cash balances, the cash payments are subtracted from the sum of cash receipts and the beginning balance.

This budget can help control spending. In the case of the Rossi Wine Company, management knows that selling and administrative expenses should not exceed an average of $1,500 per month ($18,000 ÷ 12 months), while cash purchases should average only $7,000 per month ($84,000 ÷ 12 months).

The cash budget can also highlight the need for additional funds. Notice that the ending balance is only $4000, which may be considered too low to meet unexpected cash payments. Management

> **ISSUE**   RISK, INSURANCE, AND THE BUSINESS
> MANAGER (Cont.)
>
> through contractual agreements where, for example, another
> firm agrees to take over the responsibility for a particular job.
> In large firms whose facilities are geographically spread out,
> self-insurance can save the cost of insurance premiums. In this
> case, the firm sets up its own insurance reserve fund to pay for
> possible losses.
>
> In recent years, there has been a tremendous growth in
> "key person" life and disability insurance to protect the firm
> against the loss of key personnel. In addition, the increase in
> stockholders' lawsuits against inept managers and boards of
> directors has resulted in expanded liability insurance for
> officers and directors.
>
> Another major need for insurance arises from the fact that
> government requires it; for example, workmen's compensation
> must be carried unless a particular employer is large enough to
> qualify as a self-insurer. Social security is another type of
> compulsory national insurance. Interestingly enough, the cost
> of fringe benefit insurance (group life, health, and disability),
> corporate pension plans, social security insurance, and
> workmen's compensation greatly exceeds the cost for most
> companies of their entire fire and casualty insurance premiums.
>
> *Written by Alex Pappas, a partner in Argo Insurance, Walnut Creek,
> California. Used with permission.

may decide to build up this balance by negotiating a bank loan,
reducing dividends, or increasing cash sales.

TABLE 7.5   Cash Budget Rossi Wine Company Cash Budget
for the Year Ending December 31, 1989

Estimated Cash Receipts		Estimated Cash Payments	
Cash Balance, 1–1–89	$ 20,500	Cash Purchases	$ 84,000
Cash Sales	210,000	Wages	110,900
Collection of Accounts	30,500	Selling & Administration	18,000
Receivable		Expenses	
		Taxes	5,000
		Payment of Accounts Payable	15,100
		Dividends	9,000
		Repayment of Bank Loan	15,000
TOTAL	$ 261,000	TOTAL	$ 257,000
		Cash Balance, 12–31–89	4,000

TABLE 7.6   Projected Income Statement for Zoe's Candy Company, January–December, 1989

	1988 Results	1989 Projections	1989 Percent of Sales
Sales	$ 320,000	$ 400,000	100
Cost of Goods Sold	210,000	265,000	66
Gross Profit	$ 110,000	$ 135,000	34
Operating Expenses	84,400	100,000	25
Net Profit	$ 25,600	$ 35,000	9

Projected Income Statement

Another useful tool for budgetary planning is the projected (or *pro forma*) income statement. It shows estimated income and expenses over a specified period. Suppose the management of Zoe's Candy Company (see Table 7.4) wants to develop a projected income statement for 1989. Based on past performance and future projections, management forecasts a sales increase of 25 percent and estimates that cost of goods sold will remain at about 66 percent of sales. Operating expenses are expected to be 25 percent of sales. Table 7.6 shows a projected net profit of $35,000.

Break-Even Analysis

Business managers seek to earn profits and avoid losses. The relationships among sales, costs, and profits can be studied through the use of break-even analysis.

The first step is to divide costs into two categories: fixed costs and variable costs. *Fixed costs* (sometimes called *overhead*) are those costs that do *not* change as the level of production changes. Examples include rent, insurance, bond interest, management salaries, and so forth. *Variable costs* vary directly with the level of production. Typical examples of variable costs are total wages of factory workers, the cost of materials, and fuel.

Suppose the Carter Widget Company has fixed costs of $60,000 per week and variable costs of $3 per unit. Each unit is sold for $5. The question is: How many units must be produced and sold each week to cover total costs? In other words, how many units are required to break even? The *break-even point* may be computed using a simple formula:

$$\text{Break-Even Point in Units} = \frac{\text{Fixed Costs}}{\text{Selling Price per Unit} - \text{Variable Costs per Unit}}$$

$$= \frac{\$60,000}{\$5 - \$3} = \frac{\$60,000}{\$2} = 30,000 \text{ Units}$$

The break-even point is 30,000 units per week. If fewer than 30,000 units are produced, the firm will lose money; it will not cover its

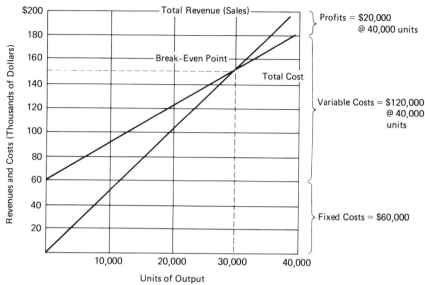

FIGURE 7.1   Break-Even Chart for the Carter Widget Company

fixed costs. At any output over 30,000 units per week, the Carter Widget Company will earn a profit. For example, if 40,000 units are produced, the profit will be $20,000 ($5 — $3 = $2 per unit; 10,000 units × $2 = $20,000).

This analysis can be shown graphically in the form of a break-even chart. The vertical axis in Figure 7.1 shows sales revenues and costs in thousands of dollars. The horizontal axis shows units of output. Fixed costs are illustrated by the horizontal line at $60,000, while variable costs are plotted on top of fixed costs at the rate of $3 per unit of output. Total cost is the sum of fixed costs and variable costs. Therefore, at an output of 20,000 units, total cost would be plotted by adding fixed costs to variable costs.

Fixed Costs   +   Variable Costs   = Total Cost
  $60,000   + (20,000 units × $3) = Total Cost
  $60,000   + $60,000   = $120,000

The total revenue line is plotted by multiplying the price per unit ($5) by the output. Therefore, when output is 20,000 units, total revenue is $100,000 ($5 × 20,000 units). The break-even point occurs when the total revenue and total cost lines intersect. In Figure 7.1 the break-even point is 30,000 units and $150,000 (note total revenue equals total cost).

SUMMARY

Accounting is the process of recording, classifying, summarizing, and interpreting business transactions. Accounting reports are used by management, creditors, investors, and various government agencies.

ISSUE THE BILLION DOLLAR RIP-OFF: EMPLOYEE THEFT

Each year employees steal between $50 and $100 billion from business firms. The major types of white-collar crime include the theft of cash and merchandise, kickbacks in the form of under-the-table "gifts" from suppliers to purchasing agents, embezzlement, and the theft of industrial secrets. Estimates range from 2.5 to 10 percent of the price paid for goods and services goes to cover the cost of dishonesty. Other startling facts:

- According to the Justice Department, 10 to 30 percent of employees steal from their employers. However, another major study revealed that half of the workers surveyed admitted to stealing.

- Employees steal two to four times as much as shoplifters.

- The greatest amount of theft is by supervisors and managers because they have more opportunities for dishonesty.

- Employee crime has more than doubled in the last decade.

- Computer crime is on the rise with employees and outsiders alike using sophisticated techniques to illegally transfer funds and access data.

The reasons employees steal are difficult to pinpoint. Some are pressured by unexpected expenses; others feel they are making up for low pay; still others have deep psychological motives. In

The two major accounting statements are the balance sheet and the income statement. The balance sheet reveals the financial condition of the business firm on a certain date. It is organized according to the accounting equation:

Assets = Liabilities + Owners' Equity

The income statement summarizes the results of operations over a period of time. It shows the firm's income and expenses and the difference between these two, which is profit or loss.

Financial analysis provides information for management decision making. Ratio analysis is a convenient method of comparing

---

ISSUE THE BILLION DOLLAR RIP-OFF: EMPLOYEE
THEFT (Cont.)

---

every case, however, widespread employee crime is a
reflection of poor management. The failure to establish
effective controls creates opportunities for dishonesty at every
level in a company.

Experts who specialize in preventing employee theft offer
several suggestions for business firms:

- Insure that honesty begins at the top. Management
must set an example and create an atmosphere that
encourages honesty.

- Ban all gift giving and receiving.

- Establish controls and procedures that remove
temptation.

- Set realistic performance standards so that workers
won't be tempted to cheat.

- Treat employees fairly by rewarding outstanding
performance.

Perhaps the most costly and controversial employee "crime" is
called "time theft." According to a recent survey conducted by
Robert Half International, a large employment recruiter, the
average employee "steals" over four hours a week by goofing
off and taking care of personal business at work. Other
"counterproductive behavior" includes getting to work late and
leaving early, lengthy coffee breaks, phony illnesses, and
excessive personal telephone calls. The survey concludes that
time theft costs American business over $150 billion a year.

---

items from the balance sheet and income statement. In addition,
income statements for several years may be compared to identify
significant trends.

Business forecasting is essential to effective planning. Three
major forecasting techniques are subjective forecasting, based on
educated judgments; simple projections, which are extensions of
current trends; and causal models, which use the relationship among
different variables to make predictions about the future.

Budgets are used to plan future operations and as control
devices that enable management to compare actual performance to
budgeted estimates. A cash budget lists estimated cash receipts and
expenditures over a period of months or years. It can serve to

highlight the potential need for additional funds. The projected income statement shows estimated income and expenses for a future period.

Break-even analysis is a useful planning tool that illustrates the relationships among sales, costs, and profits. The break-even point, where total revenue just equals total costs, may be found by using the following formula:

$$\text{Break-Even Point in Units} = \frac{\text{Fixed Costs}}{\text{Selling Price per Unit} - \text{Variable Costs per Unit}}$$

SELF-EXAMINATION QUESTIONS

The following questions are based on the Chapter Objectives listed at the beginning of the chapter. Test yourself by circling the letter preceding the answer that *best* completes the statement or answers the question. The answers to the Self-Examination Questions are in the appendix at the end of the textbook.

1. Which of the following groups would be interested in a firm's accounting reports? (A) management; (B) creditors; (C) owners; (D) government agencies; (E) all of these.

2. The accounting statement that shows the assets, liabilities, and owners' equity of a firm on a certain date is the: (A) cash budget; (B) balance sheet; (C) break-even chart; (D) income statement; (E) all of these.

3. A ratio that measures the ability of a firm to pay its short-term debts is the: (A) current ratio; (B) inventory turnover; (C) equity-to-debt ratio; (D) rate of return on investment; (E) none of these.

4. A method for business forecasting that depends on mathematical techniques to calculate the relationships among variables over time is called: (A) subjective forecasting; (B) causal models; (C) simple projections; (D) all of these; (E) none of these.

5. Cash budgets: (A) show income and expenses over a period of time; (B) provide a record of last year's cash payments and cash income that can be checked against bank statements; (C) are used to forecast a firm's flow of funds in the form of cash receipts and expenditures; (D) are the same as projected income statements; (E) none of these.

6. If a company has overhead of $10,000 a month and variable costs of $100 per unit, what is the break-even point if the product sells for $140 each? (A) 250; (B) 40; (C) 100; (D) 71.4; (E) none of these.

Student _____

BUILDING A BUSINESS VOCABULARY

Directions: Match the terms with their definitions by writing the letter in the appropriate blank.

a. Income Statement
b. Assets
c. Current Ratio
d. Balance Sheet
e. Cash Budget
f. Retained Earnings
g. Subjective Forecasting
h. Assets = Liabilities
   + Owners' Equity
i. Gross Profit
j. Owners' Equity
k. Current Assets

l. Break-Even Point
m. Fixed Assets
n. Simple Projections
o. Inventory Turnover
p. Accounting
q. Projected Income
   Statement
r. Long-term Liabilities
s. Current Liabilities
t. Depreciation
u. Causal Models

 1. A report that shows the financial condition of a business firm on a certain date.

 2. Recording, classifying, summarizing, and interpreting business transactions.

 3. The accounting equation.

 4. Anything of value owned by a business firm.

 5. The difference between sales and cost of goods sold.

 6. A financial report that summarizes a firm's operations; it shows income and expenses over a period of time.

 7. Cash and other assets that will be converted into cash in the ordinary course of business.

 8. The long-term debts of a company.

 9. Current assets divided by current liabilities; it shows how many dollars of current assets are available to pay each dollar of short-term debt.

_____ 10. The owners' share of a business found by subtracting liabilities from assets.

_I_ 11. The reduction in value of a fixed asset due to wear and tear and obsolescence.

_M_ 12. Permanent property of a business firm that is not normally converted into cash.

_F_ 13. Profits reinvested in the business.

_O_ 14. The number of times a year the average inventory is sold.

_U_ 15. A technique of forecasting that tries to develop predictive models based on cause-and-effect relationships.

_q_ 16. A statement showing projected cash receipts and expenditures.

_S_ 17. Debts that must be paid within a year.

_g_ 18. Educated judgments about the future.

_L_ 19. The output at which total revenue is equal to total costs.

_____ 20. A type of budget that shows forecasted income and expenses.

_N_ 21. Business forecasts based on extensions of past and current trends.

Student _____

REVIEWING MAJOR CONCEPTS

1. Briefly explain the difference between the income statement and the balance sheet.

   The balance sheet sumarizes the condition of a firm at a specific date, while the Income statement assesses the operations of a firm over a period of time, a year.

2. Name four groups that use business accounting statements.

   1. government agencies (IRs)
   2. Management
   3. CReditors (Bankers)
   4. investers stock holders
   5. auditors

3. Of what value are budgets to management?

   Bugets are very important not only do they allow Management to project the future, but budgets also act as a controling mechanism to make sure sales expenditures are not exceding the constraints.

4. Briefly explain the accounting equation.

assets = Liabilities + owners equity

assets are anything owned by the company
liabilities are what are owed by the company and owners equity or
net worth is the owners share of the business. the equation is in order
by who recieves Funds First if the business fails.

5. If a firm has assets of $250,000 and liabilities of $100,000, what is owners' equity?

150,000

6. A firm has owners' equity of $110 million and liabilities of $50 million. What is the amount of its assets?

160 million

7. A manufacturer purchases a new machine tool for $25,000 that has an expected life of 10 years. Using the straight-line method, how much will the machine tool depreciate each year?

$$\frac{25,000}{10} = 2,500 \text{ depreciates per year}$$

Student _____

SOLVING PROBLEMS AND CASES

1. The following information was taken from the accounting records of Overfield's Stationery Store on June 30, 1988. Prepare a balance sheet for the firm.

Accounts Payable	$ 6,000	Accounts Receivable	$ 5,000
Plant and Equip-ment	20,000	Common Stock (1,000 shares)	12,000
Inventory	12,000	Cash	4,000
Long-term Bank Loan	10,000	Accumulated Depreciation	4,000
Wages Payable	1,000	Retained Earnings	8,000

Current Assets			
Cash		4,000	
Accounts recievable		5,000	
Inventory		12,000	
total current assets			21,000
Fixed Assets			
Plant + equip	20,000		
Less depreciation	4,000	16,000	
total Fixed assets			16,000
Total assets			37,000
Liabilities and Owners equity			
Current liabilities			
Accounts payable	6,000		
Wages payable	1000		
Total Current liabilities		7,000	
Long term liabilities			
Long term bank loan	10,000		
Total Long term		10,000	
Total liabilities			17,000
Owner equity			
Common stock (1000)	12,000		
retained earnings	8,000		
total owners eq			20,000
Total liabilities + owners eq			37,000

2. From the following data covering the year ended June 30, 1988, prepare an income statement for Overfield's Stationery Store, Inc.

Operating Expenses	$ 40,000
Federal Income Taxes	1,000
Sales	120,000
Cost of Goods Sold	75,000

Sales	120,000	
Cost of goods sold	75,000	
Gross profit		45,000
operating expenses		40,000
Net profit		5,000
Federal income Taxes		1,000
Net profit after Taxes		4,000

Using the information in problems 1 and 2, compute the:

a. Current ratio.

b. Equity-to-debt ratio.

c. Inventory turnover.

d. Rate of return on investment.

e. Profit per share.

Student _____

3. Construct a cash budget for the Harper Toy Company for the month of September using the following estimates: Beginning Cash Balance, $17,000; Payment of Accounts Payable, $35,000; Repayment of Bank Loan, $50,000; Cash Sales, $120,000; Operating Expenses, $82,000; Collection of Accounts Receivable, $13,000.

Estimated Sources of Cash	Estimated Uses of Cash

Do you have any recommendations for the management?

4. The Stark Manufacturing Company has fixed costs of $160,000 per month and variable costs of $12 per unit.

a. What is the firm's break-even point if the selling price per unit is $16?

b. How much profit will the firm earn if it sells 55,000 units?

c. Draw a break-even chart for the Stark Manufacturing Company.

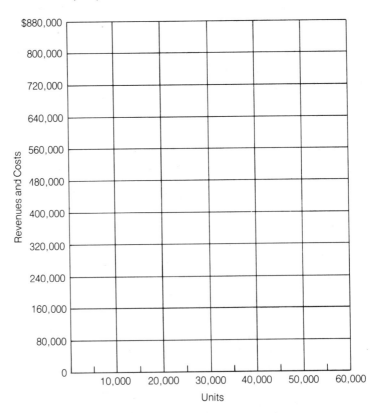

chapter 8

STATISTICS AND DATA PROCESSING

Human beings need timely information to make decisions. Since the dawn of history, people have gathered, organized, analyzed, and summarized information for decision making. Thousands of years ago, cave-dwellers used different colored stones to count and "store" information. Ancient Babylonian merchants developed the first accounting system to record sales, inventories, expenses, and other useful data. The abacus is a calculating device consisting of movable beads on a frame. This forerunner of the modern computer was developed centuries ago in Asia and is still widely used in China and Japan.

As the twentieth century draws to a close, the United States is being transformed into an information society. Nearly half the work force is employed in services related to collecting, transforming, and distributing information. The major tool of the information society is the electronic computer.

CHAPTER OBJECTIVES

1. Name and briefly describe three major sources of business statistics.

2. Identify three types of averages and demonstrate how each is calculated.

3. Explain what index numbers measure.

4. List four ways of presenting statistical data.

5. Name the major components of a computer's central processing unit.

6. Differentiate between computer hardware and software.

7. Identify three nonroutine computer applications in business.

Statistics are facts expressed as numbers. Sound management decisions are based on accurate and timely information, and much business information can be expressed in the form of quantitative data. One purpose of this chapter is to help you become familiar with some statistical concepts and tools used by business managers.

Data processing refers to any system for handling and organizing numerical data. Here we are concerned with the use of the electronic computer to process raw data into usable information. Clearly, there is a close relationship between the study of statistics and electronic data processing.

SOURCES OF STATISTICAL INFORMATION

Business statistics may be defined as collecting, analyzing, presenting, and interpreting quantitative data to assist in decision making. Statistical data may originate from sources both inside and outside the firm.

Internal Sources

Much statistical information is available from a firm's own records and reports. Accounting data, employee records in the personnel department, and production and sales reports are valuable sources of statistics. Suppose a manager is developing a new employee pension plan and needs to know the average age and length of service of employees. This information should be readily available from the firm's personnel files.

External Sources

Many management decisions require information that is not available from internal sources. For example, the manager of a machine-tool company may be faced with the question of whether or not to expand production facilities. The decision must be based in part on the forecasted level of economic activity.

The federal government produces a wealth of statistical information that is of value to business managers. The annual *Statistical Abstract of the United States* contains hundreds of pages of statistics. Up-to-date economic statistics are available from the monthly *Survey of Current Business* and *Federal Reserve Bulletin*. In addition, private firms produce thousands of publications containing valuable statistical information.

Surveys

If required information is unavailable from the firm's records or from published reports, it may be necessary to gather data directly either through observation or interviews. A relatively simple way to collect firsthand information is through direct observation of some activity. For example, a pedestrian traffic count may be helpful in selecting a location for a retail store. Another method is surveying, which normally involves the collection of data using a statistical technique known as sampling.

We use sampling every day as a handy way to gather data. Examples include squeezing fruit and vegetables at the market to test for ripeness, tasting a glass of wine before buying a case, and putting a toe in the bath to check the temperature. Statistical *sampling* is the process of selecting a small number of items from a large group in order to make generalizations about the group as a whole (called the population or universe). *Random sampling* involves ensuring that each item (or individual) in the universe has an equal chance of being selected.

Suppose the advertising manager for a newspaper wants to find out how many subscribers read the classified advertising section. Questioning every subscriber would be very expensive and time consuming. Instead, the manager can select a random sample of perhaps 100 subscribers from a total of 40,000. The next problem is how to contact the individuals in the sample. There are three major methods:

1   *Personal Interviews* are effective in getting the respondents (interviewees) to answer questions, but are time consuming and costly.
2   *Telephone Interviews* are fast and inexpensive, but are ineffective in reaching individuals without telephones.
3   *Mail Questionnaires* are the cheapest method of reaching respondents, but typically only 10 to 20 percent of the questionnaires are returned.

If the sample is truly random and care is exercised in interviewing, the responses from the sample subscribers should accurately reflect the reading habits of all subscribers.

STATISTICAL ANALYSIS

Raw data are little more than jumbles of numbers. To be of value, data must be processed, summarized, and measured. A widely used tool of statistical measurement is the average.

Averages

An average is a measure of central tendency. It is a summary number used to represent a group of figures. There are three major types of averages: the *mean,* the *median,* and the *mode.*

Suppose the supervisor of Department 10 wants to study the amount of overtime worked by employees last month. The first step is to collect the data from the payroll department and arrange it in an array—that is, in numerical order from the highest to the lowest —as shown in Table 8.1.

The supervisor next decides to compute the mean, which is found by totaling the values and dividing by their number. In this case, the supervisor adds the hours of overtime for the department and divides by the number of workers:

83 Total Hours ÷ 11 Workers = 7.55 Hours

The mean number of hours of overtime is 7.55 per worker.

TABLE 8.1   Hours of Overtime in Department 10 for May

Worker	Hours of Overtime
Johnson	15
Black	14
Chu	11
Harris	8
Cohen	8 ← Mean = 7.55
Gary	7 → Median = 7
Spinnato	6
Vatt	6 } Mode = 6
Allen	6
Poe	2
Smith	0
Total	83

The median is the middle value in a group of numbers arranged in numerical order. Since there are 11 workers, the sixth worker divides the group in half, and the median is 7 hours. If the number of values in an array is even, the median may be found by taking the mean of the *two* middle values.

The mode is simply the number that occurs most frequently. In our example, 6 hours occurs three times, and this is the mode.

Which average is best? The mean is the most commonly used average, but it is subject to distortion by extreme values. Suppose, for example, four students have the following annual incomes: $3,200, $3,600, $4,400, $4,800. Their mean income is $4,000 ($16,000 ÷ 4 = $4,000). Now a fifth student with an annual income of $34,000 joins the group. The mean income is now $10,000, a figure that is not representative of the first four students' incomes. In this case the median would be more representative. A good procedure is to compute all three averages for a group of figures.

Index Numbers

Index numbers measure the relative changes in numerical data. Suppose the marketing manager of Conn Paper Products wants to compare the performance of Sales District C to that of the firm as a whole. Table 8.2 shows the sales of District C and the firm.

TABLE 8.2   Sales in Dollars for District C and Conn Paper Products, 1984–1988

Year	District C Sales	Company Sales
1984	$210,000	$1,570,000
1985	340,000	1,850,000
1986	350,000	2,200,000
1987	410,000	2,640,000
1988	450,000	2,900,000

TABLE 8.3   Sales Indexes for District C and Conn Paper
Products, 1984–1988 (1984 = 100)

Year	District C	Company
1984	100	100
1985	162	118
1986	166	140
1987	195	168
1988	214	185

This type of data is difficult to evaluate. It is helpful to convert the dollar sales into index numbers. This conversion is accomplished by first selecting a *base year* (we will use 1984), dividing each year's sales by the base year's sales, and expressing the result as a percentage. The formula is:

$$\frac{\text{Given Year's Sales}}{\text{Base Year's Sales}} \times 100^{1}$$

The results are shown in Table 8.3.

The use of index numbers makes it clear that District C has outperformed the company as a whole over the 5-year period. Between 1984 and 1988, District C increased sales by 114 percent, while the firm as a whole managed only an 82 percent gain.

The federal government publishes many indexes that measure economic activity. The most widely known is the *Consumer Price Index* (CPI), which is published every month by the U.S. Bureau of Labor Statistics. The CPI measures the changes in retail prices of goods and services purchased by the typical city family. Another important gauge of economic activity is the *Index of Industrial Production,* which measures percentage changes in the physical output of factories and mines.

**PRESENTA-
TION OF
STATISTICAL
DATA**

Most business reports contain numerous statistics. These statistics may be presented in the body of the report, in tables, or in the form of charts. Tables 8.1 and 8.2 represent examples of statistical tables. There are three major types of charts: line charts, pie diagrams, and bar charts.

Line charts are widely used because they are simple to

[1]For District C Sales in 1984:

$$\frac{\$210,000}{\$210,000} = 1 \times 100 = 100\%; \text{ in 1985: } \frac{\$340,000}{\$210,000} = 1.62 \times 100 = 162\%; \text{ etc.}$$

For Company Sales in 1984:

$$\frac{\$1,570,000}{\$1,570,000} = 1 \times 100 = 100\%; \text{ in 1985: } \frac{\$1,850,000}{\$1,570,000} = 1.18 \times 100 = 118\%; \text{ etc.}$$

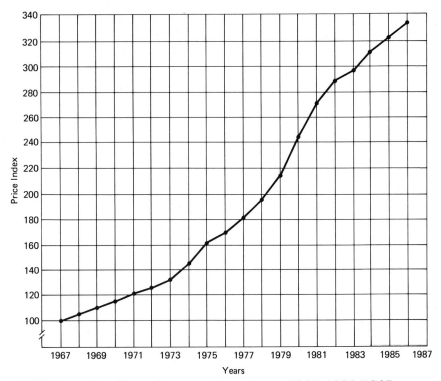

FIGURE 8.1   Line Chart: *Consumer Price Index, 1967–1986* (1967 =
100)
Source: Department of Labor, Bureau of Labor Statistics.

construct and easy to understand. Figure 8.1, which shows the
Consumer Price Index for the years 1967–1986, is a typical line chart.

Pie diagrams are often used to show different parts of a whole;
for example, how a firm's income is spent. Figure 8.2 shows a pie
diagram.

Bar charts are useful for comparing two or more sets of data.
Figure 8.3 shows the net profit for Data-Tron, Inc., for the years
1984–1987, and how the profit was distributed among federal income
taxes, retained profits, and dividends.

INTERPRETATION OF STATISTICS

Without accurate interpretation, all the statistics in the world won't
lead to good decisions. Needless to say, the interpretation of
statistical data is a highly useful management skill. The experienced
manager always approaches numerical data with caution, because
statistics can lie. They are subject to mathematical errors and
human bias. An advertising campaign may claim that three out of
four doctors recommend "Product X," but this is not a very
convincing statistic if only four doctors were asked for their
opinions.

FIGURE 8.2   Pie Diagram

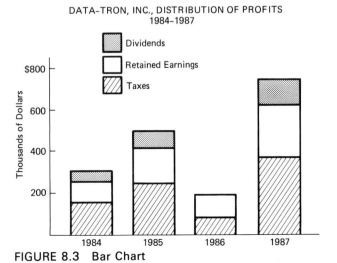

FIGURE 8.3   Bar Chart

ISSUE IS "BIG BROTHER" WATCHING YOU?

In his terrifying novel of the future entitled *1984*, George Orwell described a world without privacy where an all-pervasive government (called "Big Brother") spied continuously on every citizen. Today, a growing number of voices are warning that the computer threatens to deprive all of us of our freedom and privacy.

Everyone knows the computer is a potent tool for collecting, analyzing, and storing vast quantities of information. But is the computer more than a powerful labor-saving device for reducing tedious work and boosting productivity? Is the computer a monster that will rob Americans of their freedom, humanity, and privacy?

There is little doubt that the expanding use of computers has resulted in a growing volume of information being made available in centralized locations. Think for a moment how much information about you is stored in computer memory devices. Computers:

- Keep track of your birth and hospital records.
- Record your school and college grades.
- Compute your wages and process your paycheck.
- Calculate your taxes and bank balance.
- Compile your bills and record your credit rating.
- Maintain records of your traffic tickets as well as any criminal arrests and convictions.

What worries many people is that more information leads to more power, and this power may be used for evil purposes. Could not this growing pool of information be used to blackmail, coerce, and manipulate human beings? Does not the increasing volume of information impinge upon the individual's right to privacy?

These are difficult questions for which there are no easy answers. However, in the final analysis, it is not so much the computer itself that threatens the right to privacy as it is the morality of the people who control it. A computer—indeed, any machine—is neither good nor evil. It is only the people who control the computer who can direct its power toward moral or immoral ends. Thus, the problem is not a new one: We must be on our guard against evil people, not evil machines. In this less-than-perfect world, we must strive to maintain safeguards against infringement of individual rights.

COMPUTERS AND DATA PROCESSING

If every computer in the world were to suddenly go dead, planes would not fly, trains would not run, traffic lights would not change, banks would have to close, space projects would be aborted, and department stores and grocery stores would not be able to sell . . . If computers were suddenly silenced, the world would be thrown into instant chaos.

> David F. Webber and Noah Hutchings, *The Computers are Coming,* as quoted by Shelly and Cashman, *Introduction to Computers and Data Processing*

Data Processing refers to any system for collecting, processing, and reporting numerical data. The word *system* means an organized set of procedures. In this sense, data processing is thousands of years old. A simple pencil-and-paper bookkeeping system is a method of data processing. The term *electronic data processing* refers to the use of a computer to process numerical data.

A *computer* is a high-speed electronic machine that manipulates data mathematically according to programmed instructions in order to produce useful information. It is a mistake to view the computer as a mysterious and magical wizard superior to human beings. Rather, the computer is merely a tool that enables individuals to process data quickly and accurately.

Although the modern computer was developed little more than 40 years ago, it has gained widespread use in business and nonbusiness applications. As our society has become increasingly complex and interdependent, there is a growing demand for accurate and timely information. The computer can provide this information faster and often at a lower cost than alternative systems of data processing. Today, nearly all large corporations, and many smaller firms, use computers to perform a variety of jobs.

Computer Components: Hardware

How does a computer work? Perhaps the easiest way to answer this question is to divide the computer into its component parts. Figure 8.4 illustrates these components. The arrows show the flow of data and information through the computer.

Input Device   The computer must receive both instructions and raw data through some input device. Input may be recorded on magnetic or optical disks, punched cards, magnetic tape, or in magnetic ink on paper documents such as checks. The input unit may be a display terminal with typewriterlike keyboard, a disk reader, or an optical scanning device capable of reading printed or coded material and inputting the data into the computer. Some computers are capable of interpreting vocal input.

Memory   The memory, often called the computer's storage, may be viewed as an electronic filing cabinet. Here, instructions and data are stored until needed. There are several methods of storing

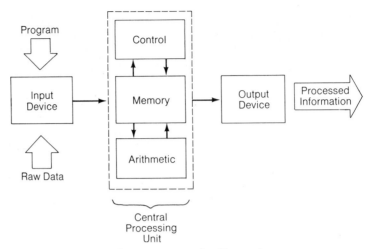

FIGURE 8.4   The Components of a Computer

external memory such as magnetic disks, magnetic tape, and optical disks. The computer's internal memory consists of tiny silicon chips etched with microscopic electronic circuits. The capacity of a computer is measured in terms of the size of its internal memory.

Arithmetic-Logic Unit (ALU)   The arithmetic component of the computer is an electronic calculator—it adds, subtracts, multiplies, and divides. In addition, it performs certain tasks of logic such as comparing quantities.

Control Unit   The control section directs and coordinates the operations of the computer. It may be viewed as an electronic traffic cop that directs the step-by-step processing of data by the computer according to the programmed instructions.

Output Unit   Output is data that has been processed by the computer. A *monitor* or *video display terminal,* which resembles a television screen, may be used to display processed information. Output may be recorded on magnetic disk and tape or on paper through the use of a printer.

The term *hardware* is used to refer to the five components of the computer. The control unit, memory, and arithmetic-logic unit together are called the *central processing unit* or CPU.

Programming: Software

The computer cannot think for itself. In order to do useful work, it requires a detailed set of instructions called a *program.* The individual responsible for writing computer instructions is called a *programmer.* Computer programs are often referred to as *software.*

ISSUE THE SUPERCOMPUTER

It vaguely resembles an old-fashioned juke box. The C-shaped cabinet is finished in red Naugahyde with black steel columns, and its transparent panels are filled with blue-tinted liquid coolant. It costs $17.6 million dollars and is the fastest computer in the world.

The Cray-2 also boasts the world's largest internal memory with 2 billion bytes. It can perform 1.2 billion arithmetic operations per second, which is 40,000 to 50,000 times faster than the typical microcomputer. As its first customer pointed out, "What took a year in 1952, we now do in a second."

Why the incredible speed? The demand for faster computers is coming from researchers in science and engineering. Supercomputers help design new products, forecast the weather, discover oil, and analyze data from spy satellites. The "Star Wars" defense system will be built around supercomputers.

The limiting factor in designing supercomputers is the time it takes electricity to travel from one part of the computer to another. Seymour Cray, the creator of the Cray-2, reduced this problem by packing 240,000 computer chips into a semicircular cabinet only 45 inches high and 53 inches in diameter. The heat generated by the flow of electrons would have melted the computer if Cray hadn't flooded the circuits with 200 gallons of liquid coolant.

The Cray-3, due out in 1988, will have four times the memory capacity of the Cray-2.

The job of programming a computer is complicated by two factors. First, since the computer cannot think like a human being, the instructions must be written in great detail and each step must be in logical sequence. Second, the program must be written in a language the computer can understand. The most widely used computer languages are FORTRAN, COBOL, and BASIC. FORTRAN (short for FORmula TRANslation) is primarily used in the area of science and mathematics. COBOL (COmmon Business Oriented Language) finds its greatest application in business data processing. BASIC (Beginner's All-purpose Symbolic Instruction Code) is a simpler language used by many microcomputers.

Software transforms the computer. By switching programs, a computer is changed from an inventory control machine to a payroll

SPEAKING THE LANGUAGE: A FEW COMPUTER TERMS

BITS, BYTES, and K   A bit is an electronic signal (current on or off) that represents a piece of data. A byte is a collection of eight bits and is used as a measure of the storage capacity of a computer. One byte is one character such as a letter or numeral. Therefore, 256K means the computer can store programs and data amounting to approximately 256,000 characters. Actually, K is the value of 2 to the tenth power or 1024 but is rounded off to 1000.

CPU   The central processing unit is the part of the computer that interprets programs and performs arithmetic and logic operations.

DATA BASE   Refers to a group of stored information needed by an individual or organization. For example, a list of a firm's customers is a data base.

DISKS   Revolving plates on which data and programs are stored. Major types include floppy disks (or diskettes), hard disks, and optical (or laser) disks.

HARDWARE   The computer and its related equipment.

MEMORY   The part of the computer that stores the program and data needed to solve a problem. There are two kinds of internal memory: (1) Read-Only Memory, or ROM, is stored permanently in the computer by the manufacturer. ROM is used to control the internal operation of the computer and cannot be changed. (2) Random-Access Memory, or RAM, is used to store programs and data for a particular task and is lost when the electricity is turned off. RAM measures the capacity of the computer. For example, 512 RAM means approximately 512,000 characters can be inputted and stored.

MICROPROCESSOR   A fingernail size silicon chip that holds up to millions of pieces of information.

MODEM   A device that connects the computer to a telephone line and allows the computer user to contact information services and other computer users.

MONITOR   A TV-like screen that displays data in the form of words, numbers, and graphics.

NETWORKING   Linking together computers so they can communicate with one another, thereby increasing the availability of information to employees.

SOFTWARE   Computer programs or machine-readable instructions that direct the computer.

DISPLAY TERMINAL   A device for inputting and outputting data often with a keyboard and monitor.

machine. Rapid developments in software have been as important as advances in hardware in making computers more useful in business.

Types of Computers

Computers are commonly divided into three classifications: (1) mainframe computers; (2) minicomputers; and (3) personal computers, also called microcomputers. The major differences among the three are speed, memory size, and cost.

Mainframe computers at one time were physically large, often filling an entire room. Today, mainframes are distinguished by their huge memory capacity, high speed, and price tags that often run to several million dollars. Typically, mainframe computers can handle complicated tasks and can accommodate several users at the same time.

Minicomputers are middle-size computers that cost up to $100,000 or more. While minicomputers are slower in operation and have smaller memories than mainframes, one CPU can handle several terminals.

Personal Computers (PCs), also known as microcomputers, are small enough to be portable and cost anywhere from a few hundred dollars to $30,000 and more. The personal computer was made possible by the development of the microprocessor, sometimes called "a computer on a chip." The microprocessor is a silicon wafer about one-fourth of an inch square containing a maze of electrical circuits. Figure 8.5 illustrates a personal computer and peripheral equipment.

The distinction among the three types of computers is becoming blurred due to rapid advances in technology. Each year, computers become more powerful, smaller in size, and less expensive.

The Personal Computer Revolution

The 1980s witnessed rapid growth in the popularity of personal computers as millions of machines were produced by such firms as Apple, Commodore, IBM, Texas Instruments, and Tandy Corporation's Radio Shack. These microcomputers were sold to two markets: households and business firms. Initially, most PCs were purchased by home users, the majority of whom were primarily interested in computer games. However, as the game craze diminished in the mid-1980s, sales to households declined. Personal computer manufacturers have increasingly focused on business users.

How do business firms use personal computers? Among the most popular applications are:

Electronic spreadsheets display data on a large grid consisting of columns and rows with totals and subtotals. When the value of a number in a grid location is changed, the program automatically changes all the numbers in related grids. Spreadsheets facilitate financial planning, forecasting, and preparation of accounting statements.

A Simple Microcomputer System

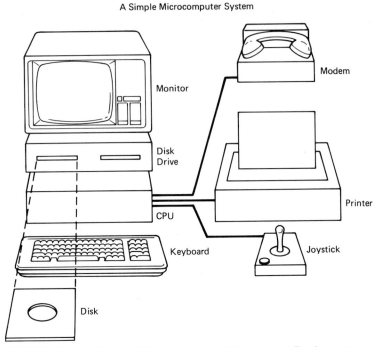

FIGURE 8.5 A Personal Computer and Peripheral Equipment

Word processing allows the user to electronically type, edit, change sentences, and reposition blocks of text. The word processor has become a valuable tool for facilitating business communications.

Data base management permits the user to sort, organize, retrieve, and summarize information. It has been likened to an electronic filing system. Major business applications include customer mailing lists, inventory control, and maintenance of accounts receivable and payable.

Graphics allow the user to display the relationship among numerical information in the form of bar charts, pie diagrams, and line charts.

Communications with other microcomputers, as well as with mainframe computers, is a major trend that will be discussed later in the chapter.

COMPUTERS IN BUSINESS

The use of computers by business firms is a fairly recent development, beginning about 40 years ago. Today, virtually no large or medium-sized business operates without the assistance of a computer, and some giant corporations have thousands. How do business firms use computers?

Basic Applications

Computers have been called "electronic paper pushers." The majority of computer time is devoted to routine clerical activities that require the processing of large amounts of information rapidly. In accounting, the handling of payrolls, accounts receivable, and accounts payable are relatively easy to adapt to electronic data processing. Consumer services firms such as insurance companies, utilities, and banks use computers to maintain customer records and to handle billing.

Other business applications of the computer include inventory control and production scheduling. Management is continuously seeking to keep the firm's inventory of goods in line with sales. Too little inventory may result in lost sales due to shortages. Too much inventory is expensive to store and increases the risk of being caught with out-of-date merchandise if sales decline. Many retailers have installed computer systems that input sales data directly from the store's checkout stand. The computer compares the sales of thousands of items to inventory levels and automatically reorders merchandise. By eliminating delays, this system can reduce inventory costs by thousands of dollars per store.

Another application of the computer is in the area of scheduling production. The computer can keep track of a highly complex production system such as automobile assembly and develop a schedule that will make maximum use of equipment and employees while avoiding bottlenecks and delays.

Office Automation

Perhaps the area of greatest potential for computer applications is in the office. According to one forecast, half the office work force will be using electronic work stations by the year 2000. This forecast is based on the rapid growth in communications both within and among business firms and other organizations.

The fastest growing use of computers in business is word processing. The speed and efficiency of handling written communications is improved through the use of automatic typewriters, programmed instructions, and video display terminals that enable operators to compose, edit, reproduce, and transmit business documents. Word processing can lead to major gains in office productivity by speeding production, increasing accuracy, and reducing filing costs.

But office automation is more than merely adding more personal computers and word processors. The key to automating the office is tying all computers together into a coherent system so that users can have common information, instantly retrieve data, and quickly exchange memos. This requires linking existing machines in companywide networks, developing software for a broad range of applications, and acquiring additional input devices or terminals so

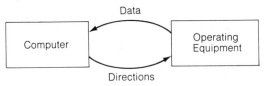

FIGURE 8.6   The Information Feedback
Principle

that virtually every employee has access to the system. The cost can exceed $5000 per employee. For giant corporations, this can add up to a billion dollars or more.

Automated Production

In the factory, *automation* refers to the use of computers to automatically control production processes. An example is the modern oil refinery, which converts petroleum into gasoline, lubricants, and petrochemicals. A computer is programmed to control the refining process to yield the maximum quantities of selected products from the least amount of petroleum.

Automation is based on the *information feedback principle,* which permits the computer to give "orders" based on information received from measuring devices that monitor production operations. Figure 8.6 illustrates this principle, which is similar to a thermostat controlling a heater.

The most dramatic use of computers in production is a new field called Computer-Aided Design/Computer-Aided Manufacturing (CAD/CAM). This approach permits products to be designed on a video display terminal and the specifications transferred to computer-controlled manufacturing equipment. CAD/CAM is discussed in greater detail in Chapter 12.

Management Decision Making

Computers have expanded management's ability to make accurate decisions by providing increasing quantities of up-to-date information. This information reduces uncertainty, thereby placing more emphasis on rational analysis and less on intuition and guessing. Some firms have worked to design *Management Information Systems* (MIS), which are computer-based networks for gathering, processing, and storing data to provide managers with timely and accurate information for decision making.

An interesting development is the use of *simulation* for management problem solving. This tool allows management to build a computer model of a business operation to compare the consequences of different decisions. For example, suppose an oil company wants to open a new service station in a certain city. It can choose several likely sites and simulate (duplicate) the operation of a model station at each site. The factors that influence profitability such as traffic volume, competition from nearby stations, and operating expenses can be expressed in mathematical terms and fed into the computer. The stations can be "operated" for a period of several years using only a few seconds of computer time. The site whose model offers the greatest potential profit is then selected. Of course, the accuracy of the prediction depends on how closely the model duplicates the real world.

The Future

Since the first electronic computer was built little more than four decades ago, three major trends have shaped the evolution of computers: (1) a reduction in size, (2) an increase in speed and flexibility, and (3) a dramatic drop in cost. These trends promise to influence future computer development. Tiny microprocessors are found in a growing range of products from automobiles to toys. By the year 2000, the pocket computer will be replacing the pocket calculator as costs continue to decline.

The development of optical disks that use laser light beams to read information will expand the storage capacity of personal computers while dramatically reducing the cost of storage. Compact disc (CD) players have already revolutionized the way people listen to music, and the same technology will impact on computers by permitting access to hundreds of thousands of times more information at a fraction of the cost.

A major trend in business is toward *distributed data processing* (DDP) which disperses the power of the computer throughout the business organization. DDP entails putting computers next to the people who need them and linking the computers together into networks so that the computers can communicate with each other. Networks that link personal computers to mainframes and share peripheral equipment, such as modems and printers, will become increasingly common. This will bring low-cost computing and instant information to all employees. The result will be huge gains in worker productivity.

Electronic mail is a worldwide computer message network. Faster and less expensive than traditional telegraph and telephone communications, there are already one million electronic "mailboxes" in use. The number of subscribers is growing at an annual rate of 60 percent. The major advantage of electronic mail is that computers can squeeze hours into seconds, thereby reducing transmission time. As a result, it is possible to transmit a page of text between two distant cities for a few pennies.

SUMMARY

The term *statistics* refers to the collection, analysis, presentation, and interpretation of numerical data. Statistical data may be collected from the firm's own records, from government or nongovernment publications, or by conducting a survey. Most surveys involve sampling. A sample is a small number of items selected from a large group for the purpose of making generalizations about the population as a whole.

ISSUE COMPUTER CRIME IS ON THE ROLL

The computer revolution has given birth to a variety of computer crimes that cost business as much as $3 billion a year. Computer-related crime comes in many shapes and sizes:

- Teenage hackers break into company data bases, often altering or destroying information.

- Computer operators steal money by ordering payments to dummy corporations.

- Modern bank robbers break into electronic funds transfer networks and divert millions to their own accounts.

- Industrial spies steal trade secrets by accessing company files.

- Software pirates cost software firms an estimated $800 million in lost sales.

There are two reasons for the rapid growth in computer theft: opportunity and pay-off. The expanded use of computers —especially personal computers—at every level in business has vastly expanded the opportunities for employees and others to gain access to computer information. Stealing is easy because many owners and managers do not know how to protect computer information. The average take in a reported computer crime is $500,000, and the thief has only a 15 percent chance of prosecution.

How to provide security for computer systems is one of the major challenges facing business today. There are three basic approaches to preventing computer theft.

Tools for statistical analysis include averages and index numbers. The three types of averages are the mean, the median, and the mode. Index numbers measure relative (or percentage) changes in numerical data.

Statistics are often summarized and presented in tables or charts. Three major types of charts are the line chart, the pie diagram, and the bar chart. Quantitative information must be interpreted with caution because statistics are subject to both mathematical errors and human bias.

Electronic data processing involves the use of computers to process and modify quantitative data. The term *hardware* refers to the five major components of the computer: (1) an input device, (2) a memory, (3) an arithmetic unit, (4) a control unit, and (5) an output

---

ISSUE COMPUTER CRIME IS ON THE ROLL (Cont.)

1 *Divide Access* The four elements essential to computer fraud are company assets, computer hardware, the program library, and data files. By dividing access to these four elements among different employees, fraud requires a conspiracy of several workers, which is difficult to organize and easier to detect.

2 *Install Safeguards* A growing industry specializes in providing hardware and software to protect data and detect illegal computer entry. The use of passwords (coded keys that permit entry to data), encryption (encoding stored data), and locking devices that require insertion of a hard-to-duplicate key before software can be used are being adopted by a growing number of firms. As one Justice Department attorney warns: "It's time for companies to put locks and burglar alarms on their computers the way they would on the front door of a jewlery store."

3 *Prosecution and Tougher Laws* Some firms have been reluctant to prosecute computer criminals fearing bad publicity, lawsuits, or alerting others to the vulnerability of computer systems. However, many firms have decided that a reluctance to prosecute only encourages criminals and snoopers. Another problem is that most states and the federal government have no specific laws against computer trespassing. This is changing rapidly as legislation providing stiffer fines and longer sentences is being pushed at both federal and state levels.

---

device. The computer needs a detailed set of instructions, called a program, to process data. Programs, or software, are written in computer languages such as FORTRAN, COBOL, and BASIC.

Computers may be classified into three catagories: (1) mainframe computers, which are expensive, fast, and have very large memories; (2) minicomputers, which are slower machines with smaller memories; and (3) personal computers or microcomputers, which are small and inexpensive and may be linked together to improve communications and increase productivity.

The use of computers in business continues to expand rapidly. Most computer time is devoted to recordkeeping activities, particularly the processing of accounting data. Routine applications include customer billing, inventory control, and production scheduling. Computers are also used to automatically control production processes. Office automation is moving toward linking personal computers, terminals, and word processors together so that virtually any employee can share information, retrive data, and exchange memos.

An expanding area of computer utilization is in management decision making. Simulation is a technique for building mathematical models of business activities to test the consequences of different decisions.

Future computer trends are likely to include expanded memories through the use of optical disks, distributed data processing (DDP) which links computers together into networks, and electronic mail that speeds the transmission of information among regions and countries.

SELF-EXAMINATION QUESTIONS

The following questions are based on the Chapter Objectives listed at the beginning of the chapter. Test yourself by circling the letter preceding the answer that *best* completes the statement or answers the question. The answers to the Self-Examination Questions are in the appendix at the end of the textbook.

1. When a firm gathers data from published government statistics, this is known as: (A) a random sample; (B) an internal source; (C) an external source; (D) a survey; (E) none of these.

2. The average calculated by summing a group of values and dividing by the number of items in the group is called the: (A) mean; (B) median; (C) mode; (D) random center; (E) all of these.

3. If company records show five employees are absent 5, 11, 14, 15, and 15 days, respectively, during the year, what is the median number of absences? (A) 11; (B) 12; (C) 14; (D) 15; (E) there is none.

4. Index numbers: (A) are the same as averages; (B) require the selection of a base year; (C) show percentage changes in numerical data; (D) both B and C; (E) all of these.

5. A method of presenting statistical data that does *not* involve the use of charts is a: (A) pie diagram; (B) table; (C) line graph; (D) bar chart; (E) none of these.

6. Computer software includes the: (A) control unit; (B) programs; (C) high-speed printer; (D) CPU; (E) all of these.

7. Which of the following is the best example of a nonroutine business application of the computer? (A) inventory control; (B) production scheduling; (C) simulation; (D) billing; (E) payroll accounting.

8.   A computer's central processing unit includes: (A) an input device such as an optical scanning unit; (B) the arithmetic unit; (C) a high-speed printer; (D) all of these; (E) none of these.

9.   The least expensive and most popular type of computer is the: (A) minicomputer; (B) microcomputer; (C) mainframe computer; (D) word processor; (E) none of these.

Student _____

BUILDING A BUSINESS VOCABULARY

Directions: Match the terms with their definitions by writing the letter in the appropriate blank.

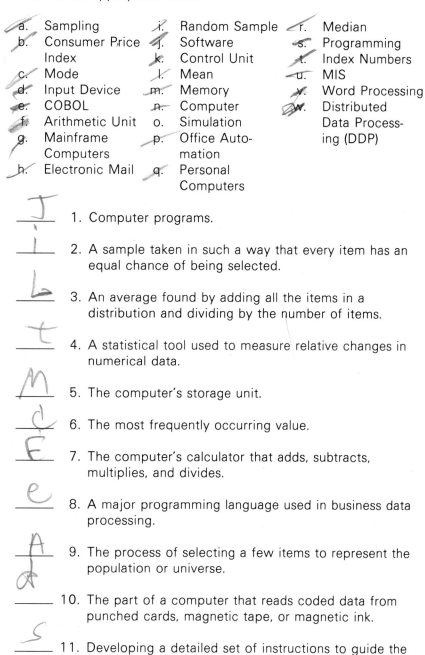

a. Sampling
b. Consumer Price Index
c. Mode
d. Input Device
e. COBOL
f. Arithmetic Unit
g. Mainframe Computers
h. Electronic Mail

i. Random Sample
j. Software
k. Control Unit
l. Mean
m. Memory
n. Computer
o. Simulation
p. Office Automation
q. Personal Computers

r. Median
s. Programming
t. Index Numbers
u. MIS
v. Word Processing
w. Distributed Data Processing (DDP)

__J__ 1. Computer programs.

__i__ 2. A sample taken in such a way that every item has an equal chance of being selected.

__L__ 3. An average found by adding all the items in a distribution and dividing by the number of items.

__t__ 4. A statistical tool used to measure relative changes in numerical data.

__M__ 5. The computer's storage unit.

__d__ 6. The most frequently occurring value.

__E__ 7. The computer's calculator that adds, subtracts, multiplies, and divides.

__e__ 8. A major programming language used in business data processing.

__A__ 9. The process of selecting a few items to represent the population or universe.

_____ 10. The part of a computer that reads coded data from punched cards, magnetic tape, or magnetic ink.

__S__ 11. Developing a detailed set of instructions to guide the operation of a computer.

_____ 12. Measures the change in prices of goods and services purchased by the typical city family.

_____ 13. The middle value in a group of numbers arranged in numerical order.

_____ 14. A system designed to provide managers with accurate and up-to-date information for decision making.

_____ 15. A high-speed electronic machine that manipulates data according to programmed instructions.

_____ 16. A system that improves the handling of written communications through the use of automatic typewriters, programmed instructions, and video display terminals.

_____ 17. The section of the computer that directs the processing of data according to the program.

_____ 18. The use of a computer to build mathematical models of business operations to assist in management decision making.

_____ 19. Inexpensive, limited memory computers often called microcomputers.

_____ 20. An electronic message network that reduces the cost of transmitting information among regions and nations.

_____ 21. The extensive use of personal computers and/or terminals linked together into networks to promote communications and improve productivity.

_____ 22. Large memory, high-speed, expensive computers capable of handling complicated tasks and accommodating several users simultaneously.

_____ 23. The use of electronic work stations linked together into companywide networks so that employees share common information, can instantly retrieve data, and can quickly exchange memos.

Student _____

REVIEWING MAJOR CONCEPTS

1. Name two internal sources of business statistics.

2. How are index numbers used?

3. Briefly describe the components of a computer.

4. What is the difference between computer hardware and software?

5. Briefly explain the information feedback principle.

6. What are the three main methods of contacting survey respondents? Which one is the most effective in getting answers to questions? Which is usually the least expensive?

7. Describe three routine and three nonroutine business applications for the computer.

Student _____

SOLVING PROBLEMS AND CASES

1. The students in an accounting course received the following grades on an examination: 67, 98, 54, 72, 78, 84, 75, 72, 65, 93, 72, 70, and 84.

    a. Compute the mean, median, and mode.

    b. If your grade is 75, what is your position in the class?

2. Suppose you want to construct a price index to measure changes in the prices of goods and services typically purchased by college students. You have collected the following data:

Item	1985 Price	1988 Price	Index
Textbook	$ 30.00	$ 43.50	
Bus Ride	0.60	0.90	
Notebook	1.20	1.20	
Cafeteria Lunch	1.80	2.25	

    a. In the space provided in the table, compute an index number showing the relative price change for each item. (*Hint:* Assume that 1985 is the base year, and show the 1988 price as a percent of the 1985 price.)

    b. Total the index numbers and find the mean.

c. On an average, how much did prices rise between 1985 and 1988?

d. Is your price index an accurate measure of changes in the cost of living for college students? Why or why not?

3. *Case:* P–Q Enterprises

P–Q Enterprises, a food service firm, was recently selected to operate the cafeteria at Westport College. In the past 5 years two other firms were forced to terminate their contracts in the face of mounting losses and student complaints about poor food quality and high prices.

Mary Ellen Thompson, the new P–Q manager for Westport, wants to operate a successful cafeteria that will satisfy the customers and, at the same time, be profitable. Ms. Thompson feels she needs more information before making decisions on how to build a successful operation at Westport. However, she is uncertain as to what types of information would be helpful, and how and where it might be found. What would you suggest?

part **4**

BUSINESS OPERATIONS

CHAPTER	TITLE
9	Marketing Management
10	The Marketing Mix
11	Finance
12	Production

Part 4 focuses on the three major functions of business—marketing, finance, and production. Marketing is satisfying human needs. Chapter 9 describes how firms identify needs of different groups of consumers and develop strategies for fulfilling these needs. Chapter 10 explores in greater detail the key areas of product planning and development, selecting channels of distribution, advertising and personal selling, and pricing strategies. Chapter 11, Finance, covers financial management, sources of funds for business firms, and corporate securities and markets. The concluding chapter in Part 4 discusses different production systems, examines the areas of responsibility of production managers, and describes the trend toward computer-based production systems.

chapter 9

MARKETING MANAGEMENT

Marketing, sometimes called distribution, is the payoff for business. Marketing activities generate the revenue necessary to cover expenses and provide profit. To put it bluntly, efficient production may be desirable, but effective marketing is essential.

From the consumer's point of view, marketing means the right goods are available at a convenient time and location at a price he or she is willing to pay. Marketing has been described as delivering a standard of living to consumers.

There are several ways of studying the broad area of marketing. This chapter attacks the subject from the manager's viewpoint.

CHAPTER OBJECTIVES

1. Define the marketing concept.
2. Describe the steps involved in developing a marketing strategy.
3. List and briefly explain the tools that make up the marketing mix.
4. Contrast and compare time, form, place, and possession utilities.
5. State the nature and purposes of market research.
6. Distinguish between market segmentation and market positioning.
7. List and define five marketing functions.

THE KEY ROLE OF MARKETING

Marketing has been defined as all activities involved in moving goods from the producer to the consumer. This definition encompasses a host of activities such as advertising, personal selling, retailing, wholesaling, market research, storage, transportation, and so forth. However, in a sense this definition is limited. In recent years, many business managers have broadened their view of marketing into what has been termed the marketing concept.

The Marketing Concept

Prior to about 1950, most managers considered marketing as the simple process of selling the goods and services produced by the firm. Emphasis was placed on production, not distribution. However, in the rapidly expanding economy following World War II, it became increasingly apparent that the major challenge had shifted from producing goods to marketing them. In order to support mass production industries, it has become necessary to develop mass markets. For this reason, many firms have become marketing oriented—that is, they have placed primary emphasis on marketing.

The *marketing concept* holds that business firms must focus on determining consumer needs and then develop a marketing strategy for fulfilling those needs. In other words, the business firm must become consumer oriented, for the failure to meet consumer needs can lead to failure. Marketing begins and ends with the consumer.

General Foods applied the marketing concept in the creation of its dog foods, Cycle 1, 2, 3, and 4. The firm wanted to broaden its line of pet foods by adding a cat food. However, research aimed at identifying the needs of pet owners revealed there was limited potential for a new cat food, but a great opportunity for a different type of dog food. The market study discovered that many people think of their pets as humans. It was concluded that dog owners should react favorably to food products specifically formulated for their pets' age and life-style. Cycle 1 would be for puppies, Cycle 2 for growing dogs, Cycle 3 for overweight dogs, and Cycle 4 for older dogs. The firm conducting the study for General Foods created the names of the products, prepared sales promotional materials, and designed the packages. This was done prior to actual production. All General Foods had to do was formulate the products and distribute them through its existing channels of distribution.

The Importance of Marketing

Approximately 50 percent of the retail price of goods and services you buy represents marketing costs. For some goods, such as fashion merchandise, marketing costs are much higher.

Does marketing cost too much? If consumers would be satisfied with a limited number of standardized products sold at a few centralized locations, then marketing costs could be slashed. But American consumers want both variety and convenience, and they are willing to pay for them.

Today, nearly 30 percent of the labor force is engaged in marketing activities, and if current trends continue, this proportion should grow. For one thing, this means there are an increasing number of career opportunities in marketing.

MARKETING STRATEGY

Some managers have carried the marketing concept one step further by suggesting that marketing considerations should control (or at least influence) all other business functions including production and finance. They argue that marketing is the essential function because it alone brings in the bread.

The purpose of marketing is to satisfy the needs of a group of consumers with a product. The task of the marketing manager is to develop a plan or strategy consisting of two parts:

1   *Identifying the target market*—the group of consumers at which the firm will aim its marketing efforts.
2   *Developing a marketing mix*—the combination of tools that the firm will employ to satisfy the target market.

The Target Market

No business firm can hope to satisfy all consumers. Consumers fall into groups according to age, income, geographic location, sex, marital status, and so on. It may also be possible to classify consumers according to social and psychological characteristics such as desire for social acceptance, personal pride, and need for status. Market research is employed to define these market segments. The marketing manager then selects the target market—those groups of consumers that offer the greatest potential for the firm.

The Marketing Mix

Once the target market is determined, the next step is to select the best combination of marketing tools for hitting the market. These tools may be divided into categories called "The Four Ps":

1   *Product.* Here we are concerned with developing the best product (either a good or service) to satisfy the consumers in the target market. Included in this area are decisions about packaging and branding.

2   *Place.* This category includes all the institutions and activities necessary to move the product to the target consumers. It involves choosing the right channels of distribution for the product.
3   *Promotion.* The major promotional tools are advertising and personal selling. The purpose of promotion is to inform the target consumers (as well as selected wholesalers and retailers) about the firm's product and to persuade them to purchase it.
4   *Price.* The fourth P refers to establishing the right price,

don't forget to answer question

FIGURE 9.1   Marketing Strategy: The
Consumer Target and the Four Ps

which will make the product attractive to consumers at which
the firm will aim its marketing efforts.

The concept of marketing strategy is summarized in Figure 9.1. The
starting point is the identification of the target market or those
consumers at which the firm will aim its marketing efforts. The
marketing mix involves developing the right product, with the right
promotion, sold in the right place, at the right price to satisfy the
target consumers.

**Marketing
and Utility**

Utility refers to the power goods and services have in satisfying
human wants. The essence of the marketing concept is to identify
and satisfy the wants and needs of consumers. Marketing
contributes to four types of utility:

1   *Form Utility* refers to the basic nature of the product.
2   *Place Utility* is created by transporting products to
locations *where* consumers want to buy.
3   *Time Utility* involves having goods available *when*
consumers want to buy. Heavy winter coats have greater value
in October than in June.
4   *Possession Utility* means helping transfer ownership of
goods by providing information about what products are
available, where and when they can be purchased, and how
much they cost.

Convenience stores with extended hours create time utility.
Wholesalers and retailers provide place utility. Advertising creates
possession utility. And, while most form utility is created by

production, marketing contributes to form utility through marketing research.

CONSUMERS: THE TARGET MARKET

Mass marketing is no longer the most effective or cost-efficient way to sell. Most companies have to aim their product at more discrete segments of the population. To do this right, you can't know too much about the consumer.

Mark S. Albion,
Assistant Professor of Marketing,
Harvard Business School

The success of any business firm depends on its ability to satisfy consumer needs. It follows that all a business firm must do to be successful is to discover what consumers want and provide them with it. Of course, this is easier said than done. First, consumers are human beings, and each individual has unique needs. Second, consumer wants tend to change over time. Finally, consumers may have difficulty in describing what they want.

Consumer wants and behavior differ according to social class, income, age, sex, marital status, education, and other factors. The marketing manager may classify consumers into groups according to these factors.

Suppose, for example, we take two families, A and B. Family A consists of a childless couple in their forties, one is an attorney and the other is a bank executive, with a combined income of $75,000. Family B is a 22-year-old single parent earning $14,000 a year, with two small children. Which family is the better market for luxury cars? For disposable diapers? For country club memberships? For toys? For personal computers? For laundry detergents? For vacation trips to the Caribbean?

Market Research

Gathering and analyzing information about consumers is called *market research.* Large firms may spend millions of dollars on market research to determine consumer wants and define their target markets. However, all business managers attempt to learn who their customers are and what they want.

There are several types of market research commonly used today:

1 *Informal Research* involves talking with customers, retailers, and wholesalers in order to gather information about the firm's marketing strategy. The proprietor of a restaurant may want to check customer reactions to a change in the menu or to new decor. A trip to the library to study census data may provide information helpful in locating a new business. Salespersons who call on customers in the field are a valuable source of marketing information.

2 *Statistical Surveys* are widely used to measure

ISSUE   HIGH TECH COMES TO MARKET RESEARCH

More than half of all new products fail within the first year. Consumers are demanding higher-quality products that more precisely meet their needs. Market research firms have been busy developing new techniques aimed at discovering more about consumers, improving test marketing of new products, and evaluating alternative advertising strategies.

The leader in electronic market research is Information Resources, Inc. (IRI) whose BehaviorScan system monitors the buying patterns and cable TV viewing habits of 30,000 households in 12 cities. A microcomputer is attached to television sets of volunteer families enabling IRI to keep track of what each home views. Moreover, IRI can cut into a regularly scheduled broadcast with special test commercials. The sample families use a coded plastic ID card when they shop so that their purchases can be recorded. An IRI computer compares commercials transmitted to each home with the family's purchases. Changes can be made in price, advertising, and even the product, and the results measured in terms of sales volume.

This system enables IRI to quickly and accurately determine how successful new products are likely to be, which ads work best, and how much advertising is cost effective. Moreover, BehaviorScan is quicker and less expensive than traditional test marketing. Using this system, a new product can be tested in 12 months at a cost of less than $2 million compared to 18 to 20 months and over $3 million for traditional test marketing. So far, only large food and packaged goods companies have used the system.

Consumer advocates complain that as BehaviorScan is expanded it will provide too much information about consumers, thereby invading their privacy. Participants receive annual gifts and monthly prize giveaways. There is no shortage of volunteers.

---

consumers' attitudes, confidence, and reactions to products. Many companies specialize in conducting market research surveys for business firms. Such surveys usually involve selecting a sample, designing a questionnaire, and contracting respondents by mail, telephone, or through personal interviews.

3   *Test Marketing* is a common method of evaluating new products. By selecting one city or section of the country as a test market, a firm can gain firsthand information on consumer reactions. If those reactions are unfavorable, the firm may abandon the product or redesign it. Test marketing may also help a firm to develop place, promotional, and price strategies.

4   *Motivational Research* is based on the assumption that the reason people buy one product over another is often subconscious and deeply emotional. This type of research often involves in-depth interviews aimed at uncovering the psychological bases for consumer behavior. Interviewers are usually psychologists or behavioral scientists who are trained to identify subconscious motives.

A carefully planned marketing strategy based on market research cannot guarantee success, but it can reduce the chances of failure.

Types of Markets

A *market* is a group of people with the desire and ability to purchase a product. Those individuals that want a product but are unable to purchase it are not part of the market. Also excluded are individuals that have the purchasing power but no desire for the product. There is no sense in directing marketing activities to those unable or uninterested in buying.

Markets may be divided into five categories:

1   *Consumer Markets* include people that purchase goods and services to satisfy their own needs or wants. Generally, people in consumer markets are the final users of products (e.g., they do not buy products for resale). Consumer markets tend to be large in size and often spread geographically throughout the country. People in this market are motivated by emotional or psychological factors such as prestige, fear, and pride. For example, many cosmetics and body care products are aimed at the individual's desire to be attractive to the opposite sex.

2   *Industrial Markets* are composed of individuals and firms that buy products (such as raw materials, equipment, and supplies) that are required in the production of other goods and services. Industrial buyers tend to be relatively few in number and geographically concentrated. If a firm produces specialized machine tools used in manufacturing domestic automobiles, its market would be limited primarily to the four major automobile makers located in and around Detroit. Buyers in the industrial market tend to be more rational and less emotional than those in the consumer market. There is greater concern for reliability, economy of operation, assurance of continuous supply, and availability of service.

3   *Reseller Markets* are made up of individuals or companies that buy products with the intention of reselling them. Included are wholesalers and retailers such as automobile dealerships, department stores, and tire distributors.

4   *Government Markets* include governmental units that buy and use products in city, state, and federal operations. Individuals in this market buy products ranging from accounting services to military hardware.

5   *International Markets* are consumer, industrial, reseller, or government markets located in other countries. International marketing is both lucrative and risky. Chapter 14 discusses international business in greater depth.

MARKET SEGMENTATION AND MARKET POSITIONING

Identifying the target market may be viewed as a three-step process:

1. Market Segmentation	→	2. Market Targeting	→	3. Market Positioning
Dividing the market into different groups of buyers with different needs.		Choosing the best market segment(s) for the firm.		Creating a distinctive and desirable place for the firm's product or service relative to the competition.

Broad markets (such as the markets for laundry detergents, automobiles, or machine tools) may be subdivided into different groups of consumers (or users) with varying needs. *Market segmentation* refers to dividing a market into distinct groups of buyers who require separate products and/or marketing mixes. Figure 9.2 illustrates the hypothetical market for automobiles divided into segments according to two sets of characteristics: (1) economy versus high cost and status on the vertical axis, and (2) traditional transportation versus high performance and sportiness on the horizontal axis. An automobile manufacturer planning to bring out a new line must first decide which segment to enter and how to enter it. Given competitors' positions, the firm has two choices: (1) position next to one or more competitors and fight for a share of the market, or (2) find a "hole" in the market and try to fill it. This latter approach requires the firm to develop a new product that is significantly different from existing products, and then convince buyers of its desirability.

Market positioning means attempting to occupy a clear and desirable place in the market and in buyers' minds relative to the competition. Therefore, the position of a product is the image that product projects in relation to competitive products.

What brand name comes to mind for the following products: computers? colas? car rentals? photocopiers? Did you think of IBM, Coke, Hertz, and Xerox? Most people do. Each of these companies has created a distinct image for their product relative to their competition. Firms unable to compete directly with well-entrenched, dominant corporations should concentrate on narrow market

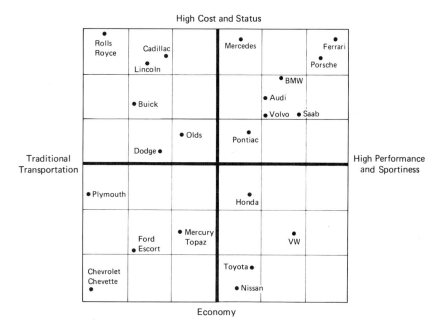

FIGURE 9.2   Market Segmentation: The Auto Market
(Hypothetical Data)

segments. For example, Xerox failed to meet the needs of people requiring small, inexpensive copiers. Savin, therefore, positioned itself as a firm serving this market segment.

Figure 9.3 represents an effort by the Ford Motor Company to position its new automobile, the Merkur. By referring to Figure 9.2, you can determine the market segment that Ford selected for the Merkur.

Effective positioning may determine the success or failure of a firm's efforts to enter a new market. For example, Xerox, the world's largest manufacturer of copiers, brought out a line of computers in the late 1970s. However, Xerox failed to position itself in buyers' minds as a computer manufacturer, and the firm was forced to withdraw from the computer market.

The critical importance of positioning is emphasized by marketing consultant Regis McKenna in his recent book *The Regis Touch:* "At the heart of every good marketing strategy is a good positioning strategy. Modern marketing is, to a large extent, a battle for positioning."

Successful market positioning depends on developing an effective marketing mix—the right combination of product, place, promotion, and price strategies. Chapter 10 provides a more detailed explanation of the "Four Ps."

Marketing Functions

Selling is only a part of marketing. All the activities involved in moving goods and services from producers to consumers (or users) are referred to as *marketing functions.*

FIGURE 9.3   Market Positioning Through Advertising

1   *Marketing information* is gathered by all marketing firms to detect new trends, identify target consumers, and develop marketing strategies.

2   *Buying* the right goods in the correct amounts is critical to the success of retailers, wholesalers, and manufacturers. Buying

---

ISSUE MARKET SEGMENTATION–COKE VS. COKE VS. COKE VS. . . .

Nearly everyone remembers the great Coca-Cola marketing blunder. In the 1980s, Coca-Cola's management became increasingly worried about Coke's share of the $25 billion soft drink market, which had dropped from 25 percent in 1973 to 22 percent by 1984. Meanwhile, arch-rival Pepsi-Cola was gaining customers with aggressive marketing, capturing a 19 percent market share in 1984. To make matters worse, Pepsi was more popular among younger drinkers, who are heavy consumers of soft drinks.

Coke's management decided to fight back using a new product strategy. After 3 years of market research involving 200,000 taste tests, the company launched New Coke in April, 1985. The sweeter-tasting product was intended to replace the old Coca-Cola whose formula had been unchanged for 99 years.

Consumer response was overwhelming. Tens of thousands of Coke lovers angrily complained, demanding the return of old Coke. Within three months the company capitulated, announcing that the old product would return as Coca-Cola Classic while retaining New Coke. This brought to six the number of products bearing the Coke name.

Does the entire episode represent a marketing disaster for the Coca-Cola Company? Not according to some experts who see the result as a successful marketing segmentation strategy where the firm satisfies its die-hard customers while gaining consumers who prefer sweeter soft drinks. According to one analyst, "They've backed into one of the most powerful strategic positions in the consumer marketplace."

Others disagree, claiming that New Coke and Coca-Cola Classic are so similar that they will cannibalize sales from each other. Moreover, the company faces a multitude of problems including double inventories, production scheduling difficulties, and trying to get increased shelf space from retailers.

Is New Coke a powerful weapon in an increasingly segmented market or a superfluous brand that will boost costs without significantly increasing sales?

---

often involves forecasting fashion trends six months or more in the future.

3 *Selling* entails the use of advertising, personal selling, and sales promotion to inform and persuade consumers, users, or middlemen.

4   *Transporting and storing* refers to the physical distribution of goods to create place and time utilities. Storing or warehousing means keeping adequate inventories on hand.

5   *Financing* in marketing means granting credit. Most manufacturers provide credit to wholesalers, who often grant credit to retailers, who, in turn, may attempt to boost sales by offering credit to consumers (or users).

6   *Standardization and grading* refers to developing uniform size and quality standards for products so that light bulbs will fit into electrical sockets and each 10-penny nail is the same weight and size. Many agricultural goods are graded into weight and size categories.

7   *Risk-taking* is central to marketing. Manufacturers introduce new products that may fail. Wholesalers and retailers take risks when they buy inventory and grant credit.

These marketing functions add value to the goods and services purchased by consumers and users.

SUMMARY

Marketing is all the activities necessary to move goods from the producer to the consumer. The marketing concept holds that business firms should concentrate on discovering consumer needs and then focus on fulfilling these needs.

Marketing strategy consists of two steps: (1) identifying the target market, and (2) developing the marketing mix. The target market is the group of consumers the firm wishes to serve. The marketing mix refers to developing product, place, promotional, and price strategies to reach the target consumers.

Consumer needs differ according to age, sex, occupation, social class, income, and psychological factors. Market research is used to gather and analyze facts about consumers. Markets are groups of people with the desire and ability to purchase a product. Five market categories are consumer, industrial, reseller, government, and international.

As consumers have become more quality conscious and selective, business firms have turned increasingly to market segmentation and market positioning strategies. Market segmentation refers to dividing a broad market into groups of buyers, each of which requires a separate product or marketing mix. Market positioning involves selecting an attractive market segment by creating a desirable image in the buyers' minds relative to competitive products.

Economists often measure consumer satisfaction in terms of utility. Marketing can create form, place, time, and possession utility. Marketing can also be viewed as a group of related activities or functions required to move goods from producers to consumers or users. The marketing functions are marketing information, buying, selling, transporting and storing, financing, standardization and grading, and risk-taking.

SELF-EXAMINATION QUESTIONS

The following questions are based on the Chapter Objectives listed at the beginning of the chapter. Test yourself by circling the letter preceding the answer that *best* completes the statement or answers the question. The answers to the Self-Examination Questions are in the appendix at the end of the textbook.

1. The marketing concept: (A) focuses on consumer needs; (B) involves developing a marketing strategy; (C) assumes that business firms should be marketing oriented; (D) all of these; (E) none of these.

2. Developing a marketing strategy entails: (A) identifying the target market; (B) developing a marketing mix; (C) hiring an advertising agency; (D) both A and B; (E) none of these.

3. Which of the following is *not* a part of the marketing mix? (A) product; (B) profit; (C) place; (D) promotion; (E) price.

4. Market research: (A) involves gathering and analyzing information about consumers; (B) is useful in developing a marketing mix; (C) can be used to identify target markets; (D) may include test marketing, motivational research, and statistical surveys; (E) all of these.

5. Market positioning: (A) is the same as market segmentation; (B) refers to how consumers view a firm's product relative to the competition; (C) is the geographic location of a firm's sales force; (D) has nothing to do with a firm's marketing mix; (E) none of these.

6. Which of the following is not a marketing function? (A) selling; (B) financing; (C) risk-taking; (D) grading; (E) producing.

Student _____

BUILDING A BUSINESS VOCABULARY

Directions: Match the terms with their definitions by writing the letter in the appropriate blank.

a. Marketing Mix
b. Target Market
c. Utility
d. Industrial Markets
e. Consumer Markets
f. Reseller Markets
g. Market Research
h. Marketing
i. Market Segmentation
j. Market Positioning
k. Marketing Functions

_____ 1. A selected group of consumers at which the firm aims its marketing efforts.

_____ 2. Gathering and analyzing information about consumer needs and behavior.

_____ 3. Dividing a market into distinct groups of consumers who require different products or marketing mixes.

_____ 4. Activities such as marketing information, buying, selling, transporting and storing, financing, standardization and grading, and risk-taking that add value to goods and services.

_____ 5. The combination of tools (known as the "Four Ps") the firm uses to satisfy the target market.

_____ 6. Individuals that purchase goods and services that directly satisfy human wants.

_____ 7. All the activities necessary to move goods from the producer to the consumer.

_____ 8. An economics term referring to the ability of goods and services to satisfy human wants.

_____ 9. Attempting to occupy a desirable market segment relative to the competition.

_____ 10. Purchasers of raw materials, equipment, and parts used in the production of other goods.

_____ 11. Wholesalers and retailers who purchase goods for resale.

Student _____

REVIEWING MAJOR CONCEPTS

1. Briefly explain the marketing concept.

2. What are the two steps in developing a marketing strategy?

3. Give two examples of how dry cereal producers attempt to position different brands of cereal.

4. Explain how the cost of marketing could be reduced. Is the current trend toward reducing or increasing marketing costs? Explain why.

5. Which type of utility is being created in each of the following examples?

    a. Ford Motor Company advertises 7.7 percent financing for its line of automobiles.

    b. A food service firm uses catering trucks that stop at industrial plants, warehouses, and related facilities on a regular schedule.

    c. Apple introduces a voice-activated computer.

6. Name the marketing function involved in each of the following:

    a. Safeway Stores, a food chain, opens a new distribution center.

    b. A travel agent opens her own travel service.

    c. A department store offers its own credit card to qualified customers.

    d. Procter & Gamble test markets a new detergent in El Paso, Texas.

    e. Government inspectors label sides of beef as fancy, choice, and prime.

Student _____

SOLVING PROBLEMS AND CASES

1. *Case:* Apple Computer

   By the early 1980s, Apple Computer had become one of the most successful corporations in the world with annual sales of $1.5 billion. No company could match Apple's growth record of doubling its size each year since its founding. The firm's greatest success had been in the home and school markets, which were dominated by the Apple II computer. However, by the mid-1980s, there was a slowdown in home computer sales.

   Apple had been slow to recognize the importance of the business market for personal computers, which by 1985 accounted for two-thirds of all personal computer sales. Its first two business computers, the Apple III and the Lisa, were costly failures. In 1984, Apple introduced the Macintosh computer. The new machine sold well, but to individuals, not business firms. Meanwhile, IBM had moved aggressively to capture 65 percent of the large business market for personal computers, while Apple's share was only 10 percent.

   In 1985, Apple introduced a group of new products aimed at making the Macintosh more attractive to corporate buyers. The new products, called the Macintosh Office, included an enlarged memory, a laser printer, and a "local area network" that allowed personal computers (IBMs as well as Apples) to work together. Most experts agreed that the Macintosh enjoyed several advantages over the IBM PC including smaller size, better graphics, and ease of use. However, a survey of large corporate buyers found that 72 percent favored IBM while only 4.5 percent preferred Apple. Apple had a national sales force of 65 compared to IBM's 6000.

   Apple's management was uncertain about its marketing strategy.

   Identify three market segments for Apple Computers. On which segment should Apple concentrate its marketing efforts? Explain your choice.

2. Macho Taco, a fast food chain, is considering opening an outlet in your area. What type of market research do recommend they undertake?

Student _____

3. *Case:* Honda Motorcycle Company

In 1960 a Los Angeles advertising agency called GB & D was selected to represent Honda Motorcycle Company of Japan. The firm was asked to create a marketing strategy designed to sell Honda Motorcycles in the United States. The marketing budget for this job was quite small.

In 1960, GB & D had to face up to the fact that total sales for all brands of motorcycles in the country were only 40,000 units, of which Honda's share was just over 5 percent. Honda had only 137 dealers in the United States. Added to this was the generally unfavorable image of hare-brained youths in black leather jackets speeding around the countryside on cycles.

Honda and GB & D had one thing in their favor: a first-rate product. It was decided to shy away from the prevailing "black leather jacket" motorcycle image and create an entirely new idea in the two-wheel field. Motorcycling was to be promoted as a very pleasant and healthy activity for the entire family.

GB & D's initial marketing strategy aimed at identifying Honda's prime markets. Who were its best prospects, and where were they located? The advertising agency did its market research the hard way: interviewing field representatives, dealers, purchasers, and the general public.

GB & D decided to try a region-by-region advertising campaign using magazines for its main medium. The campaign stressed the joys of motorcycling for everyone, particularly the family. The agency also started an extensive dealer-education campaign to improve dealer selling methods and service.

In 2 years, Honda's share of the market increased from 5 to 52 percent; its dealer network went from 137 to 767; and sales from $979,000 to $17 million.

a. Why did the advertising agency (GB & D) use market research?

b. Why do you think GB & D started with a region-by-region marketing campaign instead of going for the entire national market at once?

    c. From a marketing standpoint, what was wrong with the "black leather jacket" image of motorcycling that prevailed in 1960?

    d. What were the roles played by advertising and personal selling in marketing Honda motorcycles?

4. *Case:* Playboy Enterprises, Inc.

In late 1953, Hugh Hefner, a young magazine writer, quit his job and invested $600 in the first issue of a new magazine called *Playboy.* The magazine, with its symbol of a tuxedo-clad rabbit, was aimed directly at the young male market and featured what was then considered sexually explicit photographs. *Playboy* achieved rapid success with circulation topping 7 million by 1972. Hefner branched out into other enterprises including Playboy clubs, resorts and hotels, a movie company, a modeling agency, and gambling casinos in England.

    In the middle 1970s, *Playboy* ran into difficulty as circulation dropped to under 5 million and profits declined from $11 million to only $1 million in 1975. *Playboy* steadily lost readers to its raunchier rivals such as *Penthouse* and *Hustler.* Hefner hired a new president, who closed down some unprofitable operations and reduced staff, in an effort to cut overhead costs. These efforts were successful in boosting profits, but in the early 1980s, Playboy lost its gambling license in England and was forced to sell its very profitable casinos.

In 1982, Hugh Hefner named his 29-year-old daughter, Christie, president of Playboy Enterprises. A key problem facing the new president was how to boost *Playboy*'s circulation. Ms. Hefner was hesitant to engage in a battle to outdo competitive magazines in sexual explicitness because such a move would harm the sophisticated image of *Playboy* and drive away many advertisers. Yet one of her major goals was to increase circulation and expand advertising revenues.

a. Describe *Playboy*'s target market. Be specific.

b. What factors caused *Playboy*'s circulation to decline in the 1970s?

c. What action should the president take?

d. List the possible conflicts and problems Ms. Hefner may encounter as a woman president and daughter of the chairman of the board of Playboy Enterprises.

chapter 10

THE MARKETING MIX

In the preceding chapter, we described how management develops a marketing strategy. The starting point is the target market—those consumers or users at which the firm aims its marketing efforts. Next, management must develop a marketing mix—also known as the Four Ps—intended to satisfy the target market.

Chapter 9 briefly described the Four Ps. This chapter examines product, place, promotion, and price strategies in greater detail.

CHAPTER OBJECTIVES

1. Explain the importance of product planning and development.

2. Describe a typical product life cycle.

3. List the major channels of distribution.

4. Compare and contrast merchant wholesalers with agent middlemen.

5. Identify the three components of the promotional mix.

6. Distinguish between skim-the-cream pricing and penetration pricing.

PRODUCT

A product may be viewed as a combination of consumer satisfactions and benefits. Strange idea? Not at all. When a consumer purchases a new Ford Thunderbird, does the buyer think of the car as a certain number of pounds of steel, aluminum, glass, rubber, and other materials? Of course not! The owner views the car in terms of benefits—transportation, comfort, status, and driving pleasure. In other words, customers buy a product because of the satisfaction they expect to gain from it. A basic rule in marketing is to "sell the sizzle, not the steak." One restaurant chain with outlets in 50 states and abroad took this rule to heart. Its name, of course, is Sizzler Family Steakhouse.

Product Planning and Development

Product planning and development is the process of creating new products and improving existing ones. Market research aimed at determining what consumers want often plays an important role in product development. In this sense, marketing precedes production.

Our society is characterized by accelerating change. Developments in technology are making possible a host of new products. A few years ago computers were bulky and expensive, but with the development of the microprocessor, the "computer-on-a-chip," new markets have opened up. Automatic teller machines, compact disk players, and personal computers affect the way we live, what we buy, and how we work.

Changes in technology have been matched by rapid changes in consumer tastes and incomes. This means that business firms must develop new products in order to survive. If the market changes, the product must change. The Model-T Ford, vacuum-tube radios, and wooden skis hardly meet the needs of today's consumers. Half the profits earned by all U.S. business firms come from products that did not exist 10 years ago.

Product planning and development is a difficult and hazardous process. It has been estimated that 80 percent of all new products fail to earn a profit. RCA's video disk player lost $500 million. The process of developing and introducing a new product may require years of careful research and testing.

Product Life Cycle

Products, like people, pass through several stages of development. Figure 10.1 illustrates a seven-stage life cycle for a successful product. Some products such as record albums and toys move through these stages in only a few weeks or months, while others (for example, freezers and stereos) have life cycles that extend over many decades.

Product Development

The first three stages occur before a product is introduced to the market. *New product ideas* come from both market research and from within the firm. According to one

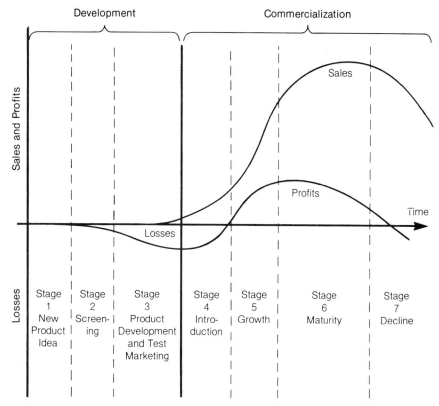

FIGURE 10.1   Product Life Cycle

study, only 1 out of 58 new product ideas results in a successful product. The *screening stage* involves determining if the product idea meets the needs of the target market as well as the objectives of the firm, which may include profit, sales volume, and consumer safety. During the third stage of development, there is a considerable investment of time and money in design, engineering, production, packaging, and testing. As you can see in Figure 10.1, the firm can realize a significant loss while engaged in *product development and test marketing.*

Commercialization   When a new product is introduced to the target market, it goes through four stages in its life cycle. During the *introduction stage* the firm spends heavily on promotion and attempts to develop channels of distribution to reach the target consumers. Cellular car telephones are an example of a product in the introductory stage of its life cycle.

In the *growth stage,* sales and profits increase rapidly as the successful new product gains widespread acceptance. Marketing strategy may call for product improvements and price reductions to gain greater sales volume, and to compete with similar products from other firms. In the middle 1980s, video tape players entered the growth stage in their life cycle.

In the *maturity stage,* the market becomes saturated as customers who want the product have purchased it, and there is widespread competition from rival firms. Sales level off and profits begin to decline due to high promotional costs and price competition. The maturity stage may last for many years as in the case of color television sets and electronic calculators. However, sooner or later products move into the market *decline stage* of their life cycles where sales fall off and profits decline to the point where products are abandoned. Black and white television sets and nonfilter cigarettes are examples of products that have entered the final decline stage.

PLACE

Even the best product will not sell unless it is available at the time and place consumers wish to buy it. The marketing manager must determine where and how the product should be distributed to reach the target market.

Channels of Distribution

The routes that products take as they move from the producer to the consumer (or user) are called *channels of distribution.* These channels often involve middlemen—wholesalers and retailers—who perform a host of marketing services. Four major channels of distribution are shown in Figure 10.2.

Producer → Consumer   At first glance this channel would appear to be the cheapest and most efficient means of distribution. However, for consumer goods, it is relatively unpopular and

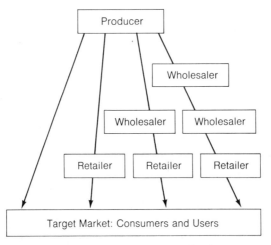

FIGURE 10.2   Channels of Distribution

expensive. Several firms such as Avon, Mary Kay, and Amway have been highly successful in distributing their products door to door. These firms enjoy vigorous selling from their sales forces and their products command a premium price.

Some manufacturers sell consumer goods from their own retail outlets. See's Candies is an example. Other firms employ direct mail distribution using catalogs and magazine advertising to solicit orders.

Direct selling from the manufacturer to the user is very common in the industrial market. Since industrial users are few in number and often geographically concentrated, manufacturers can reach the market through their own sales force with relative ease.

Producer → Retailer → Consumer   This channel is used when retailers purchase in large quantities or when the product has a high dollar value. Retail chains such as Safeway, Sears, and Woolworth prefer to purchase directly from manufacturers and to undertake the services normally performed by wholesalers. The producer may employ salespersons to contact retailers directly when the sales volume justifies the expense. Furniture and appliance manufacturers typically use this channel.

Producer → Wholesaler → Retailer → Consumer   This is the most common channel of distribution for many types of consumer goods. When a product such as cigarettes requires widespread distribution to many different retailers, it is economically efficient to use wholesalers. The wholesaler provides a sales force for the manufacturer. Since the wholesaler may distribute thousands of different products, the marketing cost per item may be very low. Because most wholesalers operate in a limited geographic area, producers often employ salespeople to contact the wholesaler.

Producer → Wholesaler → Wholesaler → Retailer → Consumer
Sometimes a manufacturer cannot afford to maintain even a small sales force to contact wholesalers. The producer may distribute through certain types of wholesalers such as agents who sell to other wholesalers. A *manufacturers' agent* may represent several producers of noncompeting goods. The agent contacts wholesalers and major retailers in a territory that may cover several states. In essence, the manufacturers' agent is the producer's sales force working on a commission basis.

There is no law requiring a producer to use only one channel of distribution. Many firms distribute through two or more channels at the same time. For example, a cake-mix manufacturer may sell its product directly to large food chains and use wholesalers to reach the small grocery stores.

Retailing

Retailing is the sale of merchandise to final consumers. Today there are approximately 1.6 million retailing firms with combined annual sales of $1.1 trillion.

It would appear from these figures that retailing is a small-scale operation with the average retailer having sales of under $700,000 per year. However, the averages are deceiving. Only 6 percent of the retailers account for over 60 percent of the total sales. This means the vast majority of retailers are small, but a few giant firms account for a major proportion of sales. The "big-time retailers" include the chain stores, some of which have hundreds of outlets.

What are the advantages of large-scale retailing? In the first place, large retailers have a buying advantage. They purchase merchandise in volume, thereby realizing quantity discounts—lower costs per unit. The chain stores also enjoy an advertising advantage since they can spread the cost of advertising over many stores. For example, if Safeway operates 10 stores in a city, a $1,000 newspaper ad costs only $100 per store. Large retailers have the added advantage of specialization of management. For example, the department store gets its name from the fact that merchandise is divided into departments, each of which is managed by a buyer. By concentrating on one type of merchandise such as kitchenware, the buyer can become highly knowledgeable about the customers' needs, the best sources of supply, and the most effective merchandising methods.

Small retailers also have some advantages, which may include a close relationship with their customers, extensive services, and specialized merchandise. Some men and women prefer to buy their clothing from small shops because of the distinctive styles and the personal attention.

Retailing is subject to very rapid changes, and the firm that fails to adapt to change is likely to face declining sales and profits. The past several decades have witnessed the decentralization of retailing as stores have followed their customers to suburban locations. The downtown shopping areas have experienced declining sales coupled with rising costs. Shopping centers with plenty of parking and one-stop shopping have proved to be very popular with consumers, but not all shopping centers have been successful. Self-service retailing was introduced by supermarkets and then copied by discount houses, variety stores, and other retailers. The trend toward self-service has forced manufacturers to spend large sums on advertising in order to presell consumers before they enter the store.

It was once popular to classify retailers by types—such as general stores, supermarkets, specialty shops, discount houses, and so forth. However, the distinction between types of retailers is fading, largely due to *scrambled merchandising*. Prior to World War II, most retailers tended to specialize in one type of merchandise. Grocery stores sold food. But no more. Today the rule is scrambled merchandising—the mixing of many different types of merchandise together in one store. Supermarkets sell hardware, toiletries, and clothing as well as food. Drug stores carry cameras, small appliances, and automotive supplies. Today the aggressive retailer is likely to add any line of goods that offers an attractive profit. Scrambled merchandising leads to increased competition, and some single-line retailers have been unable to survive.

Nonstore Retailing   A major trend in retailing is nonstore shopping. With the growing number of single-person households and working couples, many people no longer have the discretionary time for traditional shopping. Furthermore, it is expected that as much as a quarter of the U.S. population may work at home by the end of the century. These trends are already reflected in increasing sales from catalogs, coupons, and radio and television offerings, which have been growing at twice the rate of store sales.

Although catalog sales have reached $50 billion a year, the field has become overcrowded and the competition fierce. The first firm to sell by catalog, Montgomery Ward, recently abandoned catalog selling as unprofitable.

More exciting is the potential for *videoshopping,* the use of cable television to sell directly to consumers. "Shopping Channel" is a cable program transmitted to subscribers 7 days a week, 16 hours a day. Merchandise displayed on the show can be ordered by dialing a toll-free telephone number. The next step is two-way cable, which enables viewers to order goods direct through a calculator-type device operating through the cable system. Ultimately such interactive devices will permit shoppers to summon to the screen goods they want to buy. One forecast predicts that one-fourth of all retail sales will be nonstore by the end of the century.

Computerized shopping kiosks, about the size of a refrigerator, are beginning to appear in shopping malls. Sometimes called interactive retailing systems, these devices consist of a microcomputer, keyboard, a touch-sensitive display screen, and a credit card reader. Shoppers can call up TV-type commercials and use the keyboard to order thousands of items. Orders are electronically transmitted to distribution centers where the shoppers' credit card is checked and the orders shipped.

Franchising   Although franchising dates back to the nineteenth century, its real expansion in the United States started about 25 years ago. Today, about one-third of all retail sales are accounted for by franchise outlets, and the proportion is expected to reach 50 percent by the end of the century.

Nearly every type of retail operation can be franchised. Franchising is common in such diverse fields as beauty salons, art galleries, schools, variety stores, pet shops, and car washes as well as such traditional operations as fast-food outlets, motels, and service stations. The fastest growth is expected in home services, such as repair, remodeling and decorating, business services, and nonfood retailing.

The basic idea behind *franchising* is simple. It is an agreement that gives an independent business operator (called the franchisee) the right to sell a standardized product or service in a certain area. The parent company (or franchisor) is usually a successful firm that offers a proven method of operation and widely advertised brand name, plus training and management services to the franchisee. In return, the franchisee normally agrees to purchase equipment and supplies from the parent company and to pay a monthly fee based on sales or gross profit. In addition, most franchise arrangements call for an initial investment that ranges from $1,000 to $1 million or more.

Franchising offers significant advantages to both parties. The franchisor can gain rapid distribution of the firm's product or service with little capital investment. The problem of finding hard-working managers is reduced because each franchise operator has a built-in motivation for success.

From the standpoint of the small business owner-manager, the major advantage of franchising is that it reduces the chances of failure. Only about 4 percent of franchised businesses fail compared to a failure rate of over 65 percent for all small firms.

The franchisee receives assistance in site location, construction methods and layout, an intensive training program, the advantages of a large-scale purchasing operation, advertising support, a widely known brand name, and management services such as inventory control and accounting systems. However, a franchise is no guarantee of success. Even the strongest franchise cannot overcome poor location, inadequate financing, or incompetent management.

Wholesaling

The wholesaler performs a variety of marketing activities in moving goods from the producer to the retailer. Wholesalers also sell to industrial users and other wholesalers. What services do wholesalers offer to retailers and producers?

Wholesaling Functions   Wholesalers maintain a sales force to contact customers. Distributing through wholesalers may be the most economical channel for many manufacturers. One drawback, however, is that wholesalers do not provide a vigorous sales effort for individual products.

Often wholesalers will store and deliver merchandise for manufacturers and retailers. This relieves the manufacturer of transportation and warehousing problems. The retailer can keep his inventory low by depending on the wholesaler for rapid delivery of small quantities of merchandise. Furthermore, wholesalers often extend credit and provide merchandising assistance to retailers.

Some retailers and manufacturers prefer to bypass the

wholesaler and deal direct. It must be emphasized that the wholesaler may be eliminated, but wholesaling functions cannot be eliminated. When a manufacturer sells direct to a retailer, one or the other must undertake the jobs performed by the wholesaler. For example, Safeway acts as its own wholesaler by maintaining extensive warehousing facilities and a fleet of delivery trucks.

Types of Wholesalers   There are dozens of different types of wholesalers operating in many industries and handling a variety of merchandise. However, most wholesalers fall into two general categories—merchant wholesalers and agent middlemen.

1   *Merchant Wholesalers* take title to the merchandise they sell. This means they purchase goods for resale. Most, but not all, merchant wholesalers offer a full line of services to manufacturers and retailers. Although costs vary with the type of merchandise and the services provided, merchant wholesalers typically charge 10 to 25 percent of the retail price.

2   *Agent Middlemen* are limited-service wholesalers who do not take title to the merchandise they sell. An example is the manufacturers' agent who represents several producers. The agent covers a sales territory and charges a commission of roughly 5 percent of sales. Another type of agent middleman is the broker who negotiates transactions between buyers and sellers for a commission.

In determining the type of wholesaler to use, both the manufacturer and the retailer must measure the services offered against the costs. It is foolish to pay for unneeded services.

Figure 10.3 illustrates how the wholesaler simplifies the movement of goods from the producer to the retailer.

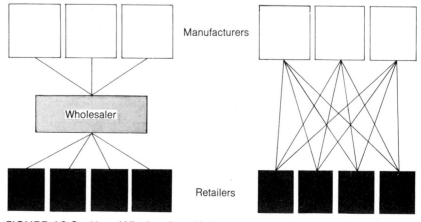

FIGURE 10.3   How Wholesalers Help

PROMOTION

Doing business without advertising is like winking in the dark. You know what you are doing, but nobody else does.

Daniel J. Boorstin

Promotion refers to any method of persuading or informing consumers about the product, place, or price. There are three promotional tools—personal selling, advertising, and sales promotion. *Personal selling,* the most widely used type of promotion, involves face-to-face or telephone contact between the salesperson and the customer. *Advertising* is nonpersonal selling on a mass basis. *Sales promotion* supplements personal selling and advertising through such promotional techniques as point-of-purchase displays, coupons, samples, and contests.

The Promotional Mix

The *promotional mix* is the combination of advertising, personal selling, and sales promotion used by a firm. Most firms use all three but place primary emphasis on advertising or personal selling.

What determines the promotional mix? Basically there are two considerations: the target market and the nature of the product. For example, in the industrial market, personal selling is the dominant promotional tool because the target market is relatively easy to reach with a sales force, and the customers want detailed information and assistance that can only be provided through personal contact. Would a business firm purchase a $200,000 industrial robot by clipping a coupon from a newspaper advertisement?

Advertising is often the major promotional tool in the consumer market where there are many thousands of buyers and the product is usually simple to use and inexpensive. The promotional mix for laundry detergents is dominated by advertising due to the huge market, low price, and simple product.

Sales promotion tools are of secondary importance in the promotional mix. They are used to supplement personal selling and advertising.

Sales Promotion

Sales promotion activities include point-of-purchase displays, coupons, samples, and contests used to complement and support the firm's advertising and personal selling. Point-of-purchase displays are intended to gain the buyers' attention and interest especially in self-service retailing. Often manufacturers and wholesalers will provide retailers with display stands for store use. L'eggs pantyhose displays in supermarkets are an example. Coupons are intended to encourage buyers to try a product by offering price discounts. Samples are often given away to promote new products. Contests may be directed at consumers to generate interest in a good or service. Often sales contests are used to motivate salespersons employed by manufacturers, wholesalers, or retailers.

Personal Selling

There are several advantages to promoting a product through personal selling. A salesperson can focus his or her efforts by calling only on good prospects. In contrast, much advertising is wasted because it reached individuals who have no interest in the product. In this sense, advertising is like a shotgun while personal selling is a rifle.

The salesperson can tailor the sales message to the customer, demonstrate the product, answer questions, overcome objections, and close the sale.

The key disadvantage of personal selling is the high cost per contact. A good salesperson may cost $60,000 per year or more in compensation and expenses. Since the salesperson can only call on a limited number of prospective customers, the cost per call may be prohibitively high.

Advertising

When a firm is attempting to reach a large and widespread market, it is almost forced to rely on mass selling through advertising. Over the past 10 years, spending on advertising has more than doubled to $110 billion per year. Although advertising through mass media such as network television and large circulation magazines can be expensive, the cost per contact may be very low. For example, if a firm spends $100,000 to sponsor a television program that reaches 10 million viewers, the cost per viewer is only a penny.

Types of Advertising   Advertising tends to fall into two broad categories, product and institutional. *Product advertising* primarily aims at informing and persuading consumers about a good or service. *Institutional advertising* attempts to create a favorable image for the business firm. Some retail stores use institutional advertising to increase customer goodwill by stressing the store's prestige, personal service, and quality merchandise.

The Advertising Agency   Most advertising campaigns are planned with the help of an advertising agency, which provides specialized assistance in creating copy and selecting media. The term *copy* refers to the advertising message, both written and visual material. *Media* is the means of delivering the advertising message to the target consumers. The agency may also perform market research and assist in developing marketing strategy.

Advertising agencies are normally paid 15 percent of the media price for their services. Suppose, for example, the XYZ Corporation spends $1 million to purchase advertising space in magazines. The magazine bills the XYZ Corporation for the cost of the space and remits 15 percent or $150,000 to the agency employed by XYZ. In other words, the agency, although employed by the advertiser, is compensated indirectly by the media.

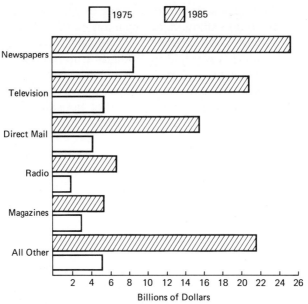

FIGURE 10.4   Spending on Advertising by Medium,
1975 and 1985
Source: Advertising Age.

Advertising Media   In planning an advertising campaign, the
marketing manager attempts to select the best media to reach the
target consumers. The manager must also consider which medium is
most effective in presenting the advertising message. The most
popular advertising media are newspapers, television, direct mail,
magazines, and radio. Advertising expenditures by medium are
shown in Figure 10.4.

  1   *Newspapers* are the most widely used advertising
medium. They offer widespread coverage in specific geographic
areas since a large percentage of households subscribe to a
newspaper. Moreover, newspaper advertising is highly flexible
because ads can be submitted and printed within a few hours.
For these reasons most retail advertising is carried in
newspapers.
      One disadvantage of newspapers is the lack of reader
selectivity by interest group. Newspapers are read by all
different types of people, and it is difficult to reach a specific
target market without wasted circulation. Why doesn't Rolls
Royce advertise in local newspapers?
  2   *Direct Mail* is highly selective. It can be used to zero in
on the target consumers. The effectiveness of direct mail
advertising is largely dependent on the mailing list. Some firms
specialize in selling mailing lists broken down by location,
income, age, occupation, special interests, and other

characteristics. A good mailing lists permits the advertiser to direct the advertising message at prime prospects.

The major disadvantage of direct mail advertising is "waste paper circulation." This means that many people throw away the advertisements unopened.

3 *Television* is the fastest growing advertising medium. Since television appeals to two senses—sight and hearing—the impact of the advertising message is increased. Television can be used to reach a limited geographic market through local stations. Some selectivity by interest group can be achieved through program and time selection.

The key drawback of television advertising is its cost. One-minute spots on prime time network television can cost $150,000 to more than $1,000,000. However, the cost of local commercials is much less.

4 *Magazines* are published for nearly every special-interest group, enabling the advertiser to pinpoint the target market. Moreover, magazines can print high-quality color advertisements and each copy may be read by several consumers. Magazines tend to be an inflexible medium since copy must be submitted 1 to 2 months before publication.

5 *Radio* offers the advertiser a relatively low-cost medium with geographic selectivity through local stations. It is also possible to achieve some listener selectivity by choosing the station, program, and time. As in the case of television, radio advertising must be heard when it is broadcast or it is lost forever.

6 *Other media* include outdoor signs, catalogs, point-of-purchase displays, and business publications.

PRICE

Price is the fourth element in the marketing mix. The importance of pricing cannot be overestimated, for it affects both sales volume and profits. Of course, some firms that operate in highly competitive markets have virtually no control over price. For example, most farmers must sell their products at the current market price, which is determined by the forces of supply and demand. However, the vast majority of producers and retailers exercise some control over price.

Pricing Considerations

A basic law of economics is that more of a product will be sold at a low price than at a high price. For this reason, some firms rely on low price to generate sales. This is the strategy used by discount stores and many supermarkets that are willing to accept a lower profit margin in order to gain increased volume. An old saying in retailing is, "A fast nickel is better than a slow dime."

Let's take an example. You will recall that the gross profit margin (or markup) is the difference between the selling price of a product and its cost. It is usually expressed as a percent of the

---

ISSUE   ADVERTISING: CONSUMER FRIEND OR FOE?

Nearly each new year brings a record in business expenditures on advertising. This mass-marketing tool has proven to be highly effective in promoting a wide variety of goods and services. But is advertising beneficial or harmful to the buying public? A growing number of critics, including many consumer advocates and economists, are convinced that advertising is generally wasteful and misleading. On the other hand, the defenders of advertising are quick to claim that both individual consumers and society as a whole realize significant benefits from advertising. Their main arguments fall into four major categories.

   1   Advertising provides valuable information to consumers. How can shoppers make intelligent buying decisions unless they have information about product features, prices, and buying locations? According to *Printers' Ink,* a trade magazine, "advertising is the most economical way of bridging the gap between the man with an idea, a product, or a service for sale and the man who can benefit from buying it."
   2   Advertising promotes competition by making it easier to introduce new products and services to the buying public.
   3   Advertising leads to lower production costs and therefore to lower prices by encouraging mass production. Without advertising, many firms would not generate sufficient sales volume to realize the advantages of mass production.
   4   Advertising pays for mass media. "Free" radio and television, as well as most of the costs of newspapers and magazines, are paid for through advertising expenditures.

---

selling price; for example, a product selling for $1 that cost $0.70 would have a markup of 30 percent. Suppose the Super-Value Toy Store can generate sales of $200,000 with an average gross profit margin of 30 percent and $500,000 with a 20 percent margin. The difference between the 30 percent and 20 percent markups represents a 10 percent price reduction.

Sales	×	Gross Profit Margin	=	Gross Profit
$200,000	×	30%	=	$60,000
500,000	×	20%	=	100,000

ISSUE ADVERTISING: CONSUMER FRIEND OR FOE? (Cont.)

The critics are unconvinced by these arguments. They claim most advertising is not informational but persuasive. For example, the majority of television commercials are designed to persuade consumers to buy without providing significant information. Some detractors complain that much advertising is misleading and attempts to manipulate consumers through emotional appeals.

Some economists believe advertising increases rather than reduces the price of goods. They point out that most advertising is competitive—that is, it is intended to increase the sales of one brand at the expense of another. Therefore, competitive advertising campaigns often cancel each other, but the costs are passed on to the consumer in the form of higher prices.

The critics also blame advertising for the "dismal programming" offered by the television networks. They argue that most people would prefer pay television if the right programs were available.

Finally, the opponents believe advertising reduces the level of competition in our economy. According to Ralph Nader and Aileen Cowan, "Competition in the marketplace is rapidly being reduced to competition in advertising as businessmen spend more and more money on inflated and deceptive claims rather than improving products or lowering prices. The result is both the exploitation of the consumer and the undermining of serious, meaningful competition."

There you have the arguments. Is advertising your friend or foe? More to the point, do you favor less advertising by business firms?

In this case the lower profit per dollar of sales is more than offset by the increase in sales. The result is an increase in gross profit.

Another factor influencing price is cost. Over the long run, prices must be high enough to permit the firm to cover its costs. Consistently selling below cost results in losses, which will ultimately lead to failure.

Competition also affects prices. A single service station in a small isolated town can charge a high price for gasoline, but a dealer located in a city with hundreds of service stations must gear the price to meet competition.

Some firms are able to charge higher prices because of superior product or promotion. Fuller Brushes command premium prices because of the high product quality plus vigorous promotion through door-to-door selling.

Pricing Strategies

Two extreme pricing strategies are skim-the-cream pricing and penetration pricing.

Skim-the-Cream Pricing   This strategy involves charging a high price in order to achieve large profits per unit. Skim-the-cream pricing is typically used when a firm introduces a new and unique product with strong consumer appeal. Mercedes Benz follows this strategy in pricing its automobiles.

Skim-the-cream pricing offers several advantages. A high price may suggest superior quality to the consumer, thereby enhancing the image of the product. Since consumers welcome price reductions, a high initial price may be lowered at a later date to broaden market appeal.

Penetration Pricing   Charging a very low price for products may permit a firm to capture a significant portion of the total market in a very short time. Penetration pricing is also effective in opening a new market segment or in discouraging competitors from entering a market.

In 1985, Dac Software advertised a new accounting software package at a special introductory price of $49.95. Similar software sold from $100 to $800. The company was swamped with 15,000 orders after its ads appeared in computer magazines. Moreover, the low price generated a great deal of publicity in the form of articles and comments in the computer and business press. Dac's pricing strategy apparently tapped a segment of the market consisting of very small businesses and home computer users that had not previously purchased accounting software.

THE MARKETING MIX

You will recall that the marketing mix is that combination of product, place, promotion, and price aimed at reaching the target market. It would be a serious mistake to think that there is an ideal marketing mix for any market. Business firms are continually experimenting to improve their marketing strategies. In fact, firms in the same industry may have vastly different mixes. Revlon and Avon both manufacture cosmetics and toiletries, but each firm uses different place, promotion, and price strategies.

Often a unique marketing mix can be very profitable. In the highly competitive washing machine market, Maytag Company earns a 10 percent return on sales, which is three times the industry average. Maytag's product strategy emphasizes quality, reliability, and service. The company is slow to introduce new models until major engineering improvements are developed. Maytag's machines sell for around $500, a $100 more than its competitors' top models. Distribution is through a sales force that calls directly on selected retail dealers. These retailers are given a high profit margin in return for which they are expected to carry a sizable inventory of Maytag parts and train their service personnel to repair Maytag machines. Consumer advertising emphasizes quality and reliability.

The result of this successful marketing strategy is a 25 percent return on investment, one of the highest of any firm in the United States.

SUMMARY

The marketing mix consists of the Four Ps: product, place, promotion, and price.

Business firms must create new products in order to meet changing consumer needs. Product planning and development is difficult and expensive. To reduce the chances of failure, many firms test new products in a limited market before committing themselves to full production.

Channels of distribution are the routes that goods take as they move from the producer to the retailer. These channels often include retailers and wholesalers.

Large retail firms are growing in importance due to their advantages in purchasing, advertising, and specialization of management. The field of retailing is subject to rapid changes, and retailers must adapt to these changes in order to survive.

Wholesalers perform a variety of services for both producers and retailers. These services include selling, storing, transporting, and financing. Some manufacturers and retailers prefer to bypass the wholesaler, but this requires undertaking the wholesaler's functions. The two major categories of wholesalers are: (1) merchant wholesalers, who take title to the merchandise they sell and typically offer a broad range of services; and (2) agent middlemen, who do not take title to merchandise and only perform the selling function.

Promotion is informing and persuading consumers about a firm's product, place, or price. The combination of personal selling, advertising, and sales promotion used by a firm is called the promotional mix. It is determined by the target market and the nature of the product.

Personal selling is effective in tailoring the sales message to the individual customer, but the cost per contact is high. Advertising is often used to reach consumer markets that consist of large numbers of potential customers. Product advertising aims at selling a good or service, while institutional advertising attempts to create a favorable image for the firm. Advertising agencies assist in creating copy and selecting media. The major types of media are newspapers, direct mail, television, magazines, and radio. Sales promotion includes point-of-purchase displays, coupons, samples, and contests.

Price influences both sales volume and profits. Two major pricing strategies are skim-the-cream and penetration pricing.

There is no perfect marketing strategy and business firms are constantly adjusting their marketing mixes. The profitability of a firm largely depends on its success in identifying consumer needs and developing effective product, place, promotional, and price strategies to meet these needs.

SELF-EXAMINATION QUESTIONS

The following questions are based on the Chapter Objectives listed at the beginning of the chapter. Test yourself by circling the letter preceding the answer that *best* completes the statement or answers the question. The answers to the Self-Examination Questions are in the appendix at the end of the textbook.

1. During which stage of a successful product's life cycle would you expect sales to level off and profits to decline? (A) product development and test marketing; (B) decline stage; (C) introduction stage; (D) maturity stage.

2. Channels of distribution: (A) are the routes that goods take as they move from producers to consumers (or users); (B) always involve wholesalers and retailers; (C) are rarely used with penetration pricing; (D) all of these; (E) none of these.

3. Firms that take title to the merchandise they sell and usually provide a full line of services to retailers and manufacturers may be classified as: (A) merchant wholesalers; (B) agent middlemen; (C) manufacturers' agents; (D) both A and B; (E) none of these.

4. A major part of the promotional mix is: (A) franchising; (B) commercialization; (C) channels of distribution; (D) product planning and development; (E) none of these.

5. A strategy calling for charging a high price to maximize profit per unit and enhance the image of product quality is called: (A) profit-promotion pricing; (B) cost-plus pricing; (C) skim-the-cream pricing; (D) penetration pricing; (E) none of these.

APPENDIX

SELLING
YOURSELF

Selling yourself does not imply selling out. It means persuading others that what you have to offer will benefit them. People who can effectively sell themselves are more likely to get what they want—the order, the job, the date, the promotion, and so on.

The first step in successful selling is to know your product and believe in its value. Knowing yourself is not easy; self-analysis requires honesty and courage. As Socrates said, "Know your strengths and your weaknesses, your potentialities, your aims and purposes; take stock of yourself."

Start by making a list of your positive and negative attributes. Are you interesting or boring, optimistic or pessimistic, sensitive or insensitive, enthusiastic or lethargic, dependable or untrustworthy? Next list your skills, accomplishments, and talents as well as your weaknesses and shortcomings. Do not be discouraged if your drawbacks outnumber your strengths. Most people are their own worst critics.

Build your self-esteem by focusing on your positive attributes. Each of us has special gifts, talents, and abilities. Too often we take these gifts for granted and discount their importance. Do not belittle yourself. You have something of value and importance to offer. If you do not believe in yourself, can you expect others to?

Once you have learned to know and believe in yourself, selling is a skill that can be learned by practice. There are five basic steps in selling:

1   *Prospecting* is the process of finding the person (prospect) in need of you or your product.
2   *Approaching* refers to meeting prospects, getting their attention, and giving a presentation (and demonstration) tailored to their needs.
3   *Overcoming objections* means listening to negative responses and converting resistance into acceptance.
4   *Closing* is motivating the prospect to make the decision you want. It involves asking for the order, the date, the job, and so forth.
5   *Following up* is making sure the prospect is satisfied and will buy in the future.

Ministers, politicians, parents, children, students, employees, and managers—everyone sells. Remember, selling is the act of convincing or persuading others to do what you want. The most effective salespeople honestly believe in themselves, their product, and their company.

If you are dissatisfied with your ability to influence others, consider taking a course in personal selling. Better yet, find a part-time job in personal sales. The experience will develop your selling skills, increase your confidence, and build your self-esteem while adding to your income.

Student _____

BUILDING A BUSINESS VOCABULARY

Directions: Match the terms with their definitions by writing the letter in the appropriate blank.

a. Channels of Distribution
b. Media
c. Skim-the-Cream
d. Agent Middlemen
e. Copy
f. Product Life Cycle
g. Advertising Agency
h. Merchant Wholesalers
i. Product Planning and Development
j. Scrambled Merchandising
k. Sales Promotion
l. Institutional Advertising
m. Franchise
n. Promotional Mix
o. Penetration Pricing

_____A_____ 1. The routes that goods take as they move from the producer to the consumer.

_____N_____ 2. The combination of advertising, personal selling, and sales promotion used by a firm to promote its product.

_____J_____ 3. The mixing of different types of merchandise together in a retail store.

_____H_____ 4. Middlemen who take title to merchandise that is resold to retailers.

_____F_____ 5. The stages of a product's life beginning with the product idea, moving through its development, introduction, growth and maturity, and ending with its decline and abandonment.

_____L_____ 6. The use of advertising to create a favorable public image for the firm.

_____e_____ 7. The advertising message.

_____M_____ 8. An agreement whereby an established corporation provides training, operating assistance, and advertising support to an independent business firm in return for a fee.

_____c_____ 9. A pricing strategy that calls for a high initial price to maximize profit per unit.

_____d_____ 10. Limited-service wholesalers who do not take title to the merchandise they sell.

_____ 11. A firm that provides expert assistance in preparing copy and selecting media.

_____ 12. Using low price to rapidly capture a major portion of the market.

_____ 13. Creating new products and modifying existing ones to meet changing consumer needs.

_____ 14. Promotional activities other than advertising and personal selling aimed at expanding sales through point-of-purchase displays, contests, samples, and coupons.

_____ 15. The means of carrying advertising to the target market.

Student _____

REVIEWING MAJOR CONCEPTS

1. What advantages do large chain stores enjoy over small retailers? Does the small retailer have any advantages?

2. Why has the trend toward self-service retailing encouraged manufacturers to spend more on advertising?

3. What are the advantages and drawbacks of franchising to the franchisee?

4. What services do wholesalers perform?

5. "You can eliminate the wholesaler, but you cannot eliminate the wholesaler's functions." Explain this statement.

6. What two major considerations influence the promotional mix?

7. Identify the major advantages and disadvantages of personal selling and advertising.

8. Explain how a retailer might increase total profit by cutting price.

Student _____

SOLVING PROBLEMS AND CASES

1. *Case:* Mel Roberts

   Mel Roberts is a wealthy inventor who recently developed an electronic mouse trap that lures mice and rats with an ultrasonic tone (which cannot be heard by the human ear) and kills them instantly with a tiny laser beam. Mel has tested his invention, which he calls "Rat-Zap," and found it foolproof. He has contracted with a manufacturer to produce the trap at a cost of $15 each.

   Mel is uncertain how to market the product and he has asked your advice. Outline a marketing strategy for Rat-Zap.

2. *Case:* Van Meter Candy Company

The Van Meter Candy Company, located in San Francisco, California, is a family-owned firm that produces inexpensive hard candies and chocolates. The firm is managed by two brothers— Herman, who supervises production, and Adolph, who handles sales. The firm sells its entire output to chain supermarkets and variety stores headquartered in the San Francisco area. The candy is resold to consumers by the pound or in packages with the retailer's brand name.

Last year the company's employees voted to be represented by a union and won a 25 percent wage increase. In order to offset rising productions costs, the brothers invested all available cash in automated equipment. The new equipment doubled production capacity and reduced per-unit manufacturing costs when the plant is operating at full capacity.

The company is now faced with the problem of marketing the increased output. No funds are available to employ additional sales personnel. Adolph Van Meter wants to expand distribution, but he is uncertain how this can be accomplished.

What suggestions can you offer the Van Meter brothers?

3. What advertising media are the following firms likely to use? Briefly explain your choices.

   a. A small manufacturer of fishing rods.

   b. A department store located in a city of 50,000.

   c. A large whiskey distiller.

   d. A bicycle shop located near a college campus.

   e. A stock brokerage firm with four offices located in a large city.

4. *Case:* The Computer Base

   Six years ago, Frank Wong opened a small computer store called The Computer Base in a large southern city. Only 20 years old at the time, Frank had always been interested in electronics, assembling his first computer while still a teenager. His small store, located several blocks from a suburban shopping area, at first catered mainly to hobbyists and home computer users. Most of the store's inventory consisted of computer kits and electronic components such as chips and computer boards.

Before dropping out of college, Frank had taken several engineering and technical courses, but he had no background in business. Despite his inexperience, The Computer Base was an immediate success, with expanding sales and profits in each of the first 6 years. In response to the growing demand, Frank added to his inventory and hired two hobbyists to help wait on customers.

Over the last 3 years, Frank noticed a significant change in his clientele. Fewer customers were interested in kits; most wanted to purchase fully assembled computers. Moreover, a growing proportion of his customers were small business managers and professionals who wanted to install computer systems in their firms. Typically the business buyers were unfamiliar with the technical aspects of computers. They were seeking computer applications to solve specific business problems. Moreover, these customers expected extensive support services, and they wanted help from someone who understood their problems.

Frank was unsure about the future of his business. Despite past success, there was growing competition from other computer stores, mail-order firms, and manufacturers' sales representatives. If he focused on the small business market, he would have to expand his inventory and floor space and add to his sales staff. This would require additional financing. Moreover, he had built his business by offering discount prices, but he wondered if he could continue to discount while expanding customer services.

a. List the major facts in the case.

b. What specific problems does Frank face?

c. What are the solutions to these problems?

chapter

FINANCE

In this chapter we introduce several major topics related to business finance. The first section explores the role of financial management and describes the major sources of funds to support business operations. Then we turn to a challenging problem of corporate finance—the selection of securities to raise long-term funds. In the concluding section the viewpoint shifts to that of the investor. We are concerned with how the different securities markets operate and with the procedures involved in buying and selling corporate stocks and bonds.

CHAPTER OBJECTIVES

1. Identify and briefly explain four responsibilities of the financial manager.

2. Distinguish between cash flow and profits.

3. Describe three major sources of short-term financing for business firms.

4. Name the three sources of long-term funds.

5. Contrast and compare common stock, preferred stock, and bonds.

6. Name at least four factors that determine which type of corporate security will be sold to raise additional capital.

7. Describe the role of investment bankers.

8. Contrast and compare stock exchanges and the over-the-counter market.

9. Briefly explain how investment companies operate.

FINANCIAL MANAGEMENT

Make no mistake about it, money is the lifeblood of business. Inadequate funds will limit a firm's expansion and hinder operations. Indeed, a chronic lack of financial resources can lead to termination of the firm through bankruptcy. Witness, for example, the 1984 financial collapse of Storage Technology, a major electronics firm.

Financial management includes all those activities involved in acquiring and using funds to achieve a firm's objectives. The financial manager is concerned with ensuring that adequate funds are available to carry out essential activities. The job involves not only raising money but also cutting costs, choosing among alternative uses of funds, conserving assets, and keeping records on how funds are used. The financial manager is responsible for paying bills, collecting accounts receivable, borrowing money, investing idle cash, and developing financial plans. Depending on the firm, the chief financial officer is known by any of a variety of titles—treasurer, controller, financial vice-president, and so on.

Cash Flow

Inexperienced managers often overlook an important fact: *A profitable firm can go broke!* This is because profits and cash are *not* the same thing. A profitable company may use its cash to build up inventories, purchase additional equipment, and expand credit sales. However, if the financial manager is not careful, the firm may find itself short of cash to pay wages, accounts payable, taxes, and other expenses. On the other hand, it is possible for a firm to have surplus cash beyond the immediate needs of the business. Idle funds are a financial waste since they could be invested and earn a return.

Cash management attempts to balance estimated cash receipts against expected cash payments in order to keep cash on hand at an ideal level. Figure 11.1 illustrates a firm's cash flow. Cash is received from cash sales, payments from credit customers, and funds from creditors such as bank loans. The outflow of funds consists of cash purchases, wages, payments to creditors, and other cash expenses. The difference between cash receipts and cash payments represents the firm's cash flow. The cash manager must ensure that there are adequate funds to take care of day-to-day transactions plus a safety stock for unexpected needs. Any cash over and above these requirements should be invested. Temporary surplus cash is often used to purchase interest-paying U.S. Treasury securities that mature in a few weeks or months.

The major device for controlling cash flow is the cash budget, which was introduced in Chapter 7. This budget shows the cash balance at the beginning of the period, the estimated cash receipts and payments during the period, and the ending cash balance.

Sources of Short-Term Funds

Short-term funds are used to finance the day-to-day operations of the firm—to purchase inventory, finance accounts receivable, and pay wages and other expenses. The source of much of these funds is

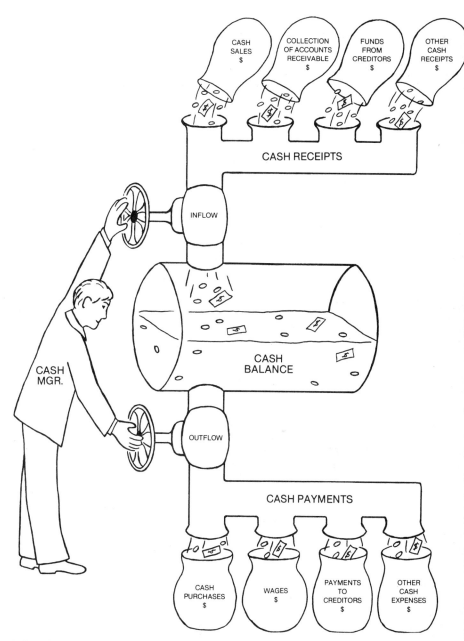

FIGURE 11.1   The Firm's Cash Flow

debts that must be paid off within a year. In contrast, long-term financing is used to purchase fixed assets such as equipment and buildings. It would be foolish to finance the purchase of a machine tool with a 5-year life by borrowing from a bank on a 90-day note. The debt would be due long before the machine had generated sufficient revenues to pay for itself.

The major sources of short-term financing for business firms are: (1) trade creditors, (2) banks, (3) factors, and (4) certain other sources such as sales finance companies, the Small Business Administration, and retained profits.

Trade Creditors You may recall that the balance sheet lists a current liability called *accounts payable,* which represents short-term debts owed to suppliers. These debts are commonly referred to as *open-book accounts,* and they reflect the purchase of merchandise, supplies, or other assets on credit. The vast majority of business transactions involve purchases on credit; open-book accounts are the major sources of short-term funds.

Suppose Waterbeds Unlimited, a retailer in Sacramento, places an order for waterbed equipment and supplies with I. A. M. Waterbeds, a distributor. The materials are delivered, and the store receives an *invoice* (bill), as illustrated in Figure 11.2.

The credit terms on the invoice, $^3/_{10}$; $^n/_{30}$, mean that if the bill is

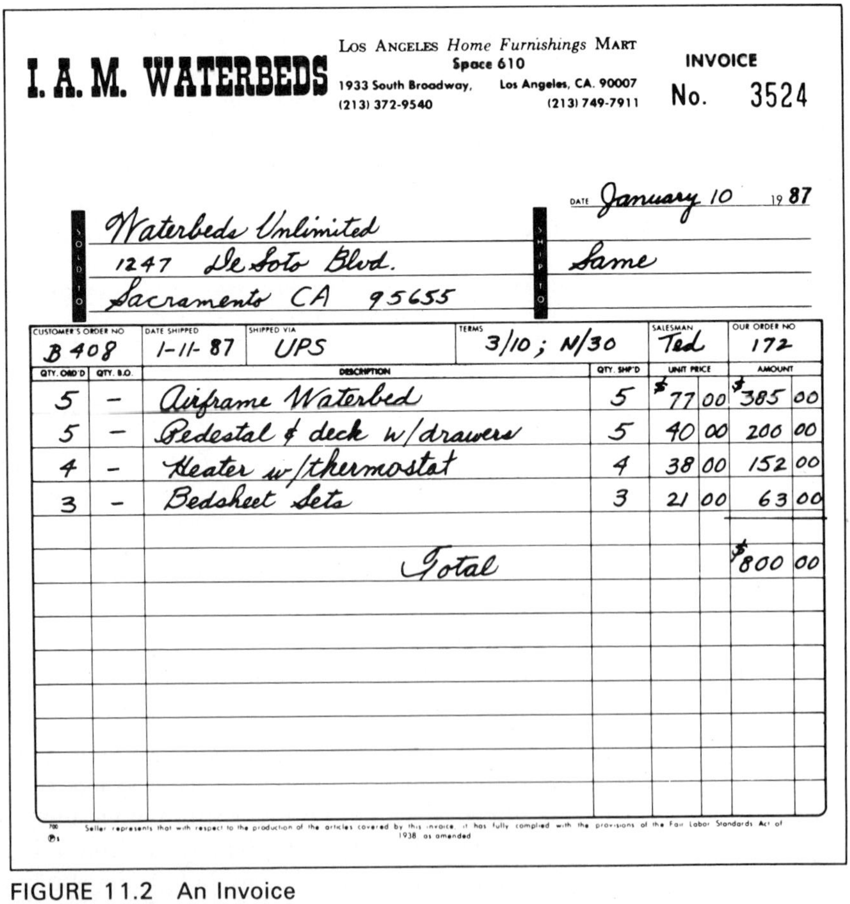
I. A. M. WATERBEDS

Los Angeles *Home Furnishings* Mart
Space 610
1933 South Broadway, Los Angeles, CA. 90007
(213) 372-9540 (213) 749-7911

INVOICE
No. 3524

DATE January 10 19 87

SOLD TO: Waterbeds Unlimited, 1247 De Soto Blvd., Sacramento CA 95655
SHIP TO: Same

CUSTOMER'S ORDER NO	DATE SHIPPED	SHIPPED VIA	TERMS	SALESMAN	OUR ORDER NO
B 408	1-11-87	UPS	3/10; N/30	Ted	172

QTY. ORD'D	QTY. B.O.	DESCRIPTION	QTY. SHP'D	UNIT PRICE	AMOUNT
5	–	Airframe Waterbed	5	$77 00	$385 00
5	–	Pedestal & deck w/drawers	5	40 00	200 00
4	–	Heater w/thermostat	4	38 00	152 00
3	–	Bedsheet Sets	3	21 00	63 00
		Total			$800 00

Seller represents that with respect to the production of the articles covered by this invoice, it has fully complied with the provisions of the Fair Labor Standards Act of 1938 as amended

FIGURE 11.2 An Invoice
Courtesy I. A. M. Waterbeds.

paid within 10 days of the date on the invoice, the retailer may take a 3 percent cash discount; but the bill must be paid in any case within 30 days. If Waterbeds Unlimited elects to pay on or before January 20, it will remit $776 ($800 less the $24 discount), but thereafter the entire $800 is due and must be paid by February 9.

The purpose of the cash discount is to encourage early payments. Business firms always try to take advantage of cash discounts because of the substantial savings. In the above example, failure to pay within 10 days means that the retailer has use of the funds for an extra 20 days at a cost of 3 percent. On an annual basis, this is 54 percent interest.[1]

Banks   Commercial banks earn interest income by loaning out a part of their customers' deposits to individuals and business firms. Often banks will grant a business firm a *line of credit* to meet short-term financial needs. For example, the Old Wave Boutique expects to experience strong demand for its fall fashions. An additional $25,000 is needed to build up inventory to handle the anticipated increase in sales. The store, which has a good credit rating, arranges a line of credit with a commercial bank. The bank agrees to make available up to $25,000 in loans on demand. The loans are repaid as cash income is realized from sales.

Most bank loans are secured by *promissory notes,* which are written promises to repay a certain sum of money plus interest on a specific date. Promissory notes are often used by trade creditors because they are more formal than open-book accounts. In Figure 11.3,

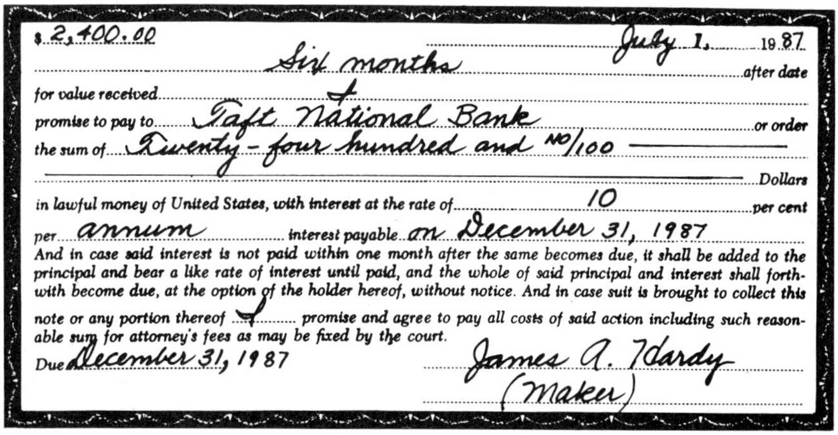

FIGURE 11.3 A Promissory Note
Courtesy of W. M. S. Lloyd Co., Inc.

---

[1]The real rate of interest is the cost of borrowing money for a year. Using a 360-day "interest year," 3 percent for 20 days equals 54 percent for 360 days (360 ÷ 20 = 18 × 3% = 54%). It would make sense to borrow funds at up to 53% interest to take advantage of the cash discount.

what sum of money will James Hardy pay to the Taft National Bank on December 31?

Factors   Accounts receivable represent charge account debts owed to a business firm by its customers. *Factors* are collection agencies that purchase accounts receivable at less than face value. Suppose, for example, that the Value Furniture Company has $70,000 in accounts receivable and needs to raise cash to pay bills. A factor may be willing to purchase the receivables at a discounted price, say $60,000. The factor is concerned with the age of the receivables (how long the debts have been outstanding) and the credit standing of the customers. There is a risk of losing money if the collection expenses (including bad debts) exceed the difference between the face value of the receivables and the purchase price.

It should be noted that some firms borrow money using their accounts receivables as collateral (or security) for the loan. Such loans are made by banks, factors, and finance companies. In this case, the risk of bad debts and collection expenses are borne by the borrower.

Other Sources   There are a variety of institutions that provide short-term financing to business. Commercial finance companies make short-term loans to business firms using the borrower's inventory, accounts receivable, or other assets as collateral. A retailer may sell customers' installment contracts to a sales finance company to raise funds.

The Small Business Administration makes loans to small businesses that are unable to secure financing elsewhere. Other government agencies, such as the Veteran's Administration, guarantee certain types of business loans made by commercial banks and other financial institutions.

Some companies use retained earnings to meet short-term financial needs. The portion of net profits reinvested in the business may be used for financing current assets or paying current liabilities. However, it is generally considered a good practice to reserve retained earnings for long-term financing.

Sources of Long-Term Funds   Money raised through long-term financing is normally used for the purchase of fixed assets—equipment, buildings, and land. There are three major sources of long-term funds: (1) equity, (2) debt, and (3) internally generated funds. *Equity* refers to ownership. Additional funds may become available through increased investment by the proprietor or partners, or through the sale of more shares of stock by a corporation. Sources of long-term loans include banks, insurance companies, and savings and loan associations. Corporations may borrow by selling bonds to the public.

The phrase *internally generated funds* refers to retained earnings and depreciation. Most successful firms plow back a part of

ISSUE ELECTRONIC BANKING COMES OF AGE

Back in the good old days before money was invented, people traded by barter—directly swapping goods and services. Slowly, over the centuries, coins and then paper money were developed to serve as a more convenient means of paying for goods and services. Then, back about the time of Columbus and Queen Isabella, someone figured out that checks would be an even more convenient way of making payments. Today, 40 billion checks are processed each year at an average cost of about 50¢ per check. The next logical move is to do away with most of the costly paper, and this is where electronic banking comes in.

The first step was the automatic teller machine (ATM) that enables customers to make deposits and withdrawals of cash at convenient times and locations. There are now more than 60,000 ATMs, and this figure is expected to nearly double in the next 5 years. Banks are hard at work creating electronic networks that link up ATMs nationally and permit retail funds to be transferred among computers at different banks. Such networks encourage the use of point-of-sale (POS) terminals in retail outlets. It is hoped that customer debit cards will largely replace checks. The debit card is inserted into the POS terminal, and the amount of the purchase is electronically transferred from the customer's account to that of the store.

A number of banks are offering electronic home banking. These systems allow customers with a personal computer to communicate with the bank's data base through ordinary telephone lines. Users can switch funds among accounts and direct the bank to pay bills.

Electronic payments is both an opportunity and a threat to banks. A growing number of nonbank firms are creating computer networks to capture a share of the electronic payments market. For example, Sears has moved aggressively into the field.

Electronic payments is not without its critics. Opponents claim that the systems are vulnerable to theft. Electronic banking also poses a threat to personal privacy since computers will have to keep detailed records of each individual's financial activities. Finally, electronic payments eliminates "float"—the delay between the time a check is written and the time the money is taken out of the account—which some people and businesses depend on to stay solvent.

net profits into the business. But why add depreciation and net profits together? *Depreciation* is an expense representing the estimated annual decline in value of plant and equipment. However, depreciation is a noncash expense that is subtracted from income to find net profit. The business firm does not give up any cash for depreciation as it does with other expenses. After all, the plant and equipment being depreciated were paid for when they were acquired. Therefore, depreciation lowers accounting profits without reducing cash income. For this reason, depreciation is added to net income to determine total sources of funds from operations.

How important are internally generated funds? Over the past 20 years, retained earnings and depreciation have averaged 60 percent of all corporate financing.

Managers must be extremely careful making long-term financial decisions. A poor decision may saddle the firm with problems for many years. For example, a 10-year, high-interest loan may be so costly that the borrower is unable to earn profits.

Both proprietorships and partnerships are extremely limited in their ability to raise long-term funds. Banks and other financial institutions are hesitant to make long-term loans to these firms because of their limited life. On the other hand, large and established corporations may raise long-term funds by marketing corporate securities.

CORPORATE SECURITIES

There are two major categories of corporate securities: stocks and bonds. Stocks may be further divided into preferred stock and common stock.

Although corporations may borrow long-term funds through term loans that mature (come due) in 1 to 20 years, a more common method of debt financing is the sale of bonds.

Bonds

A *bond* may be considered a special type of promissory note with a long-term maturity. Corporations normally sell bonds with maturity (or due) dates of between 5 and 50 years, although the majority of bonds mature in 10 to 30 years.

The bondholder is a creditor of the corporation. Bonds carry promises to repay the amount borrowed (called the *principal*) on a specific date and to pay a fixed amount of interest usually computed on an annual basis. Most corporate bonds are sold in denominations of $1000 each.

Bondholders stand ahead of stockholders (owners) in case the corporation fails. In other words, if the firm goes bankrupt and if funds are available after paying off current liabilities, the bondholder must be repaid before stockholders receive any payment. In addition, bondholders have a legal right to interest payments. If a corporation fails to pay bond interest, the bondholders may take legal action.

There are many different types of corporate bonds. We shall explore only a few of the major ones.

1 *Registered and Bearer Bonds.* A registered bond has the owner's name on the face of the bond certificate and is recorded in the corporation's books. Interest payments are made by checks mailed to the bondholder. In contrast, bearer bonds (also called *coupon bonds*) carry no evidence of ownership. To receive interest, the bondholder merely removes a dated coupon attached to the bond. The obvious advantage of the registered bond is that the owner is protected from loss or theft of the certificate.

2 *Mortgage and Debenture Bonds.* Mortgage bonds are secured by property owned by the corporation. Large and successful corporations may sell debentures, which are backed by the general credit of the corporation rather than any specific collateral.

3 *Callable Bonds.* Many bonds contain a *call option,* which permits the issuing corporation to redeem the bond before the maturity date. For example, suppose that in 1980 the XYZ Corporation sold $20 million worth of bonds with a 14 percent interest rate. The bonds mature in 20 years (2000). Each bond has a call price of $1025 (that is, $25 above the maturity value or par value of the bond). If the XYZ Corporation "calls" the bonds, it must pay the bondholders $1025 for each $1000 bond. Should interest rates decline below 14 percent, it may benefit the corporation to redeem the bonds and sell a new issue at a lower interest rate.

4 *Convertible Bonds.* Some corporations make their bonds exchangeable for a fixed number of shares of stock. This convertible feature is intended to make the bonds more attractive to investors. For example, a $1000 bond might be convertible into 20 shares of common stock. If the price of the stock is less than $50 a share, it would not pay the bondholder to convert. However, if the stock price rises above $50 per share, the price of the bond would be expected to increase proportionally. At $60 per share the bond would be worth approximately $1200 (20 shares $\times$ $60 = $1200). All convertible bonds are callable so that the corporation can force conversion. If bondholders convert their bonds to stock, the corporation is no longer faced with the problem of repayment of the debt.

Figure 11.4 shows a typical corporate bond. Notice that the par value (or maturity value) is $1000 and the stated rate of interest is 16¼ percent. When does the bond mature?

Common Stock

Common stock represents ownership of the corporation. The funds received by a corporation from the sale of common stock are not

FIGURE 11.4 A Corporate Bond
Courtesy Pacific Gas and Electric Company.

repaid as in the case of bonds. A common stockholder can sell his or her shares to other investors, but there is no guarantee against loss. Figure 11.5 illustrates a common stock certificate.

Par value is the dollar amount printed on the stock certificate. It is a confusing term because there is no relationship between par value and the market price of the stock. To avoid confusion, some corporations issue "no par" stock.

The common stockholder may receive a share of the corporation's profits in the form of dividends. However, the stockholder is not guaranteed a dividend. The board of directors, after considering the amount of profits and the firm's financial needs, may vote to declare a cash dividend. One alternative to a cash payout is a stock dividend, whereby common stockholders receive additional shares of stock instead of a cash payment.

Common stock nearly always carries voting rights. As the voting owners of the corporation, common stockholders elect the board of directors.

Preferred Stock

A second type of ownership security is *preferred stock,* which received its name because of certain preferences and priorities over common stock. Should the corporation fail, the preferred stockholders stand ahead of common stockholders for any remaining assets. Moreover, preferred stockholders must be paid their full dividend before common stockholders may receive any dividend.

The dividend on preferred stock is nearly always a fixed amount.[2] Most preferred is sold in denominations of $100 per share. Therefore, the XYZ Corporation's 15 percent preferred would have a dividend of $15 per share. In most cases, preferred stock does not carry the right to vote.

Preferred stock may be either *cumulative* or *noncumulative.* In the case of cumulative preferred, missed dividends accumulate and must be paid before common stockholders receive any dividend. Suppose, for example, the XYZ Corporation earned no profits in 1986 and 1987 and did not declare dividends on its 12 percent cumulative preferred stock in those years. In 1988 a large profit was earned and both preferred and common dividends were paid. Each share of preferred would receive a $36 dividend since a $12 per year dividend, missed in 1986 and 1987, accumulated and was paid in 1988. With noncumulative preferred, missed dividends are not carried forward to future years.

Both common and preferred stock represent ownership, while bonds are debt. In a sense, preferred stock stands between common stock and bonds with some of the characteristics of each. Table 11.1 outlines the major features of bonds, preferred stock, and common stock.

[2]An exception is participating preferred, which is very rare today.

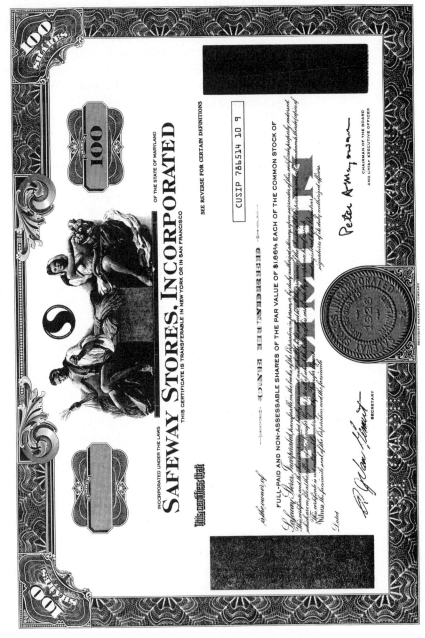

FIGURE 11.5   A Corporate Stock
Courtesy Safeway.

TABLE 11.1 Summary of Corporate Securities

Bonds	Preferred Stocks	Common Stocks
1. Represent debt.	1. Represent ownership.	1. Represent ownership.
2. Must be repaid.	2. No repayment.	2. No repayment.
3. Pay interest.	3. Pay dividends if declared.	3. Pay dividends if declared.
4. Interest is a fixed amount.	4. Dividends normally fixed in amount.	4. Dividends are not limited in amount.
5. Interest is an expense paid before taxes.	5. Dividends are a distribution of profits.	5. Dividends are a distribution of profit paid after preferred dividends.
6. No voting rights.	6. Usually no voting rights.	6. Voting rights.
7. First claim on assets.	7. Second claim on assets.	7. Last claim on assets.

MARKETING CORPORATE SECURITIES

In our expanding economy, corporations often require additional long-term funds beyond those available from internal sources. One basic decision is choosing between additional debt or equity. If the firm decides to borrow, it may attempt to negotiate a long-term loan from a bank, insurance company, or other financial institutions. Both debt and equity capital[3] may be raised by selling corporate securities to the public. Once the decision is made to sell a new issue of securities, there is still the problem of selecting the best type of security—bonds, preferred stock, or common stock. Then management must make arrangements for marketing the new issue.

Selection of Corporate Securities

At this point it is worth reemphasizing that long-term financial decisions are critically important because the firm must live with the consequences for years. Also, keep in mind that management is concerned with the interests of the corporation's owners. Financial decisions are made with an eye toward increasing the rate of return for stockholders, particularly for common stockholders.

In deciding which type of security to sell, management must carefully analyze the firm's financial needs and future prospects in terms of several major factors. These factors include: (1) cost and repayment, (2) taxation, (3) voting control, (4) expected profits, and (5) market conditions.

[3]The term *capital* has several meanings. In economics, *capital* refers to plant and equipment used to produce goods and services. In common business usage, the term refers to the funds available for investment in the firm.

Corporation A—$50,000 in Interest		Corporation B—$50,000 in Dividends	
Sales	$600,000	Sales	$600,000
Expenses	500,000	Expenses	500,000
	100,000	Profit Before Taxes	100,000
Less: Bond Interest	50,000	Income Tax (40%)	40,000
Profit Before Taxes	50,000	Net Profit	60,000
Income Tax (40%)	20,000	Less: Dividends	50,000
Retained Profit	$ 30,000	Retained Profit	$ 10,000

FIGURE 11.6   Tax Treatment of Interest and Dividends

Cost and Repayment   There are advantages and disadvantages to selling both stocks and bonds. Since bonds represent debt, the corporation must pay annual interest charges as well as repay the principal. In the case of stock no repayment is involved, and there is no legal obligation to pay dividends. However, the sale of additional stock means that profits must be divided among more shares, raising the possibility that profits per share may decline.

Taxation   Bonds offer a major tax advantage to the issuing corporation. Bond interest is considered a business expense deductible before paying corporation income taxes. In contrast, dividend payments are not an expense, but a distribution of profits after taxes.

To illustrate the significance of this point, consider a simplified example of two corporations with identical sales and expenses, except that one pays annual bond interest of $50,000 and the other dividends of $50,000. Figure 11.6 shows that interest is deducted prior to computing the corporation income tax. As a result, Corporation B pays over twice as much income tax as Corporation A. This is one reason that the sale of new issues of corporation bonds has far exceeded financing by stock in recent years.

Voting Control   If additional shares of common stock are sold, existing owners may lose voting control of the corporation. On the other hand, bonds do not carry voting rights, and most preferred stock is nonvoting.

Expected Profits   Many firms, such as public utilities, enjoy steadily rising sales and earnings year after year. These firms can afford to sell large quantities of bonds because income is available to meet fixed charges, that is, interest and repayment of principal. On the other hand, the sales and profits of steel and construction companies tend to fluctuate with changes in economic activity. A firm with unstable income cannot afford a high debt-to-equity ratio because in poor years it may have difficulty in meeting fixed charges.

As a general rule, bonds should not be sold unless the expected rate of return from the investment of proceeds exceeds the interest rate. For example, suppose the XYZ Corporation sold $10 million of 12 percent bonds to finance the construction of a new factory. The expected increase in aftertax earnings from the factory is $2 million a year, which exceeds the annual interest payment of $1.2 million (12 percent of $10 million). The difference of $800,000 reflects an increase in earnings for the stockholders. The process of increasing profits by investing borrowed funds at a rate of return higher than the interest rate is called *trading on equity* or *leverage.*

Market Conditions   If stock prices are rising and investor confidence is high, it may be relatively easy for a corporation to sell a new issue of stock. On the other hand, when stock prices are falling, corporate bonds may be more attractive to investors. When interest rates are high, a corporation may be forced to pay a high rate of interest on its bonds to attract investors. During the early 1970s, large corporations could sell bonds with a 10 percent or lower interest rate, but a decade later the same firms were forced to pay 12 to 18 percent. The higher the interest rate, the greater the interest expense. In the middle 1980s, interest rates eased somewhat, reducing the cost of borrowing.

How Corporate Securities Are Marketed

The sale of a new issue of corporate securities to the public normally involves an *investment banker,* also called an *underwriter.* The primary job of an investment banker is to market new securities to the public.

After careful analysis, the management of the Hailwood Department Store has decided to raise additional long-term capital by selling $5 million of cumulative preferred stock at $100 per share. The investment banking firm of Dobbs and Dartmore is invited to underwrite the new issue. Dobbs and Dartmore first conducts a thorough investigation into the financial condition and operations of Hailwood, using a team of accountants, merchandising experts, and financial analysts. If everything is found to be in good order, the investment banking firm enters into negotiations to purchase the preferred stock for resale to the public. A key area of negotiation is the *spread,* which is the difference between the price paid for the stock by the underwriter and the market price. In this case the two firms agreed to a 5 percent spread amounting to $250,000 (5 percent of $5 million). The spread represents a fee paid to the investment banker to cover expenses and provide a profit.

Another area to be settled is the dividend rate on the preferred stock. The underwriter wants a high dividend to make the stock attractive to potential buyers, while Hailwood's management would prefer a low rate. After studying comparable preferred stocks of other corporations, it is decided that a dividend of $12 per share is appropriate.

The investment banker assists in gaining approval of the issue from various government agencies including the Securities and Exchange Commission. Dobbs and Dartmore also agree to help in the preparation of the *prospectus,* a booklet that provides detailed information on the Hailwood Department Store and the new issue of preferred stock. Under federal law, each potential buyer of the new stock must be provided with a copy of the prospectus.

When all arrangements are complete, Dobbs and Dartmore will give Hailwood's management a check for $4.75 million ($5 million less the spread of $250,000) in return for 50,000 shares of $12 cumulative preferred stock.[4]

In marketing the stock the investment banker will notify stockbrokers throughout the country and offer them a commission for selling the stock to their customers. If the public fails to buy all 50,000 shares, the investment banker may be forced to hold on to the remainder until market conditions improve.

THE SECURITIES MARKETS

You will recall that one of the advantages of owning corporate securities is the relative ease of transferring ownership. Billions of dollars of stocks and bonds are bought and sold daily in securities markets. These markets include organized stock exchanges and the over-the-counter market, and they involve a variety of financial institutions such as brokerage firms, investment companies, and security dealers.

Stock Exchanges

A stock exchange is a marketplace where corporate securities are bought and sold. The exchange itself does not purchase or sell securities; rather, it provides facilities for its members to trade stocks and bonds for their customers.

The New York Stock Exchange (NYSE) is the largest and the best-known exchange. It has 1366 members, each of whom own a "seat" on the exchange. About 500 of the seats are owned by brokerage firms that represent customers in buying and selling securities. The NYSE lists about 1500 stocks and 2000 bond issues. These securities are not new issues, but are stocks and bonds already sold by corporations. In other words, stock exchanges do not provide funds for corporations.

In order to have its securities listed on the New York Stock Exchange, a corporation must meet certain requirements as to minimum size and financial resources and be approved by the board of governors of the exchange. Other major exchanges include the American Stock Exchange and Pacific Stock Exchange.

---

[4]In many states, corporations are required by law to give existing stockholders first preference in purchasing new issues of securities. This preference, called *privileged subscription,* is ignored here in order to keep the example simple.

Over-the-Counter Market

Only about 4500 different securities are listed on organized exchanges, but over 10 times that number of stocks and bonds are traded over the counter. These unlisted securities include government and foreign bonds, many insurance company and bank stocks and bonds, as well as securities of medium-sized and smaller corporations. The over-the-counter market consists of about 4000 *security dealers* who buy and sell securities for their own accounts. Each dealer normally maintains an inventory of several unlisted stocks and bonds and makes a market by standing ready to buy and sell these securities.

There are two prices for over-the-counter securities, the *bid* and the *ask*. For example, the common stock of the XYZ Corporation may be quoted at 25 bid and 26 ask by a dealer on a particular day. This means that the dealer is willing to buy the stock at $25 per share and to sell it for $26 per share. The difference between the bid and ask prices represents the dealer's markup or gross profit.

A computer-based national quotation system known as NASDAQ (National Association of Securities Dealers Automated Quotations System) is used to provide instantaneous bid and ask prices on 3000 major over-the-counter stocks. These "representative quotations" are available to 30,000 stockbrokers through desk-top electronic quote machines.

Brokerage Firms

A *stockbroker* buys and sells securities for customers and charges a commission for this service. Large brokerage firms are normally members of the New York Stock Exchange and other major exchanges. Some brokerage houses also serve as over-the-counter dealers. In addition to buying and selling listed and unlisted securities for customers, some brokers also act as investment bankers in underwriting new issues.

Brokerage firms provide a variety of services to their customers. They collect and distribute financial information and provide research reports on corporate securities. Most brokerage houses make loans to customers who maintain margin accounts. Buying on *margin* means that the customer need not come up with the full cash amount of the transaction. For example, if an investor buys 100 shares of a stock at $20 per share, the amount due is $2000 (omitting commissions and taxes). If the margin rate is 70 percent, the investor must deposit $1400 (70 percent of $2000) and the broker will lend the remainder using the customer's stock as collateral for the loan.

Opening an account with a brokerage firm is a relatively simple process similar to opening a checking or savings account with a bank.

A Typical Transaction

Suppose you want to purchase shares of General Electric common stock, which is listed on the New York Stock Exchange. You call or visit your broker and ask for a quote on GE common. Using an electronic quote machine connected to the floor of the NYSE, the broker discovers that the last sale of General Electric was at 61¼ ($61.25 per share). You decide that you can afford to purchase 100 shares. This is called a *round lot.* Anything less than 100 shares is an *odd lot.* You then enter an order to buy 100 shares of GE at the *market*—that is, at the best price available when the order is received. A *limit order* sets a maximum price you are willing to pay —say $61 per share. Of course, a limit order may not be filled if there are no sellers at the limit price.

Your market order is sent to the floor of the NYSE by teletype where a floor broker employed by your brokerage firm takes it to the trading post where General Electric is bought and sold. At the trading post, the floor broker asks for a quote on GE and discovers it is 61 bid and 61¼ ask. This means that there is a seller willing to take $61.25 per share for the stock and a buyer willing to pay $61.00 per share. Your floor broker bids 61⅛ and another broker representing a seller accepts the bid. Confirmation of the purchase is teletyped back to your broker's office. The entire process has probably taken less than 5 minutes.

You have purchased 100 shares of General Electric common stock at a net cost of $6112.50 ($61⅛ per share × 100 shares). To this amount you must add your broker's commission plus federal and state taxes.[5]

Investment Companies

Another way to invest in corporate securities is through the purchase of investment company shares. Investment companies sell their securities to the public and invest the proceeds in the stocks and bonds of other companies and government agencies.

Investment companies may be either closed end or open end. A *closed-end investment company* sells its securities only when first organized. Thereafter, the securities are traded over the counter or on an organized exchange. *Open-end investment companies,* better known as *mutual funds,* are by far the more popular type. Mutual fund shares are sold on a continuous basis—that is, the fund issues new shares whenever there are buyers. The money received from the sale of shares is used to purchase corporate and government securities. The value of the mutual fund shares is based on the value of the securities it owns. Suppose, for example, that on December 12, 1987, the Go-Go Fund owns a portfolio of common stocks with a current market value of $2.7 million. If the fund has 90,000 shares outstanding, the liquidation price of each share is $30 ($2,700,000 ÷ 90,000 shares = $30 per share). This is the price that the shareholder would receive if his or her Go-Go Fund shares were sold on December 12.

---

[5]Brokerage commissions vary by firm and depend on the dollar amount of the transaction. Commissions range from 1 to 2 percent of the net cost. Taxes amount to only a few cents a share.

High interest rates in the 1970s and early 1980s made *money market funds* very popular. These mutual funds invest in short-term, interest-paying securities issued by corporations and government. Investors in money market funds earn a large return on their investment as long as interest rates remain high.

There are two major advantages of investing in a mutual fund: diversification and professional management. Since the investor's money is spread among many different securities, the risk of losing the entire investment is minimized. The managers of the open-end investment company keep a close watch on the fund's portfolio and make purchases and sales intended to increase the value of the fund's shares. To some extent, the individual investor is relieved of the necessity of keeping close watch on his or her investment.

Mutual funds also have certain disadvantages. When purchasing shares, the investor must pay a commission, called a *front-end load,* which amounts to about 9 percent.[6] In addition, there is an annual management fee, which usually averages ¼ of 1 percent of the portfolio's value.

Stock Quotations

About 50 million Americans own corporate securities. Since many of these investors want timely information on their investments, financial news reporting is an important part of most news media.

Most newspapers present a daily summary of stock transactions on major exchanges. This summary may appear confusing at first glance, but with a little practice it is easy to read. Figure 11.7 presents a portion of the stock quotations for the New York Stock Exchange together with a section-by-section explanation.

Can You Beat the Market?

One way to make (and lose) money is to purchase corporate securities. Basically, there are two types of security buyers—speculators and investors. The speculator is interested in quick profit. Usually the speculator buys a company's stock, which is subject to wide and rapid price changes, with the hope of buying low and selling high in a relatively short period of time (a few hours, days, weeks, or at most, a few months). The investor is interested in long-range appreciation (growth) of his or her funds. This person normally purchases a portfolio of securities in several corporations, and often holds these securities for years with the objective of steady (if not spectacular) appreciation and/or income.

If you are considering the purchase of stocks or bonds you should first determine your objectives. Are you primarily interested in current income, steady appreciation, or fast profits? Investment objectives must relate to your personal circumstances—your financial resources, knowledge, personality, and willingness to accept risk. It is important to understand that there is a close

[6]Some funds do not charge a commission and are called *no-load funds.*

1. The highest and lowest price of the stock during the last year.

2. The abbreviated name of the corporation: Aetna Life & Casualty Company.

3. The annual dividend paid over the last twelve months: $.60 per share.

4. The abbreviation "pf" stands for preferred stock.

5. The letter "t" before the dividend refers to a footnote which gives additional information.

6. The annual yield is computed by dividing the dividend by the price per share.

7. This column shows the ratio between the price of the common stock and the earnings (profit) per share.

8. The number of shares traded on June 29 in hundreds: 460,800 shares.

9. The highest price of the day for this stock: 29 7/8 or $29.875 per share.

10. The lowest price of the day.

11. The price for the last trade of the day, called the closing price.

12. The difference between the closing price on June 29 and the closing price on the previous day. In this case, the price per share increased 1/2.

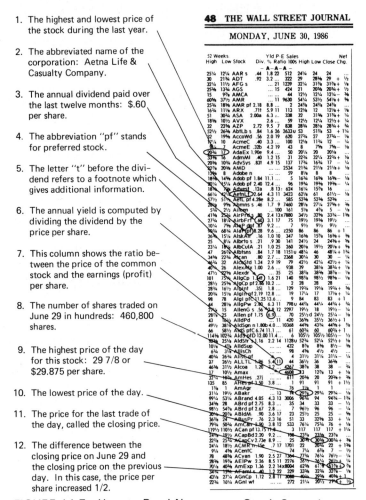

FIGURE 11.7   How to Read Newspaper Stock Quotations

relationship between the potential profit from an investment and the degree of risk involved. In other words, the greater the potential profit, the higher the risk of loss.

Successful investors and speculators carefully evaluate a possible investment before committing their funds. They attempt to answer a variety of questions through careful research. In what type of industry does the firm operate and what are the future prospects for the industry? What products and/or services does the firm produce? What is the corporation's earnings record? Does the firm have good management? What has happened to the price of the stock or bond over the past few years?

If you think it is easy to make a quick fortune on the stock market, perhaps you should consider the advice of Bernard Baruch, one of the most successful speculators of all time:

ISSUE   CORPORATE RAIDERS PLAY THE TAKEOVER GAME

During the first half of the 1980s, there were close to 50 corporate mergers each worth over $1 billion. This is four times the number that took place during the entire decade of the 1970s. The dramatic increase is partly due to corporate raiders who attempt to buy controlling interest (usually 51 percent of the voting stock) in corporations they consider undervalued and poorly managed. Raiders claim to be helping stockholders whose share prices are depressed due to inept management.

The most famous corporate raider is T. Boone Pickens. Typically, his strategy is to buy shares of a corporation's stock, claim that the firm is badly managed, and offer to pay remaining stockholders more than the current market price for their shares. An intense propaganda war ensues, and stockholders must choose whether to support management or accept Pickens' offer. Often, the target company will sell out to a "white knight," a friendlier corporation with better terms of acquisition. While the takeover by Pickens may be thwarted, he can realize tremendous profits on the increase in the market value of his shares. Although T. Boone Pickens has made millions of dollars as a corporate raider, he has never successfully taken over a large corporation.

Stockholders have mixed reactions to corporate raiders. Some welcome them because stock prices are bid up dramatically. However, prices may collaspe after the acquisition is over and the raiders sell out.

Are corporate raiders good for the economy? They force corporations to spend great amounts of time, energy, and money fighting takeovers. These resources might be better used in boosting productivity and profits. Moreover, takeover attempts may cause firms to borrow heavily to pay high acquisition and settlement costs. Yet, acquisitions do have a positive side. According to the annual report of the President's Council of Economic Advisors:

> The available evidence is that mergers and acquisitions increase national wealth. They improve efficiency, transfer scarce resources to higher valued uses, and stimulate effective corporate management.

The presence of corporate raiders may force poorly run firms to become more concerned about management, productivity, and the welfare of stockholders.

If you are ready to give up everything else—to study the whole history and background of the market and all the principle companies whose stocks are on the board as carefully as a medical student studies anatomy—if you can do all that, and, in addition, you have the cool nerves of a great gambler, the sixth sense of a kind of clairvoyant, and the courage of a lion, you have a ghost of a chance.

SUMMARY

Financial managers are primarily concerned with acquiring sufficient funds to finance operations and using these funds to achieve the firm's objectives. Part of their job is cash management, which involves balancing cash receipts against expected cash payments in order to maintain an adequate cash balance. Short-term funds are employed in financing the day-to-day operations of the firm, while long-term funds are normally invested in fixed assets.

The major source of short-term funds is from open-book accounts, which are debts owed to trade creditors. Most trade creditors offer a cash discount for early payment of the amount owed. Banks may extend a line of credit to established firms, which specifies the maximum amount the bank will loan. Most bank loans are secured by promissory notes, which specify the repayment date and the rate of interest.

Factors are companies that purchase accounts receivable at a discount. Other sources of short-term funds include sales finance companies and various government agencies such as the Small Business Administration.

Long-term funds are available from owners, creditors, and internal sources such as retained earnings and depreciation. Corporations may sell additional shares of preferred and common stock or bonds to raise long-term capital.

Bonds are formal, interest-bearing debts with long-term maturities. Bondholders stand ahead of stockholders in their claim to the assets of the corporation, and bondholders have a legal right to interest payments. Registered bonds, which have the name of the bondholder recorded on the certificate and in the corporation's books, are protected from loss or theft, but bearer bonds are not. Mortgage bonds are secured by property owned by the corporation, while debentures are backed only by the good credit standing of the firm. Many corporate bonds may be redeemed prior to maturity by paying a call price. Some bonds are convertible into shares of stock.

Common stockholders are the voting owners of the corporation. As such, they bear the greatest risks, but enjoy the greatest opportunities for gain if the corporation is profitable. Dividends are a distribution of profits paid to stockholders at the discretion of the board of directors.

Preferred stock, another type of ownership security, enjoys

preferences over common stock as to assets and dividends. In most cases, preferred stock is nonvoting, and the dividend is limited to a fixed amount.

In deciding which type of corporate security to sell to raise additional capital, management must consider the problems of cost and repayment, the tax treatment of interest and dividends, the effect on the voting control of the firm, the amount and stability of future earnings, and current market conditions. New issues of stocks and bonds are normally marketed through an investment banker, who purchases the securities from the issuing corporation and resells them to the public.

Corporate securities are traded on organized exchanges and over the counter. The largest exchange is the New York Stock Exchange, which provides facilities for its members to buy and sell securities for their customers. In contrast, the over-the-counter market consists of security dealers who trade for their own accounts.

Stockbrokers act as agents for their customers in the purchase and sale of securities. Investment companies sell securities to the public and reinvest the funds in corporate and government securities. Open-end investment companies, better known as mutual funds, sell their shares on a continuous basis, as opposed to closed-end investment companies, which only sell securities when first organized.

Corporate securities are purchased by both speculators and investors. The speculator attempts to earn a quick profit by buying low and selling high within a short period of time. On the other hand, the investor is interested in long-term appreciation and/or current income. Successful investors and speculators carefully study possible purchases in light of their own objectives.

Fortunes have been made and lost in the stock market. Successful investing is more a matter of careful study, knowledge, and skill than it is of luck. On the other hand, good luck never hurt anyone!

SELF-EXAMINATION QUESTIONS

The following questions are based on the Chapter Objectives listed at the beginning of the chapter. Test yourself by circling the letter preceding the answer that *best* completes the statement or answers the question. The correct answers to the Self-Examination Questions are in the appendix at the end of the textbook.

1. With regard to financial management, which statement is *false?* (A) The goal of cash management is to build up cash surpluses; (B) The financial manager is responsible for developing financial plans, raising funds, cutting costs, preserving assets, and keeping financial records; (C) It is possible for a profitable company to go broke; (D) None of these statements is false.

2. Cash flow is: (A) the difference between sales revenues and expenses; (B) an abstract concept of no concern to the practical business manager; (C) the amount of money in a checking account; (D) all of these; (E) none of these.

3. Which of the following is *not* a source of short-term financing? (A) banks; (B) factors; (C) trade creditors; (D) bondholders.

4. Internally generated funds: (A) are the proceeds from the sale of common stock; (B) refer to retained earnings and depreciation; (C) are borrowed from bondholders; (D) can be obtained through a line of credit; (E) none of these.

5. A type of corporate security that typically carries no voting rights and pays a fixed dividend is: (A) common stock; (B) preferred stock; (C) convertible bonds; (D) debentures; (E) none of these.

6. If a corporation selling a new issue of securities is primarily concerned with tax savings, retention of voting control by current owners, and the opportunity for trading on equity, it would probably select: (A) common stock; (B) preferred stock; (C) bonds; (D) convertible widgets; (E) none of these.

7. Investment bankers: (A) market new issues of corporate securities; (B) grant lines of credit to business firms; (C) is another name for factors; (D) negotiate loans for foreign nations; (E) none of these.

8. The largest number of corporate securities are traded: (A) on the New York Stock Exchange; (B) on the American Stock Exchange; (C) in the over-the-counter market; (D) through the Federal Reserve Bond Market.

9. Investment companies: (A) sell securities to the public; (B) purchase stocks and bonds; (C) are sometimes called mutual funds; (D) offer diversification to the investor; (E) all of these.

10. In contrast to the investor, the stock market speculator is interested in: (A) long-term growth; (B) high current income from dividends or interest; (C) short-term profits; (D) low-risk investments; (E) none of these.

APPENDIX

MONEY, THE
BANKING SYSTEM,
AND THE
FEDERAL RESERVE

Money may be defined as coins, paper currency, and demand deposits (or checking accounts).[7] Demand deposits are by far the most important form of money since over 80 percent of the dollar value of all payments are made by check.

The Role of Money

Money is an essential requirement in a modern economy. The most important function of money is to serve as a *medium of exchange;* it is used as a "go-between" in the exchange of goods and services. Think for a moment what would happen if all money were to disappear or become valueless. We would be forced to rely on *barter*—the direct exchange of goods and services for other goods and services. Barter is time consuming, inconvenient, and complicated. How could a research physicist trade for a restaurant meal? Without money, people cannot focus on specialized occupations or activities and hope to be compensated for their efforts. Our modern, highly specialized economy depends on money to facilitate the exchange of goods and services.

The Banking System

The U.S. banking system is comprised of more than 14,000 *commercial banks.* Although banks perform a variety of services for their customers, these financial institutions have two key functions: (1) they accept and hold deposits from individuals and business firms, and (2) they make loans. In a sense banks merely recycle money by lending out other people's deposits and charging interest for these loans.[8] This means that banks hold only a fraction of total deposits in the form of cash reserves. The remainder is loaned out or used to purchase interest-paying securities. If all depositors decided to withdraw their deposits at the same time, there would not be sufficient cash reserves to pay the depositors. The bank would fail unless it were able to borrow additional reserves. The amount of cash reserves that banks must hold against deposits is called the reserve requirement. For large banks, the reserve requirement is set by a government agency called the Federal Reserve. Commercial banks are the major source of short-term business loans.

The Federal Reserve System

When banks have plentiful reserves to lend out, individuals and business firms find credit or loans easy to obtain and interest rates are low. With easy credit, consumers are encouraged to finance the

---

[7]This is a narrow definition. Sometimes other items are considered money. For example, NOW (negotiable orders of withdrawal) accounts, which pay interest on checkable deposits may be defined as money. "Plastic money" in the form of debit and credit cards does not fit neatly into our definition.

[8]Interest can be thought of as a rental charge for money. More precisely, it is an amount paid for borrowing money. Interest is expressed as a percent of the amount borrowed and is calculated on an annual basis. Therefore, the interest on $1000 at 15 percent for half a year is $75 ($1000 $\times$ 0.15 $\times$ 0.5 years = $75).

purchase of "big ticket items" such as automobiles, homes, and major appliances. Business firms can borrow to invest in additional plant and equipment and expand inventories. Unfortunately, if credit is too easy to obtain, total spending by individuals and firms may grow so rapidly that inflation results. Inflation is a general rise in prices, and one of the causes is too many dollars chasing too few goods.[9]

Tight credit means banks are short of reserves to make loans. This pushes up interest rates. Individuals and businesses find it difficult and costly to borrow funds for purchases and investment, leading to a reduction in total spending. Tight money can be effective in slowing inflation, but soaring interest rates reflecting a shortage of loanable reserves may plunge the economy into a recession or even a depression.

The Federal Reserve, often referred to as the "Fed," is the government central bank responsible for controlling the *money supply*—the total of coins, paper currency, and demand deposits. Created in 1913, the *Federal Reserve system* consists of a board of governors, 12 Federal Reserve banks each serving a section of the country, and approximately 5000 member banks.

The board of governors, consisting of seven members appointed by the president of the United States for 14-year terms, is responsible for formulating monetary policy and supervising the banking system. *Monetary policy* refers to controlling the nation's money supply to achieve the goals of steady prices, full employment, and economic growth. The Fed has three major tools for manipulating the nation's supply of money and credit: (1) the reserve requirement, (2) open market operations, and (3) the discount rate.

The *reserve requirement* is the percent of deposits that commercial banks must hold in the form of cash reserves. The Federal Reserve may vary the reserve requirement, on deposits between certain limits. If the Fed wants to encourage bank lending, it may reduce the reserve requirement thereby freeing bank reserves for additional loans. Conversely, a boost in the reserve requirement forces banks to hold more cash reserves and reduces loanable funds.

Open market operations refers to the purchase and sale of U.S. government securities by the Federal Reserve for the purpose of manipulating the availability of bank credit. When the Fed purchases government securities from banks, it pays for the securities by providing banks with additional cash reserves. This enables banks to expand their loans. When the Federal Reserve sells government securities, banks lose reserves, thereby reducing their ability to make loans. Open market operations is the Federal

---

[9]Inflation is measured by price indexes that show the percentage change in prices from some base year. The Consumer Price Index (CPI), which measures changes in prices paid by the typical city family, is the most widely used measure of inflation. A graph of the CPI is shown in Figure 8.1.

Reserve's most important monetary tool. Each week the Fed buys and sells hundreds of millions of dollars of government securities in an attempt to keep commercial bank reserves in line with money supply goals.

The *discount rate* is the rate of interest charged by the Federal Reserve for loans to commercial banks. If the Fed wants to discourage bank lending, it raises the discount rate, making it more expensive for banks to borrow reserves. An easy money policy is often signaled by a cut in the discount rate to encourage bank borrowing of reserves.

Student _____

BUILDING A BUSINESS VOCABULARY

Directions: Match the terms with their definitions by writing the letter in the appropriate blank.

a. Convertible Bond
b. Load
c. Security Dealer
d. Promissory Note
e. Cash Management
f. Registered Bond
g. Factor
h. Trading on Equity
i. Federal Reserve System

j. Line of Credit
k. Invoice
l. Call Price
m. Bearer Bond
n. Prospectus
o. Preferred Stock
p. Odd Lot
q. Debenture
r. Open Book Accounts

s. Depreciation
t. Stockbroker
u. Equity Capital
v. Round Lot
w. Spread
x. Underwriting
y. Margin
z. Open-end Investment Company

_____ 1. Short-term debts reflecting purchases from trade creditors.

_____ 2. One hundred shares of stock.

_____ 3. A firm that provides short-term funds to a business by purchasing accounts receivable.

_____ 4. A mutual fund.

_____ 5. An itemized list of merchandise including prices and terms sent by the supplier to the buyer.

_____ 6. A stated amount of short-term funds that a bank is willing to loan to a firm.

_____ 7. An individual who represents customers in buying and selling securities and charges a commission for this service.

_____ 8. A written promise to repay a sum of money plus interest on a certain date.

_____ 9. Funds from owners.

_____ 10. A bond whose owner receives interest payments by check.

_____ 11. One to 99 shares of stock.

_S_ 12. A noncash business expense that may be considered a component of internally generated funds.

_A_ 13. A special type of bond that can be exchanged for a set number of shares of stock.

_Y_ 14. Credit available for the purchase of securities.

_B_ 15. The commission charged for purchasing shares of a mutual fund.

_M_ 16. A bond with attached coupons that are used to collect interest payments.

_C_ 17. Balancing expected cash receipts against cash expenditures in order to maintain the cash balance at a suitable level.

_O_ 18. A security that represents ownership but normally receives a fixed dividend and usually carries no voting rights.

_d_ 19. One who makes a market in over-the-counter securities by buying or selling for his or her own account.

_i_ 20. A government-operated central bank charged with controlling the money supply.

_g_ 21. A bond with no specific security other than the general credit standing of the issuing corporation.

_W_ 22. The difference between the price an investment banker pays for securities and the price at which he or she sells them.

_H_ 23. Increasing stockholders' earnings by investing borrowed funds at a higher return than the interest rate.

_L_ 24. A price at which a corporation may redeem its bonds prior to the maturity date.

_X_ 25. The purchase of a new issue of securities by an investment banker for resale.

_N_ 26. A booklet published for potential investors that provides detailed information about a new issue of securities.

Student _____

REVIEWING MAJOR CONCEPTS

1. Briefly, why are long-term financial decisions considered more important than short-term financial decisions?

2. What are internally generated funds?

3. Explain why short-term funds should not be used to finance the purchase of fixed assets.

4. What is the difference between cumulative and noncumulative preferred stock?

5. From the viewpoint of the corporation, what tax advantage do bonds have over stock?

6. Briefly, what does an investment banker do? What risk does the investment banker assume in underwriting an issue of securities?

7. What are the major advantages and disadvantages of buying mutual fund shares?

8. Suppose you own a 9 percent convertible bond callable at 103 ($1030). The bond is convertible into 30 shares of common stock which has a current market price of $36 per share. If the corporation calls the bond, what should you do? Explain your decision.

Student _____

SOLVING PROBLEMS AND CASES

1. *Case:* Vargas Hardware Store

   On September 15, 1987, Vargas Hardware received a shipment of lawnmowers together with an invoice for $1200. The terms on the invoice were 2/20; *n*/60.

   a. If Vargas pays the bill on or before October 5, how much does the store owe?

   b. If Vargas elects to wait until October 30, how much should be paid?

   c. If Vargas can negotiate a short-term loan from a bank at an annual interest rate of 14 percent, would it pay to borrow funds and take the discount? Explain why or why not.

2. *Case:* Zenith Widget Company, Inc.

The Zenith Widget Company has decided to go out of business due to declining sales and profits. After selling its assets and paying off current liabilities, $3 million in cash remains. The firm's outstanding securities are shown below:

Common Stock	$2,000,000
Bonds	1,600,000
Preferred Stock	1,200,000

a. How much will the owners of each type of security receive?

b. What would your answer be if the remaining cash were only $1 million? Explain.

Student _____

3. *Case:* Home Run Products Company

Spike Hanson is the owner and manager of the Home Run Products Company, a small but profitable manufacturer of baseball equipment. Recently he has become concerned about his firm's shortage of cash. Since sales are expected to increase rapidly in the next few months, he feels that additional funds are needed to purchase more inventory and meet operating expenses. A simplified balance sheet for the firm is reproduced below.

Assets		Liabilities & Owner's Equity	
Cash	$ 5,000	Accounts Payable	$ 10,000
Accounts		Note Payable to Bank	15,000
Receivable	80,000	Taxes Payable	5,000
Inventory	30,000	Spike Hanson,	
Fixed Assets	100,000	Owner's Equity	185,000
	$215,000		$215,000

Mr. Hanson has turned to you, his accountant, for advice. What suggestions do you have for raising additional funds?

4. *Case:* Fun-Rite Toys, Inc.

In 1985, Fun-Rite Toys sold 10,000 shares of $12 cumulative preferred stock at $100 per share. The $12 preferred dividend was paid in 1985. The firm experienced losses for the next 2 years due to poor economic conditions plus increased competition. No dividends were declared on either common or preferred stock during 1986 and 1987. In late 1988, a new line of toys was introduced that proved highly successful, and profits reached record levels. If the board of directors declared $800,000 in dividends in 1988, how much would the preferred stockholders receive?

5. *Case:* Harriet Silvers

Ms. Harriet Silvers is a young stockbroker recently employed by a leading brokerage firm. One afternoon, a Mr. Martin Kingman introduced himself and asked Ms. Silvers to suggest some "hot" common stocks.

In talking with Mr. Kingman, Ms. Silvers learned that he had recently retired at the age of 65 from his job as sales clerk with a department store. He lives with his wife in a small apartment near the brokerage office. His income from social security and a pension fund is $800 per month. In addition, he has a savings account of $30,000 on which he earns 8 percent interest.

Mr. Kingman mentioned that he wants to "make a little quick money on the market" by investing his $30,000 in common stocks. He feels that his profits from the stock market will permit him to live more comfortably on his retirement income.

What advice should Ms. Silvers offer to Mr. Kingman?

Student _____

6. *Special Challenge Case:* Barton Machine Tools, Inc.

Late in 1987, the finance committee of Barton Machine Tools was considering the best source of long-term funds to finance the purchase of a foundry that would cost $12 million. The financial vice-president had prepared a report that estimated that the new foundry would increase the firm's pretax profits by an average of $4 million each year for the next 15 years. However, this estimate did not include the cost of the funds needed for the purchase. The committee members were in full agreement that the foundry would be a good investment, but there was some difference of opinion as to how the $12 million should be raised.

One committee member recommended that Barton issue debenture bonds, which he felt could be sold at a 12 percent interest rate. The head accountant proposed a $13 cumulative preferred ($100 par value) stock issue, while two other committee members favored the sale of additional shares of common stock at the current market price of $20 per share. The current common stock dividend is $1.50 per share.

Barton Machine Tools had earned profits every year for the past 20 years with the exception of 1980. Dividends on common and preferred stock have been paid each year since 1983. The firm's current capital structure (long-term debt and shareholders' equity) is shown below:

8 Percent Mortgage Bonds due 1998	$1,000,000
$9 Noncumulative Preferred	5,000,000
Common Stock (1,000,000 shares)	10,000,000
Retained Earnings	8,000,000

As assistant to the president, you have been asked to write a brief report analyzing the alternatives and presenting your recommendations.

chapter **12**

PRODUCTION

Production means making things. In a broader sense, production is the creation of goods and services by combining people, materials, machines, and management.

Production managers perform the same functions as managers in other parts of the firm. However, they are particularly concerned with decisions relating to location and design of plant facilities, selection of production equipment, planning and control of production operations, and materials handling.

This chapter provides a brief overview of the American production system, describes the different types of production processes, and introduces the major phases of production management. It concludes with a description of Computer-Aided Design/Computer-Aided Manufacturing (CAD/CAM), which promises to transform the American production system.

CHAPTER OBJECTIVES

1. Describe four major characteristics of the U.S. production system.

2. Contrast and compare the five production processes.

3. Distinguish between mass production and custom production and explain how these systems influence plant layout and the selection of production equipment.

4. Differentiate between motion study and time study.

5. Describe the purchasing process.

6. Given the rate of consumption, the minimum inventory, the time to process an order, and the minimum order size for a part or material, determine the reorder point and maximum inventory.

7. Briefly explain CAD/CAM and describe how this system affects factory productivity.

PRODUCTION: A BIRD'S-EYE VIEW

The American production system has evolved over a period of more than 2 centuries and delivers one of the highest standards of living in the world. Its major characteristics include large-scale production, mechanization, standardization, specialization, and diversification.

Large-Scale Production

Bigness can mean efficiency. In the United States, three-quarters of total production is accounted for by 500 giant corporations, most of which own and operate several huge plants. Large-scale mass production permits the cost of expensive equipment to be spread over many units of output. Suppose, for example, that a machine tool costs $1 million. If the firm produces only 100,000 units, the cost per unit of the machine is $10. However, if production is 2 million, the unit cost of the machine is only $0.50.

Large-scale operations also encourage specialization of labor, which may lead to increased productivity. Moreover, giant corporations can spend millions of dollars on research to develop improved products and to streamline production.

Of course, bigness is not an unmixed blessing. For one thing, management problems become increasingly difficult and complex as firms grow in size.

Mechanization

Mechanization means the substitution of machinery for humanpower. Obviously, the more capital equipment a worker has on the job, the greater the worker's productivity. Capital investment per worker in the United States exceeds $50,000, one of the highest figures in the world. Management substitutes machinery for workers when it reduces costs.

Automation is an extension of mechanization. The essence of automation is machines directing machines. It involves the use of electronic computers to control operating machines through information feedback systems.

Standardization

The term *standardization* actually has two related meanings: (1) making parts interchangeable and (2) limiting the number of types and sizes of a product. Standardization is a necessary ingredient of mass production. Each left front fender for a Ford Escort is identical to all others. This keeps down inventory costs for dealers as well as for the manufacturer. Standardization also permits long production runs, which reduce manufacturing costs and improve quality.

Specialization

Years ago managers discovered that productivity could be boosted by dividing work into simple jobs or tasks and assigning workers to perform each job over and over again. *Specialization* of labor permits an unskilled worker to become expert in performing a simple task in a few days.

Unfortunately, specialization is not an unmixed blessing. It can lead to boredom and inefficiency because workers lose interest in their jobs. For this reason, some firms have initiated job-enlargement programs, which assign employees a variety of tasks. One electronics company has its workers assemble entire components, requiring 20 or more different operations.

Diversification

Many firms continuously seek to add new products in order to expand sales and profits. Campbell's line of "Chunky Soups" was introduced to gain broader market appeal. *Diversification* may also lead to better utilization of plant, equipment, and by-products. For example, Armour and Company brought out Dial Soap to utilize animal by-products from its meat-packing operations.

The opposite of diversification is *simplification,* which means eliminating products that are no longer profitable. In the 1970s, General Electric stopped producing computers, electric fans, vacuum cleaners, blenders, integrated circuits, and television camera equipment. The objective of this massive simplification program was to abandon markets in which GE was not earning satisfactory profits. As a result, General Electric's profits nearly doubled over a 3-year period. John F. Welch, GE's chairman, summed up his firm's policy on simplification this way: "The managements and companies in the eighties that don't do this, that hang onto losers for whatever reason—tradition, sentiment, their own management weakness— won't be around in 1990."

PRODUCTION PROCESSES

The word *production* may conjure up images of huge automobile assembly plants pouring out thousands of cars daily. But production means more than assembly. To understand the scope of production, it is useful to define five production processes: (1) extraction, (2) analytic, (3) synthetic, (4) fabrication, and (5) assembly.

Extraction

The *extraction* process involves taking materials from the earth or water. Typical examples include mining of coal and iron ore. Drilling for petroleum and claiming salt from sea water also represent extraction.

Analytic

The term *analytic* refers to the process of breaking down a material into component products. An example is oil refining, in which crude petroleum is broken down into oil, gasoline, petrochemicals, and other products. In meat packing, a steer carcass is divided into various cuts of meat; even the bones and hooves are separated and sold for feed and glue.

Synthetic

The opposite of analytic is *synthetic,* which means to chemically combine several materials into a product. Steel is produced by combining iron ore, coke, manganese, and other materials at high temperatures. The production of glass is another example of the synthetic process.

ISSUE   AUTOMATION: IS YOUR JOB NEXT?

For progress there is no cure.

John Von Neumann

In broad terms, automation refers to any use of computers or other self-regulating devices that replace human control over processes or machines. Does this mean that automation displaces human beings? You bet it does!

There is little doubt that automation is causing dramatic social changes. Some observers fear that the computer is increasing productivity so rapidly that the nation's economy cannot create new jobs fast enough for the people who are displaced. They foresee a future with massive technological unemployment where a large percentage of the work force is permanently without jobs. However, before we push the panic button perhaps we should consider the other side of the story.

In the first place, the computer industry is creating thousands of new jobs each year in manufacturing, programming, and maintaining the expanding number of computers. Beyond this, automation creates jobs indirectly by boosting productivity and workers' incomes. The result is a growing demand for goods and services, which generates more output and employment. Today, for example, the increasing demand for services has created millions of jobs for beauticians, salespersons, lawyers, airline flight attendants, and repairers.

Automation is twisting the structure of the labor market by putting more emphasis on brainpower and less on musclepower. There is an expanding demand for technicians, managers, and accountants while job openings for unskilled or semiskilled workers are dwindling.

In the long run, automation offers another bonus—more leisure time. This will mean shorter working hours, longer vacations, and earlier retirements. The increased free time will further boost the demand for leisure-time products and services.

If you are concerned about losing your job to automation, now is the time to protect yourself through a carefully planned program of education and training. Also, when choosing a career, be sure to consider the probable long-term impact of automation on alternative occupational fields.

Fabrication

When a material has its form changed, it has been *fabricated*. Typical examples are converting cotton into thread and sheet steel into shaped body panels for automobiles.

Assembly

When different parts are put together to form a final product we have an *assembly* process. An obvious example is the television production line, on which various circuits, tubes, and other components are assembled to produce a television receiver.

MANUFACTUR-ING SYSTEMS

Manufacturing refers to the production of goods in factories or plants. Manufacturing may be divided into two broad categories: (1) mass production and (2) custom production.

Mass Production

Mass production is the manufacture of standard products in large quantities. The purpose of mass production is to reduce unit costs through long production runs, emphasizing mechanization, standardization, and specialization. Mass production requires heavy investment in equipment and a limited range of products.

Custom Production

Custom production is manufacturing products to customer specifications. Custom manufacturers are often called *job shops* because each order or job is usually different. The costs of production are high due to short production runs and the problems of scheduling and setting up for each different job.

PRODUCTION MANAGEMENT

The job of the production manager is to produce goods of acceptable quality in the most efficient manner. This requires the careful planning, organizing, and controlling of production operations. The production manager must make decisions regarding a host of factors that influence the production process. These factors include: (1) plant location, (2) plant layout, (3) production equipment, (4) production planning and control, (5) make-or-buy decisions, (6) job design, and (7) quality control.

Plant Location

The location of physical facilities may be a critically important decision for the business firm. Once the decision is made, it is difficult and expensive to change location. For some companies, the location of the plant may make the difference between success and failure. The major considerations in selecting plant locations are: (1) nearness to market; (2) nearness to raw materials; (3) availability of labor; and (4) other factors such as transportation, taxes, and community facilities.

Nearness to Market   When a firm produces perishable goods or when the transportation cost of finished goods is high, the primary factor determining plant location may be nearness to the market.

Bakeries tend to be located close to their customers. Automobile manufacturers have followed the practice of locating assembly plants near large population centers. It is less expensive to ship parts to these plants than to transport assembled automobiles to the market.

Nearness to Raw Materials   When raw materials used in production are heavy or bulky, it is likely the plant will be located near the source of these materials. For this reason, canneries and frozen food plants are usually located near agricultural areas. Why are there so many oil refineries in Texas?

Availability of Labor   A century ago the American textile industry was concentrated in New England. Today, most textile plants are located in the southeastern part of the country. One reason for the move was to get nearer to the source of raw cotton. Another factor was the availability of a large supply of inexpensive, nonunionized labor in the South.

When the production process requires highly skilled workers, their availability may determine location. This is one reason that many electronics firms are located near universities.

Other Factors   Plant location is influenced by a host of other considerations, including power supply, taxes, transportation facilities (highways, railroads, and airports), climate, land cost, and community services. Some localities are willing to give business firms major tax concessions for building a plant in their community. Why?

General Motors used a computer to analyze the key variables in deciding where to locate its $3.5 billion Saturn Corporation manufacturing complex. The highly sophisticated computer model compared all cost data related to alternative sites. However, the final decision was made by executives after considering subjective factors such as community relations and educational facilities available for training employees.

Plant Layout

Layout refers to the arrangement of equipment and facilities in the plant. The objective of plant layout is to attain maximum production efficiency by speeding the flow of work and materials.

Planning the layout of a factory begins with an engineering study to determine the number of workers and machines and the amount of space needed for production. Cardboard templates and scale models may be used in planning the layout design. More recently, computers have been employed to determine the most efficient arrangement of floor space.

There are two basic types of layouts—process and line. The choice between the two depends on the nature of the production system.

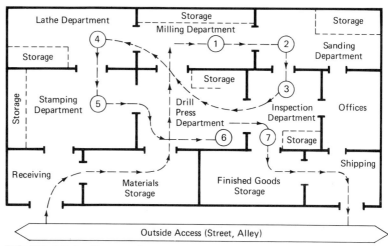

FIGURE 12.1   Process Layout

Process Layout   *Process layout* is typically found in custom production where a variety of different products are manufactured to customer specifications. In the process layout, machines of the same type are grouped together in a section of the factory. Figure 12.1 presents a simplified process layout.

The dotted line shows the progress of a typical order; each number represents a different operation. Figure 12.1 illustrates the major disadvantages of the process layout—excessive materials handling as the order moves from department to department, and the need for large amounts of storage space for goods in process.

Line Layout   In mass-production manufacturing, machines are arranged according to the sequence of operation rather than by separate sections. This has the advantages of reducing handling and saving space. However, the *line layout* is inflexible; once established, it is difficult to alter. Moreover, the breakdown of one machine can stop all production.

Figure 12.2 illustrates a line layout. Notice that the equipment is arranged according to the operations to be performed on the product. This permits work to flow in a straight line. Can you explain why two lathes are required after the milling operation?

Production Equipment   There are two broad categories of production equipment—general purpose and special purpose.

1   *General-purpose* machines are capable of performing a variety of operations. A general-purpose lathe, for example, can shape many types of materials that come in different sizes. Although general-purpose equipment is cheaper to buy, it operates at a relatively slow speed. Moreover, general-purpose

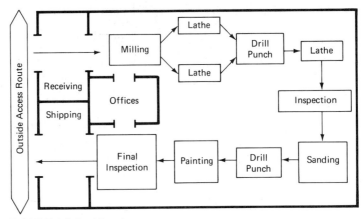

FIGURE 12.2   Line Layout

machines normally require skilled operators who are capable of setting up and adjusting the equipment for each operation.

2   *Special-purpose* equipment is designed to perform a single operation at high speed. An example is a special lathe designed to grind automobile cam shafts to close tolerances. Special-purpose equipment is expensive, but it can often be operated by unskilled or semiskilled workers.

As a general rule, special-purpose equipment is used in mass-production systems, while general-purpose equipment is commonly found in job shops.

When the production manager selects equipment, he or she must consider not only the cost of the machines but also the type and volume of production and skills of the factory work force.

Production Planning and Control

The planning and control of production operations aims at the efficient use of resources—employees, machines, and materials. The production manager is haunted by a single overriding fact: Idle workers and machinery cost money. Therefore, the manager attempts to plan and control work to avoid delays and downtime.

The production plan is based on a sales forecast or on actual orders received from customers. After deciding what is to be done, the production manager must determine how and when the work is to be accomplished. *Routing* involves deciding how an order will move from operation to operation as raw materials are converted into finished goods. In other words, routing means establishing a sequence of operations required to process goods. Figure 12.1 illustrates the routing of one job.

Scheduling is the process of setting up a timetable that shows when each job is to begin and end. The schedule is both a planning and a control device. It can be used to check how closely actual production is conforming to the production plan.

The complexity of production scheduling is illustrated by the modern automobile assembly line, where thousands of different parts must come together at the right time and place. Today, many large factories use an electronic computer to assist in planning and controlling production. The computer can schedule complex operations to ensure a steady flow of work through the plant and, in addition, provide up-to-date information on the status of work in process.

Make-or-Buy Decisions

A key part of the production plan is the determination of which parts should be purchased from outside suppliers and which should be manufactured by the firm itself. The basis for a *make-or-buy* decision is a cost analysis of alternative courses of action. In theory the decision is a simple one: The costs of manufacturing the part are compared to the costs of buying from suppliers, and the most economical method is selected. However, make-or-buy decisions can involve large sums of money, and a host of factors must be carefully evaluated. A decision to make a part might require a substantial investment in new tools and equipment. Are there funds available to finance this investment? Does the firm have the expertise and personnel to undertake expanded production? Can quality standards be met? If the firm elects to buy the part, can suppliers be relied on to meet delivery dates? What are the possible effects of inflation on suppliers' prices and manufacturing costs?

A firm may decide to manufacture a part even when the cost analysis shows that it would be less expensive to buy from a supplier. Such a decision could be based on a desire to use idle plant capacity or to retain employees who might otherwise be laid off.

Job Design: Motion-and-Time Study

The production manager is interested in reducing the time and effort required to do a job, thereby boosting worker productivity. Late in the nineteenth century, a pioneer of modern management named Frederick Taylor carefully studied how workers performed their jobs and attempted to develop ways of redesigning jobs to increase efficiency. Taylor called his methods *scientific management;* today they are known as *motion-and-time study.*

Motion study is used to find the most efficient way of performing a job. Without going into detail, motion study begins by breaking a job into parts called *elements* and carefully analyzing the motions used for each element. Then the job is redesigned to eliminate wasteful or unnecessary movements by pre-positioning tools, avoiding delays, and emphasizing efficient motions. The basic purpose of motion study is to make a job easy and fast.

Time study is used to determine the time required to perform a job. Each element of a job is timed with a stopwatch. After adding an allowance for fatigue and personal needs, a *time standard* is established for the task.

ISSUE IMPROVING PRODUCT QUALITY THROUGH
PREVENTION

Inspection is too late.

W. Edwards Deming

In the arena of international competition, many battles are
fought, but none is more important than the race for quality.
Product quality is becoming a competitive weapon that
separates the successful firm from the failures. Shoddy goods
antagonize customers, undermine a firm's reputation, and
increase operating costs.

But who is responsible for poor quality?

1 Lazy workers?
2 Rigid unions?
3 Too few inspectors?
4 Incompetent suppliers?
5 None of these?

The answer, according to a growing number of quality control
consultants, is none of these. Only management can control
the variables that determine product quality.

The traditional approach to improving quality is to add
more inspectors and exhort workers with such slogans as
"Quality Counts!" But many experts argue that the key to
quality is prevention, not inspection.

The single most influencial advocate of this view is
86-year-old W. Edwards Deming. In 1950, Deming introduced
a group of Japanese industrial leaders to his quality control
method. The rest is history. His system helped transform the
reputation of Japanese goods from "junk" to the
acknowledged hallmark of quality.

Deming claims quality failures are due to either "special
causes" or "common causes." A special cause of poor quality
could be a malfunctioning machine, a careless worker, or
inferior materials. Common causes of poor quality result from

---

Time standards are used to evaluate worker performance and
to plan and schedule production. For example, suppose the time
standard for welding a part is 10 minutes. This means that a worker
should weld 48 parts in an 8-hour day. If the production schedule

---

ISSUE IMPROVING PRODUCT QUALITY THROUGH
PREVENTION (Cont.)

---

flaws in the design of the production process or system.
Deming maintains that special causes account for only 6
percent of all product defects; the remaining 94 percent are
common to the production system.

Deming's goal is to minimize the spread or range of
deviations from the ideal standard, thereby *preventing* the
production of poor-quality products. Using statistical
techniques, he first identifies and eliminates variations due to
special causes. Then he focuses on reducing deviations from
the ideal due to the system itself.

By modifying the process and statistically measuring the
effects, product quality can be systematically improved.
However, this procedure takes time. Deming warns that there
are no quick fixes. Management must be committed to
investing time, money, and study to eliminating defects. He
recommends the use of quality circles—groups of workers and
managers—to study variations in the process and develop
suggestions for improvement.

Successful quality control requires top-to-bottom
commitment. Management must take the lead in convincing
employees that product quality is more important that output
goals. This necessitates improving worker training, redesigning
both the product and the workplace, and most important,
reshaping employee attitudes. The entire firm must accept
product quality as a major company objective, not merely a
passing fad.

Higher-quality products tend to lead to increases in
productivity. With fewer defects, less time is devoted to
adjustment, inspection, and handling of scrap, thereby boosting
efficiency and reducing costs. In addition, workers have a
greater pride in their work.

If management does not exercise its responsibility to
improve quality through prevention of defective products,
workers will be dissatisfied, consumers will buy elsewhere, and
companies will be unable to compete.

---

calls for 90 parts per day, then two workers will be required to
perform this operation.

Quality Control   The control of product quality is a two-step process: (1) the
establishment of quality standards and (2) inspection to determine if
the product conforms to these standards.

The production manager recognizes that quality costs money. It is foolish to insist on quality standards that are too high for the intended use of the product. No one expects a $2 baseball to last a lifetime. On the other hand, poor quality can antagonize consumers and cause sales to drop.

Inspection is used to reject products that fail to meet established standards of quality. In addition, a good *quality control* system attempts to detect and correct the problems that caused the production of below-standard goods.

When quality is of major importance, every unit of output may be carefully examined. However, in most cases inspection is carried out on a sampling basis, where, for example, every fifth or tenth unit is inspected.

PURCHASING AND INVENTORY CONTROL

Purchasing is the acquisition of materials, supplies, and parts required for production. In manufacturing firms, purchases often account for over 50 percent of production costs. Therefore, efficient purchasing can have a significant impact on profits.

Most large firms have purchasing departments headed by a chief purchasing agent, who is assisted by a staff of buyers. The objective of the purchasing department is to get the most for each dollar spent. This does not mean that the purchasing agent always seeks to buy at the lowest price. Other factors that affect the purchasing decision are quality, transportation costs, delivery time, reliability of the supplier, and inventory costs.

Price is dependent on the quantity purchased. Most suppliers offer quantity discounts (a reduction in unit price) for large orders. However, large orders mean increased inventory-carrying costs. For this reason, some firms prefer "hand-to-mouth purchasing"; that is, buying in small quantities at frequent intervals.

The purchasing process begins with a *requisition,* which lists the quantity and specifications of the items to be purchased. On receipt of the requisition the purchasing department explores alternative sources of supply. The selection of a supplier may require bidding or simply negotiations on price, delivery date, and quality specifications. After the supplier is selected, a *purchase order* is prepared. When the goods are received, they are checked against the purchase order before payment is made to the supplier.

Inventory control is closely related to purchasing. The objectives of inventory control are twofold: (1) to maintain an adequate supply of inventory on hand and (2) to minimize inventory costs. The first objective requires that enough materials, parts, and supplies be available to meet production needs. Halting production because of inventory shortages can be disastrous. In addition, enough finished goods must be on hand to meet customer demand.

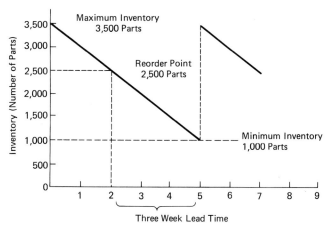

FIGURE 12.3   Inventory Chart for Part 10A

Inventory costs include the costs of handling and storage, interest on funds tied up in inventory, insurance expense, and the risks of obsolescence and deterioration. Inventory control may be viewed as a sort of balancing act—the risks of running out of inventory must be balanced against the costs of maintaining large supplies on hand.

Inventory control systems may be highly sophisticated, often involving the use of electronic computers. However, the basic principles can be illustrated with a simple example. Suppose the inventory control manager has determined that Part 10A is used at the rate of 500 per week. It takes 3 weeks to deliver a minimum order of 2500 parts. To avoid running out, the manager has decided to keep a 2-week supply on hand at all times. The manager wants to know the answer to two questions: (1) When should an order be placed for additional parts? (2) What will be the maximum inventory on hand?

Figure 12.3 summarizes the inventory levels for Part 10A. The minimum inventory is 1000 parts (2 weeks × 500 parts per week). The reorder point is 2500 parts. Why? Because it takes 3 weeks lead time before an order will be received. During that period 1500 parts will be used (500 parts per week × 3 weeks). The reorder point is found by adding the parts needed during the lead time (1500 parts) to the minimum inventory (1000 parts). The maximum inventory is 3500 parts—the order size of 2500 parts plus the minimum inventory.

CAD/CAM: THE NEW INDUSTRIAL REVOLUTION

The United States is on the verge of a second industrial revolution that promises to transform the way goods are produced. The goal of this revolution is to revitalize American industry through massive increases in productivity. The most widely recognized symbol of our

ISSUE   THE JAPANESE MANUFACTURING SYSTEM

The Japanese economic success has been attributed to a variety of factors ranging from participative management to the country's high rate of saving and investment. Often overlooked, however, is the simple fact that the Japanese are experts at running factories. Nowhere is this point more apparent than in the automobile industry where the Japanese lead the world in quality and productivity. Among the more significant manufacturing techniques are tiny inventories, production in small lots, individual responsibility for quality control, and job rotation.

Japanese automobile manufacturers keep only enough parts on hand for immediate production needs. Inventory control at Toyota Motor Company is called the "just-in-time" system. When new parts are needed, they are ordered from suppliers who deliver directly to production lines, often within a few hours. This system requires close coordination and cooperation with suppliers, most of whom are located within a few miles of the automobile plant. Maintaining minimum inventories saves storage space, reduces materials handling, and minimizes the amount of funds tied up in inventory.

According to conventional wisdom, the benefits of mass production result from long production runs where a large volume of identical products is manufactured. However, the Japanese view overproduction as waste. To keep goods-in-process and finished goods inventories at a minimum, Japan's auto manufacturers typically gear production to orders from the marketing department. This forces the factory to produce in lots as small as 50 units with frequent changeovers to different products. As a result, production workers become very fast at machine setup procedures required to change over to different parts or models. At one factory, the changeover time for an operation was reduced from 2 hours to 3 minutes.

The Japanese system encourages every employee to take responsibility for quality control. Every worker has a button to stop the assembly line if a defect is spotted. This can be costly in lost production time, but it instills a concern for quality and helps detect minor problems before they become major ones.

Training workers to do several jobs provides versatility in reassigning employees when orders change. If sales decline, employees can be shifted to maintenance and repair tasks rather than continuing production for inventory buildup.

Far more important than individual technique is the attitude that pervades the Japanese manufacturing system of continually striving to improve production operations.

changing production system is the *industrial robot,* which combines computer brainpower with the mechanical arm. But robots are only one part of the new system that goes by the name of Computer Aided Design/Computer-Aided Manufacturing, or simply CAD/CAM.

The Revitalization of American Industry

Put simply, *CAD/CAM* is an integrated, computer-controlled system of factory automation. It is the push-button factory become a reality. Early efforts at automation date back 40 years and more, while the first industrial robot was invented in the United States about 2 decades ago. Why then did the frantic race to automate U.S. factories begin only in the past few years? Two factors have given impetus to the heavy investment in CAD/CAM systems. The first is the sagging productivity of U.S. industry reflected in the growing competition from abroad. American executives have come to realize that to remain in business, they must automate. The second factor is the rapid advances in computer technology. The development of the low-cost microcomputer made automation economically feasible. Moreover, recent improvements in software have permitted the linkup of design and production activities, which is the central feature of CAD/CAM systems.

Computer-Aided Design (CAD)

CAD is the vital first step in factory automation. It permits products to be designed on a computer's video screen while accumulating the data necessary to computerize overall production planning. Using an electronic pen, design engineers sketch the outlines of a part on the screen. Based on data in its memory, the design computer assigns precise tolerances to the sketch and displays the part in three dimensions. The drawings can be tested under computer-simulated conditions to make sure the part meets performance standards. Figure 12.4 illustrates the computer-aided design of a Ford Thunderbird.

When the data for the final design have been accumulated in the CAD computer, it can be transferred to an automated machine tool or robot, which translates the electronic design into a finished part.

Computer-Aided Manufacturing (CAM)

CAM systems begin with inexpensive microcomputers that exercise control over machine tools. An example is the industrial robot. But CAM goes far beyond robot assembly. It includes the linking together of machine tools and work stations through large computers that provide managers with push-button control over factory operations. The result is faster decision making and greater flexibility, both of which translate into huge productivity gains.

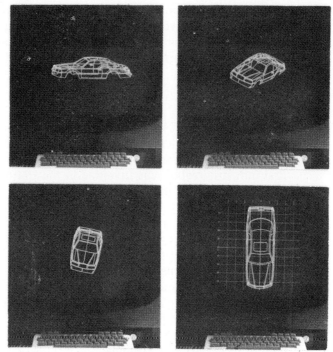

FIGURE 12.4   Computer-Aided Design:
Three-Dimensional Rotation of the Ford Thunderbird

The Impact of CAD/CAM

Automated systems offer a number of significant advantages to manufacturers. Specifically, CAD/CAM can:

- Reduce the time required to develop, design, and manufacture new products by 25 percent or more.

- Boost factory productivity fourfold.

- Speed up management decision making and improve control over manufacturing operations.

- Enhance flexibility by permitting factories to produce in small job lots without losing the economies of mass production.

- Sharply reduce inventories by cutting the time required to manufacture parts and assemble finished goods.

The benefits of CAD/CAM are so overwhelming that an estimated one-quarter of all factories will be using these systems in the next decade. At first most development and investment was done by giant firms in the automobile, aircraft, and heavy construction equipment industries that could afford large mainframe computers and elaborate software packages. However, in the past few years CAD/CAM software has been developed for low-cost

ISSUE   WHAT IS A ROBOT?

Industrial robots bear little resemblance to the robot creatures in science fiction adventures. As one writer put it, the typical factory robot looks like a large fireplug with a mechanical arm growing out of its top.

What does the robot do? It is a computer-controlled machine capable of performing several tasks and handling a variety of materials. The robot can be reprogrammed according to the job required. Actually there is a debate over the distinction between robots and automated machinery. In Japan, which leads in the production and use of robots, any device that performs simple repetitive tasks such as lifting objects and placing them elsewhere is classified as a robot. By U.S. standards, this device is automated equipment.

What makes the robot unique is its electronic brain, or microcomputer, that can be programmed to do a task repeatedly and accurately without human supervision. More advanced robots provide greater flexibility and can perform a wide variety of tasks. An example of an "intelligent" robot is the IBM RS 1 that has a six-direction, hydraulically powered arm and a two-fingered gripper equipped with both tactile and infrared optical sensors. The optical sensors tell the robot when an object is between the fingers of the gripper, and the tactile sensors enable the robot to jiggle a part into place when it is incorrectly aligned. Moreover, the RS 1 can respond to voice commands such as "grasp" and "transport." Using a robot language, AML (A Manufacturing Language), the robot can be programmed to go on to a second job when its parts feeder box is empty.

The most advanced robots are equipped with vision systems using solid-state cameras linked to computers that enable the robot to scan and sort parts as well as inspect engines and entire body assemblies for defects.

Do robots displace human workers? Yes and no. People with jobs that are systematic, routine, and mechanical such as welding and paint spraying are likely to be displaced by robots. Robots, however, may enable firms to slash costs and improve quality, thereby resulting in expanded sales and production, and a corresponding need for more human employees. Sometimes the hiring of humans increases after robots are installed.

personal computers. As a result, smaller firms producing low-technology products such as spoons and forks, shoes, hair dryers, and toys have purchased computer-aided design and manufacturing systems. Smaller companies have found that CAD/CAM boosts profits by cutting product development time, improving product quality, and reducing manufacturing costs.

The high-technology CAD/CAM systems are changing the very meaning of work for both blue-collar and white-collar employees. Most observers do not expect widespread displacement of workers by automated equipment. For one thing there is a growing demand for computer technicians to install, repair, maintain, and oversee CAD/CAM systems. Many firms are investing heavily in retraining programs aimed at providing the necessary technical skills for their employees.

SUMMARY

Production in the United States is characterized by large-scale operations, mechanization, standardization, specialization, and diversification.

Production may be divided into five processes: extraction, analytic, synthetic, fabrication, and assembly. There are two broad types of manufacturing: (1) mass production, which is the manufacture of large quantities of standard products; and (2) custom production, which is the manufacture of products to customer specifications.

Production management seeks to produce goods at the lowest cost consistent with desired quality. Plant location decisions are based on several factors including nearness to the market, availability of labor, and nearness to raw materials. The two basic types of plant layout are the process layout, typically found in custom production, and the line layout, which is used in mass production.

Production planning and control attempts to ensure the steady flow of work through the plant. The production plan determines what, how, and when work should be accomplished. Routing, scheduling, and make-or-buy decisions are important parts of the production plan.

Job design is aimed at improving worker efficiency through motion-and-time study. Motion study attempts to find the best way of performing a task. Time study is used to establish time standards for different jobs.

Quality control refers to establishing quality standards and inspecting products to ensure they conform to these standards.

Purchasing is all the activities required to buy materials, supplies, and parts for production. The purchasing agent must consider many factors such as price, quality, delivery time, transportation costs, and the reliability of suppliers.

Inventory control requires balancing inventory costs against the risks of running short of inventory.

Computer-Aided Design/Computer-Aided Manufacturing (CAD/CAM) refers to integrated systems of factory automation that can increase productivity by linking design and production activities.

**SELF-
EXAMINATION
QUESTIONS**

The following questions are based on the Chapter Objectives listed at the beginning of the chapter. Test yourself by circling the letter preceding the answer that *best* completes the statement or answers the question. The answers to the Self-Examination Questions are in the appendix at the end of the textbook.

1. Which of the following is *not* a characteristic of the U.S. production system? (A) mechanization; (B) standardization; (C) generalization; (D) diversification; (E) large-scale production.

2. The production process that involves chemically combining several materials into a product (such as steelmaking) is called: (A) analytic; (B) synthetic; (C) fabrication; (D) assembly; (E) extraction.

3. Mass-production manufacturing systems usually require: (A) the process layout; (B) the line layout; (C) general-purpose equipment; (D) special-purpose equipment; (E) both A and C; (F) both B and D.

4. Breaking down a task into parts to determine the easiest and fastest way to do the job is called: (A) motion study; (B) quality control; (C) time study; (D) make-or-buy analysis; (E) none of these.

5. The purchasing process begins with a(n): (A) invoice; (B) purchase order; (C) bid request; (D) requisition; (E) none of these.

6. If a part is used at the rate of 50 per month, and it requires a 3-month wait to receive a minimum order of 300 parts, what is the reorder point if the inventory manager wants to keep at least 100 parts on hand at all times? (A) 300; (B) 250; (C) 200; (D) 150; (E) none of these.

7. CAD/CAM: (A) is an integrated, computer-controlled system of factory automation; (B) involves product design using a computer's video display screen and an electronic pen; (C) is likely to include the use of industrial robots; (D) all of these; (E) none of these.

Student _____

BUILDING A BUSINESS VOCABULARY

Directions: Match the terms with their definitions by writing the letter in the appropriate blank.

a. Assembly
b. Standardization
c. Time Study
d. Custom Production
e. Requisition
f. Fabrication
g. General-Purpose Equipment
h. Computer-Aided Design
i. Process Layout
j. Quality Control
k. Specialization
l. Analytic
m. Scheduling
n. Mechanization

o. Routing
p. Make-or-Buy Decision
q. Computer-Aided Manufacturing
r. Extraction
s. Motion Study
t. Synthetic
u. Line Layout
v. Diversification
w. Mass Production
x. Special-Purpose Equipment
y. Industrial Robot
z. CAD/CAM

_____ 1. The substitution of machines for humanpower.

_____ 2. Manufacturing standard products in large quantities.

_____ 3. A plant design in which similar machines are grouped together.

_____ 4. Machinery designed to perform a single operation at high speed.

_____ 5. Inspecting products to determine if they conform to quality standards.

_____ 6. A form that lists the quantity, size, and description of materials, parts, or supplies to be purchased.

_____ 7. A production process that entails taking material from the earth or water.

_____ 8. A manufacturing system using computers to plan and control production as well as direct individual machine tools.

_____ 9. Making parts interchangeable.

_____ 10. A procedure used to establish standard times for jobs.

_____ 11. A production process that involves chemically combining materials into a single product; for example, the production of steel.

_____ 12. Dividing work into simple jobs or tasks to increase productivity.

_____ 13. Determining how work will move through the production process.

_____ 14. A production process in which parts are put together to form finished goods.

_____ 15. Arrangement of machines according to the sequence of operations.

_____ 16. A production process that involves changing the form of a material.

_____ 17. The determination of which parts should be manufactured by a firm and which should be purchased from outside suppliers.

_____ 18. An integrated, computer-controlled system of factory automation linking together product design and production.

_____ 19. A computer-controlled machine capable of performing several tasks and handling a variety of materials that can be reprogrammed according to the job required.

_____ 20. Manufacturing goods to customer specifications.

_____ 21. Establishing a timetable for production operations.

_____ 22. A production process found, for example, in a lumber mill, in which a basic material is broken down into several products.

_____ 23. A procedure used to find the most efficient way of performing a job.

_____ 24. Adding new products to increase sales and profits.

_____ 25. Machinery typically found in job shops that can perform a variety of operations.

_____ 26. The use of computer video screens to design and test new products.

Student _____

REVIEWING MAJOR CONCEPTS

1. Suppose every make and model of automobile came with different size tires. What problems would this create?

2. Does automation cause unemployment? Support your answer.

3. What problems may result from specialization of labor?

4. Which production processes are required to produce automobiles?

5. Is the line layout likely to be found in custom production? Explain why or why not.

6. What are the major disadvantages of the process layout?

7. Which type of equipment is typically used in mass production? In custom production? Explain why.

8. "A firm should always strive to achieve the highest quality in its products." Do you agree or disagree? Why?

9. Inventory control has been described as a balancing act. Explain why.

10. When asked about the need for factory automation, a vice-president of General Electric Company responded, "Automate, emigrate, or evaporate." Explain this statement.

Student _____

11. What do you consider the most important factors in selecting a location for the following:

   a. A soft-drink bottling plant.

   b. A computer development laboratory.

   c. A lumber mill.

   d. A brewery.

   e. A potato-chip factory.

12. The following questions refer to Computer-Aided Design and Computer-Aided Manufacturing, or CAD/CAM.

    a. How do CAD and CAM differ?

    b. In what way are CAD and CAM related?

    c. True or False? CAM is merely the use of industrial robots in manufacturing. Explain your answer.

    d. In what ways can CAD/CAM increase efficiency and reduce manufacturing costs?

    e. What effects will widespread installation of CAD/CAM systems have on the industrial work force?

Student _____

SOLVING PROBLEMS AND CASES

1. *Case:* Stanton Industries, Inc.

   Stanton Industries is a medium-size manufacturer of plumbing fixtures located near Cleveland, Ohio. The company has not been profitable in recent years, and 2 months ago the board of directors hired a new management team to revitalize the firm.
   Keith Goode, the new, young, and aggressive production manager, decided to use motion-and-time study to improve worker productivity and to develop time standards for more effective production planning. He employed a team of industrial engineers to conduct the study.
   Yesterday, the engineers appeared in the plant with clipboards and stop-watches. One engineer was assigned to each department. He stood behind workers carefully analyzing and timing their movements.
   Some of the workers became nervous and anxious, and one employee quit on the spot. Most of the older workers deliberately slowed their pace.
   At the end of the day, the union lodged a formal grievance charging management with harassment of the workers. The union threatened a strike unless the study was halted immediately.

   a. Why did the workers react as they did?

   b. How could the trouble have been avoided?

2. *Case:* Carter Container Company

The management of the Carter Container Company is considering the purchase of a new machine that costs $600,000 and has an estimated life of 5 years. The operating costs of the machine are $30,000 per year.

The machine will replace 10 workers who are paid $7 per hour under the union contract. Each employee works 40 hours per week for an average of 50 weeks per year.

a. Should the firm purchase the machine? Why or why not?

b. What factors should be considered in making the decision?

Student _____

3. *Case:* Norton Foundry Company

The Norton Foundry Company uses 10,000 tons of coal per month. A shipment of 60,000 tons of coal requires 3 months from the order date for delivery. The inventory control manager wants to keep at least a month's supply on hand at all times to avoid running out of coal.

a. At what level of inventory should the manager place an order for more coal?

b. Draw an inventory chart showing the maximum and minimum inventories and the reorder point.

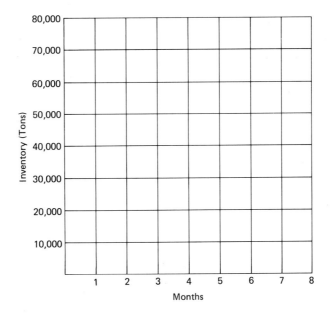

4. *Case:* Barker Manufacturing Company

You have been assigned the job of scheduling in the Production Control Department of the Barker Manufacturing Company, a job shop located in Los Angeles. The head of the department, Rocky Snark, believes in "learning by doing."

At 8:00 A.M. on August 7, you receive an order for 200 Zumpers (Jobs 123 and 124) to be delivered at 8:00 A.M. on August 11. You have a modified flow process chart for Zumpers shown below.

Before leaving for coffee, Rocky says, "Okay, kid, schedule the order on the Gantt chart. Don't forget to work backwards from the delivery date. The inspection after the milling operation takes place in the Milling Department. Get hopping!"

(*Hint:* The flow process chart shows the routing for an order of Zumpers together with time required for each operation. Note the job size is 100 Zumpers. The Gantt chart covers the period from August 7 through August 10. The scale under the dates shows hours. The numbered blocks are jobs already scheduled.)

FLOW PROCESS CHART FOR ZUMPERS—JOB SIZE: 100

Operation	Symbol	Explanation	Time in Hours
1	● ● ■	Transportation to Milling Department Milling Operation Inspection	2
2	● ●	Transportation to Drill Punch Department Drill Punch Operation	1
3	● ●	Transportation to Lathe Department Lathe Operation	3
4	● ●	Transportation to Paint Department Painting	6
5	● ■	Transportation to Inspection Department Final Inspection	2
6	●	Transportation to Storage Storage	

●	4	●	6	■	2	▼	1
	Operation		Transport		Inspection		Storage

Student _____

GANTT CHART

Departments	August 7	August 8	August 9	August 10
Milling		93		
Drill Punch	89		90 | 101	107
Lathe	Dept. Picnic ☒		93	120 | 93
Paint	117			109
Final Inspection	100		89	90

THE BUSINESS ENVIRONMENT: TODAY AND TOMORROW

In Part 5 the focus again widens. Chapter 13 explores three related topics: (a) how laws and the legal system shape business affairs; (b) the growing scope of the social responsibility of business; and (c) the controversial area of business ethics. The final chapter briefly introduces some future business trends and concludes by examining world business, international trade, and the role of multinationals.

CHAPTER	TITLE
13	The Social and Legal Environment of Business
14	International Business and Future Trends

chapter 13

THE SOCIAL AND LEGAL ENVIRONMENT OF BUSINESS

This book began with a general overview of the business system. Later chapters focused in on specific areas of business. This chapter again takes the broad view. It provides a brief and general summary of the U.S. legal system as it applies to business and examines the critical question of the social responsibility of business. Our legal system defines the "rules of the game" that govern business operations. A growing number of people believe that responsibility of business extends beyond merely conforming to the law.

CHAPTER OBJECTIVES

1. Distinguish common law from statutory law.

2. Explain the purpose of the Uniform Commercial Code (UCC).

3. List and explain the requirements of an enforceable contract.

4. Distinguish between:

   • Principals and agents

   • Personal property and real property

   • Trademarks and copyrights

   • Sales and bailments

5. State the two major purposes of bankruptcy.

6. Give three reasons why modern business managers are increasingly concerned with social responsibility.

7. Name four areas in which the social responsibility of business has expanded in the last 30 years.

8. Differentiate between laws and ethics.

BUSINESS AND THE LAW

All a business manager needs to know about the law is when to call a lawyer.

Old Saying Popular Among Lawyers

A man who serves as his own lawyer has a fool for a client.

Older Saying Popular Among Lawyers

A key function of government is to provide a legal system that prescribes the "rules of the game." Our legal system includes a body of written and unwritten laws together with a system of courts to enforce these laws. A society makes laws to protect the rights of its citizens, to promote order, and to provide a means of settling disputes.

The supreme law of the land is the U.S. Constitution. All laws —federal, state, and local—must conform to the provisions of the Constitution. Our system of law may be divided into two broad parts: (1) *common law,* or unwritten law, which is based on the principle that each court decision becomes the basis for deciding future cases of a similar type; and (2) *statutes,* or statutory law, which are legally enforceable rules passed by legislative bodies ranging from Congress to your city council. Under common law, judges attempt to reach decisions by studying previous court decisions on similar cases. Thus the basis of much law goes back to decisions made hundreds of years ago in England.

Business Law

Business law (sometimes called commercial law) is a set of rules and procedures that govern business affairs. Without clearly established rules and procedures, business operations would collapse in chaos. The most comprehensive body of business law is the *Uniform Commercial Code* (UCC), first formulated in 1952 and since then adopted by all states except Louisiana. The UCC was devised to reduce the differences in laws among states, thereby simplifying the legal rules governing business transactions and promoting commercial activity.

Some of the key areas of the law that are of major importance to business are contracts, agency, property, trademarks, patents, copyrights, negotiable instruments, sales, bailment, and bankruptcy. The following summary is necessarily brief and only touches on a few major topics.

Contracts   The law of contracts is the basis for nearly all commercial law. A *contract* is a legally enforceable agreement among two or more parties (individuals and/or business firms). Commercial contracts were common hundreds of years before the birth of Christ. Today, tens of thousands of contracts are made each day. In order for a contract to be enforceable under the law, it must meet five requirements:

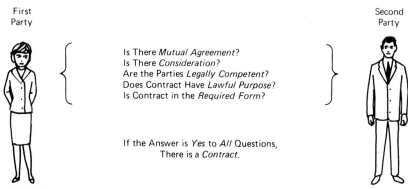

First
Party

Second
Party

Is There *Mutual Agreement?*
Is There *Consideration?*
Are the Parties *Legally Competent?*
Does Contract Have *Lawful Purpose?*
Is Contract in the *Required Form?*

If the Answer is *Yes* to *All* Questions,
There is a *Contract.*

FIGURE 13.1   Requirements for a Contract

1   *Mutual Agreement.* There must be an offer and an acceptance without fraud, duress, or undue influence. In the eyes of the law, there must be a "meeting of the minds" of the parties to a contract.
2   *Consideration.* There must be something of value (usually, but not always, money) given in exchange for a promise.
3   *Competent Parties.* In order to be valid, all parties to a contract must be of proper age, sane, and not incapacitated.
4   *Lawful Purpose.* Contracts that require illegal acts are unenforceable.
5   *Required Form.* Some contracts such as those involving the sale of real estate, or the sale of personal property in excess of $500, or those covering a period of a year or more, must be in writing.

Figure 13.1 summarizes the major requirements for a valid contract.

Agency   Agency refers to the relationship between a *principal* and an *agent.* The principal (an individual or business firm) authorizes the agent to act for the principal in dealing with third parties. Typical examples of agents include stockbrokers, automobile dealers, and real estate agents. The principal must compensate the agent for services rendered, and is liable for damages suffered by third parties that result from the authorized actions of the agent. For example, if a motorcycle dealer (the agent) sells a motorcycle after adjusting the brakes according to the manufacturer's instructions, and the customer (third party) crashes due to brake failure, the manufacturer (principal) may be held liable by the customer for damages.

No formal agreement is required to create an agency relationship. When it appears that one person is working under the control of and for the benefit of another, in the eyes of the law an agency relationship exists. An employee of a firm may become an agent of the owner-manager if specific powers such as the authority to order merchandise are delegated to the employee.

Property   The U.S. Constitution guarantees the right of individuals to own, use, and dispose of property. The law distinguishes between two categories of property—real and personal. *Real property* consists of land or anything permanently attached to the land such as buildings, mineral deposits, and trees. *Personal property* refers to everything but real estate and includes "movable" items such as stocks and bonds, clothing, and automobiles. Usually real property and personal property are subject to different tax rates.

The owner of property may use it in a variety of ways including mortgaging it, leasing it, selling it, or improving it. A *mortgage* is a written pledge of property as security for a loan. If the debtor defaults (fails to repay the loan), the lender forecloses the mortgage and sells the property to repay the loan.

Trademarks   A symbol, word, or group of words that distinguishes the goods or services of one producer from all others is called a *trademark.* Coke, CBS, *The Wall Street Journal,* and various brand names are registered trademarks. Companies having registered trademarks are legally entitled to their exclusive use for 20 years (renewable for another 20 years). If the trademark becomes generic (i.e., accepted by the public to identify a product in general as opposed to one specific company's product), the company may lose all legal rights to the name. Aspirin, cellophane, linoleum, and zipper once were product names but now have become generic. Band-Aid, Kleenex, Levi's, Vaseline, and Xerox are all registered trademarks, but are in danger of becoming generic.

Patents   A *patent* is an exclusive right to make, use, or sell a previously unknown product or process. This legal right is granted for up to 17 years and can only be renewed by an act of Congress. Patents encourage product research, development, and innovation by protecting the works of inventors. High-technology companies such as Apple, Texas Instruments, and IBM have found that even though patents may provide protection for 17 years, rapid technological changes may make their products obsolete far sooner.

Copyrights   *Copyrights* provide legal protection of the use of original work created by an author, artist, or composer. This book (and others), music, photography, and computer programs typically are protected by copyrights. Copyrights prohibit the copying of original works without permission for 50 years beyond the death of the creator(s).

Film makers, such as Universal Studios and Walt Disney Productions, felt that home taping of their movies infringed on their copyrights. In 1984, however, the U.S. Supreme Court held that such copying is not illegal provided that it is used exclusively in the home and not for personal gain.

Negotiable Instruments   *Negotiable instruments* are business documents used in place of cash. The most common type of negotiable instrument is a check. Other types include promissory notes, money orders, and certificates of deposit. Hundreds of millions of negotiable instruments are used daily in business. They facilitate business transactions by simplifying payments among individuals and business firms. To meet the requirements laid down by the Uniform Commercial Code, a negotiable instrument must be a written and signed unconditional promise to pay to order or to bearer a certain sum of money on demand or on a specific date.

The holder of a negotiable instrument may transfer it by *endorsement*—simply signing his or her name on the back. The person endorsing the instrument is called the endorser, and the person to whom the instrument is transferred is referred to as the endorsee. Three common types of endorsements are illustrated in Figure 13.2.

A *blank endorsement* occurs when the endorser signs his or her name on the back of the instrument (usually on the left end). This makes the instrument payable to the bearer (anyone who has possession of it). A *restrictive endorsement* is commonly used as a safeguard against the loss or theft of checks. By writing the words "for deposit" above the signature, the endorser prevents further negotiation of the check, and if the check is lost, it cannot be cashed by the bearer. A *special endorsement* prevents payment of the check to anyone other than the endorsee.

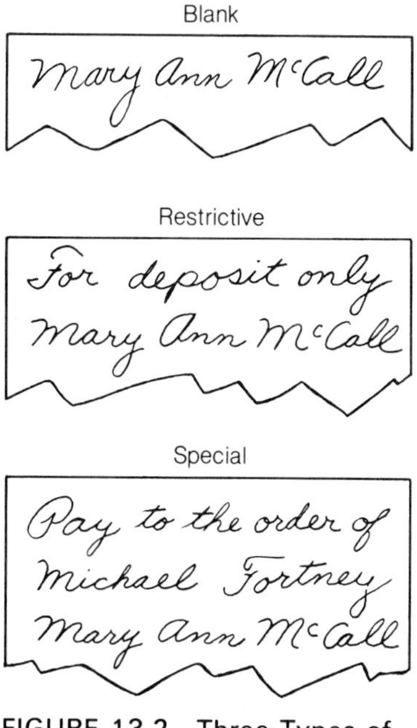

Blank

Mary Ann McCall

Restrictive

For deposit only
Mary Ann McCall

Special

Pay to the order of
Michael Fortney
Mary Ann McCall

FIGURE 13.2 Three Types of Endorsements

Sales   The law of *sales* as set forth in the Uniform Commercial Code governs transactions involving the sale and purchase of goods and services. It is largely concerned with the passage of title from the seller to the buyer. When goods are sold for cash, title passes immediately. Normally, when goods are sold on account, the title passes at the time of the sale. However, a different situation arises in the case of a *conditional sales contract,* which is typically used in the sale of durable goods such as furniture, automobiles, and appliances. The title does not pass until the goods are fully paid for, and the contract provides that if the buyer does not make the payments when due, the seller can repossess the goods.

A *warranty* is a legally enforceable guarantee by the seller as to the quality and suitability of the goods sold or services rendered. An *express warranty* is a statement by the seller (usually in writing) as to the quality and other characteristics of the goods sold. Figure 13.3 shows a typical express warranty. In contrast, an *implied warranty* is not made directly by the seller but is implied by the law. For example, there is a basic understanding between the buyer and seller that the goods are generally suitable for the purpose intended. When you purchase a shirt, you have the right to expect that it has two sleeves and a full set of buttons. If it doesn't, you have the right to return and exchange it under an implied warranty.

Bailment   Suppose you leave your television set at a repair shop, or ship merchandise by air freight to a customer, or rent a car during your vacation. In each case, a *bailment* has been created. A bailment is not a sale because no title passes. Under a bailment relationship, a *bailor* (the owner of personal property) temporarily turns the property over to a *bailee,* who takes possession, and, after accomplishing the purpose of the bailment, either (1) returns the property to the bailor, or (2) turns it over to a third party (for example, a customer). Depending on the circumstances, the bailee is required to exercise reasonable care over the bailor's property, usually receives a fee for services rendered, and may be liable for damages to the property.

Bankruptcy   Bankruptcy laws have two major purposes: (1) to help debtors who are insolvent and cannot pay their debts, and (2) to provide for an equitable distribution of the debtor's assets among the creditors. A *voluntary bankruptcy* occurs when an insolvent individual or business firm requests that bankruptcy proceedings be initiated. In the case of *involuntary bankruptcy,* it is the creditors that request the court to declare a debtor bankrupt. *Bankruptcy* proceedings include several key steps:

1   A court declares the debtor (an individual or firm) bankrupt, and a receiver (or referee) is appointed to take temporary custody of the debtor's assets.

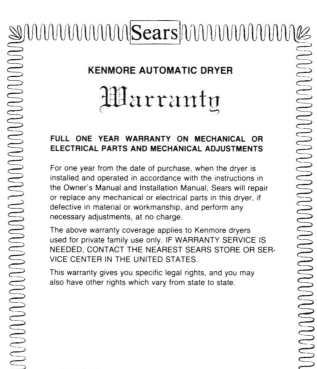

FIGURE 13.3   An Express Warranty
Courtesy of Sears, Roebuck and Co.

2   The creditors are notified of the bankruptcy and within 6 months file claims for the money owed them by the debtor.
3   With court approval the creditors select a trustee (an individual or corporation) to liquidate the debtor's assets and make a distribution to the creditors.
4   At the end of the proceedings the debtor's liability for unpaid debts is canceled.

In the case of a huge corporation, where liquidation would work a hardship on the public or a large number of employees, the court may direct the trustee to prepare a *reorganization plan,* which could provide that the creditors be paid in newly issued stocks or bonds rather than cash. The purpose of reorganization is to permit the firm to continue to operate and, if possible, make a financial recovery.

In 1982, Manville Corporation, one of the world's largest producers of asbestos insulating materials, filed for bankruptcy even though its net worth (assets minus liabilities) exceeded $1.1 billion. Manville Corporation anticipated law suits for damages exceeding $2 billion to be filed by as many as 11 million workers suffering from asbestos-related diseases. Critics believe that Manville used legal maneuvers to avoid paying a "fair" amount to injured workers. The corporation counters that if all funds are used to pay off current claims, nothing would be available for those not aware of injuries that may take as long as 40 years to surface. By declaring bankruptcy, Manville Corporation established a fund for future as well as current claimants. In addition, similar claims were lumped together, which reduced legal costs and thereby provided more funds for injured workers. Lawyers for the claimants argued that the size of the fund is too small and that cases should be determined on an individual basis. The controversy will continue for years. Do you think Manville Corporation acted responsibly?

THE SOCIAL RESPONSIBILITY OF BUSINESS

The public be damned; I'm working for my stockholders.

William Vanderbilt

Those who do not take responsibility for their power, ultimately shall lose it.

Keith Davis and Robert Blomstrom,
Business and Its Environment

Business and Society

Our business system does not operate in isolation from the rest of society. Business firms necessarily interact with many groups and individuals. Figure 13.4 illustrates the relationships between business management and six major groups of constituents. The management of a business firm is responsible to:

- *Customers*—to provide goods and services of satisfactory quality at competitive prices.

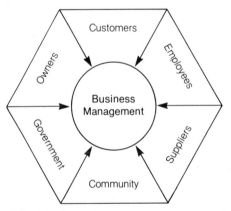

FIGURE 13.4   The Business Environment

- *Employees*—to provide fair wages and benefits, safe and healthy working conditions, and opportunities for advancement.

- *Suppliers*—to deal fairly and equitably with those firms from which it purchases.

- *The Community*—to be a good neighbor and responsible citizen by protecting the natural environment and promoting the social, economic, and cultural welfare of the community.

- *Government*—to conform to the laws and regulations laid down by the various levels of government.

- *Owners*—to conserve resources and strive to achieve an attractive rate of return on the funds invested in the business.

This is quite an order even for large and wealthy corporations. It is easy to see how some of these responsibilities may be in conflict with each other. For example, boosting employee wages and benefits may reduce the funds available for protecting the environment or providing an attractive profit on the stockholders' investment. Meeting government regulations may raise costs and require price increases to customers. In meeting its responsibilities, management must recognize the *tradeoffs*—more for one group means less for the others—and strive to achieve the best balance among the groups. Of course, this is easier to suggest than it is to achieve because each group tends to feel it is being shortchanged.

Beyond these immediate concerns, business managers must be sensitive to the changing social, political, economic, and natural environment. Our society's resources, its laws, and its social and political goals are constantly changing, and these changes exert immense pressures on business firms. Society's commitments to solving the problems of environmental pollution, eliminating poverty, providing equal opportunities for minorities and women, and protecting consumers are a reflection of the changing environment. The effective business manager must assess these changes in terms of their impact on the firm and include this assessment in making business decisions.

What Is the Social Responsibility of Business?

Until a few years ago, it was an easy task to define the social responsibility of business. Nearly everyone agreed that the role of business was to produce the goods and services society wanted as efficiently as possible. This point of view is best summed up by Milton Friedman, winner of the 1976 Nobel Prize in economics, who states: "In a (free) economy, there is one and only one social responsibility of business—to use its resources and engage in activities designed to increase profits so long as it stays within the rules of the game, which is to say, engages in open and free competition, without deception or fraud."

In the past few decades, however, this doctrine has come under increasing attack both from within and without the business community. The critics insist that business must look beyond efficient production and profits and give more consideration to those individuals and groups who are affected by the firm's actions— consumers, employees, and community neighbors. Beyond this, many people believe business has an obligation to achieve broad social goals such as curing urban ills, cleaning up the environment, hiring and training the hard-core unemployed, and fighting racial and sex discrimination. They claim that business has the power, money, and expertise to lead the fight to solve our nation's social problems.

The banner of corporate responsibility is gaining followers from a growing number of corporate managers including Lee Iacocca and David Rockefeller. Hundreds of firms are spending billions of dollars on programs ranging from pollution control to community development.

Why have so many firms embraced the philosophy of expanded social responsibility for business? In the first place, business managers recognize that society increasingly *expects* business firms to be socially responsible. Second, many managers are convinced that in the long run it is in the best interests of business to promote the social and economic welfare of society. Third, if business fails to act responsibly, government will impose more regulations creating additional red tape and boosting the cost of doing business. Finally, many managers simply feel that increased involvement in solving social problems is the right thing to do.

The major thrust of corporate efforts toward social responsibility is in four broad areas: (1) fighting poverty and discrimination, (2) protecting workers, (3) informing and protecting consumers, and (4) controlling pollution.

Fighting Poverty and Discrimination   According to federal government figures, over 10 percent of the U.S. population lives in poverty. A disproportionate number of the poor are members of various minority groups including blacks, Hispanics, and native Americans. In addition, although women now comprise about 44 percent of the labor force, female earnings average around 64 percent of what males earn.

Business is responsible for providing equality of opportunity in the workplace. Federal civil rights laws prohibit discrimination on the basis of sex, race, national origin, age, and religion. Moreover, training programs and funding for the hard-core (chronically) unemployed and minority businesses may help offset past discrimination.

Many business firms have an excellent record for hiring and training the hard-core unemployed. Given the proper training and assistance, the hard-core unemployed can become hard-working, capable employees. During the last 20 years the National Alliance of

Businessmen has assisted in the training and placement of more than 3.5 million unemployed.

In the area of plant location, the record is less impressive. As urban decay has attacked many cities, some business firms have relocated to suburban areas in an attempt to escape increasing crime, deteriorating public services, and rising taxes. This relocation has tended to compound the problem of hard-core unemployment by moving jobs away from idle urban workers. Moreover, the exodus of business firms has added to the financial woes of the cities by further reducing the tax base. Some corporations have attempted to counter this trend by deliberately locating new facilities in the central cities. They hope that the added costs of hiring and training the hard-core unemployed, paying high taxes, and providing increased security will be in part offset by government subsidies and tax incentives.

Two groups more recently protected by law from discrimination are the aged and disabled. The Age Discrimination in Employment Act of 1967 outlaws discrimination against those between the ages of 40 to 70. Prior to this act, people over 40 who were laid off often faced difficulty in finding new employment. Business firms tended to hire younger workers even though older workers might have been more qualified. The Vocational Rehabilitation Act of 1973 prohibits discrimination against the disabled (people with physical or mental disabilities that greatly hamper normal activities such as walking, talking, hearing, and seeing) if such disabilities would not prevent them from doing the required work. Business firms contracting with the government are required by law to hire the disabled and make facilities accessible to them. Many businesses voluntarily hire disabled or aged workers because most are productive, responsible, and highly motivated. Technology can and has opened many employment doors traditionally closed to the disabled. Computers and machinery have reduced the need for brawn, while sophisticated prosthetic devices lessen the effects of physical limitations. Today more than ever, one's attitude and work ethic are more important that physical stature. Many of today's best and most accomplished managers come from the "aged and disabled."

Protecting Workers   Wise management is responsive to the needs of employees. Sensitivity to employees can be justified for more than humanitarian reasons; it leads to improved morale, higher productivity, and reduced accidents, deaths, and insurance costs. Business has the responsibility to pay fair salaries, provide good working conditions, safety, and security for employees. However, some business firms have failed to adequately protect workers. This has led to government legislation and regulation. In 1970, the Occupational Safety and Health Administration (OSHA) was created to promote a safer working environment, particularly in high-risk

ISSUE HOW SHOULD MANAGEMENT DEAL WITH ON-THE-JOB ALCOHOL AND DRUG ABUSE?

Alcoholism and drug abuse are sometimes referred to as "silent problems" because many firms choose to ignore them. Management often views these problems as personal ones to be solved by the employee. Some companies have been reluctant to crack down for fear of bad publicity.

The huge and growing costs resulting from on-the-job use of drugs and alcohol are forcing many firms to reconsider their passive attitude. According to a recent congressional report, drug abuse costs business firms around $70 billion annually in reduced productivity and increased health expenses. Moreover, when compared to an average worker, employees with alcohol and drug related problems:

- have four times more accidents,
- use one-third more sickness benefits,
- have five times more compensation claims,
- are absent 16 times more often.

Many firms, including Exxon, IBM, Federal Express, and TWA require urinalysis tests as screening devices for new job applicants. In a growing number of companies, the penalty of being caught with drugs or alcohol is immediate dismissal and, occasionally, legal action. Some companies use lie detectors, drug-sniffing dogs, and undercover agents to find employees guilty of using, selling, or concealing drugs. Such actions may seem extreme but proponents argue it makes the work

jobs such as roofing and mining. Unfortunately, the results of OSHA have been mixed. Critics complain about the unclear and sometimes conflicting regulations, the mountains of time-consuming paper work, and the high cost of meeting regulations. Proponents argue that greater worker safety is worth the price and that future regulations can be more concise and understandable.

Numerous companies are implementing quality of work-life programs to make jobs more interesting and satisfying to employees. In addition, many firms are trying to help workers overcome their dependency on drugs and alcohol. Such programs benefit employees and pay for themselves by increasing productivity and reducing absenteeism and costly mistakes.

ISSUE HOW SHOULD MANAGEMENT DEAL WITH ON-THE-JOB ALCOHOL AND DRUG ABUSE? (Cont.)

---

environment safer and more productive. Moreover, employees working in hazardous areas such as nuclear or chemical plants endanger society if they are high on drugs or alcohol. According to Peter Bensinger, a top consultant on drug and alcohol abuse, "No one has a civil right to violate the law. Companies do have a right and responsibility to establish sound working conditions."

Research suggests, however, that alcoholism and drug addiction are treatable diseases. Approximately half of the Fortune 500 firms (the 500 largest industrial firms in the United States) have programs to identify and rehabilitate drug and alcohol users. Although these programs are at company expense, they pay for themselves in increased productivity and reduced accidents.

Under a typical program, all workers with poor job performance who fail to respond to traditional management methods are referred to the head of corporate counseling in the personnel department. Extensive interviews are aimed at helping employees recognize they have a drinking or drug problem. The threat of job loss jars most employees into acknowledging their problem and seeking treatment. In effect the company says, "We value you as an employee, but you must want to help yourself." If employees fail to respond and continue using drugs or alcohol, they are fired and, if circumstances warrant, arrested.

Should companies fire employees that have drug or alcohol problems or rehabilitate them at company expense? What is your opinion?

Protecting and Informing Consumers   If a business is to survive, it must provide a desired good or service at the right place, time, and price. In short, businesses must be responsive to customers or risk failure. The consumer movement gained momentum in the 1960s when consumer advocates demanded more product information and greater product safety. The government responded by passing laws to inform and protect consumers. Some of these laws are summarized in Table 13.1.

Controlling Pollution   People, creatures, and plants adapt to their environment—or die! The human race is responsible for air, water,

TABLE 13.1   Product Safety and Disclosure Laws

Year	Law	Main Provisions
1966	Truth in Packaging	Ingredients must be listed and net weight shown.
1966	Traffic and Motor Vehicle Safety	Manufacturers must notify new car owners of any safety defects.
1969	Child Protection and Toy Safety	Safer mechanical and/or electrical toys standards were established.
1969	Truth in Lending	All credit terms must be stated in clear, understandable language.
1972	Consumer Product Safety	Established the Consumer Product Safety Commission, set higher safety standards, required warning labels on potentially dangerous goods, and provides for the recall of harmful products.

land, and noise pollution of such levels that the health and survival of the inhabitants of this planet are endangered. Over 40 million tons of industrial waste is dumped or spewed into our ecological system each year. The world can no longer successfully cleanse itself.

During the 1980s business and government spent over $50 billion a year to clean up the U.S. environment. In the final analysis, it is the individual citizen as consumer, taxpayer, and worker who pays the bill for a cleaner environment. Higher costs for antipollution measures may be reflected in higher prices for consumers and fewer jobs for employees. Similarly, government efforts to halt pollution require higher taxes.

In 1980, a $1.6 billion Superfund was created by Congress to be used to clean up chemical dumps. Oil and chemical companies are to replenish the Superfund as dollars are spent to neutralize the effects of past pollution. According to the Environmental Protection Agency (EPA), it will cost more than 10 times that amount over a 10-year period to clean up the 2200 most dangerous waste sites. A recent General Accounting Office study indicated that more than 378,000 chemical dumps will eventually need cleaning up. The Office of Technology Assessment, a congressional research organization, reports clean up costs could exceed $100 billion. The EPA had only 850 dumps listed on its priority list in 1985 and cleaned up a mere 6

TABLE 13.2   Environmental Laws

Year	Law	Main Provisions
1970	National Environmental Policy	Created the Environmental Protection Agency (EPA) to protect the environment by controlling pollution.
1970	Clean Air Amendment	Established strict emission standards for vehicles and factories.
1970	Water Quality Improvement	Raised standards and strengthened water pollution regulations.
1976	Resource Conservation and Recovery	Established standards for solid-waste disposal.
1977	Clean Air Amendment	New standards and deadlines established for vehicle pollution and deterioration of air quality in pristine areas such as national parks. Additional pollution to cities limited and permitted only if offset by reduction in existing sources of pollution.

sites over a 5-year period. Critics claim the six sites were not thoroughly cleaned and environmental protection has been too little, too late.

Often it is difficult to assess which firms are harming which areas. Acid-rain results from sulfur expelled in smoke of highly industrial areas. This smoke may drift many miles before becoming acid-rain. Acid-rain that harms the lakes, rivers, wildlife, and people of one region may be caused by companies located in another state or country.

The causes of pollution are many and complex. The solutions to the problem may be so complicated and costly that government action will be necessary. If business is either unwilling or unable to solve the pollution problem, it is reasonable to expect citizens of a democracy will demand governmental action. Several important environmental laws have been passed that address the pollution problem (Table 13.2).

Many believe these laws have not been sufficient to adequately protect our environment, however. Certain chemicals should be banned or limited, additional tax revenues need to be diverted to cleaning up our environment, and dumping grounds need to be made safe. The cost of this will be staggering. Obviously the cost must be compared to benefits received. However, if we fail to make protection of the environment a top national priority today, the costs to future generations will be even higher. It is cheaper not to pollute than to pay for clean-up efforts later. In addition, some environmental damage is irreversible.

There are solutions to the problems of pollution. Waste materials can be converted into usable materials. Recycling of glass, steel, paper, aluminum, and copper is a partial solution. Conservation of our natural resources, careful production and disposal of chemicals, greater scrutiny over the use of radioactive materials, and cleaning up past pollution are also part of the answer.

The key question today is not whether business should be socially responsible. Nearly everyone agrees it should. The central problem is, and is likely to remain, defining the nature and scope of business's responsibilities to society.

BUSINESS ETHICS

In a general sense, ethics is the name we give to our concern for good behavior. We feel an obligation to consider not only our own personal well-being, but also that of others and of human society as a whole.

Dr. Albert Schweitzer

The last decade has witnessed a strong resurgence of interest in standards of behavior. There is a growing concern for morality in business, government, and society in general. Yet to many, ethics is a vague concept that is difficult to apply to the real world.

Some people mistakenly believe that ethics and the law are the same, but ethics goes far beyond the law. You cannot reduce ethical behavior to a simple set of rules. Ethical behavior is doing what you know and believe is right, not what you can get away with. Often certain acts may be legal, but their morality is doubtful.

Ethics are principles of right and wrong that provide standards of conduct. For many people, the ultimate source of ethical conduct is religious beliefs. Every religion incorporates a system of ethics. For example, the bases of Christian ethics are the Golden Rule and the Ten Commandments. Whatever the source, each individual has a set of ethics—a general sense of what is right and wrong, good and bad. Most people within a society share a general system of ethical principles, but how these principles are applied often depends on the circumstances bearing on a particular situation. For example, it is far easier to behave ethically if everyone else is doing so. On the other hand, it may be relatively easy to rationalize unethical behavior in the heat of a fiercely competitive situation. But regardless of the circumstances, honesty and responsibility are essential elements of ethical behavior.

Economic freedom requires a strong ethical foundation, and the free-enterprise system depends on trust. Today, the credibility of the system is being challenged by some individuals who are convinced

ISSUE THE WORLD'S WORST INDUSTRIAL ACCIDENT

On December 3, 1984, the worst-ever industrial accident occurred at the Union Carbide plant at Bhopal, India, killing 1757 human beings and seriously injuring another 200,000.

The preceding day, an accident or possibly an act of sabotage had caused water to be pumped into a holding tank containing 45 tons of deadly MIC, a hazardous chemical used in the production of pesticides. Because the cooling system was broken, the resulting chemical reaction caused the temperature inside the tank to rise, converting the liquid into a deadly gas. A workman noticed the problem and informed his supervisor. Four Indian workers unsuccessfully attempted to seal the tank. Five safety devices, including a vent scrubber used to neutralize toxic fumes and a flare tower that burns off escaping gas, were inoperative. As the tank pressure rose, panic seized the plant workers.

Shortly after midnight, a valve burst open and the deadly vapor leaked silently into the still, cool night air. The result: almost 1800 Indians living around the plant, many of them children and the elderly, died of heart attack or were literally drowned as their lungs filled up with fluids. Another 200,000 were injured, many of them permanently blinded.

Union Carbide is a large U.S. chemical company with operations in several foreign countries. Under an agreement with the Indian government, the Bhopal plant was 50.9 percent owned by Union Carbide, but the plant was totally managed by Indian nationals. An exhaustive investigation after the accident found that five separate safety devices were either inoperative, broken down, or shut off at the time of the accident. According to Warren Anderson, chairman of Union Carbide, "That plant should not have been operating. . . . Safety is the responsibility of the people who operate our plants. You can't be there day in and day out."

India's minister for law and justice countered: "We expected the company to palm off the blame. But Union Carbide cannot escape responsibility." Others have pointed the finger at the city officials of Bhopal who had permitted thousands of Indians to build slum dwellings next to the potentially hazardous plant.

Suits totaling over $250 billion have been filed against Union Carbide on behalf of the residents of Bhopal.

Who do you believe should be held accountable for the Bhopal disaster?

ISSUE   TESTING YOUR BUSINESS ETHICS

Assume you are the marketing vice-president for a small manufacturing firm operating in a fiercely competitive industry. In which of the following activities would you be willing to participate?

1   Embezzling funds from your firm.
2   Establishing a price-fixing agreement with competitors.
3   Accepting kickbacks from suppliers.
4   Recording "phantom" expenses to reduce taxes.
5   Applying to the government for subsidy payments for which your firm does not qualify.
6   Installing two-way mirrors in the warehouse to guard against employee pilferage.
7   Giving a job to your brother.
8   Making a "facilitating payment" to a foreign customs official to ensure your goods are delivered by the contract deadline. Such payments do not violate U.S. law.
9   Making an advertising claim that your product is special because it contains a super ingredient when your competitor's product contains the same ingredient.
10 Taking advantage of a supplier to purchase goods at less than cost because the supplier is on the verge of bankruptcy.

Hershey H. Friedman and Linda W. Friedman, two business professors, have divided business behavior into four categories:

---

that business is ripping them off. This accusation is causing grave concern among members of the business community. According to Reginald H. Jones, former chairman of the board of General Electric Company, "Shoddy goods, shoddy services, and shoddy ethics are not acceptable, and where there are problems, we've got to straighten them out without waiting to be told by the critics or government."

Many firms have developed codes of ethics to serve as guidelines for managers and employees. One survey found that 90 percent of the firms responding have formal codes of conduct for their executives, and two-thirds of the firms have fired one or more managers within the last 2 years for unethical conduct. Efforts to treat consumers fairly are reflected in growing business participation

ISSUE TESTING YOUR BUSINESS ETHICS (Cont.)

1 *Illegal High-Risk* activities include those described in the first two examples above.
2 *Illegal Low-Risk* activities may be described as "technically illegal, but everyone does it." Examples are 3, 4, and 5.
3 *Unethical* but legal practices include examples 6, 7, and 8.
4 *Possibly Unethical* behavior refers to those activities that are not illegal and are not considered unethical by many, but require careful consideration. The last two activities are examples.

According to the Friedmans' model, if you rejected the first two activities, you are "law-abiding." If you refused to accept the first five examples, then you qualify as "meticulously law-abiding." You are ethical if you would refuse to participate in all but the last two activities. The rejection of all 10 examples earns you the description of "super ethical."

The eighth example underscores the difficulty in legislating ethical behavior. The Foreign Corrupt Practices Act of 1977 was aimed at halting bribery of foreign officials by U.S. business firms. However, Congress recognized that certain types of payments are an accepted way of doing business in some countries. The law appears to exempt facilitating payments (known as "grease") made solely to expedite official actions as well as payments made to "ministerial or clerical" personnel.

in complaint mediation systems operating through better business bureaus, trade associations, and local chambers of commerce. A group of business and professional leaders have established the Ethics Resource Center to promote better industry ethics, more self-regulation, and increased professionalism of all businesses. According to William E. Simon, former Secretary of the Treasury and chairman of the Center:

The essential question facing Americans today in business, community, and government circles is not whether we can "afford" stronger ethical standards, but how much longer we can go without them. Our entire way of life, our democracy, and our treasured private enterprise system are held together by voluntary, societywide bonds of mutual trust and respect. Once these bonds of trust are broken, the whole social framework collapses and the result can only be anarchy or authoritarianism.

SUMMARY

All laws must conform to the U.S. Constitution. Common law, or unwritten law, is based on previous court decisions, while statutes are written rules passed by legislative bodies. The Uniform Commercial Code (UCC) provides a comprehensive body of business law covering such areas as contracts, agency, property, negotiable instruments, sales bailment, and bankruptcy.

A contract is a legally binding agreement among two or more parties that requires mutual agreement, consideration, competent parties, lawful purpose, and the required form. The law of agency governs the relationship between an agent and a principal, who authorizes the agent to act on the principal's behalf in dealing with third parties.

Real property is land and anything permanently attached to the land, while personal property includes all other belongings. Copyrights, patents, and trademarks are used to legally protect firms (or people) from the unauthorized use of their original works, inventions, or distinguishing symbols or names. Negotiable instruments such as checks, promissory notes, and money orders are business documents used in place of cash. Negotiable instruments may be transferred by endorsement.

The law of sales is concerned with transfer of title to goods and services from the seller to the buyer. Warranties, which are legally enforceable guarantees made by the seller regarding the quality and suitability of goods sold, may be expressed or implied. Bailment is a transaction involving a bailor who temporarily turns over personal property to a bailee. Bankruptcy laws are intended to help debtors who cannot pay their debts, and provide for a fair distribution of the debtor's assets among the creditors.

Business managers are responsible to diverse groups of constituents including customers, employees, suppliers, community neighbors, government, and owners. In meeting its responsibilities, management must contend with tradeoffs between conflicting interests of different groups. The concept of social responsibility has expanded in recent years to include such areas as cleaning up the environment, protecting workers, protecting and informing consumers, and helping to combat poverty and discrimination.

Ethics are principles of right and wrong that provide standards of conduct. Ethical standards in business are gaining renewed attention as a result of complaints about business morality and the realization that our business system depends on mutual trust and respect. A growing number of firms are adopting codes of ethics to serve as guidelines for managers and employees, and business leaders are promoting more self-regulation and increased professionalism aimed at encouraging higher standards of ethical behavior.

SELF-EXAMINATION QUESTIONS

The following questions are based on the Chapter Objectives listed at the beginning of the chapter. Test yourself by circling the letter preceding the answer that *best* completes the statement or answers the question. The answers to the Self-Examination Questions are in the appendix at the end of the textbook.

1. The UCC was devised to: (A) allow each state more freedom in establishing business laws; (B) simplify rules governing business transactions; (C) standardize laws pertaining to commercial activities; (D) both A and B; (E) both B and C.

2. Common law is: (A) written; (B) based on past court decisions; (C) passed by legislative bodies; (D) all of these; (E) none of these.

3. Which of the following is a requirement of an enforceable contract? (A) legal purpose; (B) offer and acceptance; (C) consideration; (D) required form; (E) all of these.

4. A person authorized to act on behalf of another in dealing with third parties is called a(n): (A) principal; (B) agent; (C) bailor; (D) endorsee; (E) none of these.

5. Which of the following is an example of personal property? (A) land; (B) buildings; (C) automobiles; (D) all of these; (E) none of these.

6. A symbol, word, or group of words that distinguishes the goods or services of one producer from all others is called a: (A) trademark; (B) patent; (C) copyright; (D) both A and C; (E) none of these.

7. Bankruptcy laws: (A) help debtors who are unable to pay their liabilities; (B) provide creditors with an equitable distribution of the debtor's assets; (C) allow creditors to force bankruptcy on a debtor if the debtor's liabilities exceed assets; (D) all of these; (E) none of these.

8.   Modern business managers are increasingly concerned over social responsibilities because: (A) it is in the best interest of business to be socially responsible; (B) the U.S. Constitution requires it; (C) businesses make excessive profits; (D) all of these; (E) none of these.

9.   Ethics: (A) legally protect the rights of others; (B) provide a means of settling disputes; (C) are principles of right and wrong that guide conduct; (D) both A and B; (E) none of these.

Student _____

BUILDING A BUSINESS VOCABULARY

Directions: Match the terms with their definitions by writing the letter in the appropriate blank.

a. Common Law
b. Statutes
c. Contract
d. Agency
e. Uniform Commercial Code
f. Patent
g. Real Property
h. Personal Property
i. Mortgage
j. Negotiable Instrument
k. Endorsement
l. Copyright
m. Sales
n. Warranty
o. Bailment
p. Bankruptcy
q. Ethics
r. Trademark

___q___ 1. Broad principles of right and wrong that guide human conduct.

___g___ 2. Land and anything permanently attached to land.

___p___ 3. The inability to pay one's debts.

___N___ 4. A legal guarantee of the quality and suitability of goods sold.

___d___ 5. A relationship in which a person is empowered to act as someone's representative.

___j___ 6. A business document that can be substituted for cash.

___o___ 7. A legal relationship in which one party gives possession and control of personal property to another with the understanding that the property will be returned or delivered to a customer.

___C___ 8. A legally enforceable agreement between two or more parties.

___E___ 9. A group of statutes adopted by 49 states covering business transactions.

___H___ 10. All belongings except real estate.

___M___ 11. An area of the law dealing with the transfer of title to goods from the seller to the buyer.

___B___ 12. Written laws passed by legislative bodies.

_____ 13. A signature transferring title to a negotiable instrument.

_____ 14. A written pledge of property for a loan.

_____ 15. Unwritten laws based on court decisions.

_____ 16. A symbol, word, or group of words that distinguishes a good or service of one producer from all others.

_____ 17. A legal right prohibiting others using original work created by an author, artist, or composer.

_____ 18. An exclusive right to make, use, or sell a previously unknown product or process.

Student _____

REVIEWING MAJOR CONCEPTS

1. How does the Uniform Commercial Code (UCC) benefit business firms?

2. What is the difference between a principal and an agent?

3. How do trademarks differ from copyrights?

4. How does a sale differ from a bailment?

5. What are the two major purposes of bankruptcy?

6. Give three reasons why modern business managers are increasingly concerned with social responsibility. Which do you consider the most important reason?

7. What is the difference between ethics and laws?

8. Business firms are charged with the social responsibility of fighting poverty and discrimination, controlling pollution, protecting workers, and protecting and informing consumers. Rank each of these areas by order of importance, indicating your reasons for stressing one area over another.

Student _____

SOLVING PROBLEMS AND CASES

1. Is there a valid contract in each of the following cases? Explain why or why not.

    a. Mary Eden promises her mother to stop smoking.

    b. Three large cookie manufacturers agree in writing to divide the cookie market and drive up prices.

    c. Mr. Thompson promises to sell his store for $50,000 to Mr. Harvey after Mr. Harvey threatens to set fire to the store.

    d. The Arc Record Company ships the latest punk rock album to Ms. Mabel DeVott, age 15, together with a bill for $6.95.

    e. Luke Walker agrees in writing to purchase from Darth Vonder a $10,000 home site that only Darth knows is 10 feet under water.

2. *Case:* Kenton Manufacturing Company vs. Lindell Enterprises

Two of the largest firms in the superwidget industry are Kenton Manufacturing Company and Lindell Enterprises. The managements of each firm have contrasting business philosophies.

For more than a decade Kenton's management has been highly active in a variety of social programs including community development, conservation efforts, and affirmative action. The firm has encouraged its executives and employees to devote time to working with community and government agencies in helping to solve such problems as hard-core unemployment, decay of the central city, and environmental deterioration. Kenton's sales and profits have leveled off in recent years, and its work force has remained relatively stable.

In contrast, the management of Lindell Enterprises has aggressively pursued expanding sales and profits. The firm has devoted millions of dollars to research and development in order to improve its superwidgets and find ways of reducing production costs. As a result, sales have doubled in the past 5 years, and the firm now exports superwidgets to Europe and Asia. Lindell's work force, the highest paid in the industry, has grown an average of 10 percent per year. When asked about social responsibility, the president of Lindell replied, "We believe our responsibility is to obey the law and compete like hell."

Which firm is more socially responsible? Explain your answer.

Student _____

3. Mr. Harold Mejo has written you three checks in payment for services rendered. On the back of the checks represented below, write (a) a blank endorsement, (b) a restricted endorsement, and (c) a special endorsement to Donna Gibson.

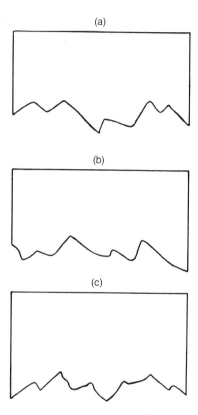

4. *Case:* IBM and Apartheid

You represent IBM in a stockholders meeting where a vote of at least 20 percent is expected demanding the termination of all IBM operations in South Africa until apartheid laws are abolished and political prisoners released. Outline what you believe IBM's position should be on this issue.

chapter 14

INTERNATIONAL BUSINESS AND FUTURE TRENDS

THE DATE: June 30, 1995

THE COMPANY: International Recreation and Health Services, Inc. (known as IRAH, Inc., for short)

YOUR POSITION: Export Manager, New Orleans Branch

You begin the day by reading the incoming mail stored in your desk-top computer. Virtually all business mail is handled electronically through international computer telecommunications, speeding up the transfer of data and reducing retrieval costs and time needed to make decisions.

Next you use the video display screen to review the latest financial reports in preparation for the afternoon conference. IRAH, Inc. markets a full line of health and recreation services in 27 countries. Today, your major concern is performance data for franchised health clinics that feature computer diagnosis of illnesses.

At 2 P.M. you "meet" with 12 Latin American branch managers using a videophone terminal and satellite communications system. Teleconferences permit "face-to-face" meetings without the inconvenience and expense of travel.

CHAPTER OBJECTIVES

1. List three major trends in business.

2. Define international business and explain its importance.

3. List the top three U.S. exports and imports.

4. Identify three restrictions on world trade.

5. Describe five ways a business can enter foreign markets.

6. Define multinational corporation and explain the benefits and drawbacks of multinational corporations to host nations.

Before leaving for the day, you recall that it is the end of the month and your pay has been electronically transferred to your bank account. You decide to use the videoshopping terminal in the company lounge to select a new personal investing program for your home computer.

While this might seem like an episode from the future, today's technology can (and has) accomplish(ed) all these activities. This chapter highlights some of the future trends in business with special emphasis on international business and the expanding world economy. The chapter appendix explores how you might choose, prepare for, and get the career you want.

FUTURE BUSINESS TRENDS

While no one can forecast the future with certainty, there is little doubt that business will change dramatically over the next decade. Among the changes most likely to occur:

- The rate of change will accelerate due to exploding technology.

- The demand for employees with backgrounds in mathematics, science, and engineering will require major changes in education and massive investment in retraining programs.

- Most employment opportunities will be in service industries.

- Computers will become as common as typewriters in business, education, and the home.

- Manufacturing will become increasingly automated with widespread use of industrial robots.

- Middle-management functions will tend to be taken over by computers and technicians; and the distinction between labor and management will fade.

- Jobs will be redesigned to capitalize on current technology; and there will be greater emphasis on quality of work-life.

- Tens of millions of employees will work at home using computer terminals (millions already do!).

- Bank debit cards will reduce the need for currency and checks.

- Most families will have two income earners.

- People will have more leisure time, and business firms will direct their marketing activities accordingly.

•   By the year 2000, an estimated 50 percent of the
population will be over 34 with important implications for
health, recreation, housing, and related industries.

•   Nations will become more economically interdependent
with a corresponding growth in world trade.

These trends pose a major challenge for the American business
system. They will require new products and services as well as new
techniques of production, marketing, finance, and management.
Perhaps no single trend has more implications for our society than
the growth of world trade. The expansion of international business
poses both a threat and opportunity for U.S. business firms.

INTER-NATIONAL BUSINESS AND THE WORLD ECONOMY

International business is world trade. It is business firms buying
from and/or selling to organizations in other countries. International
business has steadily increased since World War II. The value of
world trade exceeds $2 trillion.

International business is based on a simple fact. It is
economically beneficial for nations to specialize in the production of
goods and services in which they enjoy the greatest relative
efficiency. Economists have long recognized that specialization and
trade leads to greater total output and a rising standard of living for
consumers.

Nations also have recognized this fact. Saudi Arabia specializes
in the production of oil; South Africa provides the majority of
diamonds; and Australia concentrates on the production of wool.
Some countries have an *absolute advantage,* the ability to produce a
product more efficiently than *any other nation* because of their
natural resources, capital equipment, human resources, or culture
and work ethic. While only one country can have an absolute
advantage over all other countries in the production of a given
product, all nations have a *comparative advantage.* A comparative
advantage is the ability of a nation to produce a good or service
more efficiently than *any other product.*

Even if a country has no absolute advantage, it would still
produce those products that generate the largest return for invested
resources. Likewise, a country with an absolute advantage in two or
more products would produce the one that gives the greatest
payback per resource used. People, like nations, should specialize in
those activities that give the greatest satisfaction for the time,
money, and effort expended. Consider a commonly cited example.
Before William Howard Taft became president of the United States,
he was the nation's fastest stenographer. He had an absolute
advantage in both stenography and presidential politics. He

TABLE 14.1   U.S. Merchandise Trade, 1985 (in billions of dollars)

Exports		Imports	
Raw Materials & Supplies	$ 58.4	Petroleum	$ 50.5
Machinery	75.4	Raw Materials & Supplies	59.6
		Automobiles & Parts	65.4
Agricultural Products	23.7		
Automobiles & Parts	24.7	Machinery	63.7
		Agricultural Products	21.3
Consumer Goods	13.0	Consumer Goods	65.0
Other	23.7	Other	15.7
Total	$ 218.9	Total	$ 341.2

Source: *Survey of Current Business,* U.S. Department of Commerce, May, 1986.

concentrated his energy on becoming the president of the United States because it gave the maximum return on his time.

Every country must allocate limited resources among unlimited wants and needs. Scarcity requires nations to economize. Efficiency requires countries to conform to the law of comparative advantage.

No nation is self-sufficient. Even the United States with its wealth of resources, purchases (or *imports*) all the coffee, tea, tin, natural rubber, and nickel consumed in this country. These commodities are either unavailable in the United States or can be produced only at great cost. On the other hand, our country sells abroad (or *exports*) those goods and services in which it enjoys a competitive advantage. The difference between the dollar value of a country's exports and imports is called its *balance of trade.* If exports exceed imports, the country has a favorable balance of trade. If imports are greater than exports, there is a trade deficit or unfavorable balance of trade. Table 14.1 summarizes U.S. major exports and imports. Did we have a favorable or unfavorable balance of trade for 1985?

Sometimes companies engage in *dumping*—selling products in foreign markets at prices lower than the total cost of production. If a firm has already covered its fixed costs (costs that do not change with production, e.g., rent), it can sell its excess capacity for a little over its variable costs (costs that change with productivity, e.g., labor and materials). This firm then has two prices for a given product: the higher home price, which includes both fixed and variable costs, and the more competitive foreign price, a charge just above its variable costs. Companies are likely to use this pricing strategy when they have a dominant position in the home market, unused plant capacity, and a desire to penetrate foreign markets by offering the lowest possible price. Japanese steel manufacturers have dumped their excess steel in U.S. markets at prices U.S. steel

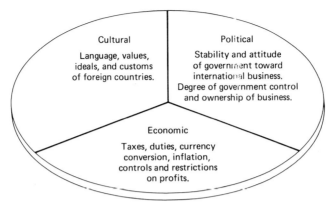

FIGURE 14.1   Factors Complicating International Trade

companies have been unable to match. U.S. steel firms felt this unfair and demanded antidumping laws.

By selling goods and services abroad, U.S. business firms may increase sales and profits, reduce unit costs through volume production, and satisfy the needs of foreign consumers. Imports provide American consumers with a wide variety of goods at lower prices. Foreign competition forces domestic producers to reduce costs and develop new and improved products. However, international business is not without problems. Some domestic producers may be unable to compete with lower-cost foreign goods. Trade makes nations more interdependent, and dependence on foreign firms may clash with political and military goals. Moreover, trade is complicated by the fact that nations have different cultures, languages, and currencies, as illustrated in Figure 14.1. Therefore, governments may impose restrictions on trade despite its many advantages.

Restrictions on Trade

Tariffs, import quotas, and embargoes limit imports and reduce exports. A *tariff* is a tax on imports. Although a tariff may be imposed to raise revenue for the government, the more common purpose is to "protect" domestic producers by raising the price of competitive foreign goods. An *import quota* is a limit on the amount of a good that can be imported. The United States has imposed quotas on foreign sugar, cattle, and textiles. Sometimes political pressure is used to force foreign producers to agree to "voluntary" export quotas. This occurred when Japanese automobile manufacturers limited their exports to the United States in the 1980s. An *embargo* is the prohibition of trade with another nation. The embargo may be complete as in the case of U.S. trade with Cuba or it may be partial as reflected in the ban on selling U.S. military technology to the Soviet Union. The purpose of an embargo is nearly always political or military.

Methods of Entering Foreign Markets

Business firms commonly choose one (or combination) of the following methods of entering foreign markets: exporting, licensing, local marketing subsidiaries, joint ventures, or total ownership.

Exporting   The easiest, least risky method is exporting. Companies selling their goods abroad may use foreign trade intermediaries (e.g., wholesalers or agents) or create their own export departments.

Licensing   Licensing involves a contractual agreement between a licensor, a company with a particular good or service, and a licensee, another firm wanting to produce and sell the licensor's product. The licensee receives information and permission regarding the manufacturing and marketing of another company's product. The licensor is able to avoid trade barriers common to exporting (e.g., tariffs), capitalize on the native company's marketing expertise, and earn royalties or fees based upon the sales or profits of the licensee.

Local Marketing Subsidiaries   A domestic corporation may open branch offices or subsidiaries in foreign lands to market goods made by the home company. The home firm has final decision-making power and usually hires local employees to market goods, thereby benefiting from these employees' cultural and ethnic background. Major marketing disasters may be averted by being aware of local traditions, beliefs, and taboos. For example, citizens of Egypt know green, Egypt's national color, is forbidden for use on commercial packages.

Joint Ventures   International joint ventures are short term partnerships between domestic firms and foreign companies or governments. Joint ventures permit the sharing of risks, resources, and rewards. For example, in 1984, American Motors Corporation (AMC) formed a joint venture with the People's Republic of China for the purpose of producing and marketing four-wheel-drive vehicles in Southeast Asia. China provided the labor, plant location, and market. American Motors provided the necessary technology and cash.

Total Ownership   The most complex, costly, and risky method of entering foreign markets is through subsidiaries totally owned and operated by parent corporations. While parent corporations have excellent control, they may be subject to criticism for exploiting the peoples and resources of foreign nations and are favorite targets for terrorists. Table 14.2 illustrates the advantages, disadvantages, and examples of five methods of entering foreign markets.

TABLE 14.2   Five Methods of Entering Foreign Markets

Method	Advantages	Disadvantages	Examples
Exporting	Increased sales, profits, and production with little risk and foreign investment.	High production and export costs (e.g., tariffs, transportation, etc.) and competition within foreign markets.	Boeing Ford General Electric
Licensing	Increased profits from royalties. Avoids tariffs and has low risk and investment.	Low returns if licensee does not sell sufficient volume of licensor's product. Licensee may compete directly after learning the production and marketing techniques of the licensor.	Avon Levi Strauss Pepsico
Local Marketing Subsidiaries	Better control over operations and services.	Higher costs. Market information may be inadequate.	IBM
Joint Ventures	Foreign and domestic companies share mutual benefits (e.g., one firm provides cheap labor and markets, the other, money and technical equipment and expertise).	Partners may disagree (methods of production, distribution of profits, required investment of people, machines, and money) and have cultural differences.	AMC/People's Republic of China Toyota/General Motors
Total Ownership	No division of profits. High control over operations. No tariffs. Foreign incentives to invest.	Greatest cost and risk. Potentially high taxes on profits. Profits may not be allowed to leave host country. Host country may nationalize or expropriate foreign firm's property. Possible problems with terrorists.	Honda's operation in the United States Polaroid's operations in the Netherlands

MULTI-NATIONALS

Corporations with subsidiaries throughout the world are more commonly called multinationals. A *multinational* is a company headquartered in one country with production and/or marketing facilities in one or more other countries. Multinationals usually have at least majority if not total ownership and control of foreign branches. Occasionally, multinationals establish joint ventures with foreign governments or firms.

Since these companies do business around the world, products are made in those countries providing the greatest economies (cheap labor, natural resources, and manufacturing facilities) and sold in countries offering the best sales and profit potential. For example, the silicon chips used in microprocessors may be manufactured in the United States, shipped to South Korea for assembly, and sold in Canada. Multinationals may place the concerns of top management and stockholders for sales and profits ahead of national interests.

The idea of firms doing business in more than one country developed from the reconstruction efforts following World War II. American companies were encouraged to start operations in Europe to promote economic recovery. These ventures proved advantageous to both Europe and the American firms.

Underdeveloped nations with high unemployment and inefficiency welcomed the technical expertise and financial backing provided by U.S. firms. Multinationals offer host nations the advantages of high technology, large capital investment, increased employment, and proven management. Without these advantages, many nations would be unable to make full use of their resources.

Exxon, McDonald's, Holiday Inn, U.S. Steel, IBM, General Motors, and ITT are examples of American multinationals. Foreign-owned multinationals include Honda, Unilever (Lever Brothers in the United States), Royal Dutch Shell, Sony, and Nestlé.

Giant multinationals have enormous economic and political power. The sales of some firms exceed the gross national product of most nations. If current trends continue through the end of this century, fewer than 200 multinationals will control over half the free world's production of goods and services. The power and size of these huge firms make governments, particularly those in smaller developing nations, vulnerable to intimidation and pressure. Critics of multinational corporations charge that these firms exert undue influence on host governments. An often cited example is ITT's support for the overthrow of the Allende government in Chile when that regime threatened to nationalize the company's Chilean operations.

Multinationals have also been accused of exploiting the human and natural resources of host nations. Critics assert that local labor is employed only in low-paying positions. When a country's natural resources are depleted, the multinational may leave. In short, multinationals have been charged with doing economic, environmental, and political damage to developing nations.

Many of the criticisms are justified. Recently, however, most multinational corporations, reacting to political pressure and adverse public opinion, have become more responsive to the interests of host nations. They have trained and promoted local labor for managerial

---

ISSUE FREE TRADE OR FAIR TRADE?

Free trade is a joke and a myth. And a government trade policy predicated on old ideas of free trade is worse than a joke—it is a prescription for disaster. The answer is fair trade, do unto others as they do to us—barrier for barrier—closed door for closed door.

George Meany
Past President of AFL-CIO

Protectionism is the inevitable response to our market's being tragically disrupted by a level of imports that no other country in the world would even consider, let alone tolerate. We are competing with industries that are being subsidized by their governments in order to get hard cash.

Roger Milliken
President and Owner of Family-Owned Textile Company,
Milliken & Co.

We have got to decide what free and fair trade is all about, and we've got to try to level the playing field—to be competitive.

Lee Iacocca
Chairman of Chrysler Corporation

Pray for work for son. After 33 years his job at Clark is dispensed with.

Message Found in the University of Notre Dame's Cathedral after
Clark Equipment Laid Off More than One-Third of Its Work Force

Today, many are protesting the actions of nations engaging in trade with the United States. Foreign countries impose ridiculously low quotas or high tariffs on U.S. goods. Yet, these countries cry "foul" whenever the United States attempts to protect domestic jobs and companies through similar tactics. Over the past two decades the average U.S. tariff rates have been below 10 percent. Our trading partners generally have much higher restrictions.

---

positions, decentralized operations, and focused on the long-term benefits for both the company and the host nation.

The Future of World Trade

The outlook for expanded foreign trade is generally favorable. The most significant growth in U.S. exports will be in service industries with data processing, telecommunications, advertising, banking, construction, insurance, lodging, and transportation leading the way.

ISSUE   FREE TRADE OR FAIR TRADE? (Cont.)

Some countries impede the sale of U.S. goods by setting unrealistic quality standards, requiring lengthy inspections, or delaying goods in customs.

Foreign firms may bribe company or government officials in other lands to close sales. U.S. firms are prohibited from making such "deals" under the provisions of the Foreign Corrupt Practices Act of 1977.

In addition, foreign firms often flood our markets with goods heavily subsidized by their government. U.S. companies cannot compete against these firms unless the foreign goods are taxed (import tariffs) or domestic companies subsidized.

Industries hurt by international trade (e.g., leather, textiles, petroleum products, furniture, plastics, steel, chemical, and automobiles) demand protection from "unfair" foreign competition. Antidumping laws, higher tariffs, and lower quotas are typically demanded to "level the playing field—to be competitive." Reciprocal trade agreements, "barrier for barrier —closed door for closed door," are also demanded.

Perhaps the United States should revert to its old tariff policy. The Tariff Act of 1930 (cosponsored by legislators Smoot and Hawley) increased the average tariff rates above 50 percent! The United States hoped this bill would protect domestic industries and jobs from "peasant and sweated labor" abroad. It triggered one of the most destructive trade wars in history, however. The tariff provoked our trading partners to retaliate and U.S. exports dropped almost two-thirds in just 2 years. By 1932 international trade collapsed and the Tariff Act of 1930 was denounced as a disaster.

Most economists favor free trade with no barriers. In contrast, *fair trade* is a vague term that implies retaliating against foreign nations that sell goods in U.S. markets below cost or erect barriers against U.S. exports. Fair trade leads to protectionism, and protectionism rewards the inefficient, increases consumer prices, and hurts export industries. In short, protectionism costs too much. Consider the following:

In addition, the demand for U.S. farm products will expand as the world's population increases. However, there are mounting pressures on governments to restrict trade. Domestic producers and labor abroad are demanding protection through import quotas and tariffs. Efforts to restrict trade are particularly strong during periods of economic depression when unemployment is widespread. Moreover, governments continue to impose embargoes for political and military

ISSUE   FREE TRADE OR FAIR TRADE? (Cont.)

• Thirty percent of U.S. corporate profits are the result of international trade.

• Four out of five new jobs created are in export industries.

• For every job "saved" through trade restrictions, three are "lost."

• Lower- and middle-income families are forced to pay higher prices to protect the jobs of those earning (possibly) higher incomes. (Consumers pay about $110,000 more a year to protect a $24,000 per year steelworker's job, $77,000 a year to save an $8,000 per year job in the shoe industry, and up to $80,000 a year to protect a $10,000 per year job in the textile industry.)

In 1983, the United States refused entry of approximately $55 million of cotton blouses from China. China responded by cancelling $500 million of grain orders from the United States. By helping textile workers, farmers were dealt a devastating blow. Indeed, the United States effectively took money out of farmers' pockets and gave it to textile workers, stockholders, and managers. Advocates of free trade believe it would be more efficient and far cheaper if markets were unrestricted and retraining and transition assistance were provided for displaced workers.

Free trade promotes specialization and exchange among countries. It allows world productivity to increase and encourages mutual interdependence. Such interdependence makes war more costly and promotes peace. Yet, nations impose trade restrictions. Should the United States do the same and use such restrictions as bargaining chips in trade negotiations or should the United States unilaterally eliminate all restrictions regardless of the actions of other countries?

purposes. Foreign trade, despite the benefits to consumers and business, is vulnerable to both political and economic pressure.

Does American Business Have a Future?

In the first chapter we described the multitude of problems plaguing the American business system. The question was raised, will U.S. business firms be able to solve these problems and meet the challenges of the future? Without doubt, the greatest strength of our

ISSUE TERRORISTS TARGET THE MULTINATIONALS

The threat of violence, or a campaign of violence (is) designed primarily to instill fear—to terrorize. . . . Terrorism is violence for effect.

Brian M. Jenkins
Terrorism: A Challenge to the State

Kill one, frighten ten thousand.

Ancient Chinese Proverb

Terrorist attacks on U.S. business abroad have been increasing at a 12 to 15 percent annual rate for the past 10 years. In 1984, there were 21 attacks on American businesses and employees worldwide, resulting in 28 deaths, 64 injuries, and property damage of $22 million. The number of attacks exceeded 35 in 1985. Bombings and related attacks on facilities is the most common form of terrorism, followed by kidnapping, assassination, and hijacking. The most dangerous location for multinational corporations is Latin America where the most feared terrorist tactic is kidnapping. In contrast, there is little risk of attack on foreign firms throughout Asia.

Terrorist groups focus on multinational firms for three major reasons. First, violent attacks on well-known corporations can create worldwide publicity, giving the terrorists an international forum for their causes. Second, damage to business property can discourage further investment, thereby undermining the economies of host nations. Finally, kidnapping multinational employees for ransom provides funds to support political and terrorist activities.

Four out of five U.S. firms that operate abroad have adopted programs to protect their employees and safeguard plant assets. According to one multinational treasurer, the cost

business system has been its adaptability—its responsiveness to change. As individuals, institutions, and systems grow older, they tend to become less flexible and more resistant to change. However, in the business world, this tendency toward rigidity is offset by the forces of competition and the profit motive, which services to spur firms to react quickly to changes in the marketplace and in the business environment. Firms that fail to react to change do not

---

ISSUE TERRORISTS TARGET THE MULTINATIONALS (Cont.)

of protection against terrorist attack averages 1 to 1.5 percent of companies' sales revenues. One of the fastest growing industries in the world consists of private firms that specialize in the protection of employees and property from terrorist attack. These companies provide training and advice as well as personal bodyguards, bullet-proof vests, and armored vehicles. Some specialize in handling negotiations with kidnappers.

Experts stress that the best defense against terrorism is careful planning. This begins by identifying and analyzing potential dangers in light of conditions that exist in host countries. Keeping up to date on local terrorist groups is a continuous process. In addition to procedures for protecting personnel and property, the plan should include crisis guidelines for dealing with terrorists. Each company should develop a corporate position statement and a negotiating strategy in advance. This plan should provide for cooperation with host country authorities as well as means for dealing effectively with the media.

The rise of terrorism creates a dilemma for management of international companies: Should the firm pay ransoms for kidnapped employees? The arguments for paying are obvious. Multinationals are morally obligated to protect the lives of their employees. Moreover, failure to pay will lead to employees refusing to accept assignments in high-risk areas. However, many experts maintain that by adopting a policy of refusing to pay ransoms, companies reduce the danger of more kidnappings. Money paid to terrorists can be used to finance more terrorism, thereby putting more lives at risk.

Most multinational firms have accepted the principle that they should pay. As a result, there has been a dramatic increase in kidnapping insurance policies, which pay part or all of the ransom. U.S. firms reportedly pay more than $80 million dollars each year in premiums for such policies.

---

survive. Anyone doubting the vulnerability of large corporations need only look at the list of the 10 largest corporations at the beginning of the century. On today's list, there is only one survivor from the 1900 top 10 corporations.

The future of American business depends on its ability to remain flexible, efficient, and productive. If the past is any clue to the future, our business system should continue its record of economic achievement. As to the importance of international trade, consider the words of James E. Perrella, executive vice-president of Ingersoll-Rand Company:

> Our economic survival now depends a great deal on our *ability to compete internationally.* . . . International trade builds trust, broadens outlook, opens communications, creates opportunities, increases understanding, reduces conflict, contributes to world peace. And, as Henry Ford once noted, "Business is never so healthy as when, like a chicken, it must do a certain amount of scratching for what it gets." Yet another reason we have no choice except to scratch for what we can get in world markets is the fact that if we do not, we will not be able to compete at home.

SUMMARY

In business, as in life, the only constant is change. Among the major trends affecting business are the rapid increase in the use of computers in offices, factories, and homes, the growth of service industries, the aging of the U.S. population, and the expansion of international business.

Specialization and trade among nations lead to greater total output and a rising standard of living. If the dollar value of a country's exports (goods and services sold abroad) exceeds its imports (products purchased from other countries), it has a favorable balance of trade. If the reverse is true, it has a trade deficit or unfavorable balance of trade.

Dumping, selling products in foreign markets at prices lower than the cost of producing such products, pays off when a firm has a dominant position in its home market, unused plant capacity, and a desire to penetrate foreign markets by charging rock bottom prices. Domestic producers, stockholders, and employees, however, demand protection from foreign competition. Governments may impose restrictions on trade in the form of tariffs, import quotas, and embargoes to protect domestic firms and to promote political and military goals.

Companies generally enter foreign markets using one or a combination of the following methods: (1) exporting, (2) licensing, (3) local marketing subsidiaries, (4) joint ventures, and/or (5) total ownership.

Multinational corporations, which are headquartered in one country and produce goods and services in one or more other countries, often have enormous political and economic power. These firms benefit host nations by introducing advanced technology, increasing investment, and creating jobs. However, some multi-nationals have been criticized for interfering in the internal affairs of developing nations and exploiting human and natural resources.

The future of our business system is dependent on its ability to adapt to change. Inflexible, inefficient, or unproductive firms cannot last. Competition and the profit motive require firms to react quickly and efficiently to changes in the marketplace.

Your future will undoubtedly be affected by how well you plan and how effectively you use your abilities. The appendix of this chapter explores how you might choose, prepare for, and get the best job for you.

SELF-EXAMINATION QUESTIONS

The following questions are based on the Chapter Objectives listed at the beginning of the chapter. Test yourself by circling the letter preceding the answer that *best* completes the statement or answers the question. The answers to the Self-Examination Question are in the appendix at the end of the textbook.

1. In the future, it is likely that: (A) most employment opportunities will be in service industries; (B) computers will be used more extensively; (C) there will be a reduction in traditional mid-management positions; (D) foreign trade will expand; (E) all of these.

2. Increased foreign trade is likely to: (A) enable all U.S. firms to increase sales and profits; (B) reduce unit production costs and expand sales in export industries; (C) lower the standard of living of American consumers; (D) all of these; (E) none of these.

3. Which of the following represents a major U.S. import? (A) wheat; (B) civilian aircraft; (C) petroleum; (D) automobiles; (E) both (C) and (D).

4. Which is a tax on imports? (A) tariffs; (B) quotas; (C) embargoes; (D) dumping; (E) none of these.

5. Which is the least risky and costly method of entering foreign markets? (A) total ownership; (B) exporting; (C) local marketing subsidiaries; (D) licensing; (E) joint ventures.

6. Multinational corporations may: (A) increase employment opportunities in host nations; (B) exert political pressure on host governments; (C) control over half the free world's production by the year 2000; (D) all of these; (E) none of these.

APPENDIX
YOUR FUTURE JOB

You can look forward to a challenging and rewarding career or you can spend your life resenting the drudgery and alienation of an unsatisfactory job. Your choice will be largely dependent upon how well you plan for your future job. The time to start is *now!*

Deciding on a Career

Begin by taking an inventory of your personal attributes, interests, and abilities. Ask yourself these key questions:

- What are my likes and dislikes?
- What are my strengths and weaknesses?
- Do I favor variety over routine?
- How hard am I willing to work?
- How much do I want to earn?

The answers to these questions will help you decide the most important question of all: What do I want out of life?

The next step is a visit to your college career or job placement center. There you should find a wealth of resources including: (a) knowledgeable job counselors; (b) diagnostic, personality, and vocational interest tests; (c) materials on interviewing, preparing resumes, and finding jobs; (d) current job announcements.

When you have decided on an occupation, try to determine if there will be a strong future in that field. It is futile to prepare yourself for a field where there will be no job openings. Today, one out of four people with college degrees are employed in jobs that do not require degrees.

Preparing for Your Future Job

Once you have determined the job you want, the education and training necessary to prepare for the job, and the cost of such training in time and money, you need to develop a plan of action to achieve your vocational goals. Begin by making a realistic timetable. List the steps necessary to accomplish your objectives and the dates when you expect to complete each step. Both your goals and your timetable may be modified as circumstances change.

Start keeping a file containing all your academic and employment records. Add recommendations, awards, club membership cards, scholarships, and any other items that might impress a prospective employer. Many employers are as interested in extracurricular activities as in grade-point averages. Becoming an officer of a club indicates responsibility and leadership.

Your file is the major source of information for your resume. A *resume* is a brief summary of your history, goals, education, and employment background. The major purpose of a resume is to sell a prospective employer on granting you an interview. Resumes may be attached to a completed application form or letter of application. The resume is the first impression you make; keep it brief, accurate,

Personal Data:	Your Name	Birthdate*
	Present Address	Permanent Address
	Phone Number	Phone Number
	Health	Marital Status*
Career Objective:	A brief statement about your immediate and long–term occupational goals.	
Education:	A list of educational institutions attended. Dates shown in reverse chronological order. Specify major areas of study and degrees or certificates awarded.	
Work Experience:	A list of past and current employers. Dates shown in reverse chronological order. Specify major responsibilities and job descriptions.	
Military:	Cite draft classification and summarize military background if applicable.	
Awards:	List any scholarships, awards, special achievements, honors, etc.	
Extracurricular Activities:	Indicate all club activities, leadership roles, and pertinent outside interests.	
References:	References will be furnished upon request.	

*Title VII of the Civil Rights Act of 1964, as amended by the Equal Employment Opportunity Act of 1972 makes it illegal for employers to ask these questions. They may, of course, be *volunteered* by the applicant.

FIGURE 14.2   A Resume Format

and grammatically correct. A typical format for a resume is illustrated in Figure 14.2.

Finding the Job

Finding the right job depends on a great deal of hard work and a bit of luck. Career centers, campus recruiters, relatives, friends, teachers, and past employers may provide leads to the job you want. State employment agencies and help wanted ads list job openings. If you cannot find an opening from these sources, consider sending letters of inquiry to prospective employers. Names and addresses of potential employers can be found in the *College Placement Manual,* through local chambers of commerce, and in the *Yellow Pages.* Sometimes you can get a job through a private employment agency. These agencies charge a fee, so make sure you understand exactly how much you must pay.

Landing the Job

Remember the purpose of a resume and application form is to get your foot in the door by securing a personal interview. The goal of the *interview* is to get a job offer.

Before interviewing, do some research. Most libraries have

annual reports of major corporations. Find out about the company's product line, reputation, philosophy, history, and future.

Try to anticipate the questions an interviewer is likely to ask. Be prepared to answer such questions as:

1   Why do you want this job?
2   What are your strengths and weaknesses?
3   What starting salary do you expect?
4   Why did you leave your last job?
5   What are your career goals and plans?

Be ready to ask some questions as well, but do not monopolize the conversation. You might ask about specific duties and responsibilities of the job, promotional opportunities, and the firm's future prospects.

Make sure you know the exact time, date, and meeting place for the interview, and arrive a few minutes early. Come properly groomed and attired. You only get once chance to make a good first impression.

During the interview, be alert and maintain good eye contact. Answer questions briefly and concisely in a friendly, businesslike manner. Stress your strengths and how your joining the company will be mutually beneficial. When the interview is completed, thank the interviewer and leave promptly. Within a week follow up with a letter or telephone call thanking the interviewer again and indicating your continued interest.

Keeping the Job

After working so hard to get a job, it is important to keep it. Be punctual and maintain good attendance. Your career advancement will depend, in part, on developing a positive attitude, communicating effectively, and working at full potential.

Student _____

BUILDING A BUSINESS VOCABULARY

Directions: Match the terms with their definitions by writing the letter in the appropriate blank.

a. Embargo	f. Multinational	k. Teleconference
b. Export	g. Import Quota	l. Law of Com-
c. Import	h. Law of Absolute	parative Ad-
d. Balance of	Advantage	vantage
Trade	i. Resume	m. Joint Venture
e. Interview	j. Tariff	n. Dumping
		o. Licensing

_____ 1. The sale of goods and services in foreign markets.

_____ 2. The use of telecommunications systems, often including videophone terminals, to conduct meetings between two or more persons who are physically separated.

_____ 3. A tax on imports.

_____ 4. A limit on the quantities of goods or services that can be purchased from abroad.

_____ 5. A written summary of a job applicant's history, goals, education, and employment experiences.

_____ 6. A prohibition on trade with a nation.

_____ 7. A company with headquarters in one country with production and/or marketing facilities in one or more other countries.

_____ 8. Face-to-face communication with a job applicant for the purpose of making an employment decision.

_____ 9. The purchase of foreign goods or services.

_____ 10. The ability of a country to produce a product more efficiently than any other nation.

_____ 11. The ability of a country to produce a product more efficiently than any other product.

_____ 12. Exports minus imports.

_____ 13. Selling products in foreign markets at prices below the total cost of production.

_____ 14. A contractual agreement between one firm with a particular product and another firm that wants to produce and sell that product.

_____ 15. Short-term partnerships that allow two (or more) organizations to share risks, resources, and rewards.

Student _____

REVIEWING MAJOR CONCEPTS

1. Name three trends that you believe will have a major impact on U.S. business in the next 10 years. Briefly explain how these trends will affect American business firms.

2. List the top three U.S. exports and the three major U.S. imports. Give a specific example of each category.

3. If international trade increases world production and benefits consumers, why do governments put restrictions on trade?

4. List and explain three restrictions on world trade.

   a.

   b.

   c.

5. Describe five methods that can be used to enter foreign markets.

   a.

   b.

   c.

   d.

   e.

6. Define multinational corporation and give two examples.

7. Explain why corporations sometimes sell their products below cost in foreign countries.

Student _____

SOLVING PROBLEMS AND CASES

1. *Case:* International Metals, Inc.

   Dr. Mbu Opelugo, Minister of Economic Affairs for the new African nation of Stotea, is considering an offer from International Metals, Inc. (IMI), an American multinational company with annual sales exceeding $25 billion. IMI wants to establish a copper mining operation in northeast Stotea complete with processing mills and smelters. The plan calls for an investment of $70 million over the next 5 years. IMI will pay the Stotean government a standard fee on each ton of copper processed. The company has promised to establish a training program for workers and ultimately will employ 18,000 Stoteans.

   As assistant to Dr. Opelugo, you have been asked to draft a brief report outlining the advantages and disadvantages of accepting the IMI offer and making suggestions that might be included in any agreement.

2. *Case:* Sparkle Toothpaste

Ms. Mary Molar, president of Sparkle Toothpaste, wishes to market her company's product in China. Domestically, Sparkle Toothpaste targets its sales to the teen and pre-teen segments, emphasizing bright, white teeth and sex appeal. What cultural, political, and economic factors should be considered before marketing Sparkle Toothpaste in China? Which of the five methods of entering foreign markets would you recommend? Why?

Student _____

3. Visit your college career or placement center, and talk with a job counselor. Based on the interview and career reference materials, answer the following:

   a. Select a career field that appeals to you.

   b. What personal characteristics make you suited for this field?

   c. What is the future demand for job applicants in this field?

   d. What are the educational and training requirements to enter this field?

   e. Name three employers in this field.

4. Prepare a one page personal resume on a separate sheet of paper.

APPENDIX

ANSWERS TO SELF-EXAMINATION QUESTIONS

CHAPTER 1:	**1.** E **2.** A **3.** B **4.** C **5.** C **6.** A
CHAPTER 2:	**1.** E **2.** B **3.** C **4.** A **5.** D **6.** C **7.** D
CHAPTER 3:	**1.** C **2.** B **3.** D **4.** B **5.** D **6.** B
CHAPTER 4:	**1.** D **2.** B **3.** A **4.** C **5.** A **6.** B **7.** E
CHAPTER 5:	**1.** A **2.** D **3.** C **4.** B **5.** A **6.** D **7.** D
CHAPTER 6:	**1.** A **2.** E **3.** A **4.** C **5.** D **6.** B **7.** B **8.** A
CHAPTER 7:	**1.** E **2.** B **3.** A **4.** B **5.** C **6.** A
CHAPTER 8:	**1.** C **2.** A **3.** C **4.** D **5.** B **6.** B **7.** C **8.** B **9.** B
CHAPTER 9:	**1.** D **2.** D **3.** B **4.** E **5.** B **6.** E
CHAPTER 10:	**1.** D **2.** A **3.** A **4.** E **5.** C
CHAPTER 11:	**1.** A **2.** E **3.** D **4.** B **5.** B **6.** C **7.** A **8.** C **9.** E **10.** C
CHAPTER 12:	**1.** C **2.** B **3.** F **4.** A **5.** D **6.** B **7.** D
CHAPTER 13:	**1.** E **2.** B **3.** E **4.** B **5.** C **6.** A **7.** D **8.** A **9.** C
CHAPTER 14:	**1.** E **2.** B **3.** E **4.** A **5.** B **6.** D

NOTES

CHAPTER 1

Productivity Is the Name of the Game

Economic Report of the President, Council of Economic Advisors, Washington, D. C., 1986.

ISSUE WHAT IS AN ENTREPRENEUR?

Patricia A. Bellew, "In Silicon Valley, L'Enfant Terrible Is Also L'Enfant Riche," *Wall Street Journal,* June 4, 1985, pp. 1, 22.

"I Can Do It! The Ed Lewis Story," The American Enterprise Series Part I, A LDL Production, Inc., Produced and Directed by Laurie Kreidler. (Available from Direct Cinema Limited, P. O. Box 69589, Los Angeles, CA 90069.)

Kathryn B. Stechert, "Making It Big by Age Thirty-five: The Millionaires," *Savvy,* April, 1984, pp. 62–68.

ISSUE THE CASE FOR COMPETITION

Adapted with permission from Clair Wilcox, *Public Policies Toward Business,* 3rd ed. (Homewood, IL: Richard D. Irwin, 1966).

ISSUE PROFITS: THE LIFEBLOOD OF THE ECONOMY

Robert Mims, "Write-Off Time: Why the Fourth Quarter Was So Bad," *Business Week*, March 17, 1986, pp. 116–140.

ISSUE ENTREPRENEURS VS. INTRAPRENEURS

John S. DeMott, "Here Come the Intrapreneurs," *Time,* February 4, 1985, pp. 36–37.

Gifford Pinchot, *Intrapreneuring, or Why You Don't Have to Leave the Corporation to Become an Entrepreneur* (New York: Harper & Row, 1985).

ISSUE CHINA TRIES THE CAPITALIST ROAD

George J. Church, "China's Deng Xiaoping Leads Far-Reaching, Audacious But Risky Second Revolution," *Time,* January 6, 1986, pp. 25–41.

John Burns, " 'Proletarian Rectitude' Runs Amok under China's New Economic Policy," *New York Times,* February 23, 1985, p. 5.

James P. Sterbu and Amanda Bennet, "Peking Turns Sharply Down Capitalist Road in New Economic Plan," *Wall Street Journal,* October 25, 1984, pp. 1, 25.

CHAPTER 2

Antitrust in Action

Christopher Byron, "Windup for Two Supersuits," *Time,* January 18, 1982, pp. 38–40.

David Pauly *et al.,* "Ma Bell's Big Breakup," *Newsweek,* January 18, 1982, pp. 58–63.

Bro Uttal, "Life After Litigation at IBM and AT & T," *Fortune,* February 8, 1982, pp. 59–61.

ISSUE IS FEDERAL SPENDING OUT OF CONTROL?

P. M. Scherschel, "Soaring National Debt—What It Really Means," *U.S. News and World Report,* September 16, 1985, pp. 33–35.

Floyd L. Spartks, *et al.,* "Deficit Control," *The Argus,* February 5, 1984, p. 20.

Evan Thomas, "Look Ma, No Hands," *Time,* December 23, 1985, pp 18–21.

ISSUE DO YOU REALLY WANT TAX REFORM?

Susan Dentzer with Rich Thomas and Gloria Berger, "The Tax Maze," *Newsweek,* April 16, 1984, pp. 62–63.

Robert E. Hall, "A Proposal to Simplify Our Tax System," *Wall Street Journal,* December 10, 1981, p. 22.

Donald T. Regan, "The Tax Reform Issue," *Vital Speeches,* May 1, 1984, pp. 21–23.

CHAPTER 3

S Corporations

Peter R. Faber, Esq. and Martin E. Holbrook, Esq., *S Corporation Manual* (New Jersey: Prentice-Hall, 1985).

ISSUE WOMEN IN BUSINESS

Joann S. Lubin, "Women Will Account for Majority of Labor-force Growth," Labor Letter, *Wall Street Journal,* November 11, 1985, p. 1.

Karen Pennar and Edward Mervosh, "Women at Work," *Business Week,* January 28, 1985, pp. 80–85.

Abigail Trafford *et al.,* "She's Come a Long Way—Or Has She?," *U. S. News and World Report,* August 6, 1984, pp. 50–58.

Cathy Trost, "The New Majorities," A Special Report: The Corporate Woman, *Wall Street Journal,* March 24, 1986, p. 15D.

ISSUE IS BIGGER BETTER?

Charles Alexander, "Let's Make a Deal," *Time,* December 23, 1985, pp. 42–49.

John Greenwald, "Bigger Yes, But Better?," *Time,* August 12, 1985, pp. 34–35.

Clemens P. Work and Jack Scamonds, "What Are Mergers Doing to America?," *U.S. News and World Report,* July 22, 1985, pp. 48–49.

CHAPTER 4

What Is Management?

Robert Townsend quotation from *Up the Organization* (Greenwich, CT: Fawcett Crest, 1970), p. 54.

Marshall E. Dimock quotation from *The Executive in Action* (New York: Harper & Row, 1945), p. 54.

ISSUE WHO IS NUMBER ONE?

Frank R. Beaudine, "So You Want to Be a Company President," Manager's Journal, *Wall Street Journal,* June 29, 1981, p. 22.

ISSUE A MENU FOR SUCCESSFUL MANAGEMENT?

Thomas J. Peter and Robert H. Waterman, Jr., *In Search of Excellence* (New York: Harper & Row, 1982).

"Who's Excellent Now?," *Business Week,* November 5, 1984, pp. 76–88.

Michael Schrage, "Search for Excellence Yields Riches," *Oakland Tribune,* May 30, 1985, pp. A1–A2.

ISSUE WOMEN IN MANAGEMENT

James Braham, "Women at the Top," *Industry Week,* March 4, 1985, pp. 106–114.

Janice Castro, "More and More, She's the Boss," *Time,* December 2, 1985, pp. 64–66.

Susan Fraker, "Why Women Aren't Getting to the Top," *Fortune,* April 16, 1984, pp. 40–45.

Carol Hymowitz and Timothy D. Schellhardt, "The Glass Ceiling," A Special Report: The Corporate Woman, *Wall Street Journal*, March 24, 1986, pp. 1D, 4D–5D.

Matrix Management

Thomas J. Peters and Robert H. Waterman, Jr., *In Search of Excellence,* (New York: Harper & Row, 1982).

"How to Stop the Buck Short of the Top," *Business Week,* January 16, 1978, pp. 82–83.

Stratford P. Sherman, "Bausch & Lomb's Lost Opportunity," *Fortune,* January 24, 1983, pp. 104–105.

APPENDIX TIME MANAGEMENT

Alan Lakein, *How to Get Control of Your Time and Your Life* (New York: Signet, 1973).

Trish Hall, "Time-Management Training: For People Who Can't Let Their Impulses Run Wild," Your Money Matters, *Wall Street Journal,* August 8, 1985, p. 21.

CHAPTER 5

Human Relations in Business

A. H. Maslow, *Motivation and Personality* (New York: Harper & Row, 1954), pp. 80–106.

Douglas McGregor, *The Human Side of Management* (New York: McGraw-Hill, 1960).

John J. Morse and Jay W. Lorsch, "Beyond Theory Y," *Harvard Business Review,* May–June, 1970, pp. 61–68.

ISSUE THEORY Z: A STEP BEYOND THEORY Y?

William G. Ouchi, *Theory Z: How American Business Can Meet the Japanese Challenge* (Reading, MA: Addison-Wesley, 1981).

Beyond Human Relations: The Quality of Work-Life Movement

For students desiring a more comprehensive explanation of the QWL movement, see Ted Mills, "Human Resources—Why the New Concern?," *Harvard Business Review,* March–April, 1975, pp. 120–134; and R. E. Walton, "Work Innovations in America," *Harvard Business Review,* July, 1979, pp. 88–98.

Quotation from Ford's Donald Peterson, "People Are Source of Corporate Strength," *Stanford Business School Magazine,* Summer, 1985, pp. 15–16.

ISSUE   MANAGEMENT JAPANESE STYLE

Jeremy Main, "The Trouble With Managing Japanese-Style," *Fortune,* April 2, 1984, pp. 76–78.

William Bowen, "Japanese Managers Tell How Their System Works," *Fortune,* November, 1977, pp. 127–138.

Christopher Byron, "How Japan Does It," *Time,* March 30, 1981, pp. 54–60.

Richard Tanner Pascale and Anthony G. Athos, *The Art of Japanese Management: Applications for American Executives* (New York: Simon and Schuster, 1981).

CHAPTER 6

ISSUE   TWO-TIER PAY: LONG-TERM TREND OR QUICK FIX?

Gail Schares, "Two-tier Pay Spreads Despite Union Opposition," *San Francisco Chronicle,* May 18, 1985, pp. 51, 54.

Paul Shinoff, "Unions' Major Shift on Two-tier Pay," *San Francisco Examiner,* March 17, 1985, pp. D1–D2.

ISSUE   DO-IT-YOURSELF FRINGE BENEFITS

Karen Southwich, "Caution About 'Flex' Plans," *San Francisco Chronicle,* June 10, 1985, p. 21.

Lance D. Tane and Michael E. Treacy, "Benefits That Bend With Employees' Needs," *Nation's Business,* April, 1984, pp. 81–82.

ISSUE   HAS ORGANIZED LABOR TURNED THE CORNER?

Leonard M. Apcar and Cathy Trost, "Realizing Their Power Has Eroded, Unions Try Hard to Change," *Wall Street Journal,* February 21, 1985, pp. 1, 25.

Aaron Bernstein and Michael A. Pollock, "The Unions Are Learning to Hit Where it Hurts," *Business Week,* March 17, 1986, pp. 112, 114.

"AFL–CIO Endorses New Labor Strategy," *San Francisco Chronicle,* February 22, 1985, p. 34.

Cathy Trost, "To the Union Chiefs, It's Still a Brotherhood," *Wall Street Journal,* November 20, 1985, p. 32.

ISSUE   THE DEBATE ON COMPARABLE WORTH

Linda Chavez, "Pay Equity Is Unfair to Women," *Fortune,* March 4, 1985, pp. 163–164.

Brock Dethier, "Equal Pay for Comparable Worth?," *Business Year* 1985, pp. 29–30.

Joann S. Lublin, "Use of Comparable Worth Idea to Fight Job Sex Bias Opposed By Rights Panel," *Wall Street Journal,* April 12, 1985, p. 52.

Tim Schreiner, "Women's Salaries Will Gain on Men's, Researchers Say," *San Francisco Chronicle,* April 2, 1985, p. 5.

CHAPTER 7

ISSUE   WHAT IS AN ANNUAL REPORT?

Cliff Pletschet, "Who Needs Annual Reports?," *Oakland Tribune,* December 10, 1984, p. B1.

Jane Bryant Quinn, "How to Read an Annual Report," Reprint from International Paper Company, no date.

ISSUE   THE BILLION DOLLAR RIP-OFF: EMPLOYEE THEFT

Sanford L. Jacobs, "Owners Who Ignore Security Make Worker Dishonesty Easy," *Wall Street Journal,* March 11, 1985, p. 25.

Milton Moskowitz, "How Employers Stop Workers from Stealing Them Blind," *San Francisco Chronicle,* December 12, 1984, p. 39.

Susan Subtle, "Preventing Theft," *Working Woman,* February, 1984, pp. 70–71.

CHAPTER 8

ISSUE   IS "BIG BROTHER" WATCHING YOU?

Lenny Siegal and John Markoff, *The High Cost of High Tech: The Dark Side of the Chip* (New York: Harper & Row, 1985).

ISSUE   THE SUPERCOMPUTER

Phillip Elmer-DeWitt, "A Sleek, Superpowered Machine," *Time,* June 17, 1985, p. 53.

Computers in Business

Microcomputers: Their Use and Misuse in Business, Price Waterhouse, 1984.

John Marcom, Jr. and William M. Bulkeley, "Computer Firms Fight to Win Market Share in Office Automation," *Wall Street Journal,* April 8, 1985, pp. 1, 15.

John Markoff, "Super Disk is Taking Off," *San Francisco Examiner,* July 21, 1985, pp. D-1, D-10.

"Electronic Mail Revolutionizing Business Activities," *San Francisco Chronicle*, February 25, 1985, pp. 51, 54.

ISSUE   COMPUTER CRIME IS ON THE ROLL

Laurie P. Cohen, "Internal Security," *Wall Street Journal*, September 16, 1985, p. 24.

Stanley Halper, "How To Thwart Computer Criminals," *Nation's Business*, August, 1983, pp. 61–62.

Mike Lewis, "Computer Crime: Theft In Bits and Bytes," *Nation's Business*, February, 1985, pp. 57–58.

Ann Reilly, "Computer Crackdown," *Fortune*, September 17, 1984, pp. 141–142.

CHAPTER 9

Marketing Strategy

Many of the concepts presented in this and Chapter 10 were developed by Alfred R. Oxenfeldt, "The Formulation of a Marketing Strategy," in E. J. Kelly and W. Lazer, *Managerial Marketing: Perspectives and Viewpoints* (Homewood, IL: Richard D. Irwin, 1958), pp. 264–271. A comprehensive examination of marketing strategy may be found in E. J. McCarthy, *Basic Marketing*, 8th ed. (Homewood, IL: Richard D. Irwin, 1983).

ISSUE   HIGH TECH COMES TO MARKET RESEARCH

Barbara Buell, "Big Brother Gets a Job in Market Research," *Business Week*, April 8, 1985, pp. 96–97.

Michael Days, "Wired Consumers: Market Researchers Go High-Tech to Home Ads, Weed Out Flops," *Wall Street Journal*, January 23, 1986, p. 35.

Kim Foltz, "Wizards of Marketing," *Newsweek*, July 22, 1985, pp. 42 – 44.

Richard Kreisman, "Buy the Numbers," *Inc.*, March, 1985, pp. 104–112.

Market Segmentation and Market Positioning

This section draws on material presented in Philip Kotler, *Principles of Marketing*, 2nd ed. (Englewood Cliffs, NJ: Prentice-Hall, 1983).

Regis McKenna, *The Regis Touch* (Reading, MA: Addison-Wesley, 1985).

ISSUE   MARKET SEGMENTATION—COKE VS. COKE VS. COKE VS. . . .

John Greenwald, "Coca-Cola's Big Fizzle," *Time*, July 22, 1985, pp. 48–52.

Scott Scredon and Marc Frons, "Coke's Man on the Spot," *Business Week*, July 29, 1985, pp. 56–61.

CHAPTER 10

Product

Management of New Product Ideas (Chicago, IL: Booz, Allen & Hamilton, 1968).

"Products of the Year," *Fortune*, December 9, 1985, pp. 106–107.

Place

John Eckhouse, "Electronic Kiosks—A New Way to Shop," *San Francisco Chronicle*, February 19, 1985, pp. 49, 55.

Sally Saville Hodge, "Franchising the American Dream," *San Francisco Examiner*, September 30, 1984, p. 37.

Teri Agins, "Owning Franchises Has Pluses, But Wealth Isn't Guaranteed," Small Business, *Wall Street Journal*, October 22, 1984, p. 31.

Mark Lacter, "Catalog Glut Swamps Mail Order Business," *San Francisco Chronicle*, February 18, 1985, p. 53.

ISSUE   ADVERTISING: CONSUMER FRIEND OR FOE?

"A New View of Advertising's Economic Impact," *Business Week*, December 22, 1975, pp. 49–50.

Ralph Nader and Aileen Cowan, "Claims Without Substance," In Ralph Nader, ed., *The Consumer and Corporate Accountability* (New York: Harcourt Brace Jovanovich, 1973), pp. 90 – 97.

"What Advertising Is, What It Has Done, and What It Can Do Now," *Printers' Ink*, September 8, 1967, pp. 39 – 60.

Price

Edward Foster, "$49.95 Dac Easy: Is It Real?," *InfoWorld*, July 15, 1985, p. 42.

CHAPTER 11

ISSUE   ELECTRONIC BANKING COMES OF AGE

Eric Gelman, "How American Pays the Tab," *Newsweek*, January 7, 1985, pp. 40–41.

Louis Rukeyser, "Consumers Balking at the 'Checkless Society'," *Puget Sound Business Journal*, September 16, 1985, p. 17.

G. David Wallace and Blanca Riemer, "Interstate Banking: Back to the Drawing Board," *Business Week*, June 10, 1985, pp. 106–107.

ISSUE CORPORATE RAIDERS PLAY THE TAKEOVER GAME

John Greenwald, "High Times for T. Boone Pickens," *Time*, March 4, 1985, pp. 52–64.

John S. DeMott, "Three Who Watch, Wait, and Strike," *Time*, March 4, 1985, pp. 65, 67.

CHAPTER 12

Production Management

"Computer to Pick GM's Saturn Site," *San Francisco Chronicle*, May 4, 1985, p. 32.

ISSUE IMPROVING QUALITY CONTROL THROUGH PREVENTION

Ed Bean, "Cause of Quality Problems Might Be Managers—Not Workers," *Wall Street Journal*, April 10, 1985, p. 27.

Jeremy Main, "The Curmudgeon Who Talks Tough on Quality," *Fortune*, June 25, 1984, pp. 118–122.

William M. Ringle, "The American Who Remade 'Made in Japan'," *Nation's Business*, February, 1981, pp. 67–70.

ISSUE THE JAPANESE MANUFACTURING SYSTEM

Evan L. Porteus, "Small Is Beautiful in Large-Scale Manufacturing," *Stanford Business School Magazine*, Summer, 1985, pp. 9–10.

Richard J. Schonberger, *Japanese Manufacturing Techniques: Nine Hidden Lessons in Simplicity* (New York: The Free Press, 1982).

CAD/CAM: The New Industrial Revolution

Bob Davis, "Computers Speed the Design of More Workaday Products," Technology, *Wall Street Journal*, January 18, 1985, p. 19.

John Eckhouse, "Computerized Factory—The Future is Now," *San Francisco Chronicle*, November 4, 1985, pp. 23, 33.

Doran Howitt, "Computer-Aided Design for All," *InfoWorld*, December 3, 1984, pp. 38–39.

ISSUE WHAT IS A ROBOT?

John Eckhouse, "Robots Reach Out to Expanding Market," *San Francisco Chronicle*, March 26, 1985, pp. 51, 58.

Doran P. Levin, "Robotics: A Special Report," *Wall Street Journal*, August 8, 1985, p. 1.

"Robots Get the Gift of Sight," *San Francisco Chronicle*, April 13, 1985, p. 53.

CHAPTER 13

ISSUE HOW SHOULD MANAGEMENT DEAL WITH ON-THE-JOB ALCOHOL AND DRUG ABUSE?

Bryan Burrough, "How G.M. Began Using Private Eyes in Plants to Fight Drugs, Crimes," *Wall Street Journal*, February 26, 1986, pp. 1, 15.

Janice Castro, "Battling the Enemy Within," *Time*, March 17, 1986, pp. 52–61.

Janice Castro, "Battling Drugs on the Job," *Time*, January 27, 1986, p. 43.

ISSUE THE WORLD'S WORST INDUSTRIAL ACCIDENT

Phillip Elmer-DeWitt, "What Happened at Bhopal," *Time*, April 1, 1985, p. 71.

Thomas M. Gladwin and Ingo Wilter, "Bhopal and the Multinational," *Wall Street Journal*, January 16, 1985, p. 24.

Leslie Helm *et al.*, "Bhopal, A Year Later: Union Carbide Takes A Tougher Line," *Business Week*, November 25, 1985, pp. 96–101.

Barry Meier and James B. Steward, "A Year After Bhopal, Union Carbide Faces a Slew of Problems," *Wall Street Journal*, November 26, 1985, pp. 1, 24.

ISSUE TESTING YOUR BUSINESS ETHICS

Michael D'Antonio, "Honesty vs. Big Business," *San Francisco Chronicle*, September 2, 1985, pp. 52, 54.

Hershey H. Friedman and Linda W. Friedman, "Ethics: Everybody's Business," *Collegiate News and Views*, Winter 1981–1982, pp. 11–13.

John S. Estey and David W. Marston, "Pitfalls (and Loopholes) in the Foreign Bribery Law," *Fortune*, October 8, 1978, pp. 182–184, 188.

CHAPTER 14

ISSUE FREE TRADE OR FAIR TRADE?

William A. Andres, "The Case for Open Trade," *Vital Speeches of the Day*, August 1, 1985, pp. 623–626.

George J. Church, "The Battle Over Barriers," *Time,* October 7, 1985, pp. 22–35.

Monroe W. Karmin, "Where the Surge of Imports Is Hitting the Hardest," *U. S. News and World Report,* May 6, 1985, pp. 45 – 46.

ISSUE TERRORISTS TARGET THE
MULTINATIONALS

Christopher Dobson and Ronald Payne, "Private Enterprise Takes on Terrorism," *Across the Board,* January, 1983, pp. 34–41.

M. B. Harvey, "Terrorists v. the MNC," *Public Relations Journal,* October, 1983, pp. 11–17.

Brian M. Jenkins, *Terrorism: A Challenge to the State* (Juliet Lodge: St. Martins Press, 1981).

Brian O'Reilly, "Business Copes With Terrorism," *Fortune,* January 6, 1986, pp. 47–55.

Does American Business Have a Future?

Quotation by James E. Perrella, from "Challenging the Hazards of International Business," *Vital Speeches,* July 1, 1984, pp. 553–555.

INDEX